FOREIGN INTEREST
IN THE
INDEPENDENCE OF NEW SPAIN

AN INTRODUCTION TO THE
WAR FOR INDEPENDENCE

By

JOHN RYDJORD

1972
OCTAGON BOOKS
New York

Copyrighted, 1935, by Duke University Press

Reprinted 1972
by special arrangement with Duke University Press

OCTAGON BOOKS
A DIVISION OF FARRAR, STRAUS & GIROUX, INC.
19 Union Square West
New York, N. Y. 10003

LIBRARY OF CONGRESS CATALOG CARD NUMBER: 72-159223

ISBN 0-374-97001-7

Manufactured by Braun-Brumfield, Inc.
Ann Arbor, Michigan

Printed in the United States of America

57756
F
1231
.R93
1972

DUKE · UNIVERSITY · PUBLICATIONS

FOREIGN INTEREST IN
THE INDEPENDENCE OF NEW SPAIN

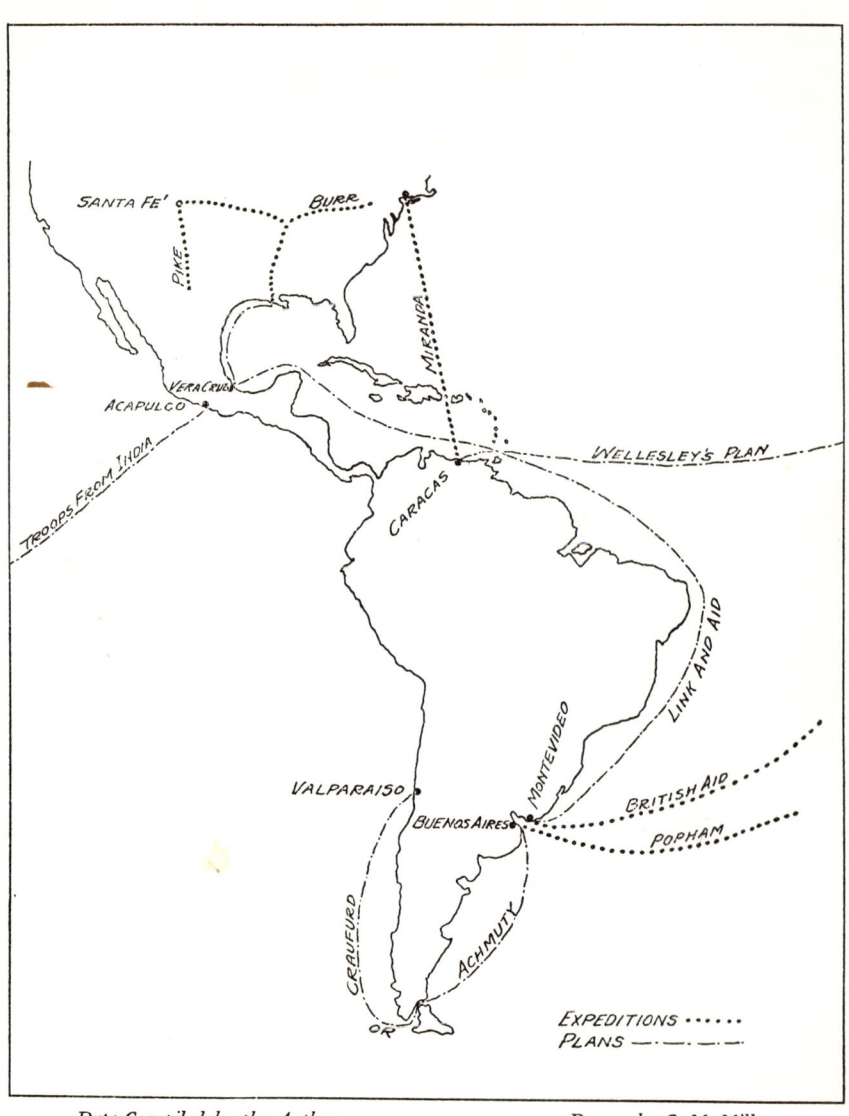

FOREIGN REVOLUTIONARY PLANS AND EXPEDITIONS
1806-1807

To My Mother

When on 11 October 1492 Christopher Columbus first sighted the outermost islet of new lands across the Atlantic, he brought into the world of affairs fresh objects for international rivalry that for the next three centuries and a half were never to be far from the centre of the struggle for world power.
—Arthur Percival Newton.

PREFACE

THE SIGNIFICANCE of the Spanish colonies in world affairs has not been well known. A few excellent studies have been made on special fields, but most of these have not been fully appreciated since they have been accepted merely as incidents. It has been the purpose of the author, therefore, to make this survey to show the scope of the foreign influence and to bring all the isolated incidents into a related whole. Some of the gaps have been filled by collecting scattered items from printed materials, and others by special studies from manuscripts in European archives. In some cases the task has been to condense special studies and fit them into the general framework. Thus a double purpose has been accomplished: that of bringing out new materials on some phases, and a general assembling and compilation of the others.

My interest in this field began at Northwestern University with a study of the viceregal administration of Iturrigaray in Mexico. In the University of California I began the study of the foreign influence on the independence movements. Further research in the archives of England, France, Spain, and Mexico, and in the Library of Congress has rounded out the work to its present proportions.

In tracing the origin of the independence movement, the author was led backward from the events of 1808 to the time of the conquest. When asked by one of the archivists in Seville where I would set the origin of the independence movement, my reply was, "With Cortés." He showed a little astonishment, and then asked me why I did not begin with Adam, a question which was reasonable enough, since the spirit of independence may be as old as man.

A whole chapter has been devoted to a description of the

colonial conditions which served as causes for revolutionary tendencies. This naturally pictures the darker side of the colonial life, because that was the side causing most of the grievances.

The revolutionary trends have been traced quite briefly for the first two centuries, since the foreign influence became most pronounced only after the opening of the eighteenth century and increasingly important from then until the climax was reached in the Napoleonic wars. While the first two chapters do not contain much material on the foreign influence, they give one an understanding of the conditions which made the foreign powers not only desire the independence of the colonies, but believe that independence might be achieved. Throughout the whole period one sees that the desire for independence in the colony would probably have to be influenced by foreign support if it were to culminate in a successful liberation movement. It is hoped that this study will make one appreciate the importance of the Spanish colonies in world affairs and that it will help to explain the international rivalries of the world, particularly in the eighteenth century and the Napoleonic period.

Two monographs have already been published from this study: "The French Revolution and Mexico" in *The Hispanic American Historical Review* (February, 1929); "Napoleon and the Independence of New Spain" in *New Spain and the Anglo-American West* (Los Angeles, 1932). The first article is reprinted with the permission of the managing editor of the *Review,* and the second was first printed by permission of the Duke University Press.

Encouragement and assistance from numerous persons have contributed to the development of this study, and the writer feels deeply indebted to all of them. Nevertheless, errors and omissions, for which the author alone must be held responsible, will undoubtedly be found in a work of this scope.

I received courteous and helpful service in the British Museum and the Public Record Office of London, in the national archives of France in Paris, in the archives of Simancas, Madrid, and Seville in Spain, in the archives of Mexico, and in the Huntington Library. The Bancroft Library staff has been especially helpful. To Professor I. J. Cox of Northwestern University I am grateful for introducing me to this field of research and for directing its foundation. For the scope and development of this subject I am largely indebted to the stimulating encouragement and vision of Professor H. E. Bolton of the University of California. Professor Cox has also read the chapters dealing with the Burr period and has made corrections and helpful suggestions. Assistance in reading parts of the manuscript and in typing has been given by Ellene Doyra, Ruth Goodsell, Laura McMullen, and Mrs. A. B. Thomas. My wife has coöperated by her sympathetic interest and patience. And finally I wish to acknowledge the aid and generous grants of institutions and individuals, particularly for the William Smith Mason Fellowship at Northwestern University and the Travelling Fellowship of the Native Sons of the Golden West in California.

J. R.

TABLE OF CONTENTS

	PAGES
Preface	vii

CHAPTERS
I. The Background of Independence	3
II. Early Plans for Independence	20
III. Bourbon and British Advance	39
IV. Reforms Against Revolutions	60
V. The American Revolution	77
VI. Aftermath of the American Revolution	94
VII. Revolutionary Plans on the Louisiana Border	110
VIII. The French Revolution and Mexico	128
IX. Revival of British Interest	149
X. Franco-American War	163
XI. Spanish Defense	178
XII. Competition for the Key to Mexico	191
XIII. Boundaries and Burr	206
XIV. Pitt and the Failures of 1806	226
XV. Castlereagh and Wellesley	241
XVI. Braganzas, Bourbons, and Bonapartes	254
XVII. The Mexican Reaction to Napoleon	272
XVIII. Joseph Bonaparte, King of Spain and the Indies	290
Bibliography	309
Index	323

ILLUSTRATIONS

Foreign Revolutionary Plans and Expeditions,
 1806-1807, map .... *frontispiece*

Proclamation of Joseph Napoleon to clergy, facsimile
 opposite page 300

FOREIGN INTEREST IN
THE INDEPENDENCE OF NEW SPAIN

CHAPTER I

THE BACKGROUND OF INDEPENDENCE

> "Dios está mui alto, el Rey en Madrid, y yo en México."—William Walton quoting a viceroy.
>
> "Learn to read, to write and to say your prayers: this is all an American ought to know."—Gil de Lemos.
>
> "Whilst they are ignorant, they are led; as soon as they get knowledge they run alone, and at their own discretion."—M. De Pradt.

IN NEW SPAIN the conquistadores found reminders of their homeland: the ruggedness of the Spanish mountains, the rich soil of Andalusia, the barren lands of Old Castile, and the sunny clime of the Peninsula. The boundary of this new land was limited at first only by the Spanish imagination, one of the early church writers holding it to extend to Greenland. In time the Kingdom of New Spain, for so it was called, was limited by foreign intrusion, by the occupied territory, and by administrative partitions until it included Anahuac, or Mexico proper, Guatemala, and the Spanish borderlands west of Louisiana. The eastern borderlands were placed under separate jurisdictions, but continued to coöperate with the viceroyalty of New Spain in matters of defense.

To this distant land Spain sent her soldiers and settlers, her religious workers, and her government officials to put the stamp of Spanish civilization on the native Americans and to exploit the land and the people for the benefit of the Spanish rulers. The clash of races and civilizations was at first destructive; later it was modified and adjusted until groups and individuals found themselves fitting into classes, their rise limited by social, economic, and political barriers. This classification, which at first aided the adjustment and the organization of Spain in America, became in time one of the great causes for discontent and, therefore, for independence.

Foremost stood the European-born Spaniard, the Peninsular or, as he was often called, the *Gachupín* or *Chapetón*. The Peninsulars were the fewest in numbers but the highest in rank. As Spain was considered superior to the colony so the Spaniard was considered superior to the colonist. The number of pure-blooded Spaniards in Mexico at the beginning of the nineteenth century was estimated by Alexander von Humboldt to be approximately 1,200,000, of which seventy or eighty thousand were Peninsulars.[1] In general, the Peninsulars represented the ruling class, holding especially the higher offices, both ecclesiastical and civil. Of three hundred and sixty-nine bishops and archbishops appointed in New Spain before 1637 only twelve were creoles,[2] and of fifty-six viceroys appointed before 1808 not more than two had been born in America.[3] Many of these favored officials were guided by self-interest, by a desire to become wealthy in order to return to Spain and live in leisure. They grew domineering and, as a result, the Spaniards became known as the oppressors of the Americans of all classes. Because of their privileged position they gained advantages in commerce and in the possession of land,[4] while the descendants of the conquerors found that their privileges and concessions were often ignored or evaded. One of the reasons for this favoritism was that the Spanish crown felt more certain of the loyalty of men from Spain than that of men who had grown up far from the homeland.[5] The Spanish rulers hoped to retain the loyalty of these by a generous bestowal of favors.[6] Their residence near the Spanish court gave them opportunities to plead for high offices, to purchase them,

---

[1] Alexander von Humboldt, *Political Essay on the Kingdom of New Spain*, trans. by J. Black, (2nd ed., 4 vols., London, 1814), I, 206, 210.

[2] William Robertson, *The History of America* (2 vols., London, 1777), II, 500.

[3] Wilhelm Roscher, *The Spanish Colonial System*, ed. E. G. Bourne (New York, 1904), p. 20.

[4] Herbert I. Priestley, *José de Gálvez* (Berkeley, 1916), p. 52.

[5] Humboldt emphasized the pecuniary interest, *Political Essay*, I, 204.

[6] Albert G. Keller, *Colonization* (Boston, 1908), p. 313.

or perhaps to court favors by politic marriages.[7] The wealth, titles, and honors of these officials served only to stimulate the envy of the Americans. As a result the Peninsulars became arrogant and haughty; and the creoles, sullen, suspicious, and jealous.

The creole, American-born Spaniard, though of pure Spanish blood, accordingly found himself relegated to a position inferior to that of the Peninsular. There was no legal basis for such a distinction, but the practice led to its acceptance until it became equivalent to an unwritten law. This was carried to such an extent that a family coming to Spanish America "held in very different regard their children who were born in Spain and those who were born later in America."[8] Being born in America was therefore a serious handicap and it explains in part the rivalry which occasionally led to open revolt and eventually to independence.[9] Thomas Gage, an English traveler in Mexico, after witnessing the government's method of punishing rebellious persons in 1625, said that the prime movers in the uprising had been the creoles, "who do hate the Spanish government, and all such as come from Spain; and reason they have for it, for by them they are much oppressed ... and are and will be always watching any opportunity to free themselves from the Spanish yoke."[10] The Abbé Raynal, calling attention to the class hatred, said: "This animosity hath often broken out in such a manner as to endanger the dominions of the mother-country in the New World."[11] Pleas and

[7] H. H. Bancroft, *History of Mexico* (6 vols., San Francisco, 1883-1887), III, 526-527.
[8] Bernard Moses, "Social Revolution in South America," *Annual Report of the American Historical Association, 1915* (Washington, 1917), p. 166.
[9] On class distinction, see also Lucas Alamán, *Historia de Méjico* (5 vols., Méjico, 1849-1852), I, 12-22.
[10] Thomas Gage, *A New Survey of the West Indies* (3rd. ed., London, 1677), p. 145.
[11] Abbé Raynal, *A Philosophical and Political History of the Settlements and Trade of the Europeans in the East and West Indies,* trans. by J. O. Justamond (8 vols., London, 1788), IV, 315-316.

complaints were sent to Spain with futile results. In 1771 a memorial was addressed to Charles III to secure greater consideration for the creoles,[12] and in 1779 the Bishop of Michoacán complained bitterly of the inequalities in New Spain.[13]

Class distinction was applied with similar results to the rest of the population—to the natives, the negroes, and the new types resulting from the mixture of races. Of the latter the most important were the mestizos, the descendants of Spaniards and Indians. The mestizo, "despised by his father, despising his Indian mother,"[14] became a disturbing factor. Without a normal outlet for his activities in life, he frequently resorted to the vices of the two races from which he sprang, and from whose society he was generally excluded, and has, therefore, been unjustly accused of inheriting the worst traits of the two. A better explanation of his character is found by considering his environment.[15] The mestizo was generally the illegitimate child of a Spanish father and an Indian mother. He was therefore a virtual outcast from society, and this ostracism placed him in such a degrading position that he sought relief in sensual vices and a livelihood, in part or wholly, by gambling and robbery. He did not adopt this mode of life from choice; he sought by two means to rise to the position of the white man; namely, by law and by war.[16]

Before the end of the colonial period their numerical strength, estimated at 1,860,000,[17] was greater than the two

---

[12] *Representacion umilde que hace la Imperial Novilisima y muy Leal Ciudad de Mexico en favor de sus Naturales a su Amado Soberano el Senor Don Carlos 3 en 2 de Mayo de 1771* (MS. Mexico, 1771, Bancroft Collection).

[13] Quoted in Humboldt, *Political Essay*, I, 190-198.

[14] T. Esquival Obregón, "Factors in the Historical Evolution of Mexico," *The Hispanic American Historical Review*, II, 152 (May, 1919).

[15] For a discussion on the influence of environment on the mixed races, see A. L. Kroeber and T. T. Waterman, *Source Book in Anthropology* (Berkeley, 1920), p. 211.

[16] Impelled by the maxim, *"Todo blanco es caballero,"* he occasionally requested and obtained a judicial decision declaring him white (Humboldt, *Political Essay*, I, 246; Roscher, *Spanish Colonial System*, p. 21).

[17] For a comparative table, see Roscher, *Spanish Colonial System*, p. 18.

white elements combined. Such a large dissatisfied group became a menace to organized society. They were ready to fight for the wealth and honor of which they were in great part deprived by the hated white man, and they became the disturbing element among the Indians, whose animosities they stirred up and encouraged in order to incite them to rebellion. Much of the turbulence and disorder in Mexico, in colonial times and since, has been caused by the efforts of the mestizos to rise to a position of equality with their fellowmen.

At the opening of the nineteenth century, by far the largest part of the population were the Indians, estimated by Humboldt as approximately 3,700,000.[18] The natives were from the first considered Spanish subjects, but not on a basis of equality with the others. Believed to be inferior in mentality to the *Gente de Razón,* they were in many respects treated like children or minors, as wards of the government. Under the encomienda system the Spanish government placed masters over the Indians to civilize and christianize them, with the privilege of collecting their tribute and exploiting their labor.[19] The result was not what the Spanish rulers had hoped, for the encomenderos neglected their duties and abused their privileges. The native soon found himself in the degraded position of a slave, without liberties and without rights. Efforts of the natives to improve their condition generally led to rebellion, their only resource. Such revolts were put down with a ruthless hand, with the view of making their fear greater than their hatred, lest the latter lead to the destruction of the Spaniard and the Spanish system. The Indian was considered a brute, who must be deprived of the means of rising to a position where he would become a greater danger than in his abject ignorance. He was held in check by fear and he remained, even

[18] *Ibid.*
[19] Representative material may be found in Keller, *Colonization,* pp. 257-280; E. G. Bourne, *Spain in America* (New York, 1904), pp. 253-268.

then, a constant threat to the whole political and social structure.

There was little hope for the natives as long as opinions of the officials resembled those of the Mexican board of trade which reported that "the Indians were a race of monkeys, filled with vice and ignorance, automatons, unworthy of representing or being represented."[20] There were others who, recognizing their deplorable condition, held the Spaniards directly responsible. Manuel Antonio Sandoval, writing in 1778, was impressed by the "humility, poverty, nudeness, and misery" of the Indians.[21] The native was looked down on socially, despised by his overlords, robbed of his liberty, and denied the exercise of initiative and economic independence; "Now, Sire," wrote Fray Antonio de San Miguel, "what attachment can the Indians have to the government, despised and degraded as he is, and almost without property and without hope of ameliorating his existence?"[22] According to the laws of the Indies, the policy of Spain really was benevolent, but, as Henry C. Lea said, these laws were an example of "how the kindly intentions of governments, expressed in beneficent legislation, may be rendered nugatory when administration is entrusted to unworthy hands or when sufficient influence is brought to bear by those who profit from abuses."[23]

Spain had adopted the old Roman practice of *divide et impera,* but the encouragement of class conflict was a dangerous method by which to control the inhabitants of New Spain. Although rivalries and differences prevented, for a time, united action, these were eventually to be subordinated by the greater hatred of the common enemy, the Peninsular. In such an event the European would find himself deprived of the land and

---

[20] Manuel Palacio, *Outline of the Revolution in Spanish America* (London, 1817), p. 21.

[21] Lillian E. Fisher, *The Background of the Revolution for Mexican Independence* (Boston, 1934), pp. 45-48.

[22] Quoted by Humboldt, *Political Essay,* I, 196.

[23] Quoted by Keller, *Colonization,* p. 257, note 2.

people whom he had exploited for his own selfish gain (and the Americans would again become divided to fight over the spoils). This odious system, encouraging class distinctions, failing to protect the natives from unscrupulous taskmasters, and ruling by fear, could not long have kept the Indians from rebellion if it had not been upheld by the powerful agency of the church.

The church became at the same time the protector of the persecutor and the persecuted. The superstitious natives, generally treated with great consideration by the church, embraced, in outward form at least, the tenets of Catholicism. The early missionaries, and the Jesuits in particular, were tireless in their efforts to convert the heathen. The result was that the church gained a powerful hold on the natives. It declined, however, towards the end of the colonial period and abused its trust. The Abbé Raynal wrote that

The Indian, whom they [the clergy] were appointed to instruct and comfort, did not dare to appear before them without some present. Such a conduct had rendered their tenets generally odious. These people went to mass as they did to labours of vassalage, execrating the barbarous strangers, who loaded their bodies and their souls with burthens equally weighty.[24]

Raynal depicts the darker side, for the clergy was frequently lenient and did not demand complete obedience, treating the natives with indulgence "on account of their ignorance and their weak minds."[25] The church developed a state of fear in the minds of these people in order to hold them in complete subjection to itself and the state. After the Tepic rebellion (1801) the clergy were warned to be on their guard and instructed to develop the proper respect for authority among the natives.[26] It also became the duty of

[24] Raynal, *A Philosophical and Political History*, IV, 278.
[25] Quoted by Roscher, *Spanish Colonial System*, p. 7.
[26] Berenguer de Marquina to Cevallos, Mexico, Feb. 26, 1801, Archivo General de las Indias (referred to hereinafter as A. G. I.), Estado, Mexico, legajo 10; Alamán, *Historia de Méjico*, I, 135.

the church to issue warnings against the irreligious and dangerous maxims of the French Revolution.[27] The church and state being combined, it was only natural to consider any disrespect towards the state as an attack on the church.[28]

The regular clergy had been the most active in converting the natives, but with the advance of civilization they had to leave their wards to the abusive treatment of those who wanted cheap labor. The Jesuit order had been a very influential agency in the process of conversion and civilization of these people, and its expulsion was followed by Indian revolts which marked the approaching storm. Spain had not only made the Jesuits themselves enemies of the Spanish Empire, but had removed a powerful agency of peace and order within the Mexican kingdom. This fact was emphasized by several of the Jesuit writers who later advocated independence for Mexico.[29] Their expulsion removed a steadying influence and loosened the firm hold of Spain "on both the material and spiritual interests of the colonies."[30]

The clergy itself was a powerful class which must be considered in connection with the preliminaries to independence. They formed the class on which Spain relied to a great extent to insure the peace and possession of her distant colonies. But in this group, too, one finds the destructive influence of favoritism. The difficulties in the way of attaining the higher grades encountered by the American-born priests were almost insurmountable. The rich benefices and high offices were granted almost exclusively to European-born churchmen. Most of the creoles who entered the service of the church were forced to

---

[27] Archbishop of Mexico, Oct. 4, 1794, A. G. I., Estado, Mexico, legajo 22.
[28] The relationship of the church to the conditions of Mexico is described by Fisher, *The Background of the Revolution for Mexican Independence*, pp. 216-258.
[29] See especially the recommendations of a former inquisitor, in Charles William Vane, 3rd Marquis of Londonderry, *Memoirs and Correspondence of Viscount Castlereagh, second Marquis of Londonderry* (12 vols., London, 1848-1853), VII, 262-265.
[30] Bernard Moses, *Spain's Declining Power in South America* (Berkeley, 1919), p. 103.

live in extreme poverty, while those who held the better positions, mostly Europeans, "possess[ed] revenues," Humboldt says, "which surpass[ed] those of many of the sovereign princes of Germany."[31] This extreme inequality caused much dissatisfaction and aroused envy and jealousy. One of the most dangerous elements with which Spain had to contend was these dissatisfied priests,[32] because the clergy were the best informed of the population and had the greatest power over the people, irrespective of race or color.

Education was carefully supervised and limited. Colleges were not lacking in the colonies. It has even been suggested that there were too many, because they seemed to be lacking in nearly everything — teachers, books, methods, and even students.[33] The chief studies were philosophy, law, and theology, the last two being principally stressed.[34] In the University of Mexico the study of theology was predominant.[35] This was to be expected because most of the opportunities for offices and honors were in the legal or clerical professions, together with the army. Manual labor was considered degrading; accordingly, the best way to attain honor and office was to prepare for a position in the church or state. Lawyers were held in great respect, since the Spaniards were fond of law-suits and judicial intricacies. The tribunals in New Spain held the people in awe, and it is said that the colonists "had a deep-rooted fear of the already remarkable entanglement of legislation."[36] The study of law was carried on in a trivial manner and contributed little to the advancement of public opinion politically.

[31] *Political Essay*, I, 229.

[32] Cardinaux's report enclosed with Governor Dalling's, Jamaica, March 26, 1780, British Public Record Office (referred to hereinafter as P. R. O.), C. O. 137, Vol. LXXVII.

[33] Gaston Desdevises du Dezert, "L'Eglise Espagnole des Indes a la fin du XVIII° Siècle," *Revue Hispanique*, XXXIX, 111-293 (Feb., 1917).

[34] Justo Sierra (ed.), *Mexico, its Evolution* (3 vols., Mexico, 1900-1904), I, 122.

[35] Desdevises du Dezert, "L'Eglise Espagnole des Indes a la fin du XVIII° Siècle," *Revue Hispanique*, XXXIX, 254.

[36] Sierra (ed.), *Mexico*, I, 123.

"Learn to read, to write and to say your prayers: this is all an American ought to know."[37] Such are the words of Gil de Lemos, viceroy of Peru, who proposed to change the three "R's" by substituting prayer for "'rithmetic." Branciforte, viceroy of Mexico, went so far as to declare that Americans should be taught only the catechism.[38] And Francisco de Miranda of Caracas, having studied in Mexico, informed President Stiles of Yale that there were "no great Literary characters in New Spain—or can be—for the Geniuses dare not *read* nor *think* nor *speak*, for fear of the Inquisition which keeps out all Books, lest it should effect sedition."[39] Though these views may be somewhat exaggerated, they give an indication of the limitations and the tendency towards repressive measures in education.

Not only was knowledge limited within this country, but also information from other countries was necessarily meager owing to the watchful eye of the Inquisition. This Holy Office exercised rigid control over the printing, sale, and introduction of all kinds of literature. Booksellers were required to keep a list of all the works on the Papal Index, and those who neglected to do this were subject to severe punishment. Orders were issued frequently for officials to burn all obnoxious literature.[40] When Europe was being stirred by the eighteenth-century philosophers, New Spain found that their ideas were forbidden fruit. After the establishment of their Bourbon rule, however, many Spaniards traveled to Paris, and some of them returned as supporters or champions of the encyclopedists and philosophers.[41] There was considerable opposition to these "Filosofos o novadores," as they were called; they were "looked

[37] Paul Leroy-Beaulieu, *De la Colonisation chez les Peuples Modernes* (5th ed., 2 vols., Paris, 1902), I, 9.

[38] Alamán, *Historia de Méjico*, I, 27.

[39] Franklin B. Dexter (ed.), *The Literary Diary of Ezra Stiles* (3 vols., New York, 1837), III, 131.

[40] Hubert Howe Bancroft, *Essays and Miscellany* (San Francisco, 1890), p. 483.

[41] Angel Salcedo y Ruiz, *Historia de España* (Madrid, 1914), p. 431.

upon by their compatriots as dangerous innovators, Voltaireans and Freemasons."[42] Once these modern ideas had entered Spain, it was difficult to keep them out of Mexico. It is difficult to discover to what extent the restrictions of the Inquisition were evaded, but there is sufficient evidence to show that there was some familiarity with modern thought. Montesquieu's *Esprit des Lois* was studied in the University of Mexico[43] until the outbreak of the French Revolution, when all his works were placed on the Index. Miranda told President Stiles of Yale that in Mexico he had been obliged to pay twenty dollars for two volumes of Locke's *Treatise on the Human Understanding,* only to burn them as soon as he had read them, and that he had done the same with many other books.[44] The *Philosophical and Political History of the Two Indies* by the Abbé Raynal, who got much of his information from Count D'Aranda, is said to have had considerable influence in developing democratic ideas and in preparing the colonies for independence.[45] It was dangerous to read the forbidden literature. A young man by the name of Antonio de Castro was sentenced to banishment for ten years to the Philippines for holding certain views against the papacy and the Inquisition, and "for reading with pleasure, as he said, the 'Letters of Abelarde and Heloise' and 'Emile' by Rousseau."[46] Miguel Hidalgo y Costilla, who finally started the revolution, was also said to be quite familiar with French literature, and he had read a number of books which aroused the suspicion of the Inquisition.[47] The Spanish government and the church made great efforts to

[42] Martin A. S. Hume, *Modern Spain, 1788-1798* (New York, 1900), p. 1.
[43] Dexter (ed.), *Diary of Ezra Stiles,* III, 132.
[44] He had lost a library of 2,000 books in Spain, *ibid.,* III, 132.
[45] Jules Mancini, *Bolivar y la Emancipacion de las colonias Españolas* (Paris, 1914), p. 51.
[46] José Toribio Medina, *Historia del Tribunal del Santo Oficio de la Inquisición en México* (Santiago de Chile, 1905), p. 451.
[47] William Spence Robertson, *Rise of the Spanish American Republics* (New York, 1918), p. 80; Arthur H. Noll and A. P. McMahon, *The Life and Times of Miguel Hidalgo y Costilla* (Chicago, 1910), p. 41.

seal Mexico against revolutionary ideas, but they were unable to establish a Chinese wall which would be idea-proof.

The economic policy of the government was as backward and prohibitive as that for education and liberal ideas. The belief that the colonies existed for the benefit of Spain and the crown caused numerous and annoying restrictions. Commerce was regulated, controlled, and directed in order to secure every possible profit for the crown. There were reforms during the reign of Charles III,[48] but these sought to make the financial system more efficient rather than to help the economic conditions of the colonies. They did, however, improve the economic condition of Mexico, which, in place of winning greater loyalty, made the colonists more self-sufficient and better prepared to support an independent state.

The government monopolies were especially obnoxious and burdensome. They prevented a free and natural development of economic interests, and the enforcement was certain to leave feelings of resentment which became the forerunners of opposition. Officials known as *guardas de tabaco* traveled about the country and destroyed the tobacco which had been planted outside of the specified districts. Farmers were not allowed to raise tobacco for their own use.[49] There were other restrictions, equally annoying, which contributed to the discontent. Extracting oils, making wine or brandy, planting vines or almond trees were prohibited in any province of Spanish America except in Peru and Chile, and these countries were prohibited from sending their products to Mexico.[50] When Hidalgo, the father of independence, became curate of Dolores, he encouraged certain industries which violated the regulations of Spain; and, as a result, officials were promptly sent to Dolores

---

[48] For the reforms of this period, see Priestley, *José de Gálvez, passim;* and Sister Mary Austin Collins, *Reforms of Charles the Third in New Spain in the Light of the Pacte Famille* (MS., University of California, 1927).

[49] Humboldt, *Political Essay*, III, 39-40.

[50] Palacio, *Outline of the Revolution in Spanish America*, p. 23.

where, among other things, they cut down his mulberry trees and grapevines.[51] Such acts, though legal, stirred up a rebellious spirit.

New Spain was also burdened by stifling duties and heavy taxes. "The tax collector was ever at the elbow of the Spanish-American vassal."[52] There were import and export duties, a convoy-tax, the royal "fifth" on precious metals, tribute from Indians and negroes, and the hated *alcabala* or sales tax; altogether there were at least sixty kinds of taxes by the end of the colonial period. Besides the heavy state taxes, there were the additional and burdensome exactions of the church. The tithe, the sale of indulgences, and the payment for masses, all drained the meager resources of the inhabitants.[53] Most of the revenue was carried to Spain, where it was often squandered for questionable purposes. Much of it was lost through peculation, thereby increasing the burden.

Besides the taxes, there were other annoying restrictions on colonial commerce. Foreign trade was forbidden, as was inter-colonial trade, until the reforms of Charles III, and the trade between Spain and the colonies was subject to the most detailed supervision. Spain, suffering from an unwise economic policy at home, was unable to satisfy her own needs and those of her colonies and was forced to seek supplies from foreigners. These goods were ordinarily supposed to go through Spanish ports, where the duties were exceedingly high. "One sees," wrote Charles Weiss, "merchants from France, England, Holland, Genoa, and Hamburgh, inundate Spain, Mexico, and Peru with the products of their manufacture."[54] Certain ex-

---

[51] Noll and McMahon, *The Life and Times of Miguel Hidalgo*, p. 37. Robertson, *Rise of the Spanish American Republics*, p. 78, however, refers to Alamán as saying that in the middle of the nineteenth century there were still eighty-four mulberry trees left of those planted by Hidalgo.

[52] Herbert I. Priestley, *The Mexican Nation, A History* (New York, 1923), p. 130.

[53] For taxation see *ibid.*, pp. 130-134; and Keller, *Colonization*, pp. 314-315.

[54] Charles Weiss, *L'Espagne depuis le régne de Philippe II jusqu'a l'avénement des Bourbons* (2 vols., Paris, 1844), I, p. 50.

ceptions were occasionally made to the exclusion of foreign trade, especially after the establishment of the Bourbons on the Spanish throne, when there was some leniency shown toward French trade, and the British gained an opening through the Asiento Treaty of 1713. Other than these exceptions, there were irregularities in trade during times of war and a constant contraband trade.

Smuggling was of great importance in puncturing the governmental monopolies. Contraband trade was lucrative and flourished in spite of Spain's efforts to prevent it. The smugglers succeeded by deceiving, bribing, or fighting the authorities. Many of the colonial officials held their offices in order to become rich as quickly as possible and found that connivance with the foreign trader was one of the best means of attaining their ends. Even after the commercial reorganization of 1778, Raynal showed that the contraband trader had an advantage of sixty-four per cent over the fair dealer.[55] This forbidden trade could not be stopped since it was to the advantage of the foreigners, the colonials, and the officials.[56] With foreign goods and foreign contact came also foreign ideas. Smuggling was one of the significant factors in preparing the colonies for independence. It gave them a taste of the advantages of foreign trade, it showed them that Spain's interest was contrary to theirs, and finally, it was an evidence of their ability to evade the law which undermined the prestige of Spanish authority and thereby weakened her control.

Foreigners, as well as foreign goods, were to be excluded from the colonies.[57] At first this even applied to the Spanish

---

[55] Raynal, *Philosophical and Political History of the Indies*, IV, 339-340.

[56] Smuggling must have been at its height during the Napoleonic wars, although Leroy-Beaulieu considers the opening of the eighteenth century as the worst period, *De la Colonisation chez les Peuples Modernes* (6th ed., 2 vols., Paris, 1908), I, 30-31; see also Keller, *Colonization*, pp. 244-251; and Vera Lee Brown, "Contraband Trade: A Factor in the Decline of Spain's Empire in America," *The Hispanic American Historical Review*, VIII, 178-190 (May, 1928).

[57] *La Recopilación de Leyes de los Reinos de las Indias* (3 vols., Madrid, 1791), III, libro IX, título xxvii.

THE BACKGROUND OF INDEPENDENCE 17

kingdoms outside of Castile, for the rulers feared "lest the new territories should be contaminated by coming in contact with the 'Aragonese liberties' which they had not been able to wholly subvert."[58] Both religious and political reasons were given for keeping out foreigners. Yet the law was not always enforced and a number of aliens drifted into the forbidden territory. Some came to trade, some came as adventurers and travelers, and a few as scientists. Whenever Napoleon or Wellesley wanted information on Mexico, they seemed able to find someone who could give it from experience. Spain made several attempts to rid the country of the dangerous foreign element.

As seen from the laws of the Indies and the general policy of the government, the colonial system has generally been considered good; certainly, at the time of its establishment, no other European country had anything equal to it. There were, however, two defects: the machine-like organization did not change with the needs of the times; and secondly, the officials did not ordinarily live up to the ideals of the rulers and the lawmakers. The viewpoint of the selfish official is well expressed in the words of one of the viceroys: *"Dios está mui alto, el Rey en Madrid, y yo en México."*[59] Distance, whether it be from God or king, might easily encourage independent action. It certainly contributed to the difficulty of governing the colonies satisfactorily. As early as the middle of the sixteenth century, Toribio de Motolinia, a Spanish priest in Mexico, expressed the opinion that this vast and remote country could not be governed well from Spain. He thought it would be necessary to have a king or ruler in the country itself.[60] A similar suggestion was later made by Count D'Aranda.[61] The

[58] R. B. Merriman, *The Rise of the Spanish Empire in the Old World and the New* (3 vols., New York, 1918-1925), II, 221.
[59] Walton, *An Exposé on the Dissentions of Spanish America* (London, 1814), p. 43, n. 2.
[60] Joaquín García Icazbalceta, *Coleción de Documentos para la Historia de México* (2 vols., Mexico, 1858-1866), I, cxvii.
[61] Alamán, *Historia de Méjico*, I, 126-127; Bancroft, *Mexico*, III, 388-390.

government was too often in the hands of men who were primarily interested in becoming rich. Many of the lower courts were notoriously corrupt, and the upper courts were exasperatingly slow, causing a great loss of money and time. The excessive number of colonial regulations defeated their own ends, for they encouraged evasions and invited resistance.

Behind all these restrictions and discriminations was the home government which, in itself, served as a cause for resentment and opposition. Seldom has a country had more promising prospects than Spain at the beginning of her colonial era. Her unification, following the marriage of Ferdinand and Isabella, and the discovery of the New World gave promise of a glorious future. But unfortunately her capable rulers too often misdirected their efforts, seeking glory by means of European intervention and wars; and her incapable rulers gradually brought the Empire to stagnation and ruin. Charles V was continually embroiled in European wars, and yet the remarkable conquests in America during his reign have given rise to the name of this period as "the era of the conquistadores."[62] Philip II took a great interest in colonial affairs, but the broader and larger principles were excluded by a conscientious regard for minor details of little importance. According to Keller, "the morbid mind of Philip II was at the bottom of many positive regulations of a harmful nature, and the positive imbecility of his successors threw a baneful influence into the hands of unworthy panders and dependents."[63] No intelligent colonial policy could be expected from the last of the Hapsburgs, the "impotent idiot," Charles II. Only because of the perfection of the colonial organization did the Spanish Empire survive during this critical period.

The establishment of the Bourbons on the Spanish throne in the eighteenth century marked the beginning of a period of

[62] Charles E. Chapman, *A History of Spain* (New York, 1918), p. 244.
[63] Keller, *Colonization*, p. 184.

reform which reached its highest point under Charles III (1759-1788). It was already too late to bring the sixteenth-century system up to date and many of the reforms served largely as a cause or an aid to independence. His efforts both in Spain and in America brought about improved conditions and gave promise of progress, but such progress in America gave rise to self-consciousness and independent views, and with these came national aspirations. Charles IV lacked the energy and vision to continue the work of his predecessor. Hume describes him as "a simple, kindly soul . . . a man of scanty mental gifts, generous and easily led; yet still with plenty of Bourbon obstinacy and a high sense of his kingly privileges."[64] He came to the throne in 1788, the year before the ideas of the French Revolution began to threaten monarchs and their possessions. Manuel Godoy, the favorite of the queen, was made prime minister at the age of twenty-five, and it became his difficult task to guide Spain during one of the most critical periods of her history. After Godoy came Napoleon, and with the removal of the royal family the vast empire received its death blow.

[64] Hume, *Modern Spain*, p. 9.

CHAPTER II
EARLY PLANS FOR INDEPENDENCE

> "They are yet babes, that cannot live without sucking the breasts of their mother-cities; but such as I mistake if, when they come of age, they do not wean themselves."—JAMES HARRINGTON.
>
> "Irked by restrictions and surveillance as well as by inaction or poverty, these sons of the sword sought again on this soil the freedom which was once the Spaniard's birthright."—HERBERT E. BOLTON.

THE IDEAS of independence in Mexico date back to the time of its conquest. When Hernando Cortés slipped away from the irate Velásquez, he made himself temporarily independent of Spanish authority, and when he defeated his pursuer, Narváez, he maintained that independence. When Cortés and his followers established their government at Villa Rica de Vera Cruz, the authority came from within the group and not from Spain nor from any higher official. It was quite in keeping with events, therefore, that some of his followers should accuse the illustrious conquistador of desiring to make himself the independent ruler of Mexico. Following the conquest and the unsatisfactory division of spoils, complaints and accusations against Cortés increased until the king's suspicion was aroused.[1]

The conqueror's bid for royal favor by sending to Spain a precious cargo of the spoils taken from the Indians served unfortunately to arouse the envy of predatory neighbors. French privateers attacked the galleons as they approached Europe, and gained possession of two ships which were rich in plunder. The French were amazed at the wealth of Spanish America, which was henceforth to arouse the cupidity of the freebooter of the northern countries.[2]

[1] Merriman, *Rise of the Spanish Empire*, III, 509.
[2] A. P. Newton, *The European Nations in the West Indies* (London, 1933), pp. 48-49.

Charles V, anxious to get full control over the vast empire which had just been conquered, sent official investigators to New Spain. Fonseca, the first minister of the Indies, directed Cristóbal de Tapia to arrest Cortés as a rebel, but a junta of the combined town councils persuaded the agent to leave without imprisoning the conqueror.[3] When one after the other of the king's agents died upon reaching their destination, suspicion was increased, and there were those who said that this was the work of Cortés who was trying to resist the authority of his sovereign.[4] The hero was not to be trusted and the king took special precautions to guard against an uprising when he gave orders for his residencia.[5] Cortés seemed to be the logical candidate for the first viceroy of Mexico; nevertheless, he was rejected because the sovereign questioned his loyalty.[6]

While acting as the governor of Mexico, Cortés created a serious problem by establishing there the encomienda system. By this method the followers of the conqueror were given extensive grants of land and control over a large number of Indians, who in turn were to be civilized, christianized, and protected while they served their masters. The first contacts with the natives were almost unrestrained and the result was shocking. The encomienda system was immediately and generally abused, and the natives became virtually slaves. Priests, with Bartolomé de las Casas taking a leading part, sent complaints to Spain regarding the mistreatment of the natives. Through the efforts of Las Casas, the home government drew up the New Laws which regulated the relationship between the Spaniards and the Indians and prepared the way for the abolition of the encomienda system. The colonists who had already become accustomed to depend on their Indian vassals

---

[3] Priestley, *The Mexican Nation*, p. 50.
[4] Luis González Obregón, *Los Precursores de la Independencia Mexicana* (Paris and Mexico, 1906), p. 91.   [5] *Ibid.*, p. 108.
[6] Priestley, *The Mexican Nation*, p. 53; Merriman, *Rise of the Spanish Empire*, III, 511.

for their livelihood and wealth realized that the enforcement of the New Laws would destroy their whole economic system.

When Tello de Sandoval of the Council of the Indies came to enforce the laws, the encomenderos planned to go in mourning to meet him as a sign of disapproval. The publication of the laws resulted in demonstrations of indignation, and the opposition was so general throughout New Spain that there was fear of open rebellion.[7] Sandoval found it expedient not to enforce the laws immediately. Representatives were sent back to Spain to plead the cause of the encomenderos and, fortunately for the peace of the country and the loyalty of the colonists, they were successful.[8] Since opposition had been rewarded, it would seem as if the government could not or dared not enforce laws for the protection of the Indians if they seriously handicapped the economic advantages of the Spaniards. The affair quieted down temporarily, but it was certain that any future attack on the encomienda system would renew the feelings of discontent and stir up ideas of rebellion.

The occasion came during the disturbed conditions after the death of the viceroyal Velasco in 1564. The sons of the conquerors were loyal only as long as they were assured of the glory and fruits of the conquest; and when these were threatened, they became united as representatives of a new nation.[9] The greatest of the encomenderos was Martín Cortés, the second Marquis del Valle and the son of the Conqueror. When he returned to Mexico in 1563, after having spent several years in Spain, there was considerable uneasiness over the rumors that the government intended to enforce its plan to abolish the encomienda system after the second generation. It has been suggested that the joy with which the Marquis was received on his arrival in Mexico might have had some connection with

---

[7] González Obregón, *Los Precursores de la Independencia Mexicana*, p. 219; Bancroft, *History of Mexico*, II, 523.

[8] For a discussion of the New Laws, see Bancroft, *Mexico*, II, 516-529.

[9] González Obregón, *Los Precursores de la Independencia*, p. 250.

the desire of the creoles for a leader for an independence movement.[10] It would have been a good choice. "In his way," Bancroft wrote, "he was the first man in America, the most famous, the wealthiest, occupying the highest social position. He could not be viceroy.... It was too dangerous to Spanish monarchy. But he could be the social sovereign of Mexico."[11] The highest officials of the country showed him constant respect until the viceroy and the Marquis clashed over their prerogatives of entertaining the visitador, Valderrama. From that time on, the people began to take sides.

Among the most prominent of the American faction was Alonso de Avila, member of an important family, son of one of the conquerors, and himself a man of influence. His home was the meeting place of relatives and friends where they enjoyed good food and excellent wine, and where they found entertainment and opportunities for conversation. Martín Cortés and his two brothers, the illegitimate sons of Hernando, were often among the guests who partook of the hospitality of Avila.[12] It was logical that the problems of the encomenderos should be discussed often and freely in the home of this good and merry host.

The mere rumors of unfavorable action on the part of the king made resistance one of the chief topics for discussion, with Alonso de Avila taking the lead. Referring to the king, he said, "He who wants all, loses all."[13] The viceroy having died during the summer of 1564, "the city council of Mexico was seized with a brilliant idea," says Bancroft. "Would the king send them no more viceroys! For howsoever good they might be in theory, they were sure to bring friends and dependents, to whom they would give the offices rightly belonging to the conquerors and their sons."[14] They went so far as to suggest

[10] *Ibid.*, p. 234. [11] *Mexico*, II, 604.
[12] González Obregón, *Los Precursores de la Independencia*, p. 271.
[13] *Ibid.*, p. 276.
[14] *Ibid.*, p. 256; Bancroft, *Mexico*, II, 602.

that if they had no viceroy, the king might appoint the Marquis del Valle, a most desirable representative, as their captain-general.[15] They felt, no doubt, that he could be trusted to look after the interests of the encomenderos.

There were those who were toying with the idea that Martín Cortés might easily be made their sovereign. The son of the viceroy, Luis Velasco, saying that they should raise the Marquis to king, "as the man who had a better right to this country than the King of Castile, and that the Marquis should then elect dukes, counts, and marqueses, and divide the land among them."[16] Rumors and reports from both Spain and Mexico indicated that neither country was safe from the machinations of the other.

On the arrival of the fleet of Pedro de las Roelas from Spain, in September, 1565, some of the rumors were confirmed and the Marquis himself was deprived of a number of his vassals as well as the privilege of using a large seal.[17] Martín Cortés had assumed some of the trappings of royalty, his social functions resembling a court, with servants and pages in livery, and a guard.[18] The encomenderos, believing that they had grievances enough to justify their resistance to the government, were encouraged by the prospects of securing a leader. The Marquis was not likely to see himself stripped of honors and privileges without a keen feeling of resentment which could be used to advantage by the dissatisfied encomenderos. Plans for the rebellion were made. In justification of their actions, the plotters declared that they owed allegiance to their sovereign only as long as he respected his pledges,[19] giving evidence of their belief in the contract theory of government.

Action was delayed, due to the hesitancy of some of the leaders, and Avila left the city for one of his estates where he remained until he was recalled to take up the plan for rebel-

---

[15] González Obregón, *Los Precursores de la Independencia*, p. 257.
[16] *Ibid.*, p. 280.
[17] *Ibid.*, p. 278.
[18] *Ibid.*, p. 239.
[19] Bancroft, *Mexico*, II, 608.

lion. He returned with a number of followers on horseback, all masked to represent various personages, Avila playing the part of Montezuma. They proceeded to the home of the Marquis where a banquet was being held. There they staged the coming of Cortés to Mexico, in which Martín played the part of his father, the Conqueror. On presenting the Aztec feather crown, the symbol of authority over the land, Avila said to the Marquis, "This is indeed becoming to your señoría!" and to his wife, "accept the crown Marchioness!" In the flowers that were distributed were couplets, the one to the Marquis saying, "Do not fear the fall, because it is for a greater rise." After the banquet they held a parade through the city, singing songs which made allusions to the proposed rebellion. Such actions seem unwise, but the plotters were probably testing the attitude of the people before executing their plan.

The details of the conspiracy were perfected two days later in the home of Alonso de Avila. Friday was the day chosen for its execution, since the leading officials were meeting with the audiencia on that day. The government offices should be guarded, certain leaders were to enter to kill the oidores and the visitador, the archives were to be burned in order to destroy all records containing the king's name, and the treasury was to be used to buy adherents. Other leaders were to take over the government in the most important cities, one going to Vera Cruz where he was also to take possession of the fleet, another to Spain to bring back the eldest son of the Marquis, for he was to become heir to the throne. In seeking foreign support they would go first to the pope to secure investiture for the kingdom, and they would ask the ruler of France for permission to cross his kingdom in sending messengers to Rome. The reward for friendship would be to open the country to trade with the world. Since the colonists had money and supplies, and could trade, they had no need for Spain.[20]

[20] For the general plan, see González Obregón, *Los Precursores de la Independencia*, pp. 280 ff.; and Bancroft, *Mexico*, II, 610 ff.

"Several learned men and ecclesiastics" were said to be supporting the movement, and Avila held open house in order that the conspirators could come and go freely; but the Marquis, who was present only occasionally, hesitated and postponed action, causing delays and excuses until enthusiasm began to change to indifference. Avila, the soul of the revolution, was taken ill, after which interest declined and the opportunity was lost.

Martín Cortés, the Marquis, had remained on friendly terms with the visitador and is even supposed to have warned him against the conspiracy. No action had been taken, however, and the affair seemed to blow over and might have ended without any investigation, but information leaked out until the government had something on which to base its action. As happens so often when the guilty are being found out, a few turned informers. The conspirators retained their liberty for some time, during which period one more regal function took place, namely, the baptism of the newly-born twins of the Marquis and the Marchioness. Then came the news of an act on the part of the Council of the Indies which again threatened the possessions of the encomenderos, and Alonso de Avila made a last effort to stir the people to rebellion. It was too late. The government had prepared to defend itself, and the plan to kill the oidores was never carried out. The leading conspirators and the Marquis were arrested and imprisoned.[21]

Alonso de Avila and his brother Gil González were tried almost immediately, found guilty of treason, and decapitated eighteen days after the arrest.[22] They were considered as the first victims of independence.[23] Alonso finally confessed, but many believed that his brother professed his innocence to the

---

[21] For a list of the arrests made, see Bancroft, *Mexico*, II, 618 and n. 15.

[22] *Ibid.*, II, 619; for a record of the trial, see Orozco y Berra, *Noticia Histórica de la Conjuración del Marqués del Valle* (Mexico, 1853), Documento Num. 1, pp. 3-53.

[23] José María Luis Mora, *Méjico y sus Revoluciones* (Vols. I, III, IV, Paris, 1836), III, 425 n.

last and they, therefore, accused the audiencia of acting too hastily and unjustly. There was considerable excitement over the affair and only by having numerous soldiers stationed in the streets and public places could the government feel secure against an uprising.

When the new viceroy, Gastón de Peralta, Marquis de Falses, came, he took precaution before landing to make certain that there was no revolution brewing. Being a man of judicious temperament and fair-minded, he stopped the proceedings of the audiencia until he could investigate the situation. He soon liberated a number of the prisoners, much to the disgust of the audiencia; and he treated the Marquis with courtesy and great consideration, although he was held a prisoner to be sent to Spain. He also refused to allow the property of Cortés to be confiscated. The oidores now became the enemy of the viceroy and went so far as to accuse him of disloyalty, of favoring the conspirators, and of planning to make New Spain independent. They also succeeded in withholding his mail to Spain so that the king received only the bad reports about his viceroy and nothing from the viceroy. This would naturally arouse the king's suspicion. Further evidence that there was an alliance between the viceroy and the Marquis del Valle was deduced from the fact that the latter had won the friendship of the French king and that the former had relatives at the French court.[24] In the trial of the Marquis del Valle efforts were made to ascertain whether he had any connection with the French expedition which came to occupy Santa Helena in Florida in 1561, and if he intended to have any commercial relations with them after coming to New Spain.[25] As the oidores developed their case against the viceroy, the public lost all respect for them and considered the informers as infamous.[26] Unfortunately for Mexico, affairs be-

---

[24] Bancroft, *Mexico*, II, 623, n. 28.
[25] Orozco y Berra, *Noticia Histórica de la Conjuración*, p. 62.
[26] Bancroft, *Mexico*, II, 623.

came worse when the king acted on the complaints of the audiencia and replaced the viceroy who was unaware of having committed any crime.

Alonso Muñoz, a haughty and cruel old man, took over the control of the government as the senior commissioner. The persecution of the political conspirators was renewed with vigor. No one was safe, for those who were apprehended became informers in order to plead for leniency, and they often involved innocent persons in their accusations. The innocent suffered with the guilty, and the more victims the old man found the more suspicious he became. In the case of Martín Cortés, the son of Marina, he resorted to torture without getting a confession. In addition to the executions, a considerable number of those who came under the suspicion of Múñoz were exiled.[27] González Obregón has aptly called this period the Reign of Terror in Mexico.[28]

The unwarranted harshness of Muñoz aroused more opposition and greater hostility than the previous actions of the government, until there was danger of renewed resistance. Feeling confident that his actions were not in keeping with the intentions of the home government, the people secretly sent complaints to Spain and petitions for the removal of the tyrant. Their requests were granted, and Philip sent two of the former oidores of Mexico to displace Muñoz and to send him back to Spain, where he received no sympathy from the king and died shortly after his arrival.[29]

Again there was peace and order in New Spain and the colony had been saved for the mother country. The actual danger from revolution was probably not as great as would appear from the reports of witnesses in the trials of the accused. And yet the affair illustrates the thoughts and aspirations of the people. Perhaps they did not plan open rebellion,

---
[27] *Ibid.*, II, 624-629.
[28] González Obregón, *Los Precursores de la Independencia*, pp. 337 ff.
[29] Bancroft, *Mexico*, II, 630-632.

EARLY PLANS FOR INDEPENDENCE 29

but there were certainly those who believed that rebellion could be expected and in many cases desired. Had Martín Cortés, the Marquis, possessed the energy and self-reliance of his father, he might have set up an independent kingdom in Mexico, since the occasion was favorable.

Insurrections and riots continued to remind the Spanish authorities of the slender bonds with which they held their vast possessions. A Negro revolt in 1609 took on the appearance of an uprising for independence. It was reported in Mexico that on the day of the kings, the negroes, free and slave, planned to start an insurrection, kill the Spaniards, and set up their own king who would appoint nobles and grandees for his court. Because of cruel treatment large numbers had fled to the mountains and forests in the vicinity of Orizaba, state of Vera Cruz. They became so numerous and dangerous that the viceroy was forced to send a military expedition against them.[30]

Another uprising occurred a few years later, 1624, which also had the appearance of being against Spanish control. It may not have been for independence,[31] but it was certainly indicative of the dissatisfaction with the government. We have already seen what Thomas Gage, the English traveler, said about this revolt, suggesting that the creoles would take the first opportunity to remove the yoke of the hated Spaniards.[32]

The unity of the Spanish Empire was threatened and the strength of the Spanish king was tested again in 1640. New Spain, troubled with political and economic problems, was in a suitable condition for revolutionary activities. The treasury had suffered losses because of shipwreck and piracy, the mines

---

[30] Luis González Obregón, *D. Guillen de Lampart. La Inquisición y la Independencia en el siglo XVIIe* (Paris, 1908), pp. 247-256.

[31] Cf. Genaro García (ed.), "Tumultos y Rebeliones Acaecidos en Mexico," *Documentos inéditos ó muy raros para la Historia de México* (35 vols., Mexico, 1905-1911), X, 9-26.

[32] *Supra*, chap. ii, n. 10.

lacked regulations, provisions were scarce and expensive, taxes were high, and religious discord prevailed.[33] Such were the conditions on the arrival in June of the new viceroy, Diego López Pacheco Cabrera y Bobadilla, Duke of Escalona and Marquis de Villena. With him came also Palafox y Mendoza, the bishop-visitador, who was to play an important part in the political affairs of New Spain. The new viceroy was not the man to restore order, and it has even been said that he made conditions worse, since he was primarily interested in seeking entertainment and in gaining wealth, his official duties being left to his friends and his courtiers. The recommendations and criticisms of Palafox, the visitador, concerning a religious controversy aroused ill-feeling between the two until an open break became inevitable. From then on popular indignation against the viceroy, in place of being hushed, was encouraged by the visitador.[34]

Disturbed conditions in Mexico were soon increased by more disturbing events in Spain. Portugal, after sixty years of Spanish domination, took advantage of the troubles caused by the Catalonian rebellion, to gain her own liberty. An attempt had been made to unite the Portuguese and Spanish people by an exchange of officials, so that a number of Portuguese were serving in the Spanish Empire.[35] In place of creating unity, this method aroused hostility and jealousy, and after the Portuguese rebellion their presence was regarded as dangerous in any part of the Empire.

Accordingly, the viceroy of New Spain was informed in April, 1641, of the Portuguese and Catalonian rebellions in the Peninsula and was warned against the former, who, because of their number, their riches, and example of their countrymen,

[33] González Obregón, *D. Guillén de Lampart. La Inquisición y la Independencia en el siglo XVII*^{e}, p. 6; Carlos María de Bustamante, "El Venerable Señor Don Juan Palafox y Mendoza," *Voz de la Patria*, Supplemento, Num. 5 (Mexico, 1831), IV, 1.

[34] Bancroft, *Mexico*, III, 99, 101-102, and 105, n. 21; Priestley, *The Mexican Nation*, p. 147.

[35] Chapman, *History of Spain*, pp. 264, 266.

might start a revolution. Many of the Portuguese held important military and naval positions, purchased arms and munitions, and, in the eyes of the Spaniards, did not live with the prudence with which those should live, who, "although not themselves guilty, were members of a guilty nation."[36] The viceroy seemed apathetic and made no effort to enforce the orders for vigilance, causing considerable murmuring and some suspicion among the Castilians. Rumors about the viceroy's favoritism towards the Portuguese spread, and suspicion increased when it was learned that he was related to the Duke of Braganza, who had just made himself independent in Portugal. There were those who believed that the Duke of Escalona planned such a step for New Spain. In talking to a chaplain he told him among other things of a possible uprising, and in such an event, he added, "I would become king and my bishop, pope."[37] He adopted the formalities of royalty, using a dais whenever he held a public function. He also distributed circulars illustrating the greatness of the House of Pacheco, emphasizing its relationship to several royal families: of England, of France, of Savoy, of Modena, and even of Philip IV. Palafox, the watchful bishop, suspected him of building a royal basis for an independent ruling house.[38]

The Portuguese took delight in supporting the turbulent sections of the Spanish Empire, the uprising in Catalonia, the independence of Portugal, the revolutions in Brazil and Cartagena. A Portuguese captain said of the situation that men were being recruited in Mexico for the king of Portugal at the expense of the king of Spain.[39] It would seem likely that they encouraged the movement for independence, and they appealed to the vanity of the young viceroy to win him to their side and

[36] González Obregón, *Guillén de Lampart*, pp. 17-19.
[37] *Ibid.*, p. 22. Bancroft, *Mexico*, III, 106, n. 23, suggests that Escalona might have said this in jest because of the suspicion of Palafox.
[38] González Obregón, *Guillén de Lampart*, pp. 24-28.
[39] *Ibid.*, p. 21.

to make him their head, because he was a cousin of their king.[40] New Spain was in danger of an open break with the mother country.

The office of the Inquisition became alarmed at the turn of affairs and began a persecution of the Portuguese. None was allowed to leave and many were imprisoned; in fact, so many were arrested that the prisons could not hold them all. The work of the Inquisition and of Palafox checked the tide which had drifted towards independence, although arrests continued to be made for two years more.[41] The viceroy finally was obliged to act, and issued an order for all Portuguese to register and to hand over their arms; nor were they allowed to live in a port city. The penalty for non-compliance was death.[42] This act was in keeping with the views of Palafox who held that the viceroy had been too lenient. In the rivalry between the two, it was natural that the visitador should picture the victory as a supporter of the Portuguese cause and, perhaps, make his neglect appear as directed action. Being a lover of horses, the viceroy was once given a choice from two, one by a Spaniard and one by a Portuguese. Having mounted each of them, he frankly declared that the Portuguese horse was the better; and this was used as proof that the viceroy favored the Portuguese above the Spaniards.[43] Furthermore, a shipload of money arrived in Portugal at the very time that it was made independent, an incident which also directed suspicion toward the government of New Spain.[44]

Finally, the Spanish government, acting on the complaints of the visitador, who had not been treated with courtesy by Escalona, turned the viceregal office over to Palafox. Fearful of resistance, Palafox and his associates made preparations for

[40] *Ibid.*, p. 28.
[41] *Ibid.*, pp. 29-30.
[42] *Ibid.*, pp. 34-35; Bancroft, *Mexico*, III, 107.
[43] Bancroft, *Mexico*, III, 105; Niceto de Zamacois, *Historia de Méjico desde sus Tiempos más remotos hasta Nuestros Días* (18 vols., Mexico, 1877-1882), V, 327.
[44] Zamacois, *Historia de Méjico*, V, 327-328.

the change with utmost secrecy. Escalona was the last to be informed, and with the news of the change he was also told that his successor desired his immediate departure. Palafox tried to make the transfer appear as if it had been necessary for the preservation of Mexico as a loyal colony of Spain, and as if he had saved it from rebellion.[45]

A third figure, Don Guillén de Lampart, alias Guillermo Lombardo Guzmán, who had come to Mexico on the same vessel as Palafox and Escalona, played his own part in revolutionary intrigue, while the more conspicuous members of this trio were unwittingly preparing the way for him. This unusual person, a beggar almost, who served as a menial in the household of Escalona, was carried away by his dreams until he sought the pompous title of "Rey de la América y Emperador de los Mexicanos."[46] He was a man of some education since he gave up his menial work to teach Latin to the children of the secretary of the ayuntamiento.[47] He was young, well informed, and possessed an imagination so fertile and expansive that it became dangerous. Some said, judging from his actions and words, that he was crazy; and others, that he might be a statesman. Lampart, observing the revolutionary tendencies and the conflict between the viceroy and the visitador, believed this was an opportune time to establish the independence of Mexico. But he lived in poverty and could do little, depending on the liberality of his pupils and his protectors. Having seen Palafox replace the viceroy, he decided that he would do the same, but wait for the next viceroy before putting his scheme into action. He would give it the appearance of legality, and false cedulas had already been prepared by a clever Indian. The support and sympathy of the masses

---

[45] Bancroft, *Mexico*, III, 109-110.
[46] González Obregón, *Guillén de Lampart*, p. 1.
[47] Henry C. Lea, *The Inquisition in the Spanish Dependencies* (New York, 1922), p. 237, speaks of him as a man of wide learning, and a linguist, knowing English, French, Spanish, Italian, Latin, and Greek.

he hoped to gain by the abolition of the ancient taxes and tributes, freedom of trade, except with Spain, suppression of slavery, promises of advancement for the natives, and, above all, "free them from the tyranny of the Spanish kings."[48]

In theory the plan seemed good, but he who would be king shared his dreams with one too many. An army officer gained his confidence and received an account of the whole scheme which he then disclosed to the Holy Office of the Inquisition. Don Guillén de Lampart, Irish, and resident of Mexico was accused of instigating a diabolical project for making himself viceroy of New Spain in the following year of 1643, rebel against the government of Spain and name himself an independent sovereign. He planned to give freedom to the Indians, Negroes, and mestizos to secure their aid. He also declared that he was the son of Philip III and, therefore, half-brother of Philip IV, who ruled tyrannically over the colonies. This accusation needs to be enlarged. He had written letters, many letters, to sovereigns, but he never sent them. He wrote to the rulers of France, England, and Portugal, as well as to the pope, asking for their aid in his effort to make Mexico independent.[49] Those to the Duke of Braganza, the usurper of the Portuguese throne, and to the pope had been read to Captain Méndez, the accuser. Lampart even wanted to take credit for having made the Portuguese independence possible, saying that the Duke would not have succeeded except for his direction. The letter to the pope was a request for investiture for which he offered complete obedience. In his letter to the king of France he complained bitterly of the actions of Philip IV, his brother, whose misdeeds had made it necessary to deprive him of the kingdom of New Spain. Finally, he read a letter to the king of Spain himself in which he asked that the Marquis de Villena be dismissed from office because of his disloyalty and un-

[48] González Obregón, *Guillén de Lampart*, p. 69.
[49] *Ibid.*, pp. 75, 117.

faithfulness.⁵⁰ Concentration on these mental vagaries had given them a touch of reality in the imaginative mind of Don Guillén, and he would have one believe that his letter to the king, which he had evidently not sent, had been the cause of the viceroy's dismissal.

On being questioned on his method of becoming ruler, Lampart said that "he could easily become king of Mexico because no one had a right to the place, except he whom the people desired." Such had been the case often in history, he said, that a man became king because he would be king—simple enough—or because the people wanted him to be king. He also explained his claim to royal blood. He was the son, he said, of Philip III and an Irish widow who had charmed the Spanish king. He therefore spoke of Philip IV as his brother.⁵¹

In addition to his treasonable political aspirations, which would have been sufficient cause for his apprehension, he was accused of acting contrary to the Holy Faith of the Catholic church. He was believed to resort to astrology, to the practice of occult powers, and the secret use of powerful herbs in order to know the future, which was God's prerogative.⁵² He was therefore placed under the jurisdiction of the Inquisition instead of the civil authorities. The final accusation by the fiscal of the Holy Office contained seventy-one charges.⁵³ Lampart must have been meditating on his predicament for some time because he seemed to answer the charges with a ready tongue. When asked if his conscience did not bother him he replied that the pope himself had no clearer conscience.⁵⁴ Many of the charges he denied outright, especially those of Captain Méndez which he characterized as lies. He did, however, admit that he had written the letters to the European sovereigns, explaining that he did so only to discover the inten-

⁵⁰ *Ibid.*, pp. 80-83.   ⁵¹ *Ibid.*, pp. 79, 91.
⁵² *Ibid.*, p. 74.   ⁵³ *Ibid.*, p. 113.
⁵⁴ *Ibid.*, p. 115.

tions of the Portuguese who were planning to take over the Kingdom of New Spain. In connection with his supposed sorcery he was accused of having a secret and mysterious means of winning the affection of the Marquis de Villena and of the women. To this charge he answered intelligently enough that his "secret" was not that of a potent herb, as supposed, but the well-known medium of money.[55] This will suffice as an example of both charges and answers.

The outcome of the trial was almost a foregone conclusion. In this period the Inquisition was doing its most effective work in Mexico, and a suspect once in their hands had very little chance of regaining liberty. For seventeen years he lingered in prison, except for a brief period when he escaped, only to be recaptured. Finally, he was condemned "for divination and superstitious cures showing express or implicit pact with the demon, besides which he plotted rebellion and was a heretic sectary of Calvin, Pelagius, Huss, Luther and other heresiarchs and an inventor and dogmatizer of new heresies."[56] Guillermo Lampart was to be burned at the stake at the celebration of the *auto-de-fé* of 1659, but he anticipated the final act by throwing himself against the iron ring about his neck with such force that it killed him.[57]

The testimonies in his trial indicate that William Lampart had made extensive preparations for revolt, although his actions were so often guided by idiosyncrasies and unreasonable declarations that he does appear to have been slightly unbalanced. Nevertheless, his ideas and plans give us an insight into the revolutionary situation at this time. In spite of all his mental flights, he seems to have had a keen insight into world problems, although lacking in the stability and firmness necessary to put his ideas into action. Writing letters and not sending

[55] *Ibid.*, pp. 117-119.
[56] Summarized by Henry C. Lea, *Inquisition in the Spanish Dependencies*, pp. 238-239; see also González Obregón, *Guillén de Lampart*, p. 201.
[57] Lea, *Inquisition in the Spanish Dependencies*, p. 239.

them are good examples of his whole imaginative procedure. He stands out as another victim of the Inquisition and perhaps a martyr of the independence movement. Some effort has been made as late as the twentieth century to raise a statue to him as one of the precursors of independence.[58]

Riots and occasional uprisings continued to disturb the tranquility of New Spain during the last half of the seventeenth century. There were revolts by the Indians and mestizos, by the Negroes and mulattoes, and occasionally creoles took part. These demonstrations of a rebellious spirit were not necessarily for the purpose of setting up an independent state, and yet they were ordinarily aimed at the Spanish government or the Spanish people.[59] One of the more important of these riots took place in Mexico City in 1692.[60]

The immediate cause for the uprising was the shortage of corn, owing to the destruction of the crop by floods and freshets. The viceroy tried to moderate the suffering of the natives by having the government take over the distribution of grain and by allowing none of it to be sold by civilians. When the supply was exhausted, the masses blamed the viceroy for their suffering. Encouraged by the rabble of the city, the hungry Indians resorted to public demonstrations of their ill-feeling toward the government. The disturbance finally culminated in open rioting during which many buildings, including the viceroy's palace, were burned. The cries of the rioters were: "Death to the viceroy and all who defend him!" and "Death to the Spaniards and gachupines who are eating our corn."[61] Some writers have tried to make the riot appear as an attempt to rid Mexico of Spanish control, and such are the views of

---

[58] González Obregón, *Guillén de Lampart*, p. 232, n. 1. A brief account of this case is given by Lea, *Inquisition in the Spanish Dependencies*, pp. 236-239.

[59] Genaro García (ed.), *Tumultos y Rebeliones acaecidos en México, Documentos inéditos ó muy raros para la Historia de México*, X.

[60] *Ibid.*, X, 230-255.

[61] Bancroft, *Mexico*, III, 240.

Sigüenza y Góngora who was an eye witness and who later described the events.[62]

Near the close of the century, 1696, Spain prevented the execution of another plot which had threatened to develop into general insurrection.[63] So far she had been successful, but she left resentment and hatred in the wake of her punishments. While the colonials were being convinced of the futility of resistance, they were storing up grievances which became a constant threat to the security of the Spanish dominions.

In the meantime foreign intrusions of various kinds were becoming an increasing menace. The French and the British were especially jealous of the Spanish in America and challenged their monopoly of the western hemisphere.

[62] Irving A. Leonard, *Don Carlos de Sigüenza y Góngora* (Berkeley, 1929), pp. 40 ff.; and Irving A. Leonard (ed.), *Alboroto y Motín de México del 8 de Junio de 1692, Relación de Don Carlos de Sigüenza y Góngora* (Mexico, 1932), *passim*.
[63] Bancroft, *Mexico*, III, 257.

CHAPTER III

BOURBON AND BRITISH ADVANCE

> "Indeed, it was France which inspired in Spain the liveliest anxiety for the safety of the Indies."—WILLIAM E. DUNN.
>
> "It well becomes a free people to place others in the same condition with themselves. To deliver so many nations from Tyranny will be truer Glory than Alexander gained by all his victories. Let me add to this, that we shall thereby greatly increase our own Riches, wch. is the end of all conquests: and we shall do it without raising the just envy of our neighbors."—*Some Thoughts relating to Our Conquests in America.*

EUROPEANS watched with envy the growth of Spanish trade and territory in the sixteenth century. The lure of Spanish gold made an irresistible appeal to adventurers, and the treasures which were enriching the Old World were an incentive for depredations in the New. Anglo-Spanish conflict in Europe was invariably connected with rivalry in the Indies. Speaking of Philip II, Richard Hakluyt the younger said:

... if you touche him in the Indies you touch the apple of his eye: for take away his treasure which is *nervus belli,* and which he hath almoste oute of his West Indies, his olde bands of soldiers will soon be dissolved, ... his power and strength diminished, his pride abated and his tyranie utterly suppressed.[1]

His narrow commercial policy, his exclusion of foreigners, and his hostility to Protestants must have stamped him as a tyrant to the British. But in those stirring times of privateering and piracy there was little chance of shutting out inquisitive and acquisitive intruders.

While the disturbances occasioned by the conspiracy of the Avila brothers and Martín Cortés were still unsettled, John

---

[1] Quoted by Harry J. Carman and Samuel McKee, *A History of the United States* (Boston, 1931), I, 27-28.

Hawkins broke through the Spanish wall of monopoly and started the commercial penetration which was to continue until independence was achieved. Smugglers, from Hawkins to Hancock, weakened Spanish authority and advertised the advantages of an open trade with Spanish America, which would be equally desirable to foreigners and colonials. The exploits of Francis Drake and others of his type warned the Spanish king that henceforth he would have to redouble his vigilance if he were to preserve his possessions in America. He would have to guard against the danger from without as well as from within and be especially watchful lest the two combine.

Walter Raleigh and his associates became a nuisance in the Spanish territories of the New World before the end of the sixteenth century, but their attempts at settlement ended in failure, to the great relief and satisfaction of Spain. The surest way of preventing these English depredations in her colonies would be to conquer England herself, seemingly a reasonable ambition on the part of the greatest power in the western world. And such was the purpose of the Invincible Armada.[2] Spanish power was already declining; nevertheless, it was the defeat of the Spanish Armada in 1588 which proclaimed the decline of Spanish strength and the rise of British seapower. As Spain's ability to defend her colonies decreased, the ability of England to intervene became greater. British adventurers made use of the opportunity at once to attempt colonization, again meeting with temporary failure.[3]

To the dangers of piracy and war in the sixteenth century was added in the seventeenth the additional one of successful British colonization. When Jamestown was settled on Spanish territory in 1607, it was allowed to remain, partly because the Spaniards expected it to fail as all the other settlements of the British had previously failed. The small force which was sent

[2] Edward Channing, *A History of the United States* (New York, 1905), I, 131.
[3] *Ibid.*, I, 124-130, 156-157.

against it in 1609 retired without striking a blow,[4] probably in respect for British fighting ability. The result was that England gained a foothold on the American continent, which marked the first step in her long process of depriving Spain of her American possessions. Later the rulers of England, in ignorance or in utter disrespect for Spanish rights, gave away sea-to-sea grants which included territories already occupied by the Spaniards.[5] Further encroachments were made by taking possession of unoccupied islands of the Lesser Antilles, which gave the British an advantageous position in the Spanish Caribbean. The numerous Spanish attempts to dislodge them were generally unsuccessful.[6]

Cromwell had no sooner become the Protector of England than he turned his attention to foreign affairs and the development of English commerce. He offered Spain an alliance against France provided that Spain would permit the English to trade with the Spanish colonies. This was too great a risk for the Spaniards and the offer was rejected, whereupon Cromwell joined France.[7] He then started a great project against Spain, "nothing less than the expulsion of the Spaniards from the Antilles and the Main, and the plantation of Englishmen in their stead."[8] He was encouraged in his schemes by Thomas Gage,[9] a converted Jesuit, and Colonel Thomas Modyford of Barbados, and he is also supposed to have consulted Roger Williams. Among the motives given for the conquest were "the temptation to fill an empty treasury with the wealth of the Indies," reprisals for Spanish aggressions, and hatred of the

[4] *Ibid.*, I, 134.
[5] Herbert E. Bolton, *History of the Americas, A Syllabus with Maps* (Boston, 1928), map, p. 99.
[6] Herbert E. Bolton and Thomas M. Marshall, *The Colonization of North America* (New York, 1921), p. 252.
[7] Chapman, *History of Spain*, p. 262.
[8] J. W. Fortescue, "The Expedition to the West Indies," *Macmillan's Magazine*, LXIX, 184 (Jan., 1894).
[9] Thomas Gage was probably influenced by having witnessed the revolt in 1624 in New Spain.

Spanish religion. "We think," he wrote in 1655, "and it is much designed among us to strive with the Spaniards for the mastery of all those seas ... to restrain and suppress the tyrannies and usurpations of the King of Spain in those countries," which he claimed by "a pretended donation of the Pope."[10] The final conquest was limited to the island of Jamaica, which was small by contrast with Cromwell's ambitious plans, but which was to be of strategic importance in any future attempt of the British to attack the Spanish colonies.

Not until 1670 did Spain recognize British rights to any territory in America.[11] On the mainland England was then allowed to extend her control to Charleston. England's advance up to this time gave proof and warning of what her progress might be in the future. The Anglo-Saxon penetration developed into an irresistible force. Others joined in the competition for America, and France was for a long time as great a menace as England.

"Indeed, it was France which inspired in Spain the liveliest anxiety for the safety of the Indies," writes William E. Dunn.[12] Her first effort to deprive Spain of territory by settling La Florida proved a failure. Quebec, the first successful colony of France on the mainland, was founded the year after Jamestown and the year before Santa Fé, and gave France a foothold from which she extended into the heart of the continent, facing Spain on a long frontier. Like England, she had her pirates and her buccaneers, who not only attacked Spanish commerce but who helped to establish French colonies in the Caribbean. The French possession of Haiti, that nest of revolution, was due largely to the incursions of the buccaneers

---

[10] Fortescue, "The Expedition to the West Indies," *Macmillan's Magazine*, LXIX, 184; see also Frank Strong, "The Cause of Cromwell's West Indian Expedition," *The American Historical Review*, IV, 228-245 (Jan., 1899).

[11] H. H. Bancroft, *History of Central America* (3 vols., San Francisco, 1882-1887), II, 598-599.

[12] *Spanish and French Rivalry in the Gulf Region of the United States, 1678-1702* (Austin, 1917), p. 9.

from the little island of Tortuga. Louis XIV made France a country to be feared in Europe, and "Spain was convinced that he merely awaited a favorable opportunity to extend his aggressions to the new world, and attempt to wrest the choicest portions of her colonial domain." The organization of the French West India Company was a challenge to Spain in America. The Spanish believed that the French would use their settlements in Española as a "stepping-stone to more formidable aggressions on her mainland colonies...."[13]

Spain was right, for France became greatly interested in Spanish America in the last quarter of the seventeenth century. Peñalosa, a renegade Spaniard, tried in 1678 to induce the French king to undertake the conquest of some of New Spain's northern provinces. He is previously supposed to have tried to enlist the aid of Charles II in aggressions against the Spanish colonies.[14] Having explored the Mississippi River, La Salle started a project which was to be a thorn in the side of Spain as long as she owned Mexico. He secured the approval of his monarch for the establishment of a French colony at the mouth of the Mississippi River which, it was said, would serve as a base from which France could deprive Spain of some of her precious colonies.[15] And after the peace of Ratisbon in 1684, Spain feared more than ever that Louis XIV, being successful in Europe, "would attempt to put into execution his long-deferred plans of conquest in America."[16]

Spain was greatly alarmed and decided to guard her treasure lands in New Spain by a defensive occupation of the frontier between New Mexico and Florida.[17] Even though La Salle failed in his colonial undertaking, his expedition to Texas was immediately followed by counter-expeditions of the

---
[13] Dunn, *Spanish and French Rivalry in the Gulf Region*, pp. 9-10.
[14] *Ibid.*, pp. 13, 32.
[15] *Ibid.*, p. 31; Bolton, *Spanish Borderlands* (New Haven, 1921), p. 209.
[16] Dunn, *Spanish and French Rivalry in the Gulf Region*, pp. 17-20.
[17] *Ibid.*

Spaniards. When his project was taken up by Pierre Le Moyne d'Iberville, the Spaniards hastened to occupy both Florida and Texas to hold back the invaders. The occupation of Florida was done partly in defense against the advancing English.[18]

While the French were thrusting a colonial wedge between the Spanish in Florida and New Spain, the Scotch threatened to sever New Spain from the southern Spanish colonies by a settlement at Darien. William Patterson, who had recognized the advantages of Darien even before the deposition of James II, called this territory "the Key of the Indies and door to the world."[19] Its threefold value, he informed the king, was that it would furnish a base for operations against Spain, it would serve as a market for the West Indies trade, and it would become a post on the trade route to India and the Far East.[20]

The colony had no sooner been established than Spain set out to destroy it in order to protect her own possessions. Having saved Florida from the French, the Pensacola expedition was ordered to proceed against the Scotch at Darien.[21] The viceroy of New Spain took an active interest in the expedition for the defense of his colony, although the greatest fear of Spain was for Peru.[22] Troubles in New Spain gave the Scotch one brief moment of hope amidst all their fears and discouragements. "Our circumstances are in some respects very good," reported one of the settlers in his diary, "for we have advise [*sic*] by way of Portobelo that there is a great rebellion in Mexico, and Captain Diego, and all the Indians about him are at war with the Spaniards."[23] But the colony was soon doomed to failure because of Spanish hostility and the lack of leader-

---

[18] Bolton, *Spanish Borderlands*, pp. 207-219.

[19] For a complete account of the Scotch colony, see Francis Russell Hart, *The Disaster of Darien* (Boston, 1929).

[20] *Ibid.*, p. 45.

[21] *Ibid.*, pp. 101-104.

[22] *Ibid.*, p. 98. For the Spanish defense see chap. vii in particular and official correspondence in Appendix, Hart, *The Disaster of Darien*.

[23] Quoted by Hart, *ibid.*, p. 70.

ship, lack of supplies, and a lack of government support.[24] For the English had not given their support to the colony, in spite of the Spanish belief that the Darien expedition had been sponsored by the English to get more territory in America.[25]

By the close of the seventeenth century, however, England was quite firmly intrenched in the Caribbean, for she held Jamaica, Barbados, Antigua, Nevis, Montserrat, Barbuda, and a part of St. Kitts. And in the eighteenth century the West Indies gained in economic importance. Temperley says that

> they were the subterranean channel which might convey to England the whole measureless volume of Spanish trade, the silks and tea of the East, carried from Acapulco to Mexico and thence to Vera Cruz, the Peruvian gold piled high on the quays of Porto Bello, the galleons laden with jewels and plate which sailed from Carthagena and Havana.[26]

The turn of the century witnessed a change of great significance in the history of the Spanish Empire. The "era of regeneration," as the eighteenth century has been called,[27] was also an era of diplomatic intrigue, of intense colonial rivalry, and of frequent wars. A contest for the throne started when Charles II, the weakest and the last of the Hapsburg rulers of Spain, died in 1701 without any direct heir.

England did not sit idly by while the rival claimants, France and Austria, struggled for possession, for she could not allow a neighbor as powerful as France to add the Spanish Empire to her own. She feared not only a greater power in Europe, but that the union of Bourbon interests in America might hinder her commerce and check her expansion. As early as 1701, the French gave evidence of such commercial rivalry when they were given the contract to introduce Negro slaves

---

[24] The decline of the colony is described in chap. vi, *ibid.*
[25] *Ibid.*, pp. 74, 87, and 287.
[26] H. W. V. Temperley, "The Relations of England with Spanish America, 1720-1744," *Annual Report of the American Historical Association, 1911* (2 vols., Washington, 1913), I, 234.
[27] Chapman, *Spain*, p. 368.

into America. The valuable contraband trade of the British might also be lost if Spain were ruled by the powerful Bourbons.[28] England, therefore, allied herself with the Dutch in support of the Austrian archduke, not because she was for the archduke, but because she was against France.

Before the struggle began the British were investigating conditions in the Spanish colonies, and "Admiral Benbow had prepared his government for the possibility of there being something like a scramble for the Indies on the death of the King of Spain." Secretary Vernon gave a report of the investigation in a letter to the Duke of Shrewsbury (June, 1699) in which he said:

Admiral Benbow was lately at Carthagena, where he found the Spaniards very much unconcerned whether the king recovered or not. Upon his death they hoped to be under the power of one that would protect them, and openly avowed their inclination to France. These are generally their sentiments in the kingdom of Peru. But in *Mexico* it may happen otherwise; the Indians there are very earnest with the Countess of Montezuma, who is descended of their race, that she would take upon her the title of queen, which she seems willing to accept; but the Conde, her husband refuses it as yet—though it is thought, if the King of Spain dies, he will set up for himself.[29]

The Conde de Montezuma was at that time the viceroy of New Spain and, therefore, in a position to threaten Philip's control over his new possession. "We hear lately," says an English report, "of an extraordinary piece of news from the West Indies, and wish it may prove true. It is said that Montezuma, viceroy of *Mexico,* would not suffer their plate to come into the hands of the French, and the orders from Spain would not be obeyed while they were looked upon to be under the influence

---

[28] *Ibid.,* p. 370. An account of the rivalry for this trade is given by Curtis Nettels, "England and the Spanish-American Trade, 1680-1715," *The Journal of Modern History,* III, 1-32 (March, 1931).

[29] From a review of *Letters Illustrative of the Reign of William III; from 1696 to 1708, The Edinburgh Review,* LXXIV, 131 (Oct., 1841).

of France." It was England's policy to encourage the colonies to "throw off all dependence on the house of Bourbon, and submit themselves to Austria."[30] The British would have preferred, quite likely, to see Mexico independent, and that the Conde would "set up for himself." This was not to be, however, for Philip had Montezuma replaced by a viceroy of his own choice, supposedly to forestall any disaffection.[31]

The position of Mexico was still uncertain because the War of the Spanish Succession had only just begun. An unusual possibility occurred when Philip was opposed by the allies of the Austrians. Fearing that he might not be able to overcome the enemy and take possession of Madrid and Spain, he considered the possibility of transferring himself to Mexico, making that the capital of his overseas dominions.[32] It was also suggested that the former colony having become an independent kingdom might reverse the situation by conquering the mother country. "You will come back in ten years," said a courtier to Philip V, "to conquer Spain with the treasures of Mexico."[33] It was evidently believed that Philip might easily maintain an independent state in America.

There had been continual danger to New Spain as long as the war lasted, although the attacks were largely confined to privateering. Spain was fortunate during this critical time in having a loyal and able viceroy in Mexico, the Duke of Alburquerque.[34] At the end of the war Philip, a Bourbon and a grandson of Louis XIV, found himself in full possession of Spain and her colonies, although under the stipulation that he renounce all right to the French throne.[35]

[30] *Ibid.*
[31] Bancroft, *Mexico,* III, 264.
[32] Alamán, *Historia de Méjico,* I, 126; Carlos A. Villanueva, *Napoleón y la Independencia de América* (Paris, 1911), p. 33.
[33] M. De Pradt, *The Colonies and the Present American Revolutions* (London, 1817), p. 339; and his *Memoires historiques sur la Révolution d'Espagne* (Paris, 1816), p. 51 n.
[34] Bancroft, *Mexico,* III, 278-279.
[35] James W. Gerard, *The Peace of Utrecht* (New York, 1885), p. 292.

It was soon evident, however, that there was to be a closer relationship between France and Spain than in the past. The former sought advantages because of the presence of a Bourbon on the Spanish throne. The extension of the French settlements in Louisiana was probably done with the knowledge and the consent of Philip V.[36] Nevertheless, the close relationship between the ruling families was not sufficient to prevent occasional hostilities and even war. In the conflict between the two Bourbon powers in 1719, France again hoped to extend her territory at the expense of the Spanish settlements in the borderlands.[37] The viceroy of New Spain requested the governor of New Mexico in 1719 to secure the allegiance of the Apaches and other Indians to prevent the French from entering the Spanish dominions.[38] In the following year the defeat of the Villasur expedition on the Platte weakened the Spanish defense and gave the French greater freedom to advance.[39]

The treaty of Utrecht by which England recognized Philip V also gave the English the right to carry to the Indies a certain number of slaves and a shipload of merchandise each year,[40] a concession which was soon abused and which prepared the way for further competition and hostility. This taste of Spanish colonial trade developed a desire for more; accordingly, British merchants were ever anxious to persuade their government to protect and aid them.

The shifting alliances and international intrigues and suspicion paved the way for another conflict, and Spain declared war on England in February, 1727. America came in for its usual share in European wars and it has been said that England's "Chief interest lay in the stopping of the Spanish treasure

---

[36] Bolton, *The Spanish Borderlands*, p. 219.
[37] *Ibid.*, p. 226.
[38] Alfred B. Thomas, "Spanish Exploration of Oklahoma, 1599-1792," *Quarterly of the Oklahoma Historical Society*, IV, 186-213 (reprint, June, 1928), p. 18.
[39] *Ibid.*, p. 16.
[40] Justin Winsor (ed.), *Narrative and Critical History of America* (8 vols., Boston, 1884-1889), VIII, 307.

fleet."[41] The British had in fact prepared for this by having Admiral Hosier blockade Porto Bello as early as September, 1726. Hostilities ceased in less than a year; in 1729 a treaty of peace was signed which recognized the provisions of the Treaty of Utrecht. A rearrangement of allies followed in which England and Austria joined to oppose France and Spain.[42] There was still some division among the colonists, since the Bourbon victory in gaining possession of the Spanish throne had not been accepted as final in Mexico. There was in 1730 a movement on foot to make Mexico independent of Spain and to give the crown to an Austrian prince.[43] This was only one of several recurring episodes which indicated the continued allegiance to the Hapsburgs or hostility to the Bourbons. Three years later the first family compact to be signed by the Bourbons contributed to the antagonism between England and Spain.[44] Henceforth British hostility to the one endangered the possessions of the other.

In addition to the commercial penetration of England there was also territorial aggression. The advance of the English has been described thus by Bolton and Ross: "Relentlessly the Carolinians advanced. In vain the Spaniards tried to hold them back. The game was played by diplomacy, trade, and war."[45] The settlement of Georgia was proof that the English did not respect Spanish colonial claims in America. The constant irritation because of commercial irregularities and the added friction on the Georgia border created hostilities beyond the control of diplomacy, and war followed. The War of Jenkins' Ear gave further proof of England's growing interest in Spanish

[41] H. W. V. Temperley, "The Age of Walpole and the Pelhams," *Cambridge Modern History* (New York, 1925), VI, 59.
[42] *Ibid.*, VI, 60.
[43] Carlos A. Villanueva, *Fernando VII y los Nuevos Estados* (Paris, n.d.), p. 2.
[44] Temperley, "The Age of Walpole and the Pelhams," *Cambridge Modern History*, VI, 63.
[45] Herbert E. Bolton and Mary Ross, *The Debatable Land* (Berkeley, 1925), p. 45.

territory. The expeditions of Admiral Vernon and of Commodore Anson were undertaken in an effort to break Spanish control in America. The former centered his interests in the Caribbean and the Gulf of Mexico, while the latter penetrated the Pacific and expected to join with the forces of Vernon at the Isthmus, thereby separating Spanish North America from South America. "If not with a conscious determination to overthrow completely the rule of Spain in South America," says Bernard Moses, the plan was "at least to open the colonial ports to British trade."[46] There were, however, more advanced ideas than that of conquest.

The author of "Some thoughts relating to our Conquests in America" took under consideration various methods of making the most out of the war with Spain. The conquest of America seemed possible, but retaining possession would entail untold difficulties, and he added, "A wise man would never grasp at what he cannot hold." The chief aim of England was to open Spanish American ports to trade, a condition which was hindered by Spanish tyranny, "a tyranny they have long groaned under, and which they are ready to shake off, whenever they shall have a proper opportunity." Therefore, as the third and last proposal, he suggested that the emancipation of the Spanish colonies would be the most advantageous policy for England. This might take a long time, but the treasures of the liberated colonies would be great enough to pay for the war. "To deliver so many nations from Tyranny will be truer Glory than Alexander gained by all his Victories." There was more in the motive than to give liberty to an oppressed people and to gain glory surpassing that of Alexander's, for the writer added: "We shall thereby greatly increase our own Riches, wch. is the end of all conquests: and we shall do it without raising the just envy of our neighbors."[47]

[46] Bernard Moses, *Spain's Declining Power in South America*, p. 312, n. 1.

[47] One endorsement on this report is in Vernon's hand, "Santiago and the Freeing of Spanish America, 1741," *The American Historical Review*, IV, 325-328 (Jan., 1899).

These were quite reasonable views, and England might well accept them as a guide for action. Admiral Vernon, too, who commanded the expedition in the Caribbean, intimated that the way to open the American trade to the British merchants was to liberate the Spanish colonies.[48] Later Lord Anson, the other great leader in the American expeditions, was to make similar recommendations. The British had been informed from other sources during the war that the desire for independence was great enough to warrant an attempt to liberate the people of New Spain, who would then "chuse their own Governors, drive out all the *Old Spaniards* and declare for us."[49]

Additional evidence that there was a desire for independence was given when a revolutionary faction of Mexico in 1742 sent a commission to General Oglethorpe to get British support in freeing Mexico.[50] The plan was to found an independent kingdom under an Austrian prince, and to reward the British for their assistance by giving them a monopoly of Mexican trade. Oglethorpe was interested and Sir Robert Walpole was also favorably impressed, but the latter's ministry came to an end before any definite action was taken. Lord Anson's plan was to destroy the Spanish power by getting support from the Indians who were to be armed for that purpose. This proposal was considered by Newcastle, but did not materialize.[51] British interest was diverted to the European phase of the struggle when the War of Jenkins' Ear merged into the War of the Austrian Succession.

Beginning with the War of Jenkins' Ear there was, therefore, a change in the British policy toward Latin America. This war occupies a "place midway between the raids of the earlier free-

---

[48] Villanueva, *Napoleón y la Independencia de América*, p. 19.

[49] *The Present State of Revenues and Forces by Sea and Land of France and Spain, compar'd with those of Great Britain* (London, 1740), p. 33.

[50] Villanueva, *Napoleón y la Independencia de América*, p. 19.

[51] *Ibid.*, p. 24; see the plan of Captain Kaye for a similar idea later, William S. Robertson, "Francisco de Miranda," *Annual Report of the American Historical Association, 1907* (2 vols., Washington, 1908), I, 198-199.

booters and the later more elaborately prepared attempts to supplant Spanish power in America."[52] The keynote of the new policy of England hereafter, then, was that of liberation rather than conquest; for by liberating the colonies from Spain and maintaining them as independent states, she could reap the benefits without antagonizing jealous neighbors. With each war the revolutionary plans became more pronounced, and one war followed another in rapid succession.

In 1756, the year of the formal opening of the war in Europe, which had already started in America, a Frenchman by the name of Bertrand wrote a memoir on the revolutionary plans of England. He referred particularly to the northern part of the Spanish possessions which he called "the occidental circle," the area from Peru to the northernmost part of Spanish North America. After considering the encroachments of English commerce in Spanish territory, he gave a warning that unless measures were taken to prevent it, the next step of England would be to effect a revolution in a great part, if not all, of the Spanish dominions in America.[53]

While the British were depriving France of her American colonies during the Seven Years' War, they were carrying on an extensive illicit trade with Spanish America. This was the "golden age of contraband." If we may trust the report of a Spanish navigator who left Cádiz for Vera Cruz, it would appear that while he was skirting the coast of Mexico to avoid corsairs and English warships, he counted about four hundred vessels which were engaged in contraband trade.[54] We may allow for some exaggeration and still accept the fact that there must have been considerable smuggling.

[52] Moses, *Spain's Declining Power in America*, p. 312, n. 1.
[53] Robertson, *Miranda*, p. 210.
[54] "*Idée générale du commerce de toutes les Indes Espagnoles Royaume de Mexique*," Beliardi Papers from Bibliotheque Nationale, Fr. 10769, p. 105, transcripts in Bancroft Collection, University of California. These papers have already been used by Sister Mary Austin Collins in her doctoral thesis, *The Reforms of Charles the Third in New Spain* (MS., Berkeley, 1927).

To deprive England of this profitable trade[55] and to save Spanish America from English dominance, France began negotiations for a closer union between the Bourbon rulers. Choiseul, who became foreign minister of France in 1758, was particularly active in arousing the fears of Spain in order to put her in a receptive mood for joint action. Charles III, probably as anxious as France to strike a blow at their greatest colonial rival, hesitated because a hostile act on his part would give England a pretext for an expedition against his colonies.[56] Eventually, however, the agreement was made which was to unite the fortunes and misfortunes of the Bourbons. The Family Compact was signed in August, 1761, but kept secret for a time, perhaps to give Spain an opportunity to prepare for the war which seemed now to be inevitable, and which England made a reality in January, 1762, a month before the second part of the treaty was signed.[57]

England was now forced to change her war plans to include her new active enemy, Spain. She had traded with the Spanish colonies during peace, but could she trade with the enemy? France hoped to divert the English in part from her own possessions in America to those of her ally. Such were the opinions of Choiseul, at least, who was proud of the alliance and said that in case they were unsuccessful in the war, "I had in view that the losses of Spain would lessen those that France might sustain."[58] Although England was actively engaged in the conquest of the vast territory of the French, she found time and means to gain a foothold in Spanish America by the capture of Havana. This point would be extremely im-

[55] In the year in which the war began Richard Rolt published a book in London on the *History of South America,* dedicated "To the right honourable, the Lords Commissioners of Trade and Plantations: and to the merchants of Great Britain." This was to guide British interest where it would have the greatest influence.

[56] François Rousseau, *Regne de Charles III d'Espagne* (Paris, 1907), I, 31.

[57] The diplomacy of the period is described in *Cambridge Modern History,* VI, 340-341.

[58] André Soulange-Bodin, *La Diplomatie de Louis XVe et le Pacte de Famille* (Paris, 1894), p. 243.

portant for the additional conquest of Mexico, if such a project were entertained, and there were those who thought that the possession of Havana was equivalent to the possession of the key to the rest of Spanish North America. The conquest of this vast kingdom would undoubtedly be followed by difficulties. Abbé Raynal tells of the more reasonable plan, which was not to take possession of Mexico, but to leave it at liberty either to choose a sovereign of its own or to form itself into a republic.[59] This would give England the advantage of its commerce without its former limitations and risks, which Admiral Vernon had lamented.

In the meantime the possessions of France were being lost. A part was, however, saved for her ally in that the western part of Louisiana was given to Spain, a gift which was accepted with considerable hesitancy. The main point of disturbance was that of having the conquering English as neighbors. If Spain did not accept the gift it might fall to the English, and under them "Louisiana would assuredly become dangerous to the peace and safety of Mexico."[60] West Louisiana was finally accepted in order to protect New Spain from an untrustworthy neighbor.

Having received the cession, Spain was somewhat at a loss as to what to do with it. A Spanish citizen of Louisiana gave an account of the possibilities for the newly acquired territory. The Spaniards might occupy it and restore it, he said, or they might "abandon it to its natural inactivity as a detached colony of little importance," or they might "destroy the settlements and demolish it completely in such a way as to leave it only a desert that can never tempt the cupidity" of their neighbor.[61]

---

[59] Abbé Raynal, *A Philosophical and Political History of the Settlements and Trade of the Europeans in the East and West Indies*, IV, 352-354.

[60] W. R. Shepherd, "The Cession of Louisiana to Spain," *Political Science Quarterly*, XIX, 438-458 (Sept., 1904).

[61] "*Reflexions sur la Louisiane par un Citoyan Espagnol*," Beliardi Papers, Fr. 10769, p. 100 (translated by Sister Mary Austin Collins from Bancroft Library transcript, *Reforms of Charles III in Spain*, Appendix, pp. 328-347).

According to Lord Rochford, the British ambassador at Madrid, the plan to make Louisiana a desert was also considered by the government. "To my certain knowledge," he informed Halifax, "it has been proposed in council to make a desert of it,—the reason, indeed, given for this was that it would put our settlements at a distance from Mexico."[62] The Spanish citizen who wrote the "Reflections on Louisiana," considered above, also referred to the English as the deciding factor. He would not abandon Louisiana, since that would be equivalent to giving it to the English at the first war. What he thought of the English can be best expressed in his own words:

> These proud islanders are well known, and they make too little mystery of their intentions for us not to have the right of presuming that they will, in time of peace, depend upon ruse to invade or usurp the whole commerce of our colonies, and that, in time of war, they will do all in their power to expand their own possessions at our expense on the side of the south and west.

No, they could not trust the English, and Louisiana could not be made a desert; nor would it be sufficient to leave a few guards there, since these could not prevent England from taking possession. Once in Louisiana, "it would be easy then to advance to Mexico." His opinion was that England would have to be blocked, and for this purpose Louisiana should be settled and defended. He portrayed the danger of English advance as follows:

> Just as water, gaining gradually, little by little undermines the dike that holds it back until it be broken, and the water spreads over the plains and floods the whole country, so the English drawing nearer and nearer and tightening more and more the circle of the sea and the desert with which we are surrounded, and which we have taken for our only defense will rush from all parts, from the east and from the west upon our rich gardens which today are the aims of their unbounded ambition.

[62] Letter of March 11, 1765, quoted by Vera L. Brown, "Anglo-Spanish Relations in America," *The Hispanic American Historical Review*, V, 345, n. 20 (Aug., 1922).

The writer supported his theory by describing the British control of trade, especially the slave trade by which they tried to weaken the Spanish resistance until they could "some day penetrate the colonies, invade, and usurp them almost without striking a blow."[63] The English menace was real and it was being recognized.

France took credit for guarding the Spanish possessions in North America by her control of Louisiana. Now, after the transfer, the Family Compact would be the means of protection for concerted action against a common enemy. The English were winning territory, as the Bourbons had just witnessed, and it was feared that they would "rush upon New Spain, even Mexico, an invasion which they were powerful enough to accomplish without any assistance from Europe."[64]

That these expressions of fear were justified by the circumstances can readily be seen from a survey of English possessions. At the end of the Seven Years' War eastern Louisiana from France and the Floridas from Spain were cessions which moved England forward in her advance to the heart of New Spain. A century of opposition to the British in Honduras had failed to expel them; and the British advance to the Mosquito Coast and their right to cut logwood on the Campeche Coast gave them additional footholds for further incursions.[65] Jamaica in the center was already in her possession and had long formed a thorn in the side of Spain, since it was the source of the smuggling with the Spanish lands of the Caribbean. Thus the links were being forged which threatened to surround Mexico and to cut her off from the mother country, a cordon which might at any time be tightened to strangle the colony into a forced independence. It was clear that England threatened Spain's

---

[63] *"Reflexions sur la Louisiane,"* Beliardi Papers, Bibliothèque Nationale, Fr. 10769, pp. 101-102, Bancroft Library transcript.

[64] *Ibid.*

[65] For the beginning of foreign interest in Central America, see Bancroft's chapter on "Belize," *Central America,* II, 623 ff.

colonies as she had formerly threatened those of France, and something had to be done to protect and to preserve them.

If France could alarm the court of Spain sufficiently, she might profit commercially as well as politically by the Family Compact. Spain was cautious and slow, fearing England but distrusting France. The prospects of British assistance for the independence of Spanish America were again emphasized as being more reasonable than conquest. In the words of a contemporary:

> It would be sufficient for her to induce the inhabitants to shake off the yoke of Spain and elect a king; she could offer to them a Catholic prince and supply them with forces to overcome the obstacles they might encounter; this would be done on condition that the Indies would carry on commerce with the English alone. The inhabitants of the Indies bear grudgingly the yoke of Spain; they recognize her authority only through the number of viceroys, governors, and alcaldes who are as so many leeches whom we send to annoy them and become rich at their expense. They suffer from not having any share in these offices, besides, all that Spain sends for their use is very expensive. It can be well understood how delighted they would be with such an offer and how much they would gain from it. There could be no doubt but that they would eagerly accept the offers of that party. Since there is no army in the Indies, the governor could not successfully oppose a secession of the kind when the inhabitants would be aided by the English. All could be over before news of it could reach Spain or even before a fleet and troops could be dispatched. Being master of the seas, the English could prevent the troops from reaching their destination.[66]

The latter statement is corroborated by A. T. Mahan who quotes: "Whatever power commands the sea may command the wealth and power of Spain."[67]

It was believed that the independence movement could easily be started in Peru and Chile, perhaps more easily than in Mexico, but Spanish South America was more inclined to

---

[66] "Idée générale du commerce de . . . Royaume de Mexique," Beliardi Papers, Bibliotheque Nationale, F. Fr. 10769, pp. 49-50 (B. L. T.).

[67] *Influence of Sea Power on History* (Boston, 1902), p. 327.

favor the French than the English. Once started the revolutionary idea would spread. The colonies most suitable for English action would undoubtedly be Mexico and those situated nearest the Caribbean, because of the possessions already in that region. The danger was that England might merely become the master of certain strategic points and thereby intercept all communication and commerce to such an extent as to make Mexico free and independent of Spain.[68]

France considered it her duty to support Spain in her efforts to check the British menace. This would be doubly advantageous since the French could work indirectly against the English while gaining economic favors for themselves. Furthermore, it was Choiseul's idea to make Spain a stronger ally by improving her economic conditions.[69] The French urged a greater freedom in trade and a greater variety of occupation and industries for the colonies. Before adopting any new program for the Indies, it was suggested that the Spanish government obtain a thorough knowledge of the country and people in order to know their "attachments and aversions for Spain, and note 'any existing facility which might enable them to follow the latter propensity'." Economic improvement it was thought might increase the loyalty and remove any desire to "shake off the yoke of Spain."[70] As an example of a necessary economic change, a memoir on the Family Compact pointed out that the cultivation of rice in the southern mainland colonies of England was profitable, largely because of Spanish and French consumption. It ought, therefore, to be developed in Spanish America "in order to prevent the prosperity of the English colony of Carolina, so favorably situated to sustain the establishments which the English have acquired

[68] *"Idée générale du commerce de . . . Royaume de Mexique,"* Beliardi Papers, Bibliotheque Nationale, F. Fr. 10769, p. 50 (B. L. T.).

[69] Jean Lemoine, "The Reversal of Alliances," *Cambridge Modern History,* VI, 351; Priestley, *José de Gálvez,* p. 38.

[70] *"Idée générale du commerce de . . . Royaume de Mexique,"* Beliardi Papers, F. Fr. 10769, p. 28 (B. L. T.).

in the Gulf of Mexico, and to favor the ultimate conquests which they intend to make upon the Spanish mainland."[71] The French believed that the Spanish colonies would be lost if Spain acted alone. And if she would not coöperate, France would look elsewhere. The writer of the *Reflexions* says: "The evolution of Empire is in the order of possible events, and, it appears, the one that threatens America is not far distant. If Spain were obliged to make way for another power in Mexico, it would be in the power of France to establish her Empire in all that part of South America which is not inferior to Mexico."[72]

The Abbé Béliardi, who had served as French agent-general of commerce and naval affairs in Madrid, had worked assiduously since his arrival in 1758 to establish a closer economic relationship between the Bourbon powers. He served chiefly as the personal representative of Choiseul in that minister's attempt to replace English with French influence in Spanish affairs.[73] He had been partially successful, and from 1763 to 1766 French goods were passing through Spain and competing with British contraband goods from Jamaica.[74] While this rivalry was causing Spain considerable worry, and showing the necessity of drastic changes both to improve and to preserve the colonies, she was too antagonistic to foreigners to accept any coöperative plans with France. Charles III, although a Bourbon, had no desire to subordinate himself to his ally and neighbor. He hoped to preserve the kingdom of New Spain by necessary reforms. And yet these very reforms may have grown from the work and plans of Béliardi and in keeping with French policy.[75]

[71] *Ibid.*
[72] Quoted by Sister Mary Austin Collins, *The Reforms of Charles the Third*, p. 146.
[73] Priestley, *José de Gálvez*, pp. 38-39.
[74] *Cambridge Modern History*, VI, 351.
[75] Priestley, *José de Gálvez*, pp. 39-40.

CHAPTER IV

REFORMS AGAINST REVOLUTIONS

> "The thought of a republic had been a rosy colored bubble of the imagination, or rather a flitting rainbow spanning the firmament of a dream, and encouraging hopes but to have them extinguished in the night of the gathering storm."—CHARLES GAYARRÉ.
>
> "Charles III (1759-1788) possessed rare qualities which his predecessors had lacked. . . . He merits a place among the greatest of Europe's benevolent despots. With the meager resources at his command . . . he gave to Spain an administration which all but restored her to her ancient prestige; he almost made a success of his colonial world."—HERBERT I. PRIESTLEY.

AT THE close of the Seven Years' War Spain faced a crisis which demanded action. Her hold on America had been weakened; France prophesied tragic results unless the colonial policy were improved, and the Spanish treasury certainly showed the need of a greater income. Grievances of the colonies were added to the threats and warnings of foreign neighbors, and isolated adventurers were ever present to take advantage of Spain's difficulties.

In 1765 deputies representing the dissatisfied element in Mexico came to Madrid to place the grievances of their people before the king, while Franklin was making a similar appeal for his people before the British parliament. They complained particularly of the domineering attitude of the viceroys and of the discrimination against the creoles. These representations may have had some influence on the king's later reforms, but on being dismissed the commissioners believed that there was little or no hope of getting relief from the Spanish crown.[1] While they were smarting under this new rebuff they were in the proper psychological mood to entertain revolutionary ideas.

Two accounts are given of their conspiracies with French-

---
[1] Report of C. L. Cardinaux to Gov. Dalling of Jamaica, P. R. O., C. O. 137, Vol. LXXVII; cf. also Villanueva, *Napoleón y la Independencia*, pp. 25-27.

men, in which plans were made for the independence of New Spain. The first of the French leaders was one D. Guiller in whose house the conspirators met.[2] Whoever suggested a satisfactory plan was to be rewarded by the title of duke and possibly the hereditary governorship of Vera Cruz.[3] Here was an opportunity for both adventurers and philosophers. A monarchy under a Mexican was not deemed advisable because they could agree on no one who would be deserving to rule the rest. The proposal to accept an Austrian prince as their monarch was also dismissed.[4] It was then suggested that they set up a republic with the aid of England, giving her the cities of Vera Cruz and Ulloa as a reward for her services. Some hesitation was shown to this proposal because it was feared that England might dominate Mexico and endanger her religion, and only by securing the support of the ecclesiastic element could they hope to succeed. Finally an agreement was made with Guiller, who stipulated certain restrictions on England. He in turn was to be rewarded by territorial possessions, comprising what is today practically the state of Vera Cruz; he should have permission to maintain a small army with fortifications and an arsenal; his title should be the Duke of Orizava; and his income, about two million pesos a year, was to be guaranteed by England.

News of the "projected uprising to throw off the Spanish yoke and to erect an independent republic" was sent to Spain from London.[5] Orders were soon directed to Croix, the viceroy of New Spain, to prevent the revolution by making full use of his military facilities. In response to this warning he in

[2] Manuel Rivera y Cambas, *Los Gobernantes de México* (2 vols., Mexico, 1872-1873), I, 414-415.
[3] Under the new plan England would receive Vera Cruz. See below, p. 63.
[4] Villanueva, *Napoleón y la Independencia*, p. 27.
[5] From a summary report of the royal action, A. G. I., 90-2-20. A man by the name of D'Edon is supposed to have revealed the conspiracy in London, Rivera y Cambas, *Los Gobernantes de México*, I, 415.

turn called a special junta to consider the danger.⁶ While the authorities were preparing their defenses another conspiracy was under way, which resembled the previous one so much as to be taken for the same, but which was probably a sequel to the previous one.

The promoter of the second phase of the conspiracy was a Frenchman known as the Marquis D'Aubarde, supposedly a military officer who had escaped from the Bastile and who sought refuge and adventure in Spain.⁷ Francisco Louis Cardinaux, a Swiss who had been a French officer, said that D'Aubarde was a member of the military order of St. Louis and that he had been sent to Madrid by the French government to solicit the office of governor of Louisiana.⁸ This would be in keeping with the opinion that French interest in Louisiana was revived in 1767. Even though the request were based merely on the personal ambition of the Marquis, it was more reasonable than might appear on first thought, especially when one considers the difficulties the Spanish had in establishing their authority over Louisiana.

When the request of the Marquis for the governorship of Louisiana was rejected by the Spanish government, he made common cause with the Mexican commissioners who had failed to win favor for their constituents. In the conferences which followed, the plans for the independence of New Spain were continued or revived. One of the banished Jesuits joined the group,⁹ a fact indicating not only the date of the conspiracy

⁶ A. G. I., 90-2-20.

⁷ Villanueva, *Napoleón y la Independencia*, pp. 25-27. A detailed manuscript account by Cardinaux was sent to London during the American Revolution by Gov. Dalling of Jamaica, P. R. O., C. O. 137, Vol. LXXVII; cf. Robertson, *Miranda*, pp. 200-202.

⁸ In Dalling's report, P. R. O., C. O. 137, Vol. LXXVII.

⁹ Villanueva gave the date for the arrival of the Mexican commissioners as 1765, and of D'Aubarde's arrival in England as 1766. Yet if the banished Jesuits took part, the final plans must have been as late as 1767. It is possible, however, that M. Guiller and D'Aubarde were the same person and that the plot continued for two years before its originators were discovered (Villanueva, *Napoleón y la Inde-*

but that Spain had created a new enemy which was henceforth to give encouragement and aid to revolutionary projects. Again the conspirators recognized their own limitations and decided to seek foreign aid.

Some opposition was shown to the selection of England as the foreign ally, seemingly based on her failure to espouse their cause earlier. England would have the same reason for opposing a republic in Mexico that Spain later had for fearing an independent republic in the British colonies. The example of a successful revolution would threaten the possessions of either country. Yet the commercial advantages to England were great enough to stimulate interest and to overcome most objections. The special inducements were to be the offer of Vera Cruz and San Juan de Ulloa, special commercial favors with the rest of Mexico, and a loan of £20,000,000 at three per cent interest.[10] In case England were drawn into the war because of her aid to Mexico, revolts would also be started in Peru and Chile to divert the attention of Spain. The weakened condition of Spain after the last two wars gave additional security to England.

D'Aubarde, the leader of the conspiracy, was to be handsomely rewarded by full possession of an independent strip of territory between the British at Vera Cruz and the Mexican republic. His little principality, resembling the proposed one for D. Guiller, would serve as a barrier and as a link between the British and the Mexicans.

Having agreed upon a plan of action, the conspirators decided to send D'Aubarde to London to lay the scheme before the British government.[11] After a careful examination of the

---

pendencia, pp. 25-27). W. S. Robertson, *Miranda*, p. 200, gives the date for the commissioners from Mexico in Madrid as being between 1767 and 1771.

[10] Cardinaux's report to Dalling, P. R. O., C. O. 137, Vol. LXXVII; Villanueva, *Napoleón y la Independencia*, p. 26, mentions merely a commercial monopoly.

[11] Villanueva gives a different account of the presentation of the plan to the British. According to his version, M. Durand, a Frenchman and a friend of the Marquis, was intrusted with the papers, which he sewed into the lining of his

plan, the Earl of Shelburne, Secretary of State, decided to adopt it. The Earl of Rochford and two secretaries were employed in making preparations for the project. According to a report from the Governor of Jamaica, "the expedition was to consist of five men of war with a sufficient number of troops and warlike stores to garrison the city of Vera Cruz and the Island of S^n. Juan de Ulua the moment it should have been surrendered." The plans were to be perfected so that "the revolution was to take place at one and the same time all over the Empire of Mexico."[12]

The great difficulty, as usual, was that of keeping the plans secret until the project was under way. The Prince of Masserano, Spanish ambassador in London, soon heard rumors of the preparations, and together with the French ambassador protested against such actions during a time of peace. When Lord Weymouth replaced the Earl of Shelburne he found it necessary to disavow the transactions of his predecessors; and when the British government came to an agreement with Spain, the project was left dormant[13]—but not dead. The British failure to get commercial freedom as requested from Spain in 1768 left England still desirous of liberating Spanish America.[14]

According to Villanueva, Marquis D'Aubarde was on hand to capitalize any favorable situation. He was at first given a pension by the British, and later he formed a company in London, ostensibly to trade with Mexico, but in reality to prepare that country for independence. He was next supposed to

---

coat. On reaching Paris he became curious about the contents of the papers, examined them, and found that the writing had been made quite illegible by perspiration. Durand then decided to turn against the conspirators, returned to Madrid, and disclosed the whole scheme to the government for a sum of money. He reported that "Aubarede" [sic] would be named Prince of the Serranías and captain-general of all the troops of the republic (*Napoleón y la Independencia*, p. 27).

[12] P. R. O., C. O. 137, Vol. LXXVII.   [13] *Ibid.*

[14] Villanueva, *Napoleón y la Independencia*, p. 28.

have gone to Mexico and Peru, to organize revolutionary juntas, after which he returned to London and continued his work by correspondence.[15]

The French in the meantime had got the idea of liberating the English colonies, based on Franklin's report in Parliament, which seemed to indicate such a possibility. But this, Durand, the French minister to England, said, would lead to the emancipation of the French and Spanish colonies also.[16] In 1769 the Count of Châtelet, the new minister to England, suggested to the Duke of Choiseul that Louisiana be made into a republic as an example of liberty and independence to the British colonies.[17] This would seem desirable from the viewpoint of France, but what would be an example to the English colonies would also be an example to those of France's ally, Spain.

Spain found the French gift of western Louisiana somewhat of a white elephant. Having accepted the gift, Spain was still very slow about establishing her authority in the new province. Not until 1766 did the first governor, Antonio de Ulloa, make his appearance, and even then he was satisfied with a dual system combining the French administration with his own. Ulloa was an experienced traveler, a scientist, a cultured gentleman, but seemingly lacking in the qualities of tact and leadership necessary for a successful administrator. On seeking information about the people he had come to rule, he discovered that nearly all the former governors represented them as being "a set of reprobates, infected with the *rebellious spirit of republicanism*." And Aubrey, the last French governor, intimated "that between the perversity and the insubordination which prevailed in the past, and that which existed in the present, there was no perceptible difference."[18]

The French inhabitants of Louisiana did not relish being

[15] *Ibid.*, p. 29.
[16] Sept. 3, 1767, *ibid.*, p. 28.   [17] *Ibid.*, p. 29.
[18] Charles Gayarré, *History of Louisiana* (4th ed., 4 vols., New Orleans, 1903), II, 165.

transferred to a foreign power, and they particularly resented the commercial restrictions of the Spanish government. Therefore they sent a delegate, Jean Milhet, to France to remonstrate against the treaty of cession. On his return in 1767 the inhabitants learned to their sorrow that his mission had failed. Yet the people were far from being reconciled to the change, and the hostility to Spain increased as time went on.

The anti-Spanish feeling was fostered by a few leaders until it grew to proportions which prepared the way for open resistance. The most conspicuous leader was Lafrénière, a native of Louisiana of obscure birth, but with eloquence, leadership, unbounded ambition, and "the majestic aspect of a king, so much so, that he had been nicknamed Louis XIV."[19] The policies and actions of Governor Ulloa were criticized and interpreted as if they were all against the people. On October 28, 1768, the conspirators entered the city with firearms and took possession. Governor Ulloa and his charming Peruvian wife took refuge on a Spanish frigate on the advice of Aubrey, the former French governor who was serving Ulloa.

At the meeting of the Superior Council, which was held on the following day, Lafrénière made effective use of his eloquence in convincing the insurgents that the Spaniards had not preserved their liberties, which he thought the provisions of the treaty guaranteed. Appeals were made to uphold liberty against despotism and to resist the slavery which threatened them. Resolutions were passed and appeals were to be made. Aubrey's protests against the actions of the rebels were to no avail.[20]

The aim of the insurgents appeared to be primarily to secure their transfer back to France and to "their sovereign Lord the King Louis the well-beloved."[21] Last of several possibil-

[19] *Ibid.*, II, 187.
[20] *Ibid.*, II, 193-206. For a recent account, see E. Wilson Lyon, *Louisiana in French Diplomacy, 1759-1804* (Norman, 1934), pp. 45-47.
[21] Gayarré, *History of Louisiana*, II, 199.

ities was probably that of winning reforms from Spain. One plan, which was necessarily kept secret, was that of seeking British aid. Two commissioners were sent to Pensacola, supposedly to get British troops to support them. Ulloa, too, believed that the rebels were contemplating "to transform this colony into a republic, under the protection of England."[22] Aubrey said they preferred English rule to Spanish, since they feared "to be governed as despotically as the Mexicans."[23] England, however, did not feel inclined at this time to embroil herself in war for the sake of an independent Louisiana, and the conspirators were left to seek another way out of their dilemma.

While the rebels were in possession of New Orleans, making an effort to put the stamp of legality on their actions, a party of merrymakers committed an act which illustrated the feelings of the populace. On their way home from a wedding, when their inhibitions had probably been submerged by the best stock of their host, a group stopped before the frigate which served as a refuge for Governor Ulloa, and derided him, and one Petit, more bold or less cautious than the rest, cut the ropes which held the vessel.[24] Intermingled with the befuddled views of the revelers there might have been a feeling that the cutting of the moorings of the Spanish frigate was a practical demonstration of cutting themselves free from Spanish jurisdiction.

The future status of Louisiana depended primarily on the attitude of Spain and secondly on the policies of England and France. The insurrection had gone too far to allow the leaders

---

[22] *Ibid.*, II, 232-233; John R. Spears and A. H. Clark, *A History of the Mississippi Valley from its Discovery to the End of Foreign Domination* (New York, 1903), pp. 164-165.

[23] Gayarré, *History of Louisiana*, II, 247.

[24] Such is the popular version given by Gayarré, *History of Louisiana*, II, 212-213. A more sober version shows how the Superior Council was responsible for Ulloa's departure. See J. W. Caughey, *Bernardo de Gálvez in Louisiana, 1776-1783* (Berkeley, 1934), pp. 15-16.

to retreat. When the report of the actions of the Council at New Orleans was read in Spain, the ministers were requested to give their opinions on the situation. The Duke of Alba urged the retention of Louisiana in order to have a barrier against the British. He recommended that there be a change in the form of government so as to leave no agency for starting another revolution,[25] wishing, no doubt, to abolish the Council. Only one of the ministers, Don Miguel de Muzquiz, favored the return of Louisiana to France. Don Juan Gregorio Muniain, on the other hand, feared that if France regained it she might extend her possessions and encourage illicit trade.[26]

That Louisiana might be made into an independent republic was the suggestion made to Choiseul by Châtelet, French ambassador to London.[27] Count D'Aranda frankly predicted the possibility of an independent republic with New Orleans as the center of the free state. To this view he added:

> The favorable circumstances in which Louisiana would then be placed, would not only increase her population, but also enlarge her limits, and transfer her into a rich, flourishing and free state, in sight of our provinces, which would present the melancholy contrast of exhaustion and of the want of cultivation.[28]

He feared an independent Louisiana, particularly for its example to Mexico; for the people of Mexico would be encouraged to show greater opposition to Spanish domination, on seeing a weak province succeed in resisting the government of Spain and gaining prosperity. D'Aranda therefore urged the government to regain possession of Louisiana, to replace undesirables by Spanish settlers, and to set up a frontier defense against the British. He would not allow New Orleans to become a place of importance, since, if it were, it might attract

---

[25] Gayarré, *History of Louisiana*, II, 249-250.
[26] *Ibid.*, II, 262-263.
[27] Letter of Feb. 24, 1769, cited by Lyon, *Louisiana in French Diplomacy*, pp. 49-50.
[28] Gayarré, *History of Louisiana*, II, 256-257.

an enemy who would send large forces to capture it, and "these very forces might ultimately serve to carry on further designs against Mexico, and our other domains in that part of America."[29]

The king supported the views of most of his ministers, not only because of the reasons they gave, but because he considered also that "if what had occurred in Louisiana remained unpunished, this bad example might have a fatal influence over our other American possessions, and even over those of the other powers, in which a spirit of sedition and independence has begun to spread. . . ."[30] The hope that Spain might allow this troublesome colony to drift back to France declined, and the critical condition of the rebels increased.

The failure of the rebels to win support from France and favor from Spain weakened their position; and they turned again to England, who, being unwilling to go to war and afraid of encouraging rebellion, rejected their overtures a second time.[31] This left them in the dangerous predicament of dealing with Spain alone; and, having committed themselves, they saw no alternative but independence. Ulloa had been driven out; and before they could proceed, they suggested that the same would have to be done with Aubrey, who had continued to support the Spanish. Then they would be free to establish a republic.

New Orleans should be a free port and the new state would become a refuge for the needy and oppressed from the whole world. The recommendation for a republic came from Captain Marquis, a Swiss, and it soon became a general topic for discussion, and a subject for printed circulars. A "Protector" would head the republic and he was to be assisted by a council of forty. Lafrénière was expected to become the "Cromwell of Louisiana" if the project were successful. This scheme was

[29] *Ibid.*, II, 259.
[30] *Ibid.*
[31] *Ibid.*, II, 274, 280.

probably second or third choice, but having exhausted the alternatives, the leaders saw no other way out of their dilemma. These actions and plans had been in keeping with the rebellious spirit of the inhabitants, their love of liberty and independence, and their irritation at restraint. Yet the world was not quite ready for such a revolution in government, and in place of getting support from European powers, their action might easily have caused intervention by France and England in addition to Spain. The fear of such opposition caused the conspirators to hesitate about putting their plan into effect, and their opportunity soon passed.[32]

After the Spanish government had decided to put down the rebellion it took measures which would insure success. Don Alexandro O'Reilly, inspector and lieutenant general of the royal armies, a military leader whose prestige commanded respect, was appointed to bring Louisiana back into the Empire, to establish Spanish rule, and to punish the leaders of the rebellion.[33] The news of his approach created a great deal of fear and excitement. Captain Marquis, who had recommended the republic, stuck a white cockade in his hat and appealed to the public for support. Petit, who had cut the cables of Ulloa's ship, took two pistols and did likewise. The response to their appeal for support was so weak that they found it prudent to withdraw. The leaders were now thoroughly frightened, and sought Aubrey's advice. He urged them to submit to the new Spanish governor. O'Reilly was well equipped to enforce submission if it were not given peacefully, and the rebels were forced to recognize that resistance would be futile. The decline of the rebel ranks and the weakening of the rebel spirit, the prestige of O'Reilly and the large size of his army, the conciliatory and moderate policy of Aubrey, all contributed to the peaceful transfer of Louisiana.

The leaders of the insurrection went in person to appeal to

[32] *Ibid.*, II, 280-282.   [33] *Ibid.*, II, 265-266.

O'Reilly and left with the impression that no action would be taken provided they gave their allegiance to Spain peacefully.[34] Considerable excitement was shown when they were later arrested, but calm was partially restored when the General declared that only the instigators of the rebellion would be held responsible.[35] The prisoners presented a fairly good defense. Since Ulloa had not officially taken over the colony, they said, their actions against him were not against Spanish authority.[36] The attorney general from Mexico, however, found numerous laws tending to indicate that the conspirators were traitors and therefore subject to punishment by death and the confiscation of their property. Twelve were found guilty on October 24, 1769, after which six were condemned to the gallows and six to imprisonment. The former were executed by a firing squad, because of the government's inability to find a white hangman.[37] Thus had Spanish rule been reëstablished over a rebellious people by the General who, because of his method, has since been known as "Bloody O'Reilly."

The governor made several changes to prevent a repetition of the insurrection, the most noticeable being the replacement of the superior council by a cabildo.[38] A new code of laws was also drawn up as a substitute for the French system. In it was specifically provided that "The authors of any insurrection against the king or the state, or those who, under pretence of defending their liberty and rights, shall be concerned in it, or take up arms therein, shall be punished with death and the confiscation of their property."[39] Superficially had allegiance been established, but the loyalty of the colonists continued to be of a doubtful nature.

While the government was counteracting the work of revolutionists in Spain and putting down a rebellion in the border

---

[34] *Ibid.*, II, 291-293; Spears and Clark, *History of the Mississippi Valley*, p. 165.
[35] Gayarré, *History of Louisiana*, II, 303-308.
[36] *Ibid.*, II, 318-320.
[37] *Ibid.*, II, 320-343.
[38] *Ibid.*, III, 2-3.
[39] *Ibid.*, III, 16.

province of Louisiana, it was also facing a crisis in New Spain. Charles III made a great effort to restore the prestige and greatness of the Empire by a series of much-needed reforms. He sent José de Gálvez as visitor-general to New Spain (1765-1771) to investigate the conditions of the colony, to make recommendations, and to direct the reform measures.[40]

One of the most difficult and significant duties of the visitor-general was the expulsion of the Jesuits. This militant order had become rich and powerful, but had at the same time aroused the suspicion of the Spanish king, the hostility of other officials, and the jealousy of rival orders. The king suspected the Jesuits of disloyalty and of opposing reforms and came to the conclusion that it would be necessary to expel them from his dominions and finally to disband the order.[41] The expulsion in Mexico was carried out with clock-like precision under the able supervision of José de Gálvez. The dismissal of an order so firmly intrenched in the life of Mexico was not done without some danger to the peace of the country. Riots occurred in several places, chiefly in Valladolid, Guanajuato, and San Luis Potosí, but were put down with the heavy hand of the visitor. At Potosí the inhabitants had gone to the extent of planning an insurrection for the purpose of setting up an independent government.[42]

A movement for independence was also started at Pátzcuaro by the governor, Pedro Soria Villaroel, or Armola, as he is sometimes called. He was reported to have received the support of one hundred and thirteen villages, a fact which indicates the dimensions of a movement which might seriously have endangered Spain's control over Mexico. José de Gálvez acted promptly and effectively. The leader and some of his chief supporters were hanged, some were to be whipped, others given life imprisonment, and a few were banished.[43] Although

---

[40] For a thorough study of this official, see Priestley, *José de Gálvez*.
[41] Moses, *Spain's Declining Power in South America*, pp. 104-107.
[42] Priestley, *José de Gálvez*, p. 217. [43] *Ibid.*, pp. 226-227.

much of the trouble was caused by the Indians, these disturbances were primarily the aftermath of the expulsion of the Jesuits. The trials of some three thousand persons uncovered a growing anti-Spanish feeling.[44]

In spite of the success of Gálvez in stamping out the ephemeral revolutions, there was a feeling of discontent among numerous classes of the people, which had been increasing since the close of the Seven Years' War. The harsh methods of the visitor became in themselves a cause for resentment. The commercial class chafed under new restrictions, the miners feared a decline in their industry, the clergy were dissatisfied, and the creoles in general were restive under the system of unfavorable discrimination. It was the representatives of the latter group which met the French adventurers, M. Guiller and the Marquis D'Aubarde, in Madrid.[45]

Among other disturbances during this period were those which arose out of the attempted reforms of the army. The Seven Years' War showed the necessity of increasing the military defense of the American colonies. Cruíllas, the viceroy of Mexico, was as much aware of the defenseless condition of his colony as the home government. The military strength was truly pitiful: a palace guard in Mexico consisting of two companies, a few artillerymen and dragoons, a handful of soldiers at Acapulco, and a regiment at Vera Cruz. These with a few poorly equipped and poorly trained militia formed the military strength for the defense of Mexico and her wealth.[46] It is not surprising then that the political observers of the time frequently stated that England could easily conquer the territory if she so desired.

To remedy this weakness, Juan de Villalba was sent to Mexico for the purpose of reorganizing, enlarging, and training the

[44] *Ibid.*, p. 228.   [45] *Ibid.*, pp. 232-233.
[46] For a summary of the military conditions, see Bancroft, *History of Mexico*, III, 401. The relation of the defense question to the advance of England is pointed out by Priestley, *José de Gálvez*, pp. 43-44.

colonial troops. He was accompanied by a considerable number of officers who were to give military instruction and help in the reorganization. There were also a number of non-commissioned officers who were to form the nucleus of new regiments.[47] Even these necessary changes were not made without dangerous disturbances. The new military commander began to act independently of the viceroy, with the result that there was soon an open feud between the two; and when the viceroy withheld the pay of the troops there was rioting and pillaging.[48] The result of the disturbances was the recall of the two leaders.

Troops were no doubt necessary to defend the country against foreign aggression, but they were not a security against internal uprisings—they might become the very means. The additional expense for the upkeep of the enlarged army became in itself a grievance. It was a similar grievance after the same war that contributed to the spirit of independence in thirteen of the British colonies. Recruiting in New Spain, notably in Uruapán and Pátzcuaro, resulted in resistance and riots which furnished one of the problems to be settled by the visitor-general. Gálvez sentenced the lower classes to pay extra taxes for the expenses of the army,[49] a questionable method of winning loyalty.

The danger from the Indians and the growing menace of European aggression made it necessary to look to the frontier defenses. In response to the recommendations of the Marquis de Rubí, who had inspected the borderlands, it was decided to establish a series of military posts along the northern frontier, forming a line of defense across the continent. This seems to

[47] Bancroft, *Mexico*, III, 403-404; G. Desdevises du Dezert, "Vice-Rois et Capitaine Généraux des Indes Espagnole a la fin du XVIIIe Siècle," *Revue Historique*, CXXV, 225-264 (July-Aug., 1917); CXXVI, 14-60 (Sept.-Oct., 1917); CXXVI, 225-270 (Nov.-Dec., 1901).

[48] Brown, "Anglo-Spanish Relations in America," *The Hispanic-American Historical Review*, V, 339.

[49] Priestly, *José de Gálvez*, p. 43, n. 60, and pp. 220, 227.

have been done primarily for protection against the Indians, but there were many who believed that the advancing wave of whites from the northeast was the real cause.[50]

"Carlos lifted his eyes to the West, and there he saw another menace."[51] Lord Anson had pierced the Pacific in 1742, and had been followed by Dutch and French adventurers; and a movement across Asia from Russia had started down the west coast of America, which gave forebodings of the coming conflict. Furthermore, England might possibly link her Pacific ventures with overland expeditions and establish a new base for her intermittent conflict with Spain. This situation led to another project by Gálvez, that tireless worker, and the result was the Spanish occupation of California.[52]

While building the defense of New Spain, Charles III considered seriously the recapture of Jamaica, the British base, which was a constant threat against his American dominions. Only with the aid of France through the Family Compact could this be accomplished; and when this aid was not forthcoming, the plan was necessarily dropped.[53] Nevertheless, both the Bourbon powers continued to build up their navies and strengthen their defenses in preparation for the next war. In 1768 Charles III wrote to Louis XV that the ambition of the restless English would not be satisfied "unless they despoiled us entirely of the commerce and the riches of the Indies." The union of the Bourbons and the increase of their navies could alone stop the English projects, he said.[54] The conflicting claims in the Falkland Islands were of sufficient importance to lead to preparations for war, and the British were planning to make use of the opportunity to attack New Orleans, which would become a new wedge into the Spanish domains. The

---

[50] Herbert E. Bolton, *Texas in the Middle Eighteenth Century* (Berkeley, 1915), pp. 377-386, and p. 381 n.
[51] Bolton, *Spanish Borderlands*, p. 258.
[52] *Ibid.*; Priestley, *The Mexican Nation*, pp. 179-180.
[53] Joseph Addison, *Charles the Third of Spain* (Oxford, 1900), Appendix E.
[54] *Ibid.*

affair passed over without open hostility when the king of Spain acceded to the British demands,[55] and England was soon too busy with her own colonial difficulties to continue the Spanish projects.

The peace which had been agreed upon in 1763 had given Spain an opportunity to check the rising tide of rebellion, to promote reforms, and to prepare for the next conflict. Military improvements and general reforms in New Spain gave that colony an outward appearance of stability. Nevertheless, there was a growing dissatisfaction with the home government, and the revolution in the British colonies gave the colonial powers cause for apprehension and the colonies a lesson for emulation.

[55] James A. James, *The Life of George Rogers Clark* (Chicago, 1928), p. 90.

CHAPTER V

THE AMERICAN REVOLUTION

> "The King our master, who possesses in the Indies domains so vast and important, should be very backward in making a formal treaty with provinces which as yet can only be regarded as rebels . . . the example of a rebellion is too dangerous to allow of His Majesty's wishing to assist it openly."—Marquis de Grimaldi.
>
> "Declare them independent and add the independence of all French and Spanish Colonies and Islands. . . . Our Presbyterian Colonies will be more than compensated for. . . ."—Hugh Elliott.

THOSE who desired the independence of the Spanish colonies found in the American Revolution a great precedent, as well as an opportunity and a pretext for action. What was a note of warning to Spain was at the same time a note of encouragement to those who sought relief from Spanish domination. The delicate situation aroused a host of sinister possibilities in the minds of Spaniards; and these were magnified and stirred to new and threatening proportions by French officials, seeking the aid of Spain against the British. Spain was in a dilemma: if England won she would have an army in America ready for additional conquests; if England and the colonies came to an agreement, they might form an alliance against the Bourbons and deprive them of their possessions; if England were unable to defeat the colonies and the latter gained their independence, there would be the extremely bad example for New Spain, with the additional danger from a new and liberty-loving rival in America. Such were the varied prospects to be faced by Spain.

The outbreak of hostilities between England and her colonies stirred France and Spain to memories of losses in the past and to thoughts of reconquest and revenge, while in the heart of the king of Spain was added the feeling of fear for his possessions in America.¹ When Grimaldi, the Spanish minister of state, learned of the extensive military preparations of England, he sought assurances that they would not be used against the Spanish colonies. The British would have him believe that they wanted only peace with Spain; yet he did not trust them. The Spanish next sought information from Vergennes, the able foreign minister of France, who tried to convince them that coming to an agreement with England was unwise, for it was merely tying their hands so that they would be unable to protect their possessions while the English had an excuse for amassing large armaments which might at any time be turned against the poorly defended colonies of the Bourbons.² In August Vergennes informed Ossun, the French minister at the Spanish Court, that England was about to resort to the political expedient of uniting the opposing factions by holding out the necessity of common action against a foreign foe; in other words, "the means to end the war in America would be to declare it on the two crowns," the Bourbons.³ The Spanish court seems to have recognized this possibility. Vergennes, who may or may not have feared such action on the part of England, certainly found the argument to be good material with which to win the support of Spain in case France should go to war. The Spaniards naturally took the threat more seriously than the French because they had a great deal more to lose in America, and because their possessions were poorly defended. On the other hand, the weakness of the colonial defense would be an argument for not going to war with England, since the first interest of Charles III was to defend his American colonies.⁴

Comte de Vergennes, quick to grasp the international situa-

[1] P. C. Phillips, *The West in the Diplomacy of the American Revolution* (Urbana, 1914), p. 37.
[2] Vergennes to Aranda, May 9, 1775, *ibid.*, p. 38.
[3] *Ibid.*, p. 38, and n. 26.
[4] Ossun to Vergennes, Oct. 30, 1775, and Dec. 28, 1775, *ibid.*, p. 39.

tion, did not wait for the colonies to declare their independence before he outlined a plan of action for the Bourbons which involved participation in the conflict.

The English Ministry, [he wrote on March 12, 1776,] beaten on the continent of America, may seek an indemnity at the expense of France and Spain, which would at once efface their shame ... the colonies, having become independent, and preserving no tie with England, may become conquerors from necessity and that surcharged with goods, they may seek a forced outlet in the sugar islands, and in Spanish America, which would destroy the ties which attach our colonies to the mother country.

If England lost, the ministry and the king, in order to save themselves, would have to resort to conquest, "which would be the price of victory, the compensation for defeat, or the pledge of reconciliation," said Vergennes. He considered a conquest entirely possible. "Such is, indeed, the state of the colonies of the two nations," he believed, "that, with the exception, perhaps, of Havannah, none is in a position to resist the least part of the forces which England is sending to America, and the physical possibility of the conquest appears but too evident."[5]

Would England do such a thing without provocation? To this the French minister answered: "Experience has but too well proved that they believe everything just and honorable which they regard as advantageous to their nation, and destructive to their rivals."[6] The French, still smarting from their defeat in the last war, were anxious to regain their lost prestige and to humiliate England. Vergennes, therefore, trying to stir Spain to support his plan, declared: "The English of all parties appear to be unanimously persuaded that a popular war against France, or the invasion of Mexico, would end, or at least lull, their domestic disputes, and extinguish their national debt."[7] The Comte de Saint Germain was quite in

---

[5] Comte de Vergennes, "Considerations," March 12, 1776, *Stevens's Facsimiles of Manuscripts in European Archives Relating to America, 1773-1783* (London, 1889-1895), XIII, 1316.

[6] *Ibid.*   [7] *Ibid.*

accord with Vergennes and believed that whatever the result of the war in America, "the King of Great Britain will then see himself forced . . . to make some advantageous operation which shall appear to compensate his people for their losses."[8] He urged the French to prepare the defense of her colonies. But France and Spain, although their positions were somewhat similar, would have to play their separate rôles, in the opinion of Madrid, since the first had almost nothing to lose, "while the vast extent of territory of the second makes her vulnerable. . . ."[9]

An appeal from General Charles Lee in America was added to the warnings and recommendations of Vergennes, and again the rulers of Spain were told that if the British were victorious, they would use their army and navy to take possession of Mexico and Cuba. And if the Americans won, the British would be too weak to molest the Spanish possessions, and the Americans need not be feared since their interests were primarily in agriculture and commerce.[10]

Count D'Aranda, Spanish minister at the court of France, was perhaps equal to Vergennes in seeing dangerous possibilities as a result of the war. He became alarmed at the large number of troops which the English were sending to America, and saw the same possible conquest of French and Spanish territory to serve as indemnity for losses or to pay the cost of the war if victorious. In considering which conquest the English could undertake with the greatest ease, he decided it would be Louisiana and the island of Santo Domingo, the first of which would prepare the way for the taking of Mexico. Moreover, he feared that the conquest could easily be accomplished and would add a great deal to British commerce. Most of the Spanish colonies were sufficiently protected, he thought,

[8] Comte de Saint Germain, March 15, 1776, *ibid.,* XIII, 1319.
[9] Henri Doniol, *Histoire de la Participation de la France a l'éstablissement des États-Unis d'Amérique* (5 vols., Paris, 1885-1892), I, 166.
[10] James, *George Rogers Clark,* p. 92.

but Santo Domingo and Louisiana ought to be given additional protection.[11]

The two Bourbon countries had decided by the spring of 1776 that they would recognize England as their common enemy and be prepared for war.[12] But they found it very difficult to agree on any plan of action, Spain generally hesitating to give cause for war because her treasure fleets[13] would immediately be subject to capture and her colonies would be exposed. They would, however, encourage the quarrel between England and her colonies.[14] This could best be done by giving secret aid to the latter in order to keep up their courage and to prevent reconciliation. The French suggested that they send supplies through Louisiana as the safest avenue of approach. Furthermore, this colony should be carefully guarded because it could also serve as a passageway to the Spanish treasure-land "where the English may well seek the compensation for their colonies," if they were lost.[15] There was a double reason for protecting the Louisiana border. Even the French recognized that "The fire of revolt which approaches that frontier is a legitimate reason for bringing there in abundance the means which could make her respected."[16] This reason could be given to avoid suspicion. However, this "fire of revolt" was probably as great a menace as the danger of English invasion.

The French and Spanish had no sooner made their plans than the English were completely informed of them. Lord Weymouth was told in a letter dated, Paris, May 1, 1776, that, after a committee meeting, D'Aranda had urged the two governments to remain inactive, although making dispositions to defend their possessions in the West India Islands. The Eng-

---

[11] Doniol, *Histoire de la Participation de la France a l'éstablissement des États-Unis d'Amérique*, I, 422-423.
[12] *Ibid.*, I, 337.
[13] See Index under "New Spain," *Stevens's Facsimiles*.
[14] Doniol, *Histoire de la Participation de la France*, I, 339, 342.
[15] *Ibid.*, I, 340.   [16] *Ibid.*, I, 343, n. 1.

lish government was also informed that the Spanish expected it to attack their colonies if it were successful in the American war. This might in itself be an encouragement to the English.[17]

The dangerous precedent of a successful colonial rebellion was considered by all three powers. Spain feared it, and England encouraged this fear lest Spain take advantage of her predicament to help the colonies.[18] While France was interested in the debasement of England, and the possibilities of punishing her so as to equalize their powers, Floridablanca considered these as "moral objects" and called them "Quixotic."[19] Spain had more practical problems to consider, and the Spanish minister, although recognizing that England's sea power was a menace, did not admit that the independence of her colonies would remove this danger, suggesting that it might even be increased.[20] Grimaldi expressed his views to Aranda as follows:

> The King our master, who possesses in the Indies domains so vast and important, should be very backward in making a formal treaty with provinces which as yet can only be regarded as rebels, an inconvenience which would not exist should the colonies succeed in really throwing off the yoke and constituting themselves an independent power . . . the example of a rebellion is too dangerous to allow of His Majesty's wishing to assist it openly.[21]

The Marquis de Castejón, member of the Spanish Royal Council, added his views in February, 1777:

> Spain is about to be left alone, face to face with one other power in the whole of North America,—a power which has assumed a national name, which is very formidable on account of the size

---

[17] *Stevens's Facsimiles,* XIII, 1333.

[18] Coxe, *Memoirs of the Kings of Spain of the House of Bourbon* (2nd ed., 5 vols., London, 1815) V, 37.

[19] Edward S. Corwin, *French Policy and the American Alliance of 1778* (Princeton, 1916), p. 106.

[20] *Ibid.,* p. 107.

[21] Doniol, *Participation de la France,* II, 192; also quoted by Corwin, *French Policy,* p. 108.

of its population and the ratio of increase thereof, and which is accustomed to war even before it has begun it. I think that we should be the last country in all Europe to recognize any sovereign and independent state in North America."[22]

In an article from Madrid, printed in the *Courrier de l'Europe,* it was suggested that the rebellion of the British colonies might become an epidemic of the nineteenth century.[23]

Vergennes, too, believed that the new states would soon become aggressive and said they would covet Florida, Louisiana, and Mexico.[24] Castejón continued to point out the dangers from an independent power and emphasized the fact that "the English and American powers would still be of one nation, one character and one religion, and would so form their treaties and compacts as to obtain the objects they both desire." And again we find that Mexico is the colony concerned, for he added that in the above-mentioned circumstances, "the kingdom of Mexico would be compromised, in fact lost."[25]

The French, although recognizing these possibilities, tried to belittle the danger from an independent state in America in order to secure aid against the greater enemy, England. When Vergennes urged the necessity of attacking England before she came to an agreement with her colonies to unite their forces against the Bourbons, Grimaldi countered with the opinion that a joint attack by the Bourbons would be the very cause for this reconciliation between the combatants in America and result in a combined attack on the Spanish possessions.[26]

While France and Spain lived in dread of the increasing British armaments in America, the English were becoming quite uneasy about the preparations of the Bourbons to defend their possessions, each suspecting the other of planning an of-

[22] Quoted by Corwin, *French Policy and the American Alliance,* pp. 108-109.
[23] Paris, April 4, 1777, Villanueva, *Napoleón y la Independencia,* p. 31.
[24] I. J. Cox, "The Louisiana-Texas Frontier," *Texas Historical Association Quarterly,* X, 38 (July, 1906).
[25] Corwin, *French Policy and the American Alliance,* pp. 108-109.
[26] Phillips, *The West in the Diplomacy of the Revolution,* p. 43.

fensive attack. The British diplomats, Stormount in Paris and Grantham in Madrid, were instructed to demand an explanation. Both insisted that the intentions of the British were peaceful and they even offered a British guarantee for the Spanish possessions in America.[27] France and Spain in turn informed the British that their actions were merely to guard the Spanish interests in America. Floridablanca, who had succeeded Grimaldi in February, 1777, added that a strong force was necessary "to hold in subjection the Spanish colonies which were being seduced by the example of the British provinces."[28]

Vergennes later gave a fuller account of the situation in a report to the king in which he argued against the acceptance of a British assurance for the security of their American possessions as being both inconvenient and useless. "It would be to tie our hands," he said, "so as not to allow us to put them of our selves in a posture of defence, and to place in the hand of our enemy a rod ever raised, whereof we should often feel the formidable effect."[29] The French minister was anticipating war and wanted perfect freedom to be prepared for it. Vergennes sent additional considerations for the information of Montmorin. Spain's interest was ten times as great as the French, he said, since England was interested in treasure which meant mainland colonies and not the island colonies like those of France of which she already had enough. He repeated his old arguments about the advantage to Spain of the separation of new and old England and added a second reflection "on the fresh advantages which Spain may obtain. Perhaps she regrets the loss of Florida," he wrote, "which gives too easy access to the Gulf of Mexico, and would see that province with

[27] Vergennes to Ossun, May 2, and Ossun to Vergennes, May 19, 1777, *ibid.*, p. 54.
[28] *Ibid.*, p. 54.
[29] Aug. 23, 1777, *Stevens's Facsimiles*, VII, 706. For additional arguments, see *ibid.*, XVIII, 1690.

as much pain in the hands of the United States of America as in those of England."[30] Against the possible chance of loss of colonies, Vergennes was holding out the prospect of conquest and reconquest.

Representatives from the newly founded state in America added their arguments to those of the French. The persistent attempts of Arthur Lee to gain admission to the Spanish court were in vain, and only irritated the Spanish authorities.[31] Both Spain and France had committed themselves by giving secret aid to the rebellious colonies. The former, however, soon ceased, and it seemed possible that the aid had been all wasted and that it might even become a boomerang. Vergennes, as we have seen, did not believe that England would necessarily need any justification for attacking the colonies of the Bourbons; but now, in case the English had risen above the French premier's low estimate, they had an excuse for doing to Spain what Spain had done to England. Charles III had made one good move towards the preservation of his dominions by making a treaty with Portugal, which, as an ally of England, might otherwise become dangerous.[32]

The war took on a new aspect after the American defeat of Burgoyne in October, 1777. The French felt assured now that independence could be won if the colonies were given support. Vergennes continued to point out the advantages to Spain of going into the war, and used as an argument the fact that the British government had already invited deputies to come to London and had offered them certain compensation in a coalition against France and Spain. He had been given to understand that they would "go as far as absolute independence, if necessary, provided doubtless that it be followed by a coalition." If the American deputies accepted, the British would have their army and navy ready for an attack on the

---

[30] Dec. 13, 1777, *ibid.*, XX, 1775.
[31] C. R. Fish, *American Diplomacy* (1923 ed.), p. 31.
[32] Coxe, *Memoirs of the Kings of Spain*, V, 26, 48.

possessions of France and Spain, and they would also have a right to do so, since these two had given aid to the former colonies. He continued to picture the possibilities of this proposed settlement. England would perhaps keep New York, he said, "to serve as a base for her expeditions against our possessions." "Eager and courageous corsairs" would "harry our commerce." England and the United States would easily be led to go further

> by the bait of the riches of New Spain, sufficient to relieve both states of the burden of their debts. The exclusive navigation of the Mississippi, which will make the possession of Mexico precarious, will in itself be powerful bait for the colonies, and they will willingly undertake everything, because they will have nothing to fear on their continent from the vengeance of the two crowns.[33]

In this manner the French minister was building up his case for Spanish participation in a war against England, using as his chief argument the maintenance of their colonies. It would certainly be safest to have the British colonies on their side instead of against them, especially since they were neighbors of their own colonies. And in case Spain was above England in seeking justification for such a step, Vergennes recalled that England under Elizabeth gave "aid to the rebels of Flanders, even when they had not yet shaken off the Spanish yoke." The United States could be bound by an alliance, and the contracting powers would "guarantee neutrality and forever their respective possessions in America." Such an alliance and agreement with England had been rejected by Vergennes, but if it were made with the new nation in America, the king of Spain could "especially feel that His Catholic Majesty's possessions in that part of the world would henceforth be sheltered from all attack . . . as we cannot suspect them of wishing to soil their first political step by a perfidious action."

[33] Jan. 7, 1778, *Stevens's Facsimiles*, XXI, 1824; Doniol, *Participation de la France*, II, 722-725.

The French minister continued to record his forebodings in an effort to stimulate fear of an Anglo-American coalition. He wrote:

This coalition being made, in whatever manner it may be, what will be the result for Spain and for us; and can we reasonably hope that England satisfied with this slight advantage, will recall to Europe immediately the mass of forces which remain to her in America, and which she will probably not delay to augment, that she will disarm and be willing only to enjoy the pleasantness of peace so dearly bought, when she sees objects of compensation within her reach? Let us not be deluded.[34]

A final summary of arguments for French participation was given in a memoir, January 13, 1778, in which it was said that if the French did not help the colonies, "the Americans will become our perpetual enemies, and we must expect to see them turn all their efforts against our possessions, and against those of Spain. . . . Thus the coalition of the English and the Americans will draw after it our expulsion, and probably that of the Spaniards, from the whole of America."[35]

Public announcement of British willingness to come to an agreement with her American colonies was made, to the amazement of both friends and enemies, by Lord North in Parliament on February 17, 1778.[36] Earlier in the month the French had finally agreed to join the Americans in their struggle against England without waiting for Spanish participation or approval. England heard about the treaty before the news reached America and promptly declared war on France.[37]

Not even this announcement could bring Spain to a decision; in fact, France was criticized for acting too hastily. In the words of Floridablanca, "between England and America there is a sort of equality of enmity that makes it difficult to

[34] Vergennes to Montmorin, Jan. 8, 1778, *Stevens's Facsimiles*, XXI, 1827.
[35] Corwin, *French Policy*, Appendix III, p. 398.
[36] J. H. Latané, *A History of American Foreign Policy* (Garden City, 1928), p. 20.
[37] *Ibid.*, pp. 19-21.

desire that either side win."³⁸ Montmorin reported later that they were already getting suspicious of the "prosperity of the colonies," meaning the success of the independence movement, and further, "one fears that they may become for Spain an enemy much more dangerous than the English."³⁹ Floridablanca also added that he considered the independence of the American colonies no less detrimental to Spain than to Great Britain herself.⁴⁰

Vergennes tried to quiet these fears and wrote to Montmorin in April, 1778, that there was no danger from the United States since it would "remain quiet with the inertia that is characteristic of all constitutional democracies."⁴¹ A similar view had been expressed by Gérard, who considered a loose confederacy unsuitable for conquest. He added, however, that even if they should threaten the Spanish possessions, that would not prove that the revolution would be prejudicial to France.⁴² This was, no doubt, nearer the real French viewpoint, but not to be given to the hesitant Spanish.

Spain refused to be drawn into the struggle in spite of the Family Compact, indicating that Vergennes had failed to convert her to the belief that her best interests would be served by fighting England. On the contrary, Spain, hoping to gain certain advantages, offered her good offices and mediation to end the war. This being rejected, she declared war on England in 1779. She had no sooner done this than she evidently began to reconsider the increased danger to her colonies. Secret negotiations were then begun with England through the agency of an Irish priest, Mr. Hussey, chaplain to the king of Spain. He traveled between London and Madrid as a private person, serving as an intermediary between the officials of the two

---

³⁸ Montmorin to Vergennes, Feb. 2, 1778, Phillips, *The West in the Diplomacy of the American Revolution*, p. 80.
³⁹ Doniol, *Participation de la France*, III, 20.
⁴⁰ Coxe, *Memoirs of Spain*, V, 37-38.
⁴¹ Doniol, *Participation de la France*, III, 82.
⁴² See *"Reflexiones," ibid.*, I, 243-249; Corwin, *French Policy*, p. 110.

countries. In addition to the safety of her colonies, Spain wanted the return of Gibraltar, and perhaps Florida. According to the preliminary plan, Spain should agree to assist Great Britain in "reducing the colonies to obedience," at least "not to harbour in her dominions any subjects of the king that are deemed rebels.... This stipulation to be mutual, and the king to make a like engagement with regard to the rebellious subjects of the crown of Spain." England could find nothing in the Spanish Empire which would compensate her for the loss of Gibraltar, the offer of Puerto Rico was inadequate, and therefore the negotiations failed. Being unable to invade England and cut her off from Gibraltar as was first planned, Spain devoted herself to the defense of her colonies and the reconquest of Florida.[43]

We have examined the diplomacy of France and Spain in connection with their American possessions, showing how they feared the loss of their colonies. There seems to be little indication of the method of this dreaded intervention, the outstanding factor being that the colonies might be lost to the mother country and that the territory in the Gulf region seemed to be the most likely objective with New Spain as the most desirable morsel. Although the anxiety of the Bourbons has been criticized as being unduly exaggerated, one has only to examine the views and plans of the enemy to see to what extent they were justified.

In 1776 a complete revolutionary plan was drawn up by Captain Kaye at Pisa and sent to Lord Germain. He proposed that the natives be armed to oppose Spain. After the war they might set up any form of government desirable, but England should be given "free and exclusive trade and commerce," as well as retain possession of her sea coasts. The natives were expected to give wholehearted support because they believed

[43] Coxe, *Memoirs of the Kings of Spain*, V, 72-73.

in a legend "that a far distant Nation Commanding the Sea, Shall Come in Ships to their deliverance, and, freeing them from the Yoke of Oppression of the Spaniards, shall Restore them to the possession of their Liberty and Country."[44] This plan which was to "annihilate universally the Spanish dominion in America" received little attention until Spain was drawn into the war as an ally of France. A similar proposal was repeatedly presented to Lord Germain by Robert White.[45]

The Jesuits, who had been so unceremoniously expelled from the New World, naturally harbored a resentment towards the country which had separated them from their work and wealth. Many of them lived on a very meager income in Italy, and were fit agents for the revolutionists as well as promoters of independence themselves. Captain Hippisley wrote from Rome:

> ... to a man, they bear implacable animosity to the Courts of Spain. The most violent are the ex-Jesuits from Peru and Mexico. ... It may be presumed that such men might prove *essential instruments* in effecting a *reduction* of New Spain, having an entire influence on their countrymen, who universally, are predisposed to revolt.[46]

A very interesting plan was submitted to Captain Hippisley by an ex-Jesuit who had formerly been an Inquisitor in both Old and New Spain.[47] By attacking both Acapulco and Vera Cruz at the same time it was shown how Mexico could easily be taken possession of with only a small force. The expedition on the west coast, which could be made from the East Indies, should first make a descent on Lower California[48] and then

---

[44] Robertson, *Miranda*, pp. 198-199.
[45] *Ibid.*, p. 199; Villanueva, *Napoleon y la Independencia*, p. 30.
[46] Hippisley to Lord Loughborough, Rome, June 18, 1779, Londonderry (ed.), *Correspondence of Castlereagh*, VII, 261-262.
[47] The memorandum of this conversation was dated Aug. 4, 1779, *ibid.*, VII, 262-266.
[48] See the *Noticia de la California* of father Buriel in Chapman, *The Founding of Spanish California* (New York, 1916), p. 56.

proceed to Acapulco.⁴⁹ In addition to taking possession of these places the British could circulate manifestoes to assure the inhabitants that the country was to be governed according to the desire of the inhabitants. The forts in the interior were, as the Jesuits had warned the government, more of a danger than a security, since they might easily be taken by a small force and become strongholds for those who wished to set up an independent government. The more powerful caciques could be relied on for help, especially if directed by a few well instructed agents who would be as important as armies.

According to Hippisley, these agents were to be former Jesuits who would gladly "expose themselves to any hazard in embarking for the Continent of America, under an assurance of a free exercise of their religion being secured to them." He also believed that it might be well to have one or two of them in England for consultations before any expedition be undertaken.⁵⁰ Others, too, proposed the use of the banished Jesuits, and one was actually sent to encourage revolts.⁵¹ These proposals were made "in the apprehension of a probable rupture with Spain." He had reason to believe that a break was imminent, because in a letter from Rome of June 18, 1779, he mentioned a letter which the king of Naples had received from his father, complaining of "the *haughtiness* of Great Britain, which would compel him speedily to declare war against her."⁵²

Governor Dalling of Jamaica had plans of his own for the conquest of Spanish territory. By the occupation of the Isthmus, Yucatan, and Pensacola, "the Spanish trade to the Bay of Mexico may be totally ruined," because the Spanish ships generally

---

⁴⁹ For similar plans see those of Colonel Fullerton which Hippisley sent to Warren Hastings, Aug. 11, 1782, Londonderry (ed.), *Correspondence of Castlereagh*, VII, 367.

⁵⁰ In another note, Nov. 28, 1779, he emphasized the importance of using the ex-Jesuits, *ibid.*, VII, 266.

⁵¹ Mr. Corneille to Mr. Hippisley, Nov. 1781, *ibid.*, VII, 267.

⁵² *Ibid.*, VII, 260.

came by way of the southern point and returned by way of the northern, he said.[53] He was apparently unaware of the Florida expedition of Bernardo de Gálvez, which was undertaken at that time. Dalling also forwarded the papers of F. L. Cardinaux, who had previously proposed the revolutionizing of Mexico, and suggested to Lord Germain that the plan might now be revived.[54] This was the link which combined the activities of D'Aubarde after the Seven Years' War with the plans of the American Revolution.[55]

From Berlin, Hugh Elliot, British minister, wrote in March, 1778, giving his opinion on the proposed conciliation with the colonies, which he thought was unnecessary. His views were as follows:

Declare them independent and add the Independence of all French and Spanish Colonies and Islands. In order to support this step, let our fleets and armies evacuate North America, fall upon St. Domingo, Martinico, Cuba, and force a free trade in the Gulph of Mexico, the straight road to the gold and silver mines, the sugar islands, and the revolt of the Spanish settlements, these will be the consequence of this vigorous measure. Our Presbyterian Colonies will be more than compensated for....[56]

He was not alone in holding such opinions as we have seen, and others supported them from time to time, justifying the fears of the French and Spanish. Governor Pownall suggested to Lord Germain in January, 1781, that England encourage the independence of the Spanish colonies to counteract her own losses by creating a new commercial field.[57] Success in any such enterprise would depend largely on the support from the colonies themselves, a condition which was still very doubtful. However, before the war was over a revolutionary society had been organized in Spanish America, whose agent, Don

---

[53] Dalling to Lord Germain, Feb. 7, 1780, P. R. O., C. O. 137, Jamaica, LXXVII.
[54] Letter of March 26, 1780, *ibid.*
[55] See above, pp. 62-64.
[56] To William Eden, Berlin, March 28, 1778, *Stevens's Facsimiles*, IV, 410.
[57] Villanueva, *Napoleón y la Independencia*, p. 31.

Juan, came to England to secure aid for their liberation.[58] The immediate opportunity for British assistance came to an end with the war and Don Juan was too late.

With the alliance of France and the indirect assistance of Spain, thirteen of the British colonies won their independence, an event which could give little comfort to Spain, since she now had two possible rivals where formerly she had but one. And the new rival was doubly dangerous, first, because of her example of a successful resistance to the mother country and, secondly, because of her revolutionary principles of government. The constant threats of France and England to the possessions of Spain were henceforth to be amplified by the United States.

[58] Chatham Papers, P. R. O., Vol. CCCXLV.

CHAPTER VI
AFTERMATH OF THE AMERICAN REVOLUTION

> "May this great monument raised to liberty serve as a lesson to the oppressor, and an example to the oppressed."—LAFAYETTE.
>
> "The example of North America is the great subject of discourse, and the grand object of imitation."—*Political Herald and Review.*
>
> "In signing the treaty which rendered America free, Europe signed the great charter of emancipation for all the colonies. . . ."—M. DE PRADT.

THE NEW, independent North American republic began to exert its influence by the great example of successful resistance to European domination, as had been predicted by Lafayette.[1] Francisco de Miranda of Caracas, traveling in the United States shortly after the war, said: "Our American kingdoms will soon experience a revolution similar to the one which you have witnessed here."[2] The best known prophecy, perhaps, is the one of Count D'Aranda, who, having signed the treaty of Paris, looked into the future and saw events which boded ill for the great Spanish Empire. His fears were expressed in a memorial to Charles III:

The independence of the English colonies has just been recognized, and this is food for thought and fear, in my opinion. This federal republic has been born a pigmy, so to speak. . . . The time will come when she will be a giant, and even a colossus, much to be feared in those vast regions. Then she will forget the benefits that she received from both powers and will only think of aggrandizing herself. Her first step will be to get possession of the Floridas to dominate the Gulf of Mexico. These fears are, Sire, only too well founded and will be realized within a few years if other more disastrous events do not previously occur in America.[3]

[1] Moncure D. Conway (ed.), *Writings of Thomas Paine* (4 vols., New York, 1894-1896), II, 283.
[2] Francois Barbé-Marbois, *History of Louisiana* (Philadelphia, 1830), p. 150.
[3] Quoted by C. L. Chandler, *Inter-American Acquaintances* (2nd ed., Sewanee, Tenn., 1917), pp. 4-5; see also William H. Trescott, *The Diplomacy of the Revolution* (New York, 1852), pp. 70-71.

Being a statesman, D'Aranda suggested a remedy. He called the king's attention to the increased danger of losing his rich possessions in America and of the difficulty of preserving them, so extensive and so far from the home government. From another continent it would be difficult to understand fully the local needs and problems or to check abuses; nor would it be easy to send them aid in case of foreign invasion. Aranda proposed then that America be divided into three kingdoms: Mexico, Peru, and New Granada, with a member of the royal family as king over each. The Spanish king should become emperor with the American kings as his subordinates. The French could be favored in commerce, but the British were to be excluded. Aranda's plan was given some consideration but was finally rejected.[4]

England, at the close of the American Revolution, was far from becoming friendly with Spain and her ally, France. The resentment against her former colonies was now concentrated against their abetters and assistants. A memoir on the subject said: "Our views to the South must still be the same I fear for a long time, viz., inevitable enmity with the Bourbon interests and friendship with all the rest. Hence Portugal our natural friend and Spain our natural enemy." It was considered better to have Spain "as a weak enemy than as a weak friend," since she would make the vulnerable part of any confederacy, and the Family Compact united her interests with France.[5] England could be depended on to lend a ready ear to those enemies of Spain who came from within the Spanish Empire.

Don Juan, the agent who had started for England before the war was over, to propose the revolutionizing of the Spanish American colonies with British aid, remained to foster the

[4] Alamán, *Historia de Méjico*, I, 126-127; Bancroft, *Mexico*, III, 388-390; Villanueva, *Napoleón y la Independencia*, p. 33, said that a similar plan had been proposed to Philip V by Vauban.

[5] "Some memoranda for treating with Spain," 1783, P. R. O., F. O. 72, I, 85 ff.

idea after peace was established. Among the Englishmen whom he interested in his project was Edmund Bott, and he also consulted Dr. Rippis and a Mr. F—. Don Juan and Mr. Bott met during the Christmas holidays to talk over the situation and to make a last effort to interest the government.[6] Another attempt to get British aid at this time was made by Don Luis Vidall who advocated the emancipation of Spanish America with New Granada as a starting point.[7] Again, in December, 1783, a memoir gave a number of reasons for British participation in a Spanish American rebellion, one of the main reasons being to transfer the resources of New Spain from the Bourbons to the British. An association between the Spanish creoles and the Indians was also mentioned, which might have been the one represented by Don Juan. Some of its members had been teaching and preparing the natives for a military resistance. The leader, who had been residing in Europe for a year, was given full power to negotiate with the British government for a supply of six thousand land forces and a proportionate squadron of ships of war. Having obtained these, he was to proceed directly to the River Plate where part of the men would land while others went on to the west coast. The war having ended before the leader reached England, he had to content himself with more moderate demands. In case the expedition should be unsuccessful, the government could disavow it and let the soldiers be treated as pirates—certainly not a generous thought. It was also suggested that they might disavow it even if they were successful and let the countries declare their independence. That Mexico was to be included in the project is shown by the reference to Acapulco, which was to serve as a trading center with the East. The writer added further: "It may be observed that the kingdom of Mex-

[6] Memoir, 1783; Chatham Papers, P. R. O., Vol. CCCXLV.
[7] Robertson, *Miranda*, pp. 206-209.

AFTERMATH OF THE AMERICAN REVOLUTION 97

ico, may be most properly attacked in the South Sea, and not as was suggested last year, by a Spaniard."[8]

The objection by the English to participation in any war for Spanish American independence was that she was exhausted by the last one. On the other hand, England might be stronger ten years later, but not necessarily proportionately, since France and Spain were equally exhausted at that time and could also gain strength. The argument for war was that success would bring to England much of the wealth of Spanish America.[9]

In 1785 a stirring pamphlet was published under the title of "La Crise de l'Europe."[10] John Adams, minister to England, epitomized the pamphlet in a letter to John Jay.[11] The theme was the emancipation of all the European colonies in America to be accomplished by a league of nations composed of Great Britain, United States, and Holland, and any others who would be willing to help, such as Russia, Denmark, Sweden, Prussia, and Austria.[12] Even France and Spain would have no reason to complain. for did not they help the British colonies in that very manner? As for Spain, it was astonishing that the resentment of Europe had not "broke[n] out against these proud monopolists."

John Adams added his own views on the subject in his letter to Jay, because, as he said:

... they form a clue for the political conduct in the future, and for the present too, for it is impossible otherwise to account for the

[8] This would indicate that the writer was very likely an Englishman, perhaps Mr. Bott, the friend of Don Juan; and, secondly, that a Spaniard had considered the project earlier.
[9] Chatham Papers, P. R. O., Vol. CCCXLV.
[10] John Sinclair said, in his *History of the Public Revenue of the British Empire* (London, 1785), p. 102, that he was the author of this pamphlet and had included many of the ideas in this second work.
[11] May 28, 1786, *The Diplomatic Correspondence of the United States* ... *1783-1789* (7 vols., Washington, 1832), V, 123-130.
[12] They could be rewarded for their efforts by a partition of the islands as follows: Cuba to Russia, Martinico to Denmark, Guadaloupe to Sweden, Porto Rico to Prussia, Spanish Hispaniola to the Emperor, and the remaining islands to Great Britain. There was none mentioned for the United States (*ibid.*, V, 123).

inattention of this country to the commerce and friendship of the United States of America; they are keeping up their navy, and sacrificing everything to seamen, in order to be able to strike a sudden blow to the House of Bourbon, by setting South America free, and they rely upon it the United States will not oppose them.[13]

John Adams reported further that one Spanish American agent had been arrested in Rouen, France, and his accomplices had attempted to get British aid, without success. He thought there were many individuals in London, "this capitol of Mammon," who would be glad to furnish war supplies were profitable prices offered,[14] and called attention to the office undertaken by Beaumarchais as an example.

He was a bit skeptical about Sinclair's plan, for he knew that Spain still had powerful allies; and to Jay he gave the following warning:

That British ambassadors will very soon endeavor to excite the two Empires and Denmark, to an alliance, for the purpose of setting the Spanish and Portuguese colonies free, is very probable. . . . The object of the next war, I think, will be the liberty of commerce in South America, and the East Indies. We shall be puzzled to keep out of it. But I think we ought if we can. England would gain the most in such a turn of affairs . . . and England, unfortunately, we cannot trust.

Such, then, were the views of one of our leading statesmen in 1786, and it is quite likely that, in keeping with his tenacity, he still held these views in 1798 when they were of such momentous importance.

Jefferson, too, seemed to think that any immediate change in Hispanic America would not be for the interest of the United States. Nevertheless, he had expansionist views several years before the constitution put any apparent legal restrictions to his ambitions. He wrote in 1786 that "Our Confederacy

[13] *Ibid.*, V, 129-130.
[14] Adams indicated that he knew more about this, but withheld his information because he did not know if it was reliable, *ibid.*, V, 123.

must be viewed as the nest from which all America, North and South is to be peopled. We should take care too, not to think it for the best interests of that great continent to press too soon on the Spaniards. Those countries cannot be in better hands." Then he made this somewhat amazing statement: "My fear is that they are too feeble to hold them till our population can be sufficiently advanced to gain it from them piece by piece."[15] Thus it would seem that the foreign policy of the United States in regard to Spanish America was to get possession of it "piece by piece." In the light of this statement, made three years after the independence of the United States, it is interesting to note Count D'Aranda's prediction in 1783 when he foresaw the development of the United States from a pigmy to a giant. The foresight of these two statesmen can be appreciated when one considers how the United States gained Spanish-American territory "piece by piece" and how the "disastrous events" predicted by Aranda came to pass.

The chance remarks of farsighted persons became common knowledge when the *Political Herald and Review* published the following in 1785: "The flame which was kindled in North America, as was foreseen, has made its way into the American dominions of Spain." After discussing the rivalry between the creoles and the Peninsulars the description goes on: "Conferences are held, combinations are formed in secret, among a race of men whom we shall distinguish by the appellation of Spanish Provincials. The example of North America is the great subject of discourse, and the grand object of imitation."[16]

These opinions were not mere idle dreams nor empty words, but ideas which were gradually gaining adherents and opponents. Mexico caused Spain increasing anxiety from this time

[15] Thomas Jefferson to Archibald Stewart, Paris, Jan. 25, 1786, P. L. Ford (ed.), *Works of Thomas Jefferson* (12 vols., New York, 1904-1905), V, 75.

[16] Quoted in *The American Register* (Part I, 1809), V, 381 n.; and in part by Chandler, *Inter-American Acquaintances*, p. 8. Parra-Pérez suggests that this article shows the influence of Miranda's presence in London, *Miranda et la Révolution Française* (Paris, 1925), p. xviii.

on. During the American Revolution she gave the outward appearance of loyalty, not by choice or interest, but because there was no alternative. The viceroy, Martín de Mayorga, was faithful in giving whatever aid in men and money he could, receiving in turn little consideration from the home government. His position in Mexico was made insecure because several of his subordinates tried to act quite independently of his authority.[17] Robert Liston reported from Spain that a recent insurrection in Mexico had been caused by the new taxes imposed by Gálvez. The report, probably exaggerated, was that a considerable number were under arms, that several judges had been killed, and that the rebellion had been quelled only after a great slaughter.[18] Such reports would undoubtedly influence British opinion whether they were based on truth or mere rumor.[19]

Those in New Spain who wanted independence still hoped to secure British aid. In 1785 three commissioners who said they represented the city and kingdom of Mexico, drew up a petition to England, asking for her protection from the oppressions of the court of Madrid which governed them with despotic tyranny and deprived them of constitutional liberty, putting them in the class of "vile slaves." Furthermore, they were forced to support the yoke which oppressed them. Now they were taking measures to secure their liberty. It was said that they had sufficient funds and that they could put forty thousand men under arms in a moment's notice, thereby becoming masters of the kingdom. They still lacked the arms and munitions of war necessary for such a great undertaking. Jamaica was considered a suitable place from which to get these indispensable supplies. They were sending Don Fran-

[17] Carlos María Bustamante, *Suplemento,* in Andrés Cavo, *Tres Siglos de México* (4 vols. in 2, Mexico, 1836-1838), III, 42-43.

[18] Robert Liston to C. J. Fox, Madrid, Dec. 25, 1783, P. R. O., F. O. 72 (Spain), I, 997.

[19] The Indian uprising in Peru had caused considerable anxiety lest it spread to the other colonies, and Spain was trying to keep it a secret.

cisco de Mendiola to England with full powers to make the necessary arrangements and to seek her protection. He was also to make a treaty of friendship and commerce. The commercial advantages to England were inconceivable, they said, and a glowing description was given of the wealth of the country and its commercial possibilities. Its commerce would more than make up for the loss of the British colonies in America, and restore the commerce of England to its former splendor. The committee indicated its willingness to approve in advance any arrangement made with the king of England and his ministers by their representative, Mendiola. They were ready to send two million piasters to Jamaica for the necessary arms. An agent could be sent there to avoid any correspondence which might fall into the hands of the Spaniards. The petition was signed in Mexico, November 10, 1785, by the Conde de la Torre Cassio, the Conde de Santiago, and the Marquis de Guardiola.[20]

While these agents were petitioning England for friendship and support, the Spanish government was being warned of their activities. It may not have believed that the agents represented large and dangerous groups, but it would have to be extremely cautious to prevent any undertaking backed by England. Circulars were sent to the authorities in Spanish America, warning them of the machinations of these rebellious spirits and urging them to capture one of the revolutionary agents in order to make an example of him.[21]

The United States was already serving as a haven of refuge for those who sought liberty. José Antonio Rojas, a Mexican who had been persecuted for having seditious ideas, fled to New Orleans where he devoted himself to picturing to his countrymen the advantages of American independence, describing the parts of the constitution which deserved to be copied

[20] Chatham Papers, P. R. O., Vol. CCCXLV; cf. Robertson, *Miranda*, p. 202.
[21] Robertson, *Miranda*, p. 209.

by the Mexicans. His works were, as a result, immediately put on the prohibited list by the Inquisition.[22] Yet it was practically impossible to prevent the world from learning about the success of the United States. M. De Pradt asks: "How, in effect, can the rest of America be prevented from seeing the United States free, flourishing, affranchised from the laws and quarrels of Europe, by the effect of their independence, and hinder them from aspiring to the same lot, by the same means?"[23] In one way or another the United States threatened the Spanish possessions.

The westward movement of the Americans by the close of the Revolution was a force to be reckoned with, and Spain took special precaution to protect herself against this growing and almost irresistible advance. Floridablanca tried to build barriers against the advancing republicans, recognizing the danger of their presence.[24] Keeping them out and at the same time preserving peace seemed impossible, for they insisted on their right to use the Mississippi River which flowed through Spanish territory and into the exclusive waters of the Gulf of Mexico. Even from London a Spanish official sent reports to the home government to warn it against the swarms of dangerous Americans who were crossing into the western country and who would become a menace to the Spanish possessions.[25] Pierre d'Argis, a Frenchman who had lived in Kentucky for several years, obtained an audience with the Spanish ambassador at Paris and repeated the note of warning, insisting that it was absolutely necessary for Spain to adopt a new policy for the Mississippi Valley if she would save her North American dominions. D'Argis proposed the absorption of the Americans in the West, which was the preliminary for the so-called "Spanish Conspir-

[22] Alamán, *Historia de Méjico,* I, 128.

[23] M. de Pradt, *The Colonies and the Present American Revolution,* p. 335.

[24] Arthur P. Whitaker, *The Spanish-American Frontier: 1783-1795* (Boston, 1927), chap. iii, *passim.*

[25] *Ibid.,* pp. 64, 67.

acy." The plan won the approval of both Aranda and Floridablanca, but was not supported by the Spanish officials in America.[26]

Another Frenchman to take an interest in the western country at this time was Brissot de Warville, whose opinions may reflect the aspirations of the West and explain the just fears of the Spaniards. Of this delicate frontier question, Brissot wrote:

> The slightest quarrel will be sufficient to throw them into a flame; and if ever the Americans shall march towards New Orleans, it will infallibly fall into their hands. The Spaniards fear this moment; and it cannot be far off. If they had the policy to open the Mississippi, the port of New Orleans would become the centre of a lucrative commerce. But her narrow and superstitious policy will oppose it; for she fears, above all things, the communication of those principles of independence, which the Americans preach wherever they go; and to which their own success gives an additional weight.[27]

This idea of the impossibility of holding back the Americans at the Mississippi was also supported by M. Saugrain, a Frenchman who had been allowed to enter Spanish America on a scientific expedition.[28] Brissot ridiculed the policy of stopping the Americans by allowing them to settle west of the Mississippi and the right of trading at New Orleans, as had been done with Colonel Morgan and his followers. "This colony," he warned, "is the first foundation of the conquest of Louisiana and of the civilization of Mexico and Peru." Clavier, his friend, had warned Brissot to "silence his imagination," and yet he gave it voice to express his enthusiasm for the spread of liberty in these words: "I see Mexicans, Peruvians, men of the United States, Frenchmen, and Canadians, embracing each other, cursing tyrants, and blessing the reign of Liberty, which leads to universal harmony." Thus he predicted "the irresistible force of democracy."[29] These views might appeal to the Amer-

---

[26] *Ibid.*, pp. 78-88.
[27] J. P. Brissot de Warville, *New Travels in the United States of America performed in 1788* (Dublin, 1792), p. 481.
[28] *Ibid.*, pp. 258, 261.   [29] *Ibid.*, p. 483.

icans who had started such a powerful movement, but most of the statesmen were more moderate in their expectations, even while sympathizing with the idea which served as the seeds of "manifest destiny."

In 1787, while in France, Jefferson informed Congress that a Mexican agent had come to him with a plan for the liberation of his country. Jefferson did not give him any encouragement, indicating that the first task was to emancipate the minds of the Mexican people since they were not ready for independence. He also informed Congress that he believed the British were encouraging revolts in Spanish America. As for the United States, he said that those who looked into the future would want Spain to retain "(not forever, but) very long her possessions in that quarter." He seemed to think that independence of the Spanish colonies was inevitable, but wanted to postpone the event until the United States could benefit by it rather than England.[30]

There were those among the Spanish Americans who were getting impatient and wanted action, in spite of their inadequate preparation for freedom. Vizcardo y Guzmán, a Jesuit, made an appeal to his countrymen in America to throw off the Spanish yoke and emulate the example of the Anglo-Americans. In his general letter to the Spanish Americans he wrote: "The valor with which the English colonies of America have fought for their liberty, which they gloriously enjoy, covers our indolence with shame; we have yielded to them the palm with which they have been the first to crown the New World by their sovereign independence."[31] With the prevalence and growth of such revolutionary ideas one can readily understand why the American Independence was to Count D'Aranda "a subject of grief and fear," and why he should say

[30] Ford (ed.), *Works of Jefferson*, V, 277-278.
[31] This letter is printed by Villanueva, *Napoleon y la Independencia*, Appendix, pp. 295-321.

that the Spanish Empire "now stands exposed to terrible reverses...."[32]

The inhabitants of the Spanish colonies had as many grievances as those of the former British colonies and perhaps more real causes for desiring independence. Little or nothing could be done, however, until there was a realization of the possibilities for improvements and for greater freedom. This realization might come from the example of the United States, the encouragement of England, or the ideas of France. Having once heard of the idealistic glories of freedom, they would be in need only of a leader and a directing force to seek the same ends. The conditions created the man, and the greatest of all the early revolutionary leaders appeared on the scene, Francisco de Miranda, who is described by Robertson, his biographer, as the "Precursor, Knight-Errant, and Promoter of Spanish-American liberty."

Francisco de Miranda,[33] a creole from Caracas, fought in the Spanish army against England during the American Revolution. He left the army immediately after the war, having aroused the suspicion of the Spanish authorities, and traveled in the United States where he met the leading political figures and made some very important connections. He admired the new Republic and began to look forward to the time when his own countrymen in the Spanish part of America could follow the example of their Anglo-Saxon neighbors.[34] He was being educated for his own part in this enterprise when he made an extensive tour of Europe between 1785-1789 to study political organizations.

[32] Trescott, *The Diplomacy of the Revolution*, pp. 70-71.
[33] Two excellent studies have been made of the life and work of Miranda by William Spence Robertson. The first was "Francisco de Miranda and the Revolutionizing of Spanish America," *Annual Report of the American Historical Association, 1907* (Vol. I, Washington, 1908). A more complete study, *The Life of Miranda* (2 vols., Chapel Hill, 1929), was based largely on Miranda's diary and other material discovered recently.
[34] *Supra*, n. 2.

Shortly after Miranda's return to England, that country became involved in the Nootka Sound Controversy with Spain.[35] The Pacific Coast of America was looked upon by Spain as her exclusive possession, and her resentment of foreign intrusion was emphasized by the arrest of British traders. The haughty attitude of the two powers seemed to make war inevitable. Here, then, was Miranda's opportunity. England had often considered propositions for the liberation of Mexico in order to open greater commercial opportunities. It had also been suggested that liberation rather than conquest would give the greater benefit to England. Miranda, expecting war, presented to Pitt and Grenville a plan for an attack on Spain by making her colonies independent. A proposal for the governments of the new states was also submitted. Miranda hoped at that time to unite all of Spanish America under one ruler. The northern boundary should be the forty-fifth parallel drawn from the Mississippi to the Pacific.[36] He suggested to Pitt that the former Jesuits could be used in the project and gave him a list of three hundred who were in Italy at the time of his visit there in 1786.[37] These, he said, might easily be "engaged for such a noble purpose." Pitt showed sufficient interest in the plan to arouse hopes that it might be approved by the government.[38] In the meantime the British sought information from other sources to verify Miranda's statements and to form a basis for action.

Mexico and Central America seemed to hold England's interest, for she continued to collect information on such places as Chagres, Panama, Guatemala, and Vera Cruz. Reports were sent to the Governor of Jamaica together with a list of "men of tried fidelity" who could be employed with the Mosquito

[35] See, in general, William R. Manning, "The Nootka Sound Controversy," *Annual Report of the American Historical Association, 1904* (Washington, 1905).

[36] Robertson, *Miranda*, p. 273.

[37] A list of names given by Miranda may be found in Villanueva, *Napoleón y la Independencia,* Appendix, pp. 305-307.

[38] Manning, "The Nootka Sound Controversy," p. 384.

Indians in any operation against the Spaniards.[39] Sir Archibald Campbell, who was, in all probability, the officer to lead one of the English expeditions, also submitted a plan.[40] Contrary to most opinions, he thought that "the march of an army from New Orleans to Mexico through Savannahs and Forests so little known to us may be attended with the most fatal consequences at this juncture."[41]

Among those who kept the English informed on conditions in Spanish America was one who signed his name as P. Allaire. He reported an uprising in Mexico in February, 1790, and concluded with the statement, "Liberty spreads her Wings from East to West."[42] He later informed the British government that the western people in the United States would aid any nation to take Florida from Spain if they were guaranteed the free navigation of the Mississippi.[43]

More active on the Florida border was the adventurer and trader, William Bowles, who also tried to arouse England's interest in the North American colonies of Spain. His report is interesting, although perhaps not entirely accurate. He informed Lord Grenville early in 1791 that he had marched seven hundred miles into the country towards Mexico, partly, as he said, "to try what influence such a movement might have." He was well pleased with the results, and continued:

> The numberless addresses I received in writing from all parts, satisfied me that I might have proceeded to the centre of Mexico and have been received as a deliverer. But the affairs of the Nation were not then ripe, according to my judgment for the experiment.
>
> Relying on these facts, I should as soon as the Floridas and the lower part of Louisiana were mastered, immediately march at the head of a strong force towards Mexico. If during the progress of

---

[39] Robertson, *Miranda,* pp. 276-277.

[40] *Ibid.,* p. 277; Londonderry (ed.), *Correspondence of Castlereagh,* VII, 288-290.

[41] Letter to Pitt, Oct., 1790, Frederick J. Turner (ed.), "English Policy toward America, 1790-91," *The American Historical Review,* VII, 716 (July, 1902).

[42] Frederick J. Turner (ed.), "English Policy toward America, 1790-91," *The American Historical Review,* VII, 711.

[43] *Ibid.,* VII, 717-718.

this march, I found it likely I should succeed in that country so well as I am led to believe I should, I would proceed without delay to Mexico, and in conjunction with Natives declare it independent of the Spaniards. In such an event I should have no fear about the state of things in the Floridas.[44]

He added that he would not waste any of His Lordship's time in pointing out the advantages of such an undertaking since they were already well understood. He was primarily interested in the method and would save the country a repetition "of such Tragedies as were acted at Porto Bello and Carthagena," where actual conquest had been attempted. He advocated the use of Creeks and Cherokees; and if it were desirable or necessary, he might also get the support of six thousand dissatisfied Americans from the West.[45] The attitude of the United States would certainly have to be considered for any border project.

The Americans were at first divided as to what policy to pursue in case England and Spain went to war. Jefferson believed that Spain might possibly allow Louisiana and Florida to become independent rather than risk their conquest by England. In that case he would be willing to support France and Spain against England. Hamilton, on the other hand, was inclined to favor England; and there was a suggestion to the effect that if the United States allowed England to cross her territory in conquering Louisiana, the latter might open the Mississippi to American commerce.[46] Miranda, who had been associating with Stephen Sayre in London, wrote to General Knox on the matter of intervention; and when Knox replied he said: "The true interests of the United States dictate a state of neutrality in the affairs between Spain and England."[47] The final decision of Washington and his cabinet was to remain

---

[44] William Bowles to Lord Grenville, Jan. 13, 1791, *ibid.*, VII, 728-733.
[45] *Ibid.*, VII, 729.
[46] Latané, *A History of American Foreign Policy*, pp. 73-74.
[47] W. C. Ford, *The United States and Spain in 1790* (Brooklyn, 1890), p. 104.

neutral as long as possible, thus establishing a policy which was to become an American tradition.

Miranda wanted war, since that was the condition necessary for the materialization of the revolutionary schemes. France became the determining factor in Spain's choice for war or peace. She did not want Spain to increase her military power, which might later be used to restore Louis XVI to the throne. Furthermore, the Family Compact was not popular in France;[48] the French Assembly was desirous of retaining allies, but felt little obligation to uphold the agreement of monarchs. Certain stipulations were therefore added before support would be given to Spain in her pending struggle with England.[49] The Family Compact had served chiefly to get Spain into trouble; when it might have proved of value, it was found useless. Spain's choice was simply to submit to England and accept a loss, or undertake a war with the possibility of a greater loss. The French reservations made Spain decide to come to an agreement with England rather than depend on her uncertain ally. The result was the settlement of the controversy in the Nootka Sound Convention, in which Spain gave up her exclusive claims to the western coast of America, marking her first setback on the Pacific coast, as her retreat to Charleston in the treaty of 1670 had marked her first setback on the Atlantic coast.

Miranda could hold France partly responsible for preventing the war which might have meant the realization of his dreams; and yet France, by her own revolution, was soon to give him another opportunity to work for the independence of Spanish America.

[48] Francis P. Renault, *Le Pacte de Famille et L'Amérique* (Paris, 1922), p. 405; in general, see pp. 397-409.

[49] Chapman, *History of Spain,* p. 400; Channing, *History of the United States.* IV, 123.

CHAPTER VII

REVOLUTIONARY PLANS ON THE LOUISIANA BORDER

"By conquering New Mexico and Louisiana, that of all Spanish America, with its mines, may, soon after, be easily achieved.—GEORGE ROGERS CLARK.
"The hour has struck, Frenchmen of Louisiana; hasten to profit by the great lesson you have received."—The Freemen of France to their Brothers in Louisiana.

HAVING failed to get England's support for his revolutionary projects, owing to the peaceful settlement of the Nootka Sound Controversy, Miranda turned to the new champion of liberty, France.[1] He thought that since France had helped the struggling colonies of England gain their independence, it might be willing to do as much for the Spanish colonies; and he was not mistaken, for the French Revolution, whose ideas knew no boundaries, made its leaders consider the Spanish colonies a field for their activities. The Girondists, with Brissot at their head, were willing to take up the cause of Spanish liberty. Shortly after he became foreign minister,[2] General Dumouriez tried to form an alliance with England to oppose despots.[3] With the aid of England, and possibly the United States, the Spanish colonies could be freed, the new world redivided, and its commerce opened to its liberators.[4] Like the English, the French sought their reward, and commercial advantages were always powerful incentives for championing the paradoxical cause of liberty and equality.

[1] In addition to the works on Miranda by Rojas and Robertson, see also Parra-Pérez, *Miranda et la Révolution Française*.
[2] March 23, 1792, five days before Miranda arrived in Paris.
[3] Albert Sorel, *L'Europe et la Révolution Française* (7 vols., Paris, 1887-1904), II, 419; III, 19-21.
[4] *Ibid.*, II, 422, 423.

[110]

It was at this time that Miranda came to France, and his arrival stimulated the revolutionists to greater activities. He soon made the acquaintance of such men as Brissot, Dumouriez, Lebrun, and Pétion. On October 13, 1792, Brissot wrote to Miranda that the time had come to revolutionize the Spanish colonies.[5] Miranda, with headquarters at Santo Domingo, was to be the leader of the expedition. But there was still some doubt about the support of Dumouriez whom they knew had cherished the idea of being the liberator of the New World.[6] Towards the end of the month Miranda informed Pétion of the project, telling him about the attitude of the United States and England, and of the ex-Jesuits in Italy.[7] Not long after this Miranda wrote to General Knox that Colonel Smith would inform him "how things are coming to maturity," and "that those schemes our patriotism suggested to our minds in our Symposiums at Boston, are not far from being realized."[8]

Miranda had reason to be optimistic for the French were making plans to support him. Brissot reminded Dumouriez, November 28, 1792, of their old purpose to leave no Bourbon on a throne, a threat to the Spanish empire. Miranda, whose name was worth an army, was the one man who could bring success to the enterprise in America. He added: "I know well that this appointment will strike Spain with terror and confound Pitt with his poor, dilatory politics, but Spain is impotent and England will not move."[9] Dumouriez, combining his European and American policy, tried to keep England neutral or as an ally by making it "choose between a maritime war and the immense benefits which the emancipation of the

---

[5] Aristides Rojas, *Miranda dans la Révolution Française* (Caracas, 1889), p. 7.
[6] Miranda was serving in the French army under Dumouriez.
[7] Miranda to Pétion, Oct. 26, 1792, Villanueva, *Napoleón y la Independencia de América*, pp. 64-69.
[8] Quoted by Robertson, *Miranda*, pp. 290-291.
[9] Rojas, *Miranda dans la Révolution Française*, pp. 2-3.

Spanish colonies would give her."[10] To Lebrun he wrote on November 30, 1792: "Once masters of the Dutch navy, we shall be strong enough to crush England, especially by interesting the United States of America in sustaining our colonies in executing a superb project of General Miranda."[11]

Admiral Kersaint had made a similar plan for the Spanish colonies, but he advocated the use of more allies; to England and the United States he added Holland, Prussia, Sweden, and Denmark, all to share in the enterprise and the plunder. Each country was assigned its sphere of action, and that of Mexico was to be the particular field of France and England.[12] It is possible that the admiral had been interested in such a project for some time, because, as early as March of that year, the Spanish government notified the viceroy of Mexico that six propagandists, headed by a Mr. Kersaint, were leaving Brest for New Spain to introduce the "maxims of independence."[13]

By December Miranda's enthusiasm for French aid had waned, and he informed Brissot that the plan was "really grand and magnificent," but he did not know if it could be executed with success, pleading his lack of knowledge of the proposed French base as a hindrance.[14] In fact, Miranda was becoming skeptical about spreading the influence of the French Revolution to America. However, he was still interested, and asked Brissot to examine the plans he had presented to Pitt in 1790 before undertaking any project.[15] Brissot, anticipating a war with England and Spain, went so far as to make an official proposal to the committee of public safety in January, 1793, for

---

[10] Sorel, *L'Europe et la Révolution Française*, III, 175.
[11] *Ibid.*
[12] Robertson, *Miranda*, p. 289, gives the date for this memoir as being in Aug., 1792; Villanueva, *Napoleón y la Independencia*, p. 69, refers to the same or a similar plan by Kersaint on Oct. 1.
[13] Revilla Gigedo to Aranda, Mexico, May 31, 1792, A. G. I., Estado, Mexico, legajo 2.
[14] Miranda to Brissot, Dec. 19, 1792, Rojas, *Miranda dans la Révolution Française*, p. 9.
[15] *Ibid.*

sending an expedition to the Spanish colonies.[16] But the French soon became too much occupied in European affairs to devote much time to America.[17]

The French now turned their attention to Louisiana where many of the inhabitants were showing interest in and sympathy for the maxims and actions of the French Revolution. These views were endangering the Spanish possessions and the Spanish officials knew it. Gayoso de Lemos, governor at Natchez, said of the inhabitants of Louisiana that "the majority are fond of novelty, have communication with France and with their possessions in America, and hear with the greatest pleasure of the revolution in that kingdom."[18] This was the fertile field in which Genêt was to sow the seeds of revolution. It promised more immediate prospects of success than the larger project of Miranda, and it might serve as an example to Mexico or as a starting point for greater undertakings.

The suggestion of Lebrun to Dumouriez that they send Genêt on this revolutionary mission[19] was followed by a large number of proposals and schemes for the independence or the acquisition of Louisiana, and many of these contained provisions for the liberation of additional Spanish territory. In an elaborate plan drawn up in 1792, the anonymous author said that, though it was a bit chimerical to include all the domain from New Mexico to Chile, he did not think this territory would remain forever under the yoke of Spain.[20] His reasons for anticipating success resemble those of the other revolutionists and give an idea of the views of the time. Ever since 1779 secret overtures had been made to the French minister at

---

[16] F. A. Aulard (ed.), *Recueil des Actes du Comité du Salut Public* (26 vols., Paris, 1889-1923), II, 10; III, 82.

[17] According to Robertson, *Miranda*, p. 293, and n. 2, the French did not give up their designs of employing Miranda until the beginning of 1793.

[18] James A. Robertson (ed.), *Louisiana under the rule of Spain, France, and the United States, 1785-1807* (2 vols., Cleveland, 1911), I, 283.

[19] Nov. 6, 1792, Sorel, *L'Europe et la Révolution Française*, III, 157.

[20] "Plan proposé pour faire une revolution dans la Louisiane," *Annual Report of the American Historical Association, 1896* (Washington, 1897), I, 945-953.

Philadelphia to get freedom from Spain.[21] Most of the inhabitants were French and Americans, needing only assurance of protection to carry out a revolt, since the "barbarous methods" of "Bloody O'Reilly," which established Spanish authority, secured no more than apparent loyalty. The weak garrison at New Orleans was still composed largely of Frenchmen, and the Anglo-Americans were "friends of liberty," all well armed. One might add to this the opinion of the Spanish governor of Natchez: "I fear that if war were declared on France, we would find but few inhabitants of Lower Louisiana who would sincerely defend the country from any undertaking of that nation."[22] Similar views were expressed by other Spanish officials, including the viceroy, Revilla Gigedo.[23]

The author of the above plan suggested that three or four agents be sent to Philadelphia to aid Genêt in setting the project in motion. One of these would seek support in New Orleans,[24] and another the aid of the adventurous westerners. General Wilkinson was thought to be the most suitable man to act as the commander-in-chief. France might well consider this "consummate artist in treason" a likely leader for a revolutionary project, and a man who could serve two countries might also serve a third as well as himself. According to the plan, manifestoes were to be spread in the name of the republic to urge the inhabitants to call assemblies, to declare their independence, and to form a government. All was to be done without the aid of the United States, because there was a possibility of getting the western states to separate from the union; and, furthermore, that country "no longer treated liberty as lovers but as husbands."

---

[21] Ten years earlier, France had considered the possibility of setting up a republic in Louisiana, according to Villanueva, *Napoleón y la Independencia de América*, p. 29.

[22] Robertson (ed.), *Louisiana*, I, 283.

[23] Mexico, April 30, 1793, A. G. I., Estado, Mexico, legajo 2.

[24] De Pauw was in New Orleans in April, 1793, apparently encouraging revolutionary plans, *Annual Report of the American Historical Association, 1896*, I, 1103.

This did not exclude the individual Americans from serving, and there were many who were willing to participate in the liberation of the Spanish American colonies. Among these were George Rogers Clark, his brother-in-law Dr. James O'Fallon, Daniel Clark, and Benjamin Logan in the United States; Thomas Paine, Gilbert Imlay, and Joel Barlow in Paris. Wherever there was a struggle for liberty against hereditary monarchs one could always enlist the support or sympathy of the champion of the "Rights of Man," the much maligned Thomas Paine.[25] He lived with a few English disciples in the old mansion of Madame Pompadour. "In the evenings they were joined by others, the Brissots (before the arrest), Nicholas Bonneville, Joel Barlow, Captain Imlay, Mary Wollstonecraft, the Rolands."[26] Even the great Miranda occasionally found his way into this fascinating circle.[27]

Gilbert Imlay, soldier of the American Revolution, western settler, writer, lover of Mary Wollstonecraft, and a member of the Paine circle, became an advocate for the emancipation of at least a part of Spanish America. In his "Observations"[28] he recommended the liberation of Louisiana, partly because it would be a blow to Spain who considered it the key to her possessions. Imlay had been introduced to several of the leading revolutionists, and it seems likely that the French intended to use him in their enterprise in America.[29] In the spring of 1793 it was suggested that four men be sent to Philadelphia to act as the nucleus of "a committee for the expedition of Loui-

[25] Thomas Paine had met Miranda in the United States and possibly in London, and must have been interested in his plan. See Robertson, *Miranda*, pp. 249, 286.
[26] Moncure D. Conway, *The Life of Thomas Paine* (3rd ed., 2 vols., New York, 1893), II, 66.
[27] Ralph L. Rusk, "The Adventures of Gilbert Imlay," *Indiana University Studies*, X, 18, n. 61 (March, 1923).
[28] Printed in *Annual Report of the American Historical Association, 1896*, I, 953-954.
[29] Rusk, "The Adventures of Gilbert Imlay," *Indiana University Studies*, X, 19.

siana and of that of the other Spanish colonies."[30] It is only reasonable to believe that Mexico was to be among "the other Spanish colonies." The revolutionary committee was to be composed of two Americans: Joel Barlow, our American poet-diplomat; Stephen Sayre, Princeton graduate, who became banker and sheriff in London, and later associated with Arthur Lee and Franklin; and two Frenchmen: Lyonnet, a former resident of New Orleans; and Beaupoils, a French military man.[31] These men were instructed, not only to seek means for overthrowing the Spanish colonies in America, both on the mainland and on the islands, but to initiate the revolution which was to be carried to completion by Miranda. There was also an indication that there might be coöperation between the proposed Louisiana expedition and revolutionists in Mexico.[32]

Sayre and Beaupoils together with Pereyrat contributed separate plans to the minister of foreign affairs.[33] They thought a war with Spain was inevitable, and not without reason, since war was declared within three days, March 9, 1793. The former plan of Dumouriez was considered with a few alterations to suit the changed conditions. The proposals of a certain general (possibly Miranda) were now too elaborate, because France, at war with England, Holland, and Spain, could not spare a fleet large enough to insure success.[34] Their own project was considered practicable because it needed no large force, "even though it had for its aim to take possession of Mexico and of stirring South America to revolt." If the taking of

[30] "Documents on the Relations of France to Louisiana, 1792-95," *The American Historical Review*, III, 491-510 (April, 1898).

[31] For the characterization of these men, see Isaac J. Cox, "The Louisiana-Texas Frontier," *Quarterly of the Texas State Historical Association*, X, 46.

[32] The document referred to a Mexican who had written to citizen Clavier, suggesting coöperation. Clavier, the minister of finance, was an intimate friend of Brissot, with whom he had traveled in America, and with whom he had been joint author of *De la France et des États-Unis* (London, 1787).

[33] Printed in the *Annual Report of the American Historical Association, 1896*, I, 954-957.

[34] They said that the republic could continue with the general's project whenever the occasion was suitable, *ibid.*, I, 955.

New Orleans did not seem important enough, the expedition could proceed down the southwest mouth of the Mississippi, along the coast of the Gulf to Pánuco, where they could offer liberty to the ill-treated Indians. Then they could proceed to Mexico, which "probably would not give as much resistance as when Cortés attacked it."[35]

Genet, who was to be chief actor in the proposed projects, was given his instructions in December, 1792.[36] The threatened break with England and Spain was considered, and the French minister was expected to get the support of the United States by suggesting that it was to the interest of the Americans to oppose the designs of George III against liberty. He was to sow the seeds of the French Revolution and to encourage the principles of liberty and independence in Louisiana and other provinces bordering on the United States. By means of an agreement between the two nations they could extend the "empire of liberty," guarantee the sovereignty of the people, and by an attack on the powers which still maintained a colonial system and commercial exclusion, their efforts would soon lead to the liberation of Spanish America, and, "perhaps, of uniting to the American constellation the beautiful star of Canada."

Of all the Americans who were involved in this revolutionary project, George Rogers Clark was probably the most important, since he was finally designated as the leader.[37] He was willing to cast his fortunes with these intriguers, because the United States had been, as he said, "notoriously ungrate-

[35] Pierre Lyonnet, too, made suggestions for a revolutionary project, March, 1793; see *The American Historical Review*, III, 496-500. For his "Additional Observations," see *ibid.*, III, 500-503.

[36] *Annual Report of the American Historical Association, 1896*, I, 957-958 and 958-963.

[37] See Lyonnet's "Additional Observations," *The American Historical Review*, III, 500-503. Clark seems also to have offered his services to Spain in 1788 in return for a land grant; see *Annual Report of the American Historical Association, 1896*, I, 932.

ful" for his services.³⁸ Dr. James O'Fallon had a personal grievance with Spain over a land question, and when he married Clark's sister he became an active supporter of his brother-in-law and the French plot.³⁹ In an intercepted letter of Dr. O'Fallon to Captain Herron, the former said of the proposed attack on Louisiana: "This plan was digested between General Clark and me last Christmas. I framed the whole of the correspondence in the General's name, and corroborated it by a private letter of my own to Mr. Thomas Paine."⁴⁰ According to Paine's reply from Passey, February 17, 1793,⁴¹ the proposal had probably been presented recently to the provisory executive council of the republic through the medium of Genêt, whose departure had been delayed until the last week in February.

Clark informed the French government in February that he was willing and able to lead an expedition against the Spanish. First, he would capture St. Louis and New Orleans. "If further aided," he said, "I would capture Pensacola; and if Santa Fe and the rest of New Mexico were objects—I know their strength and every avenue leading to them, for conquest." He had long looked for an opportunity to give Spain "a vital blow" in this quarter, and added that "by conquering New Mexico and Louisiana, that of all Spanish America, with its mines, may, soon after, be easily achieved."⁴² According to Genêt, General Clark had friends in various cities of New Spain, who kept him informed and who would be of great help to him in their proposed expedition. It was not until July 12 that Genêt informed Clark⁴³ that his plans had been

---

³⁸ Clark to French minister, Feb. 5, 1793, *ibid.*, I, 967-971.
³⁹ Louise Phelps Kellog (ed.), "Letter of Thomas Paine, 1793," *The American Historical Review*, XXIX, 503 (April, 1924).
⁴⁰ Oct. 18, 1793, Conway, *Life of Thomas Paine*, II, 156.
⁴¹ *Annual Report of the American Historical Association, 1896*, I, 967, note 2. See also Kellog (ed.), "Letter of Thomas Paine," *The American Historical Review*, XXIX, 504-505.
⁴² *Annual Report of the American Historical Association, 1896*, I, 967-971.
⁴³ *Ibid.*, I, 986.

adopted; and Michaux, who brought Genêt's letter, had now given up the scientific expedition of Jefferson to coöperate with Clark as an agent of the French republic. Clark's commission made him commander-in-chief of the "Independent and Revolutionary Legion of the Mississippi."

While the project was slowly taking form in America, events in Europe were rapidly approaching a climax. The proclamation of the French convention, November 19, 1792, promising "fraternity and aid to all peoples who wished to recover their liberty,"[44] would certainly arouse revolutionary ideas among many, but would also provoke greater opposition from European monarchs. The execution of Louis Capet on January 21, 1793, increased the danger; and on February 1, England and, on March 9, Spain were actually at war with France. The desire to attack Spain through its colonies became greater, but the opportunity to do so became less. It was, therefore, quite in keeping with the French policy to seek American aid against the Spanish colonies. The failure of the United States to come to an agreement with Spain over the Mississippi question made many of the leading Americans anticipate a war with Spain.[45] Genêt, however, endangered the whole project by his unguarded procedure.

Colonel Smith, newly arrived from Paris, informed Jefferson of the French plans which had been made together with Miranda.[46] He knew that Genêt was coming to the United States to get its support, and he was also authorized by Lebrun to deliver a letter to the president and to communicate plans to him worthy of his "great mind." He informed Jefferson further that the French intended to begin their attack at the

---

[44] Shailer Mathews, *The French Revolution, 1789-1815* (New York, 1924), p. 224.

[45] For the changing attitudes, see George L. Rives, "Spain and the United States in 1795," *The American Historical Review*, IV, 62-79 (Oct., 1898); also Samuel F. Bemis, *The Pinckney Treaty* (Baltimore, 1926), *passim*.

[46] Feb. 20, 1793, Ford (ed.), *Works of Jefferson*, I, 253-256.

mouth of the Mississippi, "and sweep along the Bay of Mexico southwardly, and that they would have no objections to our incorporating into our government the two Floridas." Even before Napoleon, France dangled the Floridas before the eyes of the United States. Jefferson, nibbling, wrote to Carmichael and Short, commissioners in Spain, to leave the United States free to act according to circumstances.[47] To Pinckney he wrote that "In the changeable scenes . . . which are passing in Europe" he should avail himself of any opportunity to gain commercial advantages; "especially in the American Colonies" he was "not to let the occasion slip by for want of previous instructions."[48]

Genêt, however, had his difficulties, and Washington was not the least of these. The president's proclamation of neutrality had put an end to Genêt's prospects for governmental aid. "Old Washington" had hindered his progress "in a thousand ways," he wrote to Lebrun.[49] He next made Jefferson his confidant, but not as secretary of state,[50] since Jefferson had to be cautious because of the negotiations then going on for a depot at New Orleans.[51] Others, such as Governor Moultrie of South Carolina and Senator Brown of Kentucky, seemed to favor the undertaking.[52] At Charleston Genêt had found an enthusiastic supporter in the French consul, Mongourit. Activities were begun on the Florida border, where expeditions were being organized under the supervision of

[47] March 23, 1793, *ibid.*, VII, 267.
[48] Philadelphia, March 16, 1793, Rufus King MSS., 263, Huntington Library.
[49] Frederick J. Turner, "Origin of Genêt's Projected Attack on Louisiana and the Floridas," *The American Historical Review*, III, 650-671 (July, 1898).
[50] "Jefferson's Minute of Conversation with Genêt," *Annual Report of the American Historical Association, 1896*, I, 984-985.
[51] This reason was later given to the westerners to prevent them from taking an active part in Genêt's project, Jefferson to Governor of Kentucky, Aug. 29, 1793, *American State Papers, Foreign Relations* (Washington, 1833), I, 455.
[52] Governor Moultrie supported the plan because he thought it would end the Indian wars on the border. Senator Brown had written a letter of introduction for Michaux. See Genêt's report of July 25, 1793, in *Annual Report of the American Historical Association, 1896*, I, 987-990.

Major-General Daniel Clark and Colonel Samuel Hammond of Georgia and William Tate of South Carolina.[53]

During the summer the revolutionary agents took the initial steps in the western country, but they had no sooner begun than they were checked by the United States government. In response to Spain's complaints, Jefferson wrote to Governor Shelby of Kentucky to prevent any hostilities against their western neighbor.[54] Lack of support did not stop Genêt and he wrote on October 7, 1793, that he had begun and would continue alone to carry out this vast project, "for I have found in Washington's cabinet only cold men, incapable of seizing such a grand idea."[55] Lyonnet, in his instructions of March, 1793, had anticipated this attitude of the Americans and made provisions for overcoming it. "One will be obliged, for example," he said, "to spend much for drink, for the Americans do not speak of the affairs of war except vis-à-vis to a bowl."[56]

Genêt might have continued in spite of the "cold men" of Washington's cabinet, but the fiery Jacobins were soon to prove an insurmountable obstacle. In June Brissot and his friends were arrested, and by the end of October the former had been guillotined. Genet had already been criticized for violating the neutrality of the United States;[57] and Washington's request for his recall, together with the attitude of the "Mountain," dominated by Robespierre, marked his fall. Genêt was recalled, but, having no desire to follow his party to the guillotine, he remained in the United States.

[53] F. J. Turner (ed.), "The Mongourit Correspondence in Respect to Genêt's Projected Attack upon the Floridas," *Annual Report of the American Historical Association, 1897* (Washington, 1898), pp. 569-679.
[54] Jefferson to the Governor of Kentucky, Nov. 6, 1793, *American State Papers, Foreign Relations*, I, 455.
[55] Genêt to minister, *Annual Report of the American Historical Association, 1896*, I, 1010-1012.
[56] *The American Historical Review*, III, 502.
[57] Deforgue's letter of July 30, 1793, Turner, "Origin of Genêt's Projected Attack on Louisiana and the Floridas," *The American Historical Review*, III, 670. For another view, see *ibid.*, III, 505-507.

During this critical period the Spanish officials had listened to rumors, read reports, made complaints, begged for aid, and waited for the worst. Baron Carondolet, governor of Louisiana and West Florida, had the difficult task of counteracting the French influence. His report on the conditions in New Orleans indicates that the revolutionists had described conditions quite accurately.[58] Carondolet was faithful, and efforts had been made to strengthen the defense against Americans as well as against the "ill-disposed and fanatical citizens of this Capital, whose intercourse with France fills it incessantly with restless, and turbulent men, infatuated with Liberty and Equality."[59] He later expressed some doubt as to his ability to defend the Spanish possessions.[60] In October he was given full information regarding the French project,[61] and in turn continued to send alarming reports to the Duke of Alcudia. On October 28 he gave an account of a Jacobin society in Philadelphia which was spreading its "pernicious and atrocious ideas" by means of a printed circular, headed "Liberty and Equality," from "The Freemen of France to their brothers of Louisiana."[62] It declared that France, having achieved its freedom, was now "ready to give her powerful assistance to those who may be disposed to follow her virtuous example. . . . The hour has struck, Frenchmen of Louisiana; hasten to profit by the great lesson you have received." The people of Louisiana were then urged to establish a republic and to form an allegiance with France and the United States.[63] Carondolet promised to continue his vigilance against ideas, since their

---

[58] De Pauw mentioned plans made at a dinner given in a house of Daniel Clark on April 20, 1793, three days before Carondolet's report; see *Annual Report of the American Historical Association, 1896*, I, 1103.

[59] Carondolet to Alcudia, April 23, 1793, *ibid.*, I, 974-977.

[60] *Ibid.*, I, 997-999.

[61] *Ibid.*, I, 1002-1003, 1005-1006.

[62] *Ibid.*, I, 1016-1017. Carondolet also wrote to Gayoso, governor of Natchez, asking him to get Wilkinson to notify them of any plans "contrary to the interests in Spain," Oct. 29, 1793, *ibid.*, I, 1019-1021.

[63] Gayarré, *History of Louisiana*, II, 337-340.

"diffusion in this province, inhabited in great part by French settlers, might have the most fatal consequences, not only here but also in the old, inland provinces of the kingdom of New Spain."[64] The viceroy, too, had recognized the difficulty of holding Louisiana because of its French inhabitants who did not offer much assurance of love and loyalty to the king. He also considered the possibility of the Americans taking possession of New Orleans, and who would then "aspire to other conquests by land and sea against New Spain."[65] The dismissal of Genêt, the neutrality of the United States, and the military activities of Carondolet promised greater security for the border provinces.

Even before Fauchet came to replace Genêt, the revolutionary enterprise seemed to be dwindling, owing to interference and a lack of support. Hammond, Tate, and Elijah Clark, all said they had enough men ready, but they could do nothing without funds. Nevertheless, the project, once considered, continued to occupy men's minds. Before the end of 1793 Joel Barlow, together with Leavenworth, wrote of the advantages of the liberation of Louisiana, which would also "give an excellent example to their neighbors in Mexico and Florida, an example which would soon banish the Spanish despotism from all of South America."[66]

When Fauchet restricted the French activities by his proclamation of March 4, 1794, it was mainly to disavow the actions of the Girondists, whose representative had violated the neutrality of the United States, and not, by any means, to indicate that France had abandoned its interest in Louisiana.[67] Nor had France given up the idea of emancipating Spanish America, for Flassau, in the foreign service section of the committee

[64] *Annual Report of the American Historical Association, 1896*, I, 1016-1017.
[65] Branciforte to Alcudia, Mexico, Oct. 3, 1794, A. G. I., Estado, Mexico, legajo 3.
[66] *The American Historical Review*, III, 508-510.
[67] Frederick J. Turner, "Policy of France toward the Mississippi Valley," *The American Historical Review*, X, 264 (Jan., 1905).

of public safety, declared in 1794 that France, having helped the British colonies, could do no less for the Spanish, and she might gain an immense field for her commercial activities.[68] The directing force might have been removed with the dismissal of Genêt, but the inflammatory material remained. Not knowing of his dismissal, George Rogers Clark wrote to Genêt on April 28, 1794, informing him of the preparations being made.[69] He had set "eavery wheele in motion" and the work of his agents in Louisiana had been done so well that

> ... the appearance of a small force in that Country would cause a Genl. revolt and upwards of two thousand men have been waiting with impatience to penetrate into that Country, declare themselves Citizens of France, and Give freedom to their neighbors on the Mississippi. ...

Perhaps they were not all ready for the invasion, but Clark probably knew that he could depend on approximately such a number. Governor Carondolet continued to recognize the danger and in a military report of November 24, 1794, he declared: "A general revolution, in my opinion, threatens Spain in America, unless it apply a powerful and speedy remedy."[70]

The various treaties at this time tended to diminish the immediate danger. Jay's Treaty with England, November 19, 1794, the Treaty of Basle, July 22, 1795, and the Treaty of San Lorenzo, October 27, 1795, settled many problems and rearranged the contestants; but the Spanish possessions continued to be a powerful factor in the diplomacy of the time. France, who had just been promoting a revolution in Louisiana to deprive Spain of the "key to her possessions," now waxed eloquent in picturing the advantages Spain would derive by giving up this "key" to its recent enemy. In the negotiations

---

[68] Villanueva, *Napóleon y la Independencia de América*, p. 75.
[69] E. C. Burnett (ed.), "Observations of London on American Trade, 1783," *The American Historical Review*, XVIII, 780-783 (July, 1913).
[70] Robertson (ed.), *Louisiana*, I, 299.

at Basle during the summer of 1795, Barthelemy, the French representative, was ordered to insist on getting Louisiana in addition to the Spanish portion of Santo Domingo.[71] Godoy, the Duke of Alcudia, was stubborn and refused to give up any territory on the mainland. But Jay's Treaty disturbed him and made him anxious to come to an agreement with the United States; for, as he said, "this treaty afforded great latitude for evil designs; it was possible to injure Spain in an indirect manner, and without risk in her distant possessions."[72]

And when Pinckney threatened to leave Madrid for London, Godoy really feared there might be an offensive arrangement between England and the United States, "leveled against Spain's colonies."[73] This made him agree to the Treaty of San Lorenzo which removed temporarily the danger from the United States and put Spain in a better position to deal with France. On the other hand, the United States had gained an advantage which was to be followed up, and the inhabitants of Louisiana became less dependent upon Spain.[74]

The year after the Treaty of Basle the French directors sent General Perignon to Madrid to arrange for an alliance and the retrocession of Louisiana.[75] Adet also knew that the cession of Louisiana was a preliminary to be insisted upon by France. The directors asked these pertinent questions: "Who can answer that England and the United States together will not divide up the northern part of the New World? Who

---

[71] Turner, "The Policy of France toward the Mississippi Valley in the Period of Washington and Adams," *The American Historical Review*, X, 266; and his "Diplomatic Contest for the Mississippi Valley," *The Atlantic Monthly*, XCIII, 676-691 (May, 1904); 807-817 (June, 1904); cf. p. 809.

[72] Quoted by Franklin L. Riley, "Spanish Policy in Mississippi after the Treaty of San Lorenzo," *Report of the American Historical Association, 1897* (Washington, 1898), p. 178.

[73] Turner, "Diplomatic Contest for the Mississippi," *The Atantic Monthy*, XCIII, 691, 809.

[74] DePradt, *The Colonies and the Present American Revolutions*, p. 329.

[75] Instruction to General Perignon, March 16, 1796, printed in the *Report of American Historical Association, 1897*, pp. 667-671.

prevents them?"[76] The opening of the Mississippi would be followed by the invasion of Louisiana and then of Florida, where there had already been, according to reports, little uprisings during the preceding October.[77] "We alone," said the directors, "can trace with a strong and respected hand the bounds of ... the United States and the limits of her territory." This, then, is the answer to the questions above. In addition to the danger of conquest by the people of the United States, "their intrigues and the example of their prosperity were daily preparing the subjects of Spain for insurrection." This new danger could be averted, for if Louisiana were given to France it would become "an impregnable bulwark for Mexico."

Spain was certainly in a dilemma: when France was her enemy she was threatened with the loss of territory by revolution, and when France became her ally she would have to give up a part to save the rest. France was playing "heads, I win; tails, you lose." Again we find that Godoy was stubborn, for even after this gloomy representation he refused to give up Louisiana.[78]

In the meantime the project initiated by Genêt had received some support from Adet, who reported that he had encouraged action along the Florida border.[79] On hearing of the peace with Spain, however, he notified Dupont to put a stop to the

[76] *Ibid.*, p. 668. The subject of retrocession had been first mentioned in the instructions of April 17, 1795, Lyon, *Louisiana in French Diplomacy, 1759-1804*, p. 79.

[77] Refers to General Clark, but evidently Elijah Clark, the filibuster; see Adet's report to Minister of Foreign Relations, Feb. 9, 1796, *Report of American Historical Association, 1903*, II, 826-831.

[78] Perignon was recalled after his failure and a successor was sent to resume the negotiations (Turner, "The Policy of France toward the Mississippi Valley in the Period of Washington and Adams," *The American Historical Review*, X, 269). These negotiations were not unknown to the United States (J. G. Adams to Rufus King, Oct. 3, 1796, Rufus King MSS., No. 1, Huntington Library).

[79] A detailed account of events was given by Adet in his report to the Minister of Foreign Relations, Feb. 9, 1796, *Report of the American Historical Association, 1903*, II, 826-831.

actions of the insurgents. This meant that the revolutionary material on the border was ready for action but was again left without support. Adet said that to abandon it would be both impolitic and unjust; it would be unjust to the individual members, and it would be impolitic because England could take over its direction and turn this revolution to her own profit. Blount's conspiracy was the materialization of the fears of Adet.[80]

The story of Louisiana intrigues has been told from various viewpoints, particularly for its influence on the United States, which was considerable, and from the viewpoint of Louisiana proper, which was its focal point. There is the third and neglected side of this episode, namely, the Mexican side. Here the border conspiracies became the work of the long arm of the French Revolution by which it threatened to undermine the authority of Spain by spreading its revolutionary system to Mexico.

[80] For "Documents on the Blount Conspiracy, 1795-1797," see *The American Historical Review*, X, 574 ff. (April, 1905); and Walter Brownlow Posey, "The Blount Conspiracy," *Birmingham-Southern College Bulletin*, XXI, 11-21 (Dec., 1928).

CHAPTER VIII

THE FRENCH REVOLUTION AND MEXICO

> "The success of the American Revolution animated the French struggle for liberty, fraternity, and equality, and the current set in motion finally swept Spanish America into the great stream of political events and economic developments which at last changed the whole trend of modern colonial theory."—HERBERT I. PRIESTLEY.
>
> "The sparks from the conflagration in Paris had meanwhile been carried far and wide, and had started fires even in places unexpected and remote, where they glowed under the surface, to burst into flame later."—W. ALLISON PHILLIPS.

WHILE the Louisiana border was being menaced by revolutionary projects, the people of New Spain had their own troubles in trying to safeguard the country against the insidious influence of France. A better appreciation of the French menace, whether in Louisiana or in Europe, can be obtained by a study of conditions in New Spain.

The French Revolution ushered in a busy season for the Holy Office of the Inquisition. A Spanish American bishop forbade, under penalty of excommunication, the reading in any of the colleges of any work relative to this "deplorable event."[1] Then there began a detailed attack on individual works. *The Rights of Man* by Thomas Paine was prohibited for having seditious doctrines.[2] Another book dealing with the controversy between Paine and Burke, *El Desengaño del Hombre* by James Puglio,[3] a Spanish instructor in Philadelphia, was evidently intended for Spanish American consumption and created considerable stir in Mexico. It was reported that three hundred copies were to be sent into the country by way of

---

[1] G. Desdevises du Dezert, "L'Eglise Espagnole des Indes a la fin du XVIIIe Siècle," *Revue Hispanique*, XXXIX, 248.

[2] Medina, *Historia del Tribunal del Santo Oficio de la Inquisición en México*, p. 438.

[3] Philadelphia, 1794. This edition may be found in the Library of Congress.

New Orleans, after which the viceroy sent orders to the frontier officials to exert the greatest vigilance to prevent the introduction of this "extremely abominable book." He thought that since many Frenchmen were finding asylum in the United States, the book was probably "the work of these pernicious characters."[4]

An edict had been passed by the Holy Office of the Inquisition on March 13, 1790, prohibiting the introduction of seditious books and papers which might excite the people to rebellion against the legitimate powers.[5] But books and pamphlets must have continued to come in, for it was necessary to publish new edicts from time to time to protect the innocent people from the new and spectacular ideas of the period. A *History of the French Revolution* was proscribed because it made scandalous, heretical, and blasphemous attacks on Divinity itself, and was injurious to the pope, to the clergy, and to the Holy Office of the Inquisition.[6] On February 2, 1798, the *Gazeta de México* published an edict,[7] largely a renewal of the prohibitions of 1790. Among others placed on the papal index in July, 1798, were *Esquisses d'un tableau historique des progress de l'esprit humain* by Condorcet; *History of the Revolution* by Servain Mereghal, for having "heretical and erroneous propositions, conducive to rebellion and anarchy"; and a three-volume work printed in Paris, 1789, called *Nouveau voyage en Espagne, ou tableau de l'état actual de cette monarchie*.[8] The volume on *Des droits et devoirs du citoyen* from Mably's works had been prohibited earlier. Although most of the prohibited books were French, the list for July included *Letters of Lord Chesterfield to his Son*, translated into French by Peyron; and *Essai philosophique consernant l'entendement humain* by Locke,

[4] Branciforte to Alcudia, Mexico, Oct. 3, 1794, A. G. I., Estado, Mexico, Legajo 3.
[5] Medina, *Historia de la Inquisición en México*, p. 440.
[6] *Ibid.*, p. 443.
[7] *Gazeta de México, Compendio de Noticias de Nueva España y Europa*, IX, 9-11.
[8] By Jean François Bourgoing.

translated by Costi; and a number of others, many of which were anonymous.[9]

One work which received special mention was *Les Ruines, ou Meditations sur les revolutions des Empires*[10] by M. Volney, deputy to the National Assembly. A few persons were given license to read certain prohibited books, but even to these this one was prohibited because it was a "summary of all the evil systems which the libertines of all times had invented and surpassed in maliciousness all the writings of Hobbes, Espinosa, Rousseau, Voltaire, and others"; and it was said to be founded on pure atheism, fatalism, naturalism, and materialism. It would not be unreasonable to believe that such a review would stir up considerable interest in the book.

Moreover, Frenchmen entered Mexico and brought in their foreign ideas which were kept alive by books and letters. In the trial of a number of these Frenchmen in 1794 it was found that one of them boasted the possession of a book so rare that not even the viceroy had a copy.[11] Another, Estevan Morel, was accused of having two trunks full of French books.[12] Juan Abadi, who was devoted to the French Assembly, reported its activities to a coterie of friends who met in the inn of Juan Aroche in Mexico. Here they discussed the new ideas of republicanism and championed the cause of the French Revolution. An address by General Lafayette was also found in the possession of one of the defendants.[13] Among the goods of Morel was discovered a letter from his nephew in France, saying that with the death of the king the country was put under a better system. Other letters conveyed the same views which Morel was accused of spreading.[14]

[9] *Gazeta de México*, X, 315; *Supplemento* (to the same), p. 321; and XII, 120, 129.
[10] Published in Amsterdam, 1795.
[11] Report of the trial by Caamaño, Mexico, Sept. 28, 1794, A. G. I., Estado, Mexico, legajo 3.
[12] Report by Valenzuela and Luzero, Mexico, Aug. 9, 1795, *ibid.*, legajo 4.
[13] Report by Caamaño, Mexico, Sept. 28, 1794, *ibid.*, legajo 3.
[14] Valenzuela and Luzero, Mexico, Aug. 9, 1795, *ibid.*, legajo 4.

The Inquisition was assisted by the government in its effort to seal Mexico against revolutionary ideas which, nevertheless, filtered in. The authorities found evidence of considerable French propaganda, and it is also possible that much eluded their vigilance. Branciforte, the viceroy, was particularly active in his efforts to save Mexico from the dangerous actions and ideas of the French. When he heard that two sets of pictorial playing cards, representing the last events in the life of Louis XVI and his family, had been sent to Vera Cruz, he ordered that a set be procured for his inspection. After examining three or four of the eight, depicting "the sacrilegious and horrible execution of the King of France and of the Royal Family," he was overcome by sorrow and the tears came to his eyes—so he says—and he ordered the rest to be taken from his sight. He would have all such pictures destroyed if possible.[15] However, as Juan Vicente said, "To prevent the arrival of papers and letters is not only most difficult, but impossible.[16] It would be difficult to examine all the letters, he added, and still more difficult to examine all the trunks and baggage that arrive every day. Even if this were feasible, those who knew what was going on would talk, especially those from Havana where they came into contact with foreigners from other islands of the West Indies. Many of the inhabitants of Mexico were poorly educated, he said, and knew little about the world, but they talked about the events in France as if most of the letters from Spain dealt with that subject.[17]

The officers of the Inquisition and the viceroy were frequently commended for their zeal in rooting out dangerous views, but the difficulty and even the impossibility of establishing a Chinese wall that would be idea-proof were recognized. The partisans of the French were also confident of their ability to penetrate the wall of exclusion, as witness this example of

---

[15] Branciforte to Principe de la Paz, Mexico, Nov. 26, 1796, *ibid.*, legajo 6.
[16] Vicente to Floridablanca, Mexico, Sept. 30, 1791, *ibid.*, legajo 1.
[17] *Ibid.*

propaganda posted on a street corner of Mexico: "The most wise are the French; to follow their suggestions is not absurd. However the laws may try, they can never stifle the cries that are inspired by nature."[18]

The Mexican authorities also learned of revolutionists who were coming directly from France to apply their maxims and systems to New Spain. On December 3, 1791, Mr. Folney, an American, was reported to have embarked at Bordeaux for New York as an emissary of French revolutionists. From New York he was expected to go to Martinique and from there to Mexico with instructions relative to an uprising in that colony. He was characterized as "a madman, capable of the most dangerous and extravagant undertaking," because his enthusiasm for the new French ideas had turned his head. He spoke English and Spanish fluently, and not only rapidly, but freely, and had informed a number of persons of his commission, showing a lack of tact which ought to make it easy to discover him. Then followed a complete description of Mr. Folney, telling about his black hair, pock-marked face, robust build, and his taste for drinks which excluded wines and favored water and certain kinds of liqueurs. He was well supplied with funds, having two letters of credit on Bordeaux, some on American banks, and three million Louis in gold.[19] The viceroy was ordered to make every effort to arrest Mr. Folney, but secretly if he could, and he was to warn other colonial governors. Thereupon Revilla Gigedo gave the strictest orders to the officials at the places where Folney might enter the country.[20] This new danger called for defense measures, and in a letter to the home government the viceroy expressed the hope that his majesty would send him troops and officers for the preservation of his dominions.[21]

[18] Copied by Bonilla, Mexico, Aug. 31, 1794, *ibid.*, legajo 3.
[19] Instructions to Revilla Gigedo, Aranjuez, Feb. 29, 1792, *ibid.*, legado 3.
[20] The governor of Vera Cruz informed the viceroy of his precautions, May 19, 1792, *ibid.*, legajo 16.
[21] Revilla Gigedo to Aranda, Mexico, May 31, 1792, *ibid.*, legajo 2.

Three days after the sending of a report on Folney, March 3, a royal order was dispatched to the viceroy informing him of the designs of six emissaries who were to embark from Brest with a number of "seductive" papers to convey the ideas of independence to Mexico.[22] At their head was Mr. Kersaint, possibly the French admiral who had advocated the building of a large navy to give strength to the revolutionary government. The viceroy expressed the opinion that by redoubling his efforts these enemies could be arrested and their papers discovered.[23] He appeared confident, but the French Revolution was beginning to create trouble for Spain in her colonies.

A new cause for disturbance came from El Guarico in Santo Domingo. The governor of the Spanish part of that island, as well as the governor of Cuba, informed the viceroy of a revolutionary plot by Mateo Coste, a Frenchman, married in New Spain, and owner of the hacienda, "El Zapo," in the province of Oaxaca.[24] Don Mateo was by profession a surgeon, but his occupation was that of a contraband trader. He was reported to have been in El Guarico in July, together with two other Frenchmen from Mexico, plotting against New Spain. He assured his associates that the inhabitants were "oppressed by the Spanish government and by the ministers of the Catholic religion," and that they were much disposed to break the yoke of both. Possessed of maps of the country, he proposed a landing at Vera Cruz as the place most suitable for their project. The persons of Guarico to whom Coste and his companions confided their plan suggested sending to the coast of New Spain a number of Negroes who had been expelled from Santo Domingo. Together with the French leaders and

---

[22] Folney, too, had spoken of other revolutionary agents. See order to Revilla Gigedo of Feb. 29, 1792, *ibid.*

[23] Revilla Gigedo to Aranda, Mexico, May 31, 1792, *ibid.*

[24] Revilla Gigedo to Floridablanca, Mexico, March 31, 1792; report of the governor of Cuba, copied in Mexico, Aug. 30, 1792; another letter from the governor, Aug. 4, 1792, *ibid.*

the Negro auxiliaries were to go a few engineers and several missionary agents to introduce and to spread the new doctrines and to prepare the way. Incidentally, they were to carry a large amount of contraband goods.[25]

The report, having come from a foreigner in Havana, seemed not to be accepted as entirely reliable by the governor;[26] but it was felt deserving of special care and action by the viceroy. He appointed Captain Ignacio Olaeta of the Coast Guard to go on a secret mission to San Martin de Acayucan to get all the information he could about the Frenchman, Coste; his associates; his ranch, "El Zapo"; and his whereabouts and occupation.[27] He was instructed to look for maps, plans and letters to be sent immediately to the viceroy, and to make a complete list of illicit goods found. He was to be given every aid necessary for the apprehension of this dangerous Frenchman or any of his associates. Even though the reports were found to be untrue, Olaeta should arrest Coste or any other foreigner he found, for the mere fact of not being a Spaniard was cause for imprisonment.[28]

Obviously, the viceroy considered the project quite serious, for he went to the extent of furnishing funds for Olaeta's mission in a manner contrary to royal orders. He gave instructions to the intendant of Oaxaca and the governor of Vera Cruz, as well as to minor officials, to give aid in men, money, or services to the captain. The expenditures should have been submitted to a superior junta of the real hacienda,[29] but the unusual circumstances and the need for secrecy made him act independently.[30] Furthermore, the viceroy was responsible for the

[25] Another letter stated that only Coste was in El Guarico and that the other two Frenchmen were in Cuba, *ibid*.
[26] Las Casas to Revilla Gigedo, Aug. 4, 1792; and Revilla Gigedo to Las Casas, copied in Mexico, Aug. 30, 1792, *ibid*.
[27] Instructions to Olaeta, Mexico, Aug. 27, 1792, *ibid*.
[28] ". . . pues solo con la calidad de no ser Español ha de ser preso," *ibid*.
[29] Aranjuez, Feb. 27, 1793, *ibid*.
[30] Revilla Gigedo to Gardoqui, Mexico, Aug. 30, 1792, *ibid*.

preservation of the kingdom, and considered his extra-legal procedure necessary. There was, however, no intention on the part of the viceroy to be extravagant, and he ordered Olaeta to do all with the greatest economy, for even saving the kingdom should be done economically. Owing to the immediate dangers to his dominions, the king soon approved the viceroy's arbitrary actions and advised him that he could continue to act independently in similar cases, being responsible only to the king.[31] In fact, he admitted that he was pleased with the prompt action of the viceroy in verifying the revolutionary reports.[32]

Captain Olaeta began his secret work at Acayucan in September, where he soon verified some of the reports about Coste,[33] but none of the suspects was there to be apprehended. From Juan Méndez, captain of the brigantine *Campechano,* he learned that Coste had departed on that vessel on March 19, 1790. Coste had said that he would return after four months to be married, but he had failed to do so, giving the Spaniards an idea as to what sort of a Frenchman he was. It was expected, however, that Don Mateo would return to a place between Guazacualcos and Alvarado with a shipload of illicit commerce.[34] Since there seemed little opportunity to apprehend Coste at Acayucan, the viceroy ordered Captain Olaeta to return to Vera Cruz by spring and resume his command of two coast guard vessels to watch for the Frenchman by sea.[35] Olaeta examined all the boats that entered Guazacoalcos and notified his superior; but neither in his report of May 31, nor of July 31, did the viceroy give any new information about Coste and his associates. Nevertheless, he ordered Olaeta to

[31] Aranjuez, Feb. 27, 1793, *ibid.*
[32] Report to Alcudia on the king's order, March 15, 1793, *ibid.*
[33] Summary of viceroy's reports, Aranjuez, Feb. 27, 1793, *ibid.*
[34] Revilla Gigedo to Aranda, Mexico, Jan. 12, 1793, *ibid.*
[35] Revilla Gigedo to Aranda, Mexico, March 31, 1793, *ibid.* This measure was also approved by the king, Aranjuez, April 27, 1793, *ibid.*

continue watching, not only for Coste, but to prevent any other project of similar purpose.[36]

El Guarico was now to take on a greater interest, for it served as a link between the project of Coste and the revolutionary schemes of Genêt. The French fleet which had been stationed at El Guarico was reported to have left to furnish naval aid for Genêt's undertaking. George Hammond, English minister to the United States, informed the governor of Cuba that the fleet had arrived and that Genêt was active in recruiting sailors, even securing Americans. It was believed that an attack would be made on the Spanish dominions within a few weeks. This report was substantiated by Ygnacio de Viar, Spanish representative in Philadelphia.[37] However, dissension among the commanders of the fleet gave the Spaniards some hope of safety, and the dismissal of Genêt must have been encouraging. Colonial officials continued to make efforts to check any new danger, and well they might, for in France, on the Mexican border, and in Mexico the ideas of the French Revolution were laying the foundation of the war for independence.

Rigid laws against foreigners had not prevented the French from entering Mexico.[38] The establishment of the Bourbon king on the Spanish throne was followed by some degree of official leniency toward the French, although they were generally disliked by the Spaniards. After the cession of Louisiana to Spain quite a number of Frenchmen were employed in the Spanish colonial service.[39] Others drifted across the Louisiana border into Mexican territory and were tolerated, some came

[36] Revilla Gigedo to Alcudia, *ibid*.
[37] Hammond to Las Casas, Philadelphia, Aug. 14, 1793, with the viceroy's report, Mexico, Nov. 6, 1793; Araoz to Las Casas, Havana, Sept. 24, 1793, *ibid*.
[38] For the evasion of the law against foreigners, see Lillian E. Fisher, *Viceregal Administration in the Spanish-American Colonies* (Berkeley, 1926), pp. 323-328.
[39] The drastic plan to punish by death any French trader found among the Indians was soon found impracticable, and toleration was followed by employment, Herbert E. Bolton (ed.), *Athanase de Mézières and the Louisiana-Texas Frontier, 1768-1780* (2 vols., Cleveland, 1914), I, 88.

with Spanish officials as their servants, and others came individually and unattached. Even the viceroys of Mexico brought French cooks to the land from which foreigners were excluded, as did several other officials. Juan Lausel (Locel), who was tried for sedition and accused of planning to poison his master, was the French cook of Revilla Gigedo;[40] Pedro Laborra came to Mexico as the cook of Bucareli; George Cap was for a long time in the service of Conde de Gálvez;[41] Nicolas Hos came as the majordomo of Cavallero de Croix; and Andres Courbiene and Nicolás Lemée had come to the Provincias Internas with Athanase de Mézières.[42] Governor Nava of the eastern provinces gave the names of several others who had come from Louisiana, most of whom he considered as good citizens. In a trial of a group of Frenchmen, two were found to be doctors, some were cooks, but most of them were said to be barbers who had entered the country without license.[43] In addition to cooks, doctors, and barbers, some served as military men, others as traders, musicians, farmers, and miners.

Revilla Gigedo had been quite lenient toward the French in Mexico and had tried to apprehend only those who were suspected or accused of encouraging the overthrow of the Spanish power. When Branciforte became viceroy, he sent a report to the home government in which he said that he admired the tolerance of his predecessor for permitting the residence of the French in Mexico, and then he proceeded to condemn him for the very tolerance which had aroused his admiration.[44] The war which Spain was then conducting against the French and their revolutionary ideas made it seem reasonable and necessary that the viceroy should carry on an investigation about these "fanatical and seductive men" whom he found living freely in

[40] Branciforte to Revilla Gigedo, Mexico, Sept. 24, 1794; and report of the trial of Frenchmen by Caamaño, Mexico, Sept. 28, 1794, A. G. I., Estado, Mexico, legajo 3.
[41] Report of George Cap, Oct. 4, 1796, *ibid.*, legajo 5.
[42] Nava to Branciforte, Chihuahua, Aug. 6, 1795, *ibid.*, legajo 18.
[43] Caamaño's report, Sept. 28, 1794, *ibid.*, legajo 3.
[44] Branciforte to Alcudia, Mexico, Oct. 3, 1794, *ibid.*

Mexico, "diametrically opposed to the wise and just" provisions of the Spanish government.[45] Branciforte read reports about the French and he heard rumors about their assemblies and disputes, but decided to postpone action until he found definite evidence of their activities.

The occasion came when on the morning of August 24, 1794, a seditious paper was found posted in one of the most conspicuous of public places.[46] In the investigation that followed the author escaped detection, but a number of Frenchmen were arrested for holding views which favored the activities of the revolutionary Assembly of France. On September 10 the viceroy sent a circular order to the intendants of Mexico, asking them to give him an exact account of all the foreigners residing in their respective districts. The conduct of each one was to be observed secretly, and suspicious characters were to be arrested.[47] Some time elapsed before they could comply with this order, but enough suspects were soon found in Mexico to provide an interesting trial. A number of Frenchmen had been arrested at the inn of Juan Aroche, where they had drunk to the health of Spain's enemy, France, and where they had played a prohibited game of cards, merely to amuse themselves by trying their luck, they said.

It was found that they were accustomed to meet in this inn and discuss the views and activities of the French Assembly. They received letters from France, from the French islands of the West Indies, and from Philadelphia, and were thus kept fairly well informed. Juan Abadi had been especially active in bringing reports from France to add zest to their conversations. In addition to letters they obtained other revolutionary material, such as a speech by Lafayette brought by Pedro Lafarga. Most dangerous, perhaps, was the presence of "La Marseillaise" with its stirring, revolutionary strains and its ap-

[45] *Ibid.*
[46] *Ibid.*
[47] Branciforte to Alcudia, Mexico, Dec. 3, 1794, *ibid.*, legajo 3.

peal "To arms!" Later the viceroy reported the introduction of a manuscript with this title: *Discurso pronunciado por Boissi d'Anglas, miembro de la Junta de Salud Pública en la Convención de 30 de Enero de 1795*.[48] The startling information revealed by this investigation showed the need for greater vigilance.

A large number of the suspects were found to be partisans of the French Assembly. Some of the more bold, such as Juan Malvert, had declared in public that "man was free and equal," that the king was different from others only in wearing a crown, that the fundamental tenets of the Assembly ought to be followed by everyone, and, finally, that it was well that the sovereigns were guillotined. In justification of this he said that the Queen had been a prostitute who had destroyed the kingdom, and that the king had been a tyrant. Similar statements had been made by Estevan Morel, a doctor, who added that the king had been a drunkard.[49] These opinions, revolting to the Spanish rulers, were shared by a number of Malvert's associates.[50] Their views on religion were also investigated and found deficient. Again Malvert was discovered to be the most depraved of a depraved lot. He was also accused of not showing the proper respect and adoration when in the presence of the divine sacrament. He admitted that he had little or no religion except that of honesty and good relations with his fellowmen, a religion he had acquired from nature.

These radical views were not merely the idle philosophies of a few Frenchmen: they were being used for the overthrow of the *ancien régime* in New Spain. Revolutionary doctrines were preparing the way for the anticipated supremacy of French arms. Abadi had received a letter, according to a wit-

[48] Branciforte to the Intendant of Puebla, Mexico, Sept. 16, 1795, *ibid.*, legajo 4.
[49] Report of the trial by Valenzuela and Luzero, Aug. 9, 1795, *ibid.*
[50] Nicolás Bardel, Juan Durrua, Manuel Guicar, Carlos del Mazo, Vicente Luye, Luis Lardo, Pedro Bonet, Juan Lausel, Pedro Lafarga, the surgeon Durrey, and Juan Savera. Two others who were not French were included, José Ximenes and Manuel Endrina (report by Caamaño, Mexico, Sept. 28, 1794, *ibid.*, legajo 3).

ness, informing him of the success of the French armies, of cities already captured, and that Cadiz and other Spanish cities would soon be taken in order to convert all to the French system. He had informed a woman that within a short time she would have French goods, and these, very cheaply. There were other evidences that France was expected to extend its control over Mexico, but, according to rumor, France was to become the mistress of the world and give liberty to all. A ship was expected to arrive in Mexico to bring "equality" to the people—a cargo that could easily stimulate the most extravagant ideas. Further investigation showed that preparations were being made to help the world movement of the French. Pedro Bonet was accused of making armor for this purpose, although he declared that it was for the protection of travelers. The surgeon, Durrey, was thought to be receiving money from his countrymen to win the support of the army by filling vacancies with his own recruits. A similar charge was made against Juan Fournier.[51] In the trial of Guerrero it was testified that Durrey was active in spreading the doctrines of the French Assembly among the common people, making them hate kings in general and their own king in particular. His efforts were directed towards securing help for the French when they should come to New Spain, as he assured the people they would.[52]

Francisco Roxas y Rocha was arrested for having written a paper in favor of the French government. He was also supposed to have been connected with the posting of the pasquinades on the street corners on August 24. Both charges were denied, and it seems that his conversations on the good points of the French government were due largely to loquacity and not to a desire to start an insurrection against the government. As one minister said, he did not think he had any ill

[51] The most complete report on the Frenchmen is by Caamaño, Mexico, Sept. 28, 1794; supplemented by Valenzuela to Branciforte, Mexico, Oct. 1, 1794, *ibid.*

[52] Valenzuela to Branciforte, Mexico, Oct. 1, 1794, *ibid.*

intent or malice, but only "a proclivity for talking on all subjects without reflection nor thought." Even talking too freely on the topics of the day could not be tolerated, for it might put dangerous ideas into the heads of more active persons. He was supposed to have had conversations with the unfortunate Guerrero, and might therefore be held partly responsible for the latter's fiasco. After he had been in prison for some time the court finally decided to free Roxas, ordering him to join his wife in Spain and never return to the Indies.[53]

Juan Guerrero, a disgruntled Spaniard who had served as treasurer of a Manila ship, being down on his luck and lacking funds, decided to head a revolt in Mexico. The insurrection should start at Vera Cruz, the key to the country. Guerrero said that he had been influenced by French ideas and his chief accomplices were found to be French.[54] His undigested plot was ridiculed as being the work of one half mad. Considering his lack of means and the small number of his associates, one can scarcely believe that he could have been serious; and yet there is a possibility that the French had convinced him that their nation was about to bring freedom and that it would be to his advantage to be among the leaders to reap the greater reward. Juan Vara, who had been imprisoned for listening to Guerrero, belittled the project, saying that the only support came from a barber without means and without friends.[55] Nevertheless, the trial led to the arrest of several persons, a few of whom were French. These may or may not have been associated with Guerrero in his plot, but in the report sent by Valenzuela it was stated that Durrey, Mexanes, and Fournier had spoken of the tyranny of kings, and of the advantages of the assembly as being in conformity with the "natural liberty

---

[53] Report of the Archbishop of Mexico, Sept. 23, 1794, *ibid.*, legajo 20. Cf. Fisher, *The Background for Mexican Independence*, pp. 354-356.

[54] The viceroy, at least, held the French largely responsible. Branciforte to Alcudia, Mexico, Oct. 3, 1794; also Luzero's report of the trial, Dec. 2, 1794, A. G. I., Estado, Mexico, legajo 3.

[55] Report of Vara's petition for liberty, July 27, 1796, *ibid.*, legajo 20.

of man and the equality of all." Such were the doctrines which had destroyed the Bourbon government of France and now threatened the government of New Spain.

The church was especially disturbed over the "unbridled fanaticism of the impious French Jacobins," who were threatening to destroy religion and all its good and noble followers. They were undermining obedience and good order by their "chimerical and detestable principles of equality and liberty," and persuading the lower classes that they themselves had the authority and power to set up a government according to their own desires. The archbishop said he saw with the greatest bitterness in his heart that the hated French had succeeded with their false principles "in seducing and infatuating, not only their own countrymen, but also many of ours."[56]

That their good God should allow these events in their Catholic country could be explained only as a punishment for their sins. The clergy was urged, by living more exemplary lives and by praying regularly for themselves and their people, to prevent the spread of pernicious ideas and the domination of the irreligious maxims of the French. In their masses of the *Oracion in tempora Belli* they were to include the appeal *contra persecutores Ecclesia.* Any evidence of French influence discovered in their confessionals or conversations should be reported with the greatest secrecy and promptness to the archbishop. The people were to be taught the "ancient and true" principles of obedience and fidelity "to the king and to all their superiors."[57]

The Inquisition played its part in the extermination of the French evil. Several of the defendants who had already been tried in the colonial courts were confronted by additional charges from the Holy Office of the Inquisition. The most prominent of these were Juan Lausel, the unfortunate cook of

[56] Report of the archbishop of Mexico, Sept., 1794, *ibid.*
[57] *Ibid.*

Revilla Gigedo, and Dr. Estevan Morel. In addition to being guilty of having favored the execution of the king of France, Lausel was found to be a member of the freemasons, as was also Morel, and it was reported that there were several others in the city. Morel had exalted the arms of France and had declared that the maxims of the Assembly would soon be transplanted to Mexico, and he had spread other views, repugnant to both church and monarchy. Furthermore, he carried on a correspondence with relatives in France who were also supporters of the Revolution.[58] The archbishop of Mexico lauded the zeal and efficiency of the Inquisition for having arrested many Frenchmen, and a few Europeans and creoles who were, "perhaps, infatuated by them."[59]

He also surveyed their "iniquitous projects" to destroy religion and to "establish in this country anarchy and the impious government of the French convention." They had planned, he thought, to gain control of the army, to liberate the prisoners, take possession of the treasury, depose the viceroy and the archbishop, and—a dreadful thought—"perhaps kill them." Revolution would be followed by the establishment of republican government. He was now thankful, however, that all had been saved by the timely intervention of God. Nevertheless, he feared that it would be difficult to restore the order and tranquility which had been disturbed by these "emissaries of Satan and others who had . . . spread and sown the most perverse doctrines against the faith, the customs, and the dutiful obedience to H. M. and other superiors." Precautious, he instructed the ecclesiastics, secular and regular, to be on the alert against the activities of the French and their accomplices. He took pride in stating that "up to the present" he did not know of any priest taking part in the foreign intrigues.[60]

[58] Report of the trial by Valenzuela and Luzero, Aug. 9, 1795, *ibid.*, legajo 4.
[59] Mexico, Oct. 4, 1794, *ibid.*, legajo 22.
[60] *Ibid.*

It was evident from the discoveries made by Branciforte and his associates that there were reasons to fear the French and that drastic measures were necessary to cleanse the country of their dangerous doctrines. The viceroy was pleased with his results so far, but was spurred on to greater activities in order to leave no trace of their seditious work. He would secure by every means possible "the public tranquility of these rich and precious dominions where flourish the most tender and true sentiments of religion, love, and loyalty to the King," and to fulfill this high-sounding purpose he instructed the officials of the provinces to apprehend every Frenchman within their jurisdictions.[61]

In order to carry out this sweeping plan he sent detailed instructions to the provincial authorities. If a Frenchman were suspected he was to be arrested and put into prison, deprived of all communication, and his property was to be seized to pay the expenses of his trial and confinement. The same was to be done with other Frenchmen of whom there was no other suspicion than "that of being individuals of that revolutionary nation," although their imprisonment was not to be as harsh. There were a few to be excepted from this general arrest, such as those who had married Spaniards, or the few who had letters of naturalization, and men owning large estates, extensive businesses, or holding important offices. These, providing they had the public recommendation of irreprehensible conduct, were not to be apprehended, nor their property seized; but they were to be notified that they were to be confined in their haciendas or business places, giving security for their person or property, and a complete inventory was to be made of their possessions.[62] Spaniards who held French views during these turbulent times were also to be seized. To insure success the

---

[61] Aguilar, "Sobre expulsión de Franceses de Nueva España, 1795 y 96," *ibid.*, legajo 5.

[62] Branciforte to the intendants of Vera Cruz, etc., Mexico, Dec. 3, 1794, *ibid.*, legajo 3.

authorities were warned to proceed with the greatest secrecy; and, as had been done with the Jesuits before, the suspects were all to be apprehended on the morning of the same day. The date was set for January 1, 1795,[63] but the viceroy reported in his letter of January 15 that on that day had taken place the arrest of the French residents of Mexico.[64]

The viceroy had already written to Alcudia to explain and to justify his action.[65] He did not have complete information on all the foreigners in Mexico, he said, but he thought he had enough on the French, who were the suspected ones, to proceed with a general arrest. Although no serious events had taken place yet, the danger from these restless persons was so great that they could no longer be tolerated in liberty. They were to be kept in the provincial prisons for greater economy and security; and they should be treated "with the humanity becoming to the noble and religious character of the Spanish nation," although the members of the nation which had overturned the system of the world with their "fanaticism and their execrable crimes" did not deserve it.[66]

Some difficulty was encountered in the Provincias Internas, owing to the large number of Frenchmen who had come there from Louisiana.[67] Pedro de Nava, the governor, suggested that special provisions ought to be made for several of these. By August, 1795, he had made a fairly long list of Frenchmen who were found in the five provinces of Nueva Vizcaya, Sonora, Coahuila, Texas, and New Mexico. This belated report included a classified description of each one with such items as: where they came from, when, their ages, and their occupations. A few had been liberated, especially those who came

[63] *Ibid.*
[64] Aguilar, "Sobre expulsión de Franceses de Nueva España, 1795 y 96," *ibid.,* legajo 5.
[65] Mexico, Dec. 3, 1794, *ibid.,* legajo 3.
[66] *Ibid.*
[67] Nava to Alcudia, Chihuahua, Feb. 5, 1795, *ibid.,* legajo 18.

with De Mézières.⁶⁸ Later he acknowledged the receipt of the royal order of May 22, in which he was instructed to prevent the introduction of "the detestable and pernicious maxims of an ill-directed liberty," and said that he had renewed his orders for vigilance.⁶⁹ The viceroy, apparently quite satisfied with the work of the frontier officials, sent a favorable report to the Duke of Alcudia on August 31.⁷⁰

The royal order of May 22, which the viceroy acknowledged on August 30, was largely a reiteration of Branciforte's former instructions for the apprehension of the French. Seditious persons were to be punished and those who were dangerous were to be sent to Spain, but those who were deserving of indulgence were to be tolerated and made to live in accordance with the laws of the Indies.⁷¹ Finding his policy approved by the home government and his orders carried out in Mexico, the viceroy continued the persecution which had begun so well. By the end of October he had twenty-one French prisoners ready for deportation.⁷² This was, however, only a part of the undesirables, for the investigations lagged and there were many yet who awaited the courts decision. One of these, Juan Fournier, died, but this interruption did not end his trial.⁷³ By December the viceroy reported that the investigations were nearly completed and that he was ready to enforce the punishments.⁷⁴ During the early part of the year 1796 the Frenchmen from the provinces were being gathered at Vera Cruz in preparation for deportation. On May 14 the governor of Vera Cruz informed Branciforte that two vessels, with twenty-one Frenchmen on the first and twenty on the second, had sailed for Cadiz.⁷⁵

⁶⁸ Report of Aug. 6, 1795, *ibid.* Athanase de Mézières, although French, had been retained by Governor O'Reilly in the Spanish service with the title of lieutenant-governor at Natchitoches, Bolton (ed.), *Athanase de Mézières*, I, 79.
⁶⁹ Nava to Alcudia, Chihuahua, Oct. 6, 1795, A. G. I., Estado, Mexico, legajo 18.
⁷⁰ *Ibid.*, legajo 4.
⁷¹ Branciforte to Alcudia, Mexico, Aug. 30, 1795, *ibid.*
⁷² Branciforte to Alcudia, Oct. 23, 1795, *ibid.*
⁷³ Branciforte to Alcudia, Sept. 26, 1795, *ibid.*
⁷⁴ Branciforte to Alcudia, Dec. 2, 1795, *ibid.*
⁷⁵ Branciforte to Principe de la Paz (Alcudia), Mexico, May 27, 1796, *ibid.*

The viceroy's efforts to rid Mexico of the French menace had met with general approval and a fair measure of success. He has been criticized for his severe methods, but the French Revolution had made Frenchmen undesirable associates, and the war which broke out between France and Spain early in 1793 made it practically a measure of self-defense to change from an attitude of toleration to one of persecution. Branciforte had to enforce the old orders against foreigners to keep out revolutionary ideas which came mostly from the French; and, secondly, he had to protect Mexico from the people of an enemy nation. The result of his investigations seem to warrant his zeal. However, before the work had been completed and the French expelled, the European war was ended by the Treaty of Basle in July, 1795. This removed only the second and perhaps the least important of the two dangers.

In the following year Spain, now allied with France, found it necessary to relax its severity against its neighbor's people. Adet, the French minister in Philadelphia, protested to Jaudenes, the Spanish minister, against the rigorous treatment of his countrymen in Mexico. He thought the Mexican clergy had contributed greatly to their distress. The victims of the persecution had written to Adet, declaring that their condition had not improved after the signing of the treaty of peace. Contrary to the agreement made with France in articles ten and eleven, they had not been given their liberty and property. Josef Yngacio de Viar, another Spanish representative in the United States, declared that the reports from the French were not in keeping with the humanity and kindness of the treatment by the Spanish government; nevertheless, he did send Adet's letter to the viceroy who forwarded it to Godoy.[76]

The reaction then set in, and the Spanish government began to comply with the French petitions for liberty and the restitu-

---

[76] Adet to Jaudenes, Philadelphia, 13 floreal An. 4ᵉ (copy signed by Viar); Viar to Adet, Philadelphia, May 7, 1796; Branciforte to Principe de la Paz, Mexico, Sept. 26, 1796, *ibid.*, legajo 6.

tion of their property. Every case seemed to be handled individually, and governmental machinery moved slowly. George Cap, who had lived in Mexico for twelve years and had said that his only crime was that of being a foreigner, requested his freedom in October, 1796,[77] and received it in April, 1798.[78] During the latter year, and for several years following, the viceroy's reports dealt with the royal orders for the release of Frenchmen.[79] Not all were granted their freedom, however. Durrey, one of the most prominent of the defendants, made repeated efforts to get permission to return to Mexico for a year to see his family and to make arrangements for his property. He was aided by the French ambassador who, between 1800 and 1805, made frequent petitions in his behalf, but without success.[80] The Spanish government, having just rid Mexico of the most bold and dangerous propagandists, had no intention of turning them loose. Others who, like George Cap, were merely guilty of being foreigners were granted their liberty and given back their property.

The Treaty of Basle in 1795 and the alliance with France in 1796 decreased the danger of French efforts to overthrow the old system in Mexico. Nevertheless, the French Revolution had already left its stamp on Mexico and would, no doubt, continue to exert its influence. Moreover, as the French menace seemed to decrease, the real danger of revolutionary projects was transferred to Spain's new enemy, England.

[77] *Ibid.*, legajo 5.
[78] Report of Branciforte, April 29, 1798, *ibid.*, legajo 8.
[79] Letters numbered 4-8, 28, 53, and 621-626 for the year 1798, *ibid.* Bancroft criticizes Zamacois for supposing that property was restored to the French after liberation, but it would seem from the viceroy's reports that this was frequently done. Cf. Bancroft, *History of Mexico*, III, 487; and Zamacois, *Historia de Méjico*, V, 705.
[80] Correspondence on Durrey, A. G. I., Estado, Mexico, legajo 23.

CHAPTER IX
REVIVAL OF BRITISH INTEREST

> "South America must soon pass through a revolution: we have an immense interest in the Event, as well as in the manner in which it shall be effected."—RUFUS KING.
>
> "Here is enough to furnish a volume of reflections. Nay, if you were to pursue all the investigations and speculations that these papers suggest, you might write as many folios as Priestly or Voltaire ever produced."—JOHN ADAMS.

THE STRICT laws of Spain had failed to keep bold and inquisitive neighbors from penetrating the barrier and securing wealth and information. Foreign ships continually pestered the colonial officials of Mexico, and report after report to the metropolis complained of the visits of these intruders. British and Americans were the most persistent violaters of the exclusion act. In 1795 Branciforte complained that the British were gaining knowledge of the coasts of Mexico, learning with what ease they might take Vera Cruz, because of its lack of proper defense. They, especially George Vancouver, who was looking after the British interests on the west coast, were also visiting San Diego, Monterey, and San Francisco. The viceroy feared that the British already knew that only a small force would be necessary to take California. He would do all he could to save the Philippines and California from the British and to prevent their trade with the coast and with the "rich and undefended province of Sonora." It would be most difficult, he surmised, to dislodge the English if they occupied California, especially if they fortified themselves and brought a fleet to the "most ample, admirable, and protected port of S^n. Francisco."[1] Such were the possibilities as seen by the viceroy of Mexico, and such were the prospects if the British were

---
[1] Branciforte to Duke of Alcudia, Mexico, July 3, 1795, A. G. I., Estado, Mexico, legajo 4.

to adopt the plans of Vansittart when war was declared the following year. Taken by themselves, such plans and prophesies might seem unreasonable; but when the two opposing sides share the same views they become quite significant.

As Adet had suspected, England was no sooner at war with Spain than she was approached by some of the western intriguers. As early as October, 1795, the British were making preparations for a possible attack on Louisiana in case of war,[2] and when war broke out a year later, they must have been willing to consider the revolutionary schemes which had been simmering on the border ever since the operations of Genêt. Blount and Chisholm had undoubtedly inherited the revolutionary projects of their predecessors, and their scheme bore considerable resemblance to the later one of Aaron Burr. Land speculation in the West was either the real purpose or the shield of the real purpose. In fact, Blount had spoken to Burr about his "Land Scheme."[3] To others he is supposed to have said that it was "quite a different thing," and that if they were successful, he would hold a high office in the government of the conquered territory.[4] In a letter to James Carry, April 21, 1797, he spoke of "the business Captain Chisholm mentioned to the British minister last winter, at Philadelphia." His high hopes, vaguely expressed, were as follows:

I believe, but I am not quite sure, that the plan then talked of will be attempted this fall, and, if it is attempted, it will be in a much larger way than talked of; and if the Indians act their part, I have no doubt but it will succeed. A man of consequence has gone to England about the business, and if he makes arrangements as he expects, I shall myself have a hand in the business, and probably shall be at the head of the business on the part of the British.[5]

[2] "Documents on the Blount Conspiracy," *The American Historical Review*, X, 575-76.
[3] Posey, "The Blount Conspiracy," *Birmingham-Southern College Bulletin*, XXI, 16; *Annals of Congress, Fifth Congress, 1797-99*, II, 2353.
[4] *Annals of Congress, Fifth Congress, 1797-99*, II, 2396-97.
[5] *American State Papers: Foreign Relations*, II, 76-77.

Whatever the "business" was, it made considerable stir in the world.

General Collot, Adet's agent on the Mississippi border, learned of Chisholm's project, in which both Senator Blount and General Clark were involved, and notified the Spanish minister, Yrujo.[6] The minister in turn warned the viceroy of Mexico, informing him that ten thousand troops were being sent from Canada by way of the Mississippi and that these were to be reënforced by British frigates, some of which were reported to be getting provisions in Baltimore.[7] To add to the disturbance, it was also reported from Nacogdoches that the United States had gone to war with Spain and that her troops were on their way to attack the border.[8] These reports must be based on what the Spaniards feared and not on the actual conditions.

The British had at first shown a natural interest. Robert Liston, the minister to the United States, reported that Chisholm's associates believed that the possession of the border provinces "might ultimately contribute to the Independence of South America,[9] if that were considered as a measure essential to the interests of Great Britain."[10] He had also been induced to pay for Chisholm's passage to London, "with much hesitation and reluctance," according to Pickering.[11] However, when Robert Liston was informed that the scheme was known, he disavowed all responsibility for the British government. He told Pickering that the government had rejected the proposition because it would violate the neutrality

---

[6] March 1, 1797, *The American Historical Review*, X, 582.

[7] *"Noticias de Filadelfia"* with letter of Pedro de Nava to Prince of the Peace, Chihuahua, Aug. 1, 1797, A. G. I., Estado, Mexico, legajo 18.

[8] J. M. Guadiana to de Nava, July 17, 1797, *ibid*. The Americans were probably merely taking possession of Natchez, as hinted, *ibid*.

[9] Meaning, very likely, Spanish America.

[10] "Documents on the Blount Conspiracy," *The American Historical Review*, X, 582.

[11] Timothy Pickering to Rufus King, Aug. 5, 1797, Rufus King MSS., No. 116, Huntington Library.

of the United States and "because the means suggested were inadequate to the object."[12] The latter reason suggests that the object must have been of considerable magnitude.

The extent of the scheme for conquest or revolution may remain uncertain since it did not materialize; and the case of impeachment against Senator Blount was dismissed as being out of the court's jurisdiction, adding to the mystery. The broad and open accusations of Yrujo were dismissed with the following retort: "His statements are as erroneous and his reasoning as feeble, as his stile and expressions are rude and unbecoming a diplomatic character."[13] There was, however, some basis for Yrujo's fear of a meditated attack on the Spanish possessions, and the danger did not end with Blount. Blount's conspiracy was not an isolated event but a link in a long chain of border intrigues and international designs against Spanish America.

The discovery of the Blount conspiracy did not end the schemes for liberating the Spanish colonies. Miranda had fared badly in France. A less energetic man would have lost faith in liberty after witnessing the crimes committed in her name, but neither imprisonment nor the atrocities of the Terror could quench his ardor for the great project. The excesses of the French Revolution made him fear rather than seek French aid. But now England was again in a position where she might to her advantage adopt his plans.

France and Spain, having signed the offensive and defensive alliance of 1796, began "the series of compromises which brought Spain to the tremendous catastrophe of 1808."[14] England could foresee a renewal of the war. Nicolas Vansittart did not wait for the formal declaration of war to draw up a plan for sending a British expedition against the Span-

[12] *Ibid.*
[13] *Ibid.*
[14] Jerónimo Becker, *Relaciones Exteriores de España durante el Siglo XIX* (2 vols., Madrid, 1924), I, 8.

ish colonies. He thought that the western coast would be the most suitable point for attack and suggested the use of troops from India, which would "render the success of the enterprise almost infallible." The south Pacific coast was to be attacked first, and then Mexico could be conquered from Acapulco.[15]

The king of Spain was aware of the British interests in his dominions across the sea; and, while Miranda was still in France, he issued an order to the colonial officials to warn them against an English expedition to Mexico, headed by Miranda, who was in England, he thought, or perhaps already departed for New Spain.[16] This order reached the border provinces at the same time as the rumors and reports of the British attack from Canada, making it doubly necessary to observe the watchfulness enjoined by the king. A description of a suspected person, spoken of as Miranda in some of the dispatches, was also sent to the various officials in order that they might identify him.[17] The local functionaries responded with zeal, and at Tampico a certain Manuel Montecino, answering to the description of Miranda, was suspected of being the revolutionist.[18] Governor Panes at Vera Cruz had complained in February about English corsairs sinking ships on the coast of Mexico.[19] By June, however, he was ready to defend the coast against foreigners and, if possible, to apprehend Miranda.

Pedro de Nava busied himself with plans for protecting the Provincias Internas. In a survey he suggested that Sonora might be attacked by land and sea forces from India, and California could also be invaded. His views coincided with the fears of the viceroy and the plan of Vansittart. De Nava thought there would be little object for the English to invade

[15] Robertson, *Miranda*, 311; see also his *Life of Miranda*, I, chap. viii.
[16] Prince of the Peace to Branciforte, San Lorenzo, Dec. 24, 1796, A. G. I., Estado, Mexico, legajo 18.
[17] Copy of the description, Chihuahua, Aug. 1, 1797, by Manuel Marino, *ibid*.
[18] Robertson, *Miranda*, p. 312.
[19] To Prince of the Peace, Vera Cruz, Feb. 9, 1797, *ibid.*, legajo 16.

Coahuila or Texas, but that Louisiana would be a more likely objective. He was, however, ready to send aid to any section in need of it.[20]

Meanwhile other plans were being suggested to and considered by the English. One of these, dated March 18, 1797, was by a person who characterized himself as being "a very young man, of little consequence in the country, only having just left the University." He advocated the separation of Mexico from Peru by a settlement in the lake region of Nicaragua, giving England an advantageous position during the war. Nor were the English averse to such proposals, and the government began to make preparations for the emancipation of Spanish America.[21]

Governor Picton of Trinidad was given a proclamation by Lord Melville, then secretary of state, to be circulated on the coast of Spanish America. Its purpose was to encourage the inhabitants of the continent to resist the oppressive authority of the Spanish government with the assurance

> that measures have been taken to support them with arms and ammunition, merely to enable them to maintain their commercial independence; without any desire on the part of the king of England, to acquire any right of sovereignty over them, or to interfere with their civil, political, or religious rights, unless they themselves should in any degree solicit his protection.[22]

The value of a policy of liberation was being recognized and supported; and conquest, characterized by Governor Picton as "Chimerical and Ruinous," was being abandoned.

With all this going on, Miranda might feel encouraged since the revolutionary ideas were already prevalent. He was no sooner set free in France than he renewed his schemes. Nor was he alone, for there were Spanish Americans with

---

[20] To Prince of the Peace, Chihuahua, Aug. 1, 1797, *ibid.*, legajo 18.
[21] Robertson, *Miranda*, p. 313.
[22] *The American Register*, V (Part I, 1809), p. 390 n.; and Walton, *An Exposé of the Dissentions of Spanish America*, Appendix, Document A.

similar opinions working in Spain, France, and London. Among the revolutionary agents from Spanish America, who were in London in 1797, were Pedro José Caro and Antonio Nariño.[23] Caro said he was from Cuba, but owned property in Mexico. For fifteen years he had traveled through Spanish America and Europe in an effort to promote the independence of the Spanish colonies.[24] He evidently worked in conjunction with Miranda, who gave him letters of introduction to influential men in England and informed them that he had papers *"de haute Importance."*[25] The letters contained the usual plans with a description of the colonies which were "on the Eve of a general Insurrection." He added that there were fourteen hundred persons, "of some Fortune and Character," throughout Spanish America who were occupied in the same manner as he. We may allow for some exaggeration, but still there is an indication of an elaborate and organized effort to liberate the Spanish colonies. Caro considered Santa Fé de Bogotá as the most suitable starting point from which the revolt could extend into the rest of South America and into Mexico by way of Central America.[26] Caro was probably preparing England for the return of Miranda, "whose reputation," he said, "was worth an army."

A revolutionary junta was at the same time working under the very nose of the Spanish king at Madrid. At least, such are the indications of a paper supposedly drawn up by agents from this junta.[27] Two of the agents, Joseph del Pozo y

[23] Nariño was the liberal from Bogotá who had translated and published Paine's *Rights of Man*, Carlos Navarro y Lamarca, *Compendio de la historia general de América* (2 vols., Buenos Aires, 1910-1913), II, 548.

[24] Caro and Nariño had possibly appealed to France for aid before coming to England, Robertson, *Miranda*, p. 306; see also Robertson, *Life of Miranda*, I, 162-163.

[25] Letters to Joseph Smith, Pitt's secretary, and to John Turnbull.

[26] Robertson, *Miranda*, p. 317, considered Caro's representation as being highly colored.

[27] This paper is printed in full by C. F. Adams (ed.), *Works of John Adams* (10 vols., Boston, 1852-1865), I, 679-684.

Sucre and Manuel Joseph de Salas,[28] who had met with the deputies from Spanish America in Madrid, October 8, 1797, had gone to Paris to negotiate with Miranda and one Pablo de Olavide. John Adams said he knew Olavide, and seems to have had some very interesting meetings with him in Paris. He was a remarkable man, but had aroused the suspicion of the Inquisition and had been obliged to flee to France for safety.[29]

On December 22 these agents met with Miranda in Paris[30] to renew, if possible, the plans of 1790. Since the Hispanic American colonies had "unanimously resolved to proclaim their independence" they would invite Great Britain to assist in this "honorable enterprise." England was to furnish both a naval force and a land force, and the United States should furnish funds to defray at least a part of the expenses.[31] This was the only hope for liberty, "so audaciously outraged by the detestable maxims of the French Republic," and it was the only means of balancing the "destructive and devastating power of France."

England was to be granted special trade advantages, and the United States rewarded by the acquisition of the Floridas and Louisiana. Both countries were to have favorable rights of navigation in the canals of the Isthmus and of Nicaragua which were to be opened to commerce. The whole project was to be under the direction of Miranda, who should have full power to negotiate with England; and if he were unable to go

---

[28] Little is known about these two agents except John Adams's statement that they were Jesuits, *ibid.*, X, 142.

[29] A description of Olavide is given by John Adams in a letter to James Floyd, March 26, 1815, *ibid.*, X, 139-143; compare also Joseph Addison, *Charles the Third of Spain*, p. 122.

[30] Olavide had not answered their invitation for some reason or other. John Adams said, "he had too much sense to have any connection with them," *Works of John Adams*, X, 142.

[31] The British force should not exceed 27 vessels of the line, 8,000 infantry, and 2,000 cavalry. There was also a suggestion that the United States furnish 7,000 infantry and 2,000 cavalry.

to England, his place could be taken by Olavide. The two agents planned to return to Madrid, thence to America where their presence would be necessary to make the uprisings simultaneous.

John Adams might well ask where was the source for all this authority and who composed the junta.[32] There seems to be no other evidence of this junta, and Robertson says, therefore, that the papers drawn up on December 22, "did not even have the appearance of legality."[33] What was back of these actions may be uncertain, but armed with these papers Miranda created considerable stir in three continents. John Adams said of the plans:

> Here is enough to furnish a volume of reflections. Nay, if you were to pursue all the investigations and speculations that these papers suggest, you might write as many folios as Priestley or Voltaire ever produced.[34]

In less than a month after the meeting at Paris, Miranda was in England, carrying out the instructions with a master hand. The favorable opportunity he had been waiting for had now come, and on January 16, 1798, he presented Pitt with the new plans.[35] He came at the opportune time, since the United States was having her own troubles with France—troubles which, if properly nurtured, might lead to war between the two and joint action on the part of England and America. Adet had already warned France what might happen if there was a rupture between her and the United States. Fauchet, too, had declared that an Anglo-American alliance would not only endanger the French colonies, but the Spanish possessions as well.[36] This would be a splendid opportunity for the revolu-

[32] Adams (ed.), *Works of John Adams*, X, 142.
[33] Robertson, *Miranda*, p. 320.
[34] Adams (ed.), *Works of John Adams*, X, 141.
[35] Miranda to Pitt, Jan. 16, 1798, printed in Villanueva, *Napoleón y la Independencia*, pp. 85-87.
[36] James Alton James, "Louisiana in American Diplomacy, 1795-1800," *The Mississippi Valley Historical Review*, I, 47 (June, 1914).

tionists. A rupture seemed imminent and nothing could be better for the revived plans of Miranda. His next step was to win the favor of Rufus King, United States minister to England. He called on King on January 30 and suggested a joint operation of England and the United States against France, and then it would be easy to liberate Spanish America.[37] At a suitable time he would send a confidential agent to Philadelphia. Two days later King spoke to Lord Grenville about Miranda's project. Grenville intimated that he did not like Miranda nor his scheme, and he feared the influence of the French Revolution, but he did not think that the independence of the Spanish colonies could be long delayed.[38] On February 7 King wrote to Pickering, the secretary of state, about Miranda's suggestion.[39] On the following day Miranda showed King a letter he had written to Hamilton,[40] and again they took up the revolutionary topic. Miranda's idea was to unite Mexico and Peru under one government which was to be "a monarchy with a House of Lords and Commons."[41] Later King was shown the plans which had been drawn up in Paris; and on being asked if he approved, he merely said he was glad to know what was going on concerning Spanish America but would not commit his government.[42]

Lord Grenville informed King that if Spain were able to preserve her independence and prevent a revolution, England would not interfere. But if Spain fell under the control of France, England would begin negotiating with the United States to execute the plan. That France might gain complete possession of the Spanish peninsula or cause a revolution there was becoming a current belief. William Smith wrote to Rufus King from Lisbon, June 20, 1798, that if Spain and Portugal

---

[37] Charles R. King (ed.), *Life and Correspondence of Rufus King* (6 vols., New York, 1894-1900), III, 556-557.
[38] *Ibid.*, III, 558.   [39] *Ibid.*, II, 278-281.
[40] He had also written to Hamilton from Paris but had received no reply, *ibid.*, III, 558.
[41] *Ibid.*, III, 559.   [42] Feb. 12, 1798, *ibid.*, III, 559-560.

were united under a strong government they would be a check to France. But he added that "perhaps they would fritter away into several small republics, stripped of their navies, colonies, and commerce like Holland and like her be so many satellites of the great monster."[43] John Q. Adams intimated that France might not be successful. "The revolution destined for Spain and Portugal," he said, "will perhaps meet with more difficulties and obstacles than might be expected. At least it will take a considerable time to effect, if the spirit of opposition to it be such as I am given to understand."[44] The future of the Spanish seemed to depend upon the unsettled conditions of Europe.

King continued to collect information on Spanish America and found "certain Jesuits . . . who with a view of its independence are and for several years have been in the service and pay of England."[45] It is quite likely that Juan Pablo Vizcardo y Guzmán gave his *"Lettre aux Espagnols"* to King.[46] The latter also informed the secretary of state of Grenville's report on the British policy. He seemed to think the revolution would take place, for he said:

The revolution of Spain is decreed; the attempt will be made, and the success is scarcely doubtful. The President may therefore expect the overture of England, and will, I am persuaded, act upon it, under the influence of that wise and comprehensive policy, which, looking forward to the Destinies of the New World, shall in the beginning by great and generous Deeds lay deep and firm the foundations of lasting accord between its rising Empires.[47]

King showed clearly that he was sympathetic, but informed Lord Grenville that he merely wanted to gain the president's

---

[43] Rufus King MSS., No. 217, Huntington Library.
[44] Letter to Rufus King, Berlin, April 9, 1798, *ibid.*, No. 7.
[45] King to secretary of state, Feb. 26, 1798, *ibid.*, II, 283-284.
[46] See *The Edinburgh Review*, XIII, 277 (Jan., 1809).
[47] King (ed.), *Works of Rufus King*, II, 283-284.

exact knowledge on this subject.[48] England had already made an offer to Spain to save her colonies, according to Grenville, but he did not think she would accept.[49] It seemed probable, therefore, that England would continue her plans.

In the following month, March, Miranda wrote a letter to President Adams in which he spoke of the danger of a war with France and of Pitt's willingness to coöperate with the United States in making the New World independent. He feared the influence of "the fatal system of republican France."[50] His letter and plans were to be taken to the United States by Pedro José Caro, the revolutionary agent who had preceded Miranda to London.[51] King was quite convinced by this time that the project would be carried out. He informed Pickering, Marshall, and Gerry, the American commissioners in Paris, that if England did not do it, France would, and then she would "introduce their detestable principles, divide it into small Republics, put bad men at their head, and by these means facilitate her meditated enterprise against us." With the French system established in Spanish America "we shall be in perpetual risque."[52]

The conditions justified the views of the American minister. France and Spain had an offensive and defensive alliance; England was at war with both; the treaty of the United States with Spain had not been fulfilled; and France, triumphant in Europe, treated the American commissioners in such a manner that Adams said peace was no longer possible. Under these conditions war with France would almost make it necessary for the United States to coöperate with England in liberating Spanish America as a measure of self-defense. Robert Liston had been "instructed to say that any proposals for concert and

[48] *Ibid.*, III, 564.
[49] *Ibid.*, III, 165.
[50] Adams (ed.), *Works of John Adams*, VIII, 569-572.
[51] *Ibid.*, VIII, 570. Rufus King wrote a letter of introduction for him to the secretary of state, April 2, 1798, King (ed.), *op. cit.*, II, 653; III, 564.
[52] *Ibid.*, II, 300-301.

coöperation would be cordially received by Great Britain."[53] Miranda hoped, through the influence of King and others, to make the liberation of Spanish America the prime object of the coalition.

King wrote to Pickering again in April, telling him that "South America must soon pass through a Revolution: we have an immense interest in the Event, as well as in the manner in which it shall be effected."[54] On the day that King wrote this, Miranda wrote to Hamilton, addressing him as if he were already familiar with the project. Hamilton had ignored his earlier letters, but with the hope of a high military command and a chance to win glory at the head of an army he seems to have looked more favorably on the schemes of the "intriguing adventurer," who now informed him that the "establishment of liberty throughout the whole world is confided in us by providence." Again there was a warning note against the introduction of French principles which might even destroy the liberty of the United States.[55] Miranda feared that Knox would not support his plan, but thought that Lee would surely take part when it was a question of the well-being of his compatriots in Peru and Mexico. Other letters followed, telling how every thing was being prepared for "our grand enterprise."

The scope of the enterprise can be seen from Miranda's instructions to Caro.[56] Hamilton was the man to be trusted above all. After making some business connections with Thomas Walling of Philadelphia in the name of Turnbull of London, he should proceed to call on the minister of foreign affairs to seek at once an audience with President Adams. If he failed to see the president, he should at least get his opinion in order that it might be sent without delay to Spanish Amer-

[53] James A. James, "French Opinion as a Factor in Preventing War between France and the United States, 1795-1800," *The American Historical Review*, XXX, 49-50 (Oct., 1924).
[54] King (ed.), *Life and Correspondence of Rufus King*, II, 305.
[55] Robertson, *Miranda*, p. 327; and *The Edinburgh Review*, XIII, 291.
[56] Fuller details are given by Robertson, *Life of Miranda*, I, 174-178.

ica and to London. The instructions ended with a warning against the employment of persons of no position or wealth, since they have nothing to lose by turning against them, while the man of property and standing would be more reliable and useful. Trusted men were to be sent both to Philadelphia and Trinidad for political and military duties. Offices were not, however, to be given to foreigners who were not perfectly known or recommended by the British or American governments, "who are as interested as we are in the success of the enterprise."[57] Having completed his duties in Philadelphia, he should go to Santa Fé.

Caro had the misfortune to miss his packet, and was unable to deliver the letters in person because he had no more time to spare before going to South America. They were therefore sent to Pickering to be delivered to the president.[58] There were also letters for Knox and Hamilton, who were both expected to play a prominent part in the undertaking. When Pickering acknowledged the receipt of these letters he added some information on the military appointments which were being made.[59] The United States was putting on her armor to be ready for any contingency which might arise out of these troubled times. Miranda's hopes must have gone up as he saw the preparation of the tools which gave increasing promise of the realization of his project.

Conditions seemed to favor a joint action on the part of the United States and Great Britain. Miranda had interested eminent officials in both countries, and his views, which had at first been considered lightly by men of affairs, were being given serious consideration. His dreams were passing from the state of idle fancy to the realm of practical reality.

[57] London, April 6, 1798, A. G. I., Estado, Mexico, legajo 4; cf. Robertson, *Miranda*, p. 325.
[58] Adams (ed.), *Works of John Adams*, X, 584.
[59] Pickering to King, Aug. 29, Rufus King MSS., No. 132, Huntington Library.

CHAPTER X

FRANCO-AMERICAN WAR

"*Tout est applani, et on attend seulement le* fiat *de votre illustre Président pour partir Comme l'Eclair—En Effet, le moment parait des plus favorables, et les derniers Evénemens semblent nous laisser un Champ Vaste et tranquille pour agir à notre entiére Satisfaction. Profitons avec sagesse de la nature des Circonstances et rendons à notre Pays le plus grand Service qu'un Mortel soit Capable d'offrir a ses semblables'.*"—FRANCISCO DE MIRANDA.

"The destiny of the new world is in our hands. We have a right and it is our duty to deliberate and act, not as secondaries, but as Principals."—RUFUS KING.

THE SUCCESS or failure of Miranda's revolutionary schemes depended largely on the relationship of the United States to the European war. The condition necessary for the project was that the United States coöperate with England, but this could be done only providing the war between the United States and France materialized. As the summer progressed the conditions became more promising. The publication of the X. Y. Z. papers in April aroused the country to the proper psychological state necessary for war. John Adams, however, was too stolid to be carried into rash actions by any popular clamor, and he had no love for the English, even though he was a Federalist. Victor Du Pont, who had been sent to the United States as consul-general in May, 1798, failed to get his exequatur, but succeeded in having a private conference with Jefferson about their disturbed relations. On his return he urged Talleyrand to avoid war with the United States, for "France and Spain would be forced to sacrifice their colonies, Mexico would be exposed, and England would become doubly powerful."[1] France acted too slowly to prevent hostilities. When authority was given in July to American vessels to capture armed French vessels, the revolutionists might con-

[1] James, "French Opinion," *The American Historical Review*, XXX, 52-53.

sider that all was in readiness for the final culmination of their dreams and desires.

Talleyrand, who had been in America as an emigré (1793-1795), was now directing the foreign policy of France. He considered the United States "hopelessly attached to England,"[2] and treated her accordingly. When Godoy gave up the disputed posts east of the Mississippi before leaving office, France denounced the action because it opened the Spanish territory to the Americans, who intended to rule alone in America. The very existence of the Spanish colonial empire would be threatened.[3] If France could only secure Louisiana she would form "a wall of brass forever impenetrable to the combined efforts of England and America." Spain was told that she had nothing to fear from France, but it was the opinion of both Englishmen and Americans that "Spain and her provinces bid fair to become appanages of France."[4]

It seemed only natural, then, that England should seek the alliance of the United States to free the Spanish colonies in order to prevent their falling into the hands of France. But even Hamilton, who seemed to favor the project, was opposed to an alliance with England. He thought England would find it to her advantage to give aid without an alliance, and had already suggested, in March, that she send a dozen frigates to be under the direction of the United States.[5] Rufus King, too, thought the United States ought to take a leading rôle in the great project. "The destiny of the new world," he wrote, "is in our hands. We have a right and it is our duty to deliberate and act, not as secondaries, but as Principals."[6] He thought

[2] Turner, "The Policy of France toward the Mississippi Valley," *The American Historical Review*, X, 276.

[3] Henry Adams, *History of the United States* (9 vols., New York, 1909-1911), I, 355-357.

[4] Turner, "The Policy of France toward the Mississippi Valley," *The American Historical Review*, X, 276. Rufus King got this idea from Lord Grenville.

[5] Hamilton to Pickering, March 27, 1798, J. C. Hamilton (ed.), *The Works of Alexander Hamilton* (7 vols., N. Y. 1850-1851), VI, 278.

[6] A forerunner of the Monroe Doctrine.

the occasion was one that "we ought not . . . to suffer to pass unimproved."⁷ When King next talked with Lord Grenville on the subject he found him more favorably disposed. He had expressed some doubts, however, about the ability of the Spanish Americans to make a successful revolution, and concluded by saying that he was "more and more confirmed in the opinion that none but Englishmen and their descendants knew how to make a Revolution."⁸

Miranda was certainly anxious to use the "Englishmen and their descendants" to perform the difficult task for him. He continued to address letters to Adams, even though he received no reply. In his letter of August 17 he declared that since his last dispatch "circumstances have become still more favorable."⁹ He thought the events in Europe and the United States had made the separation of the Hispanic American colonies indispensable. England, he said, had resolved to lay down "all spirit of commercial monopoly" in order to coöperate with the United States in this important object. He very likely realized and frankly told John Adams that his decision would largely determine the fate of Spanish America.¹⁰

On the day after Caro's dispatches had been distributed by Pickering, Hamilton wrote to King, inclosing a letter to Miranda, but requested King to give the latter only as much information as he thought expedient. Hamilton said he wished the enterprise could be undertaken, but wanted the principal agency to be in the United States, "they to furnish the whole land force necessary. The command in this case would very naturally fall upon me." He was not alone in having aspirations for the proposed military commands. Among those who were interested in Spanish America and seeking com-

---
⁷ King to Hamilton, July 31, 1798, King (ed.), *Life and Correspondence of Rufus King,* II, 657.
⁸ King to Secretary of State, Aug. 17, 1798, *ibid.,* II, 393-394.
⁹ Adams (ed.), *Works of John Adams,* II, 581-582.
¹⁰ Adams received this letter in October.

mands were Hamilton, Burr, Wilkinson, and W. S. Smith, the son-in-law of President Adams. Washington recommended Hamilton, Pinckney, and Knox to rank in the order named, but this met with considerable opposition from the president.[11] John Adams had also proposed that Aaron Burr be made a brigadier-general in the provisional army, a recommendation which failed because of Hamilton's objection. Hamilton on the other hand requested that Wilkinson be promoted to the rank of major-general, but McHenry, the secretary of war, did not trust him, and under these conditions Washington refused to make the recommendations.[12] Finally Smith, too, met with opposition, and the Senate prevented his appointment. Hamilton's place seemed assured, however, by Washington's support, and he hoped to become the liberator of Spanish America.

The United States was not quite ready for the undertaking, but Hamilton said he had already "advised certain preliminary steps to prepare the way." He intimated that the result would be to establish an independent territory under a moderate government, with equal commercial privileges among the coöperating powers. The project could not be taken up until the following spring, he informed Miranda, but added that he would be happy in his official station to be "an instrument of so good a work." He wanted Great Britain to send an agent to the United States,[13] and Miranda's presence would be "extremely essential."[14]

Hamilton, whose military position was second only to Washington's, began to make preparations for the project as

[11] Bernard C. Steiner, *The Life and Correspondence of James McHenry* (Cleveland, 1907), pp. 313, 327.

[12] Albert J. Beveridge, *The Life of John Marshall* (5 vols., Boston, 1919), III, 277, n. 1; Samuel Wandell and Meade Minnegerode, *Aaron Burr: A Biography* (2 vols., New York, 1925), I, 174-175.

[13] Yrujo believed that General Maitland, who came to the United States in the spring of 1799, was such an agent, Yrujo to Conde de Sta. Clara, April 6, 1799, A. G. I., Papeles de Cuba, legajo 1708.

[14] King (ed.), *Life and Correspondence of Rufus King*, II, 659-660.

soon as he knew there would be a decisive rupture with France. The task was slow, but "this country continues to progress in the right direction,"[15] he said. Wilkinson called on Hamilton to arrange the details of the campaign. Edward Everett Hale, who examined the correspondence between these two, was of the opinion that "This mine was ready to be sprung upon poor Spain, when the republic of the United States should make a war upon the French republic."[16] The greatest problem was that of converting the president to the plan. John Adams resented the influence of Hamilton in the cabinet, and he did not like to be led by his cabinet members. The secretary of war, James McHenry, presented the president with a plan for the liberation of Spanish America which bore unmistakable resemblances to the plans of Hamilton. He opposed an alliance with England, but in case of a rupture he suggested that they coöperate in the American possessions of Spain.[17] William Van Murray, at the Hague, on hearing the report that the French part of Santo Domingo had "declared itself independent," prophesied that in the event of a war between the United States and France, one would see changes in the other colonies which would "probably form a new commercial era for the beginning of A. D. 1800."[18]

In England Miranda was anxiously awaiting the decision of the government, and the British in turn seemed to be waiting for an assurance of help from the United States. Adams kept his opinions to himself. On the receipt of Miranda's letter he sent a copy of it to Pickering[19] with a few questions, but refrained from expressing his views. He asked Pickering to "Read it and think of it. . . . We are friends with Spain. If

[15] Hamilton to King, Oct. 2, 1798, Hamilton (ed.), *Works of Hamilton*, VI, 362.
[16] Quoted by Wandell and Minnegerode, *Aaron Burr*, II, 16.
[17] Adams (ed.), *Works of John Adams*, I, 516, n. 1.
[18] To Rufus King, Nov. 27, 1798, Rufus King MSS., No. 464, Huntington Library.
[19] In March, 1815, Adams said he showed the correspondence to no one, Adams (ed.), *Works of John Adams*, I, 516, n. 1.

we were enemies would the project be useful to us?" He did not think it would be proper for him to answer the letter, and asked, "Will any notice of it in any manner be proper?"[20]

Here it hung fire. Pickering evidently did not like to take the responsibility of answering it as long as he did not know the opinions of the president, and the latter merely neglected it. King, however, continued his correspondence in spite of the fact that he received no information on the subject from Pickering. "As England is ready," he said, "she will furnish a fleet and military stores and we should furnish the army."[21] This was quite in accord with Hamilton's views. He wrote to the latter that "there will be precisely such a coöperation as we wish the moment we are ready."[22] Miranda, too, wrote a reply to Hamilton's letter. The British had agreed to the military and naval arrangements, and, as Miranda said, "All is approved, and we await only the *fiat* of your illustrious President to depart like lightning."[23] He considered the great object to be that of saving America from the calamities of the French Revolution, and not only America, but "we will save the entire world which staggers on the edge of an abyss."[24] Miranda continued hopeful and informed Caro from time to time about his negotiations with Turnbull and King. "Especially in America," he wrote on November 9, "all is going very well," and he was happy to report that there had been a clash between French and American frigates.[25] By December he had received favorable news from his correspondent in Philadelphia, and a "friend from New York H— [Hamilton?]" assured him of the success of their commercial affairs. Miranda was

---

[20] *Ibid.*, VIII, 600.

[21] He wrote to both Hamilton and Pickering, Oct. 20, 1798, King (ed.), *Life and Correspondence of Rufus King*, II, 453.

[22] King's letter was in reply to Hamilton's of Aug. 22, 1798.

[23] Quoted by Robertson from Miranda's letter of Oct. 19, 1798, *Miranda*, p. 519.

[24] He added a postscript for Washington; see facsimile in Robertson, *ibid.*, opposite p. 330. He also wrote to Knox. See *The Edinburgh Review*, XIII, 292.

[25] Letters of Nov. 5, 9, and 13, 1798, A. G. I., Estado, Caracas, legajo 4.

now becoming quite confident and was ready to follow the suggestion of Mr. K— [King?] to leave for America, because what they needed from the British was already assured whenever the Americans should request it, and the news from Philadelphia would decide this.[26] In spite of Miranda's hopes and assertions, England was not yet quite convinced that France would overthrow the Spanish government, and John Adams certainly had not shown any tendency to support the project.

Before the end of the year France indicated a desire to settle her difficulties with the United States. Talleyrand had been warned by Fauchet and DuPont, and he, in turn, proposed to Napoleon that they seek peace with the United States for the security of the Spanish and French colonies.[27] A war with the United States would be, to say the least, inconvenient, and the American projects which revolved in his mind could be carried out only if France were at peace with the United States. On September 28, therefore, Talleyrand showed his willingness to accept any minister from the United States with the respect due to the "representative of a free, independent, and powerful nation,"[28] as stipulated by John Adams. An acceptance of this offer would, of course, put an end to the participation of the United States in Miranda's project.

Many were anxious for peace and neutrality, but a few continued their revolutionary plans. King wrote to Hamilton in January, 1799, to urge him to continue the project, and he became very emphatic, as we may see from his own words:

For God's sake, attend to the very interesting subject treated of in my ciphered dispatches to the Secretary of State of the 10th, 18th, and 19th instant.[29] Connect it as it should be, with the main object, the time to accomplish which has arrived. ... I am more confirmed

[26] Miranda to Caro, London, Dec. 8, 1798, *ibid.*
[27] James, "Louisiana in American Diplomacy," *The Mississippi Valley Historical Review*, I, 56.
[28] Fish, *American Diplomacy*, p. 136.
[29] The editor of King's correspondence says that this is probably in connection with the Miranda project, *Life and Correspondence of Rufus King*, II, 519 n.

than before, that an efficient force will be confederated to act against France. The combination is *not yet completed,* but, as I have reason to believe, will soon be. ... That will be the moment for us to settle upon immutable foundations the extensive system of the American nation. Who can hinder us? One nation alone has the power; and she will cooperate in the accomplishment in South America of what has so well been done in North.[30]

Hamilton was by this time supporting King wholeheartedly. He wanted the president to be given adequate powers to use the land and naval forces "for preventing and frustrating hostile designs of France, either directly or indirectly through any of her allies." Hamilton's idea was to organize an expedition and "attack where we can. France is not to be considered as separated from her ally. Tempting objects will be within our grasp."[31] The best way to defeat the French schemes for universal empire would be "to detach South America from Spain, which is the only channel through which the riches of Mexico and Peru are conveyed to France." But Hamilton as a leader of the expedition could do little without an army, and military preparations progressed slowly.

Hamilton, as inspector general, retained supreme command of the western army and, in order to form "a more perfect plan for present and eventual arrangements," informed Wilkinson that his "speedy presence in this quarter" was necessary.[32] He explained to Washington that this was desirable for "a more full examination of the affairs of the Western scene, and to the concerting of ulterior arrangements." The prospects of peace did not put a stop to Hamilton's preparations. He continued the organization of the army and sought something for that army to do, once organized. "It is a pity, my dear sir, and a reproach," he wrote to McHenry, "that our administration

---

[30] *Ibid.*
[31] Hamilton to Gunn, N. Y., Dec. 27, 1798, *ibid.,* II, 665; H. C. Lodge (ed.), *The Works of Alexander Hamilton* (9 vols., New York, 1885-1886), VII, 45.
[32] Lodge (ed.), *Works of Alexander Hamilton,* VII, 65.

have no general plan. Certainly there ought to be one formed without delay. . . . Besides eventual security against invasion, we ought certainly to look to the Floridas and Louisiana, and we ought to squint at South America."[33] He added that if the cabinet would take up such a subject he would be glad to come to Philadelphia to consult with them. Wilkinson did come to talk over plans, and Hamilton reported to Washington, but he was noncommital and vague. Perhaps he did not feel assured of sufficient government support to announce his plans boldly and openly, or perhaps it was not necessary. He wrote as follows:

I had previously thought of the subject, but had purposely limited myself to a few very general ideas, that I might examine with less prepossession the plan of an officer who, possessing talents to judge, has for years had his mind occupied with the scene to which he refers. . . . I adopt several of the leading ideas of the General, but I vary in some particulars.

One objective seemed certain, however, that in case of a rupture, there would be "a prompt attack on New Orleans." Hamilton wanted the main body of troops concentrated to the north on the Ohio where they would not arouse the suspicion of the Spaniards. There they "will look to various points: to the northern Indians, to the disaffection of the neighboring country, etc. etc. Enough is said."[34] Of course, "the disaffection of the neighboring country, etc. etc." might be saying a great deal. The main part of the veteran army was to be in the West, while the recruits were to be in larger units in the East. "The very great sphere of action to which the former are destined, including important and complicated objects appears to me to render it expedient that not more than two regiments shall constitute a brigade." What is this "very great sphere" and what are the "important and complicated objects"? His plan, he said, was "the result of communication with Gen-

[33] Hamilton to McHenry, New York, June 27, 1799, *ibid.*, VII, 97.
[34] Hamilton to Washington, New York, Sept. 9, 1799, *ibid.*, VII, 117-125.

eral Wilkinson and the Commander-in-Chief, and in accord with the opinion of the latter."³⁵ We may also recall his correspondence with King.

•Incidentally, this was the period in which Philip Nolan, the well-known filibuster and horse-trader, was making his intrusions into Spanish territory. Nolan was first of all serving General Wilkinson. In 1797 he spoke of Wilkinson in these words: "I look forward to the conquest of Mexico by the United States and I expect my friend and patron the General will, in such event, give me a conspicuous command."³⁶ Edward Everett Hale, relying on his memory, said that, while looking through Wilkinson's papers at the home of the latter's grandson in Louisville (1876), he found "the whole history of the proposal of John Adams, when he was President, to move an army from Cincinnati down the river and take New Orleans. This army was to be under the care of General Hamilton."³⁷ The latter, looking forward to his command of the "new army," recommended in vain, as we have seen, that Wilkinson be made a major-general, and later called him to Philadelphia for a conference on the "great sphere of action" of the western army which was "destined" for "important and complicated objects."³⁸ This would seem to make a chain with Hamilton on one end, Nolan on the other, and Wilkinson a link between.

There is still another phase of the Nolan episode. Philip Nolan had assured his men that he had permission to enter the Spanish territory, yet he was stopped, and among those who questioned the object of Nolan's expedition was one Mordicai Richards. Nolan then began to unfold a tale which, taken alone, seems fantastic and unreasonable; but which, taken in conjunction with the wars, near-wars, plots, intrigues, military

---

³⁵ Hamilton to McHenry, Trenton, Oct. 12, 1799, *ibid.,* VII, 149.

³⁶ E. E. Hale, "The Real Philip Nolan," *Publications of the Mississippi Historical Society,* IV, 281-329 (1901).

³⁷ *Ibid.,* IV, 284.

³⁸ Hamilton to McHenry, Trenton, Oct. 12, 1799, Lodge (ed.), *Works of Alexander Hamilton,* VII, 149.

preparations, and diplomatic negotiations, brings it within the realm of the possible and the probable. They would build a strong house, he said, to oppose any attack. From there they could make their trips to examine the mines, and other precious things of that country. In the meantime they would collect horses and return to Kentucky the following August or September. There, he said, he expected to be provided with a patent from the English minister in Philadelphia, and under it "there are many I know who wish to come to make the conquest of those countries," or at least to collect the riches to be found there. It was for this purpose that he was securing horses, so that they could all be mounted. At the end of two years they could return rich. They would always be supported by the English; of that he had been assured.[39] Here we have another chain, from Miranda in London, through the English government to its minister in the United States, and, again, with Philip Nolan on the other extreme end. The projects were the same, their origin the same, the objective the same. Miranda had made great efforts to reënforce the chains by linking them at the heads of the two governments, and Nolan was apparently serving as a link in the Spanish territory. Under these circumstances, then, Philip Nolan seems to be no longer an isolated horse-trader and a soldier of fortune, but the forerunner of a project which embraced not only horses and mines, but countries and continents.

The revolutionary project met with reverses, and only the most enthusiastic would continue after these were observed. In March King admitted that the president's silence gave him some "inquietude."[40] He sent a copy of the "famous map of South America," which Fayden had lately engraved, to Hamil-

---

[39] Report of Richards, Natchez, Dec. 13, 1800, copied in New Orleans, Jan. 2, 1801, in Mexico, Feb. 26, 1801, A. G. I., Estado, Mexico, legajo 10; George P. Garrison, *Texas, a Contest of Civilizations* (Boston, 1903), p. 114.

[40] King to Hamilton, March 4, 1799, King (ed.), *Life and Correspondence of Rufus King*, II, 662-663.

ton, as well as one of Mexico which was not as good but would "supply a desideratum." King had not given up the idea, but thought that some action ought to be taken at once. "I am entirely convinced," he said of Spanish America, "if it and its resources are not for us, that they will speedily be against us." As for Spain and Portugal, "the game may be terminated with them at the pleasure of France." The next step of France was plain. "What, without infatuation, can we expect of France? Why then any Reserve?"[41] This was King's ardent appeal, but in vain.

When the people in the United States heard that France sought peace, a large number were anxious to accept the offer. John Adams, whose decision might have put in motion the great project for liberating Spanish America, responded to the French offer by nominating Murray as minister to France. Professor Carl Russel Fish says of this:

Of all personal decisions in American diplomacy, this was the most important, unless it may be that Jay was justified in his suspicions of Vergennes in 1782 and so deflected the course of history at that point.[42]

In the light of the relations this decision had with the revolutionary plans for Spanish America, it is clear that it was a most momentous decision for all America, and not only for America in the narrower sense of the United States.

The Spanish American project was not dropped immediately after the minister was nominated. The terms presented to France were, according to Pinckney, what "we have a clear right to," but he doubted very much whether France would grant them. Then he added, "I am morally sure she will not; and this has put us all much at our ease."[43] It would seem as if they were all set for war which would give them an oppor-

[41] King to Hamilton, March 9, 1799, King (ed.), *Life and Correspondence of Rufus King*, II, 663.
[42] Fish, *American Diplomacy*, p. 137.
[43] Pinckney to King, March 12, 1799, *ibid*.

tunity of conquering some Spanish territory and liberating the rest.

Miranda continued to exert his influence in England. He had, however, tried to get a passport to the West Indies, but England refused his request.[44] On March 19 he presented a new memorial to Pitt, still hoping that there would be coöperation between England and the United States against France. This would be the signal for the declaration of independence in Spanish America, where Caro had prepared them for a "spontaneous and general" uprising. Miranda was somewhat disappointed because there had been no offer of aid, but there was still considerable interest in the project.

Among the sympathizers was Sir Ralph Abercromby,[45] who wrote a paper on the project, possibly during 1799. He emphasized the commercial advantages and showed clearly what was the nature of the British interest. He thought that every military enterprise should be to secure or increase their commerce and wealth. "But of all objects that ought to claim our attention," he said, "the liberation of South America from the dominion of Spain seems to stand first."[46] There should be no idea of conquest nor of exclusive commerce, and still he thought England would have nine-tenths of this great trade.[47] This view is quite in keeping with the statement of John Adams made in 1785 that, "even if the revolution were possible it would be England, and not the United States, that would reap the greatest benefit."[48] Sir Ralph Abercromby described the conditions in Spanish America quite accurately and gave the causes tending towards independence. He thought that the same views were held in Mexico as in the rest of

[44] Robertson, *Miranda*, p. 333; and his *Life of Miranda*, I, 188-190.
[45] Sir Ralph Abercromby had served in the West Indies, and it was he who captured Trinidad, over which he made Picton governor.
[46] It was in 1799, possibly the date of this plan, that he was called to London to consider a project for a descent on Holland.
[47] Londonderry (ed.), *Castlereagh Correspondence*, VII, 269-273.
[48] *The Diplomatic Correspondence of the United States 1783-1789*, V, 124.

Spanish America, but did not plan to include that territory in the enterprise unless the United States were to coöperate.[49] This would lead one to believe that Mexico was to be the special field for the activities of the United States.

Manual Gual, a friend of Miranda, presented a memorial to the British in which he said that "Spanish America can only be regarded as a colony of France." He urged the liberation of the colonies as a blow against France to deprive her of the source on which she was dependent in order to continue the war against England.[50]

In October Henry Dundas, secretary of war, drew up a memorandum which he sent with a letter to several members of the cabinet to get their opinion on the revolutionary plans. He feared to see the "world set adrift on any revolutionary system." But if a revolution took place, he thought it would be necessary for England to take part, acting as a guide and steadying force.[51] One of the cabinet members who signed his initial, "G," probably Grenville, gave the opinion that England should by no means "engage in the projects of General Miranda," nor in those of the United States. The other opinion given, probably by Mr. Windham, agreed with Mr. Dundas that in case a revolution were started, Great Britain ought to participate.[52]

Miranda's hopes had begun to dwindle during the year 1799. England had given him hopes but little aid. He made several attempts to get passports, first to the West Indies, and then to the United States.[53] By the end of 1799 England had

[49] Londonderry (ed.), *Correspondence of Castlereagh*, VII, 273.

[50] Gual referred to Raynal's *Philosophical and Political History* which spoke of the British plans during the Seven Years' War, 353-354.

[51] "Memorandum for the consideration of the Cabinet," Oct. 3, 1799, Londonderry (ed.), *Correspondence of Castlereagh*, VII, 284-285.

[52] *Ibid.*, VII, 285.

[53] Rufus King helped him and wrote a letter of introduction for him to Pickering, but it was never sent because Miranda was detained in England. See King (ed.), *Life and Correspondence of Rufus King*, II, 664, 665.

given some consideration to proposals for a general peace,[54] but Miranda was, nevertheless, detained.

When the United States showed her willingness to negotiate with France, she was closing the door to coöperation with England in the liberation project. Hamilton wanted to be the liberator of at least a part of Spanish America, and together with Pickering he made every effort to postpone the mission to France. In the meantime Napoleon had replaced the Directory. The negotiations proceeded slowly but surely to their completion in September, 1800. John Adams had very likely postponed the independence of Spanish America, but he had also restored the United States to a condition of peaceful neutrality and had felt proud of his achievement.

Having made this peace, he naturally desired to uphold his policy and therefore ridiculed the other possibility of supporting Miranda's schemes. He made some interesting comments on the project in a letter written in 1815.[55] He said that "So intuitively obvious and certain was the answer to every question that I could imagine relative to the subject, that my judgment was made up as soon as I had read the despatch."[56] He even had an answer all ready, he said in case the British minister should propose a tripartite alliance. He would plead the "juvenility of our nation," lack of financial stability, the aversion of our people to war, the uncertainty of the enterprise, and, above all, our policy of neutrality. It probably did not take John Adams fifteen years to come to these conclusions, but they were, no doubt, an after-thought or what is sometimes known as *esprit d'escalier*.

[54] A. W. Ward and G. P. Gooch (eds.), *The Cambridge History of British Foreign Policy, 1783-1815* (3 vols., New York, 1922), I, 337.

[55] John Adams to James Lloyd, March 26, 1815, Adams (ed.), *Works of John Adams*, X, 139-143.

[56] That his memory was not entirely reliable is shown by the fact that he had already forgotten that he presented the plans to Pickering. Cf. Adams (ed.), *Works of John Adams*, VIII, 600.

CHAPTER XI

SPANISH DEFENSE

> "As a piece of machinery the Spanish administration certainly surpassed anything of the sort constructed by the colonial powers of the time."—WILLIAM R. SHEPHERD.
>
> "But what most impresses one in their story is, as in the case of Muir, the ceaseless and minute vigilance with which the whole administration of New Spain, from the viceroy down, kept its eye upon all the doings of every foreigner, and struggled to preserve state and church from contaminating influences."—MARJORIE MASSON and J. F. JAMESON.

WE HAVE already seen the wide ramifications and the international aspects of the revolutionary plans for Spanish America. There remains the problem of defense—Spanish effort to avert the threatened catastrophe. One can but admire the efficiency of the Spanish colonial government, when considering its success in keeping fully informed of the conspiracies of foreign governments and of private intriguers. The promptness with which the Mexican government was warned of the revolutionary plans of Miranda and the British in 1796 is an example. A whole year before Miranda left for England to put his ideas into action, the colonial government was informed of the project and put on its guard.[1]

Foreigners were being watched with greater vigilance since the experiences with the adherents of the French Revolution. One of the interesting individuals who fell into the hands of the colonial authorities during this period was Thomas Muir, a Scotchman who had been deported to Botany Bay because of his liberal views.[2] He had been one of the leading members

---

[1] Prince of the Peace to Branciforte, San Lorenzo, Dec. 24, 1796, A. G. I., Estado, Mexico, legajo 18.

[2] The Spanish documents on the adventures of Thomas Muir are found in A. G. I., Estado, Mexico, legajos 6, 7, and 23 in particular. In legajo 6 see numbers 1, 3, 4, 340, and 352 for the reports in 1796. Thomas Muir is treated in greater detail by Marjorie Masson and J. F. Jameson, "The Odyssey of Thomas Muir," *The American Historical Review*, XXIX, 49-72 (Oct., 1923).

of the Society of the Friends of the People, a radical organization which owed its origin to the democratic principles of the French Revolution. The English government feared such societies and Thomas Muir, a lawyer from Edinburgh, was among those who were tried and deported.

He escaped from Australia in the *Otter,* a vessel of the Boston trader, Captain Dorr.[3] His intention was to seek asylum in the United States. Having reached the Pacific coast at Nootka, Dorr decided to return by way of the Orient. Thereupon Muir boarded a Spanish coast guard, the *Sutil,* a ship which had been sent from San Blas under the pilot major Don José Tovar to guard the coast against foreigners.[4] Muir hoped in this way to reach the United States in much shorter time than by Captain Dorr's ship, and perhaps also to evade the English.

The *Sutil* remained in the harbor of Monterey for over two weeks, where the governor of California, Don Diego de Borica, found the radical Scotchman to be most delightful company. Thomas Muir regaled the lonely governor with stories of his experiences, especially those of the French Revolution, with which he seemed to be quite familiar, having been in Paris in 1792 and 1793. He "painted with very vivid colors the characters of the principal personages such as Mirabeau, Condorcet, Lafayette, Dumouriez, Brisot, Robespierre, Danton, Tallien, D'Egalité, and others, and does not appear less informed on political conditions of England."[5] Such a person was certainly too dangerous to be given his freedom in Spanish territory. And Tovar who had given him refuge and a passage to San Blas was arrested for his assistance to a foreigner. The viceroy

[3] The Captain of the *Otter* is referred to not only as Dorr, but also as Dawes. Cf. article by Masson and Jameson, "The Odyssey of Thomas Muir," *The American Historical Review,* XXIX, 68. The author's copyist in Seville has also transposed it as Doux.

[4] Branciforte to Príncipe de la Paz, Mexico, Sept. 26, 1796, A. G. I., Estado, Mexico, legajo 6.

[5] Diego de Borica to Branciforte, Monterey, July 13, 1796, *ibid.*

did not believe that Tovar had any other fault than that of "stupidity and ignorance" which made it possible for the astute Muir to deceive him.[6]

While in New Spain Thomas Muir was accorded the good treatment of a man of prestige; yet he was guarded cautiously as a man who was dangerous. He was escorted to Mexico and then to Vera Cruz where he was held until the authorities secured passage for him to Spain, since they had not complied with his requests to be sent to the United States or to France. He had written to Washington and had intimated to the Spaniards that he was assured of the protection of the American president. There is greater evidence of the interest of the French government in the liberal who spread its views. Nevertheless, Muir was sent to Spain on a Spanish battleship. The ship was attacked by the British, and only by means of a wound on the face which disfigured him was he supposed to have escaped detection by the English officers who made a search for him.[7] While he was convalescing in Spain, he was constantly under the care of the French consul, and as a result of diplomatic intervention and of having been declared a French citizen by the Convention he was finally permitted to go to Paris, with the warning never again to return to any territory of the Spanish king.[8]

Somewhat connected with the Muir episode was the treatment by the Spaniards of Juan Kendrick, son of John Kendrick, the explorer of the Columbia River. Juan had joined his father in the fur trade, but on manifesting his desire to accept the Catholic religion and to serve the Spanish monarch he was given the post of pilot at San Blas. His conduct had been satisfactory, but he could no longer remain in the country because of the royal order against foreigners. It would be unwise to set him free because dangerous American neighbors

[6] Branciforte to Príncipe de la Paz, Mexico, Sept. 26, 1796, *ibid.*
[7] Report of Sept. 16, 1799, *ibid.*, legajo 23.
[8] *Ibid.*

might make use of his extensive knowledge of the coast and interior of New Spain to harm the Spanish monarch. The difficulty was solved by sending him to Spain as interpreter for Thomas Muir and five Englishmen who had been brought from Nootka.[9]

Besides the growing menace from foreigners there were increasing manifestations of unrest and threats of insurrection, spurring the officials on to greater vigilance and repression. The evidence of disaffection in Mexico tends to substantiate the somewhat exaggerated reports of Miranda and his associates. While the trials of the French were still fresh in their memories and the trial of Guerrero was still going on, a new conspiracy was discovered, the "Conspiracy of the Knives," or as it is more aptly called in the trial of its designers, the "Conspiracy of the Creoles vs. Europeans." The leader, Don Pedro Portilla, was only eighteen years old, and he had only a small number of associates, thirteen, and all under thirty years of age. They decided to call themselves *"Convención Nacional Americana"* and they were already considering whether to adopt a constitution like that of the United States or some other form. Their plan in brief was that each should secure a certain number of recruits, then liberate the prisoners for support, gain control of the garrison, win the creoles by proclamations, and finally take possession of the persons and property of the Europeans.[10]

This immature plot was an example of the ill-feeling between the creoles and the gachupines which threatened to break out at any time. In conducting the arrest and the trial the officials were warned to act quietly and secretly in order not to fan the flame of existing class hatred.[11] The next viceroy, Berenguer de Marquina, belittled the whole affair, saying

---

[9] Branciforte to Prince of the Peace, Mexico, Sept. 26, 1796, *ibid.,* legajo 6.
[10] Alamán, *Historia de Méjico,* I, 132-134; and report of the trial, Archivo Histórico Nacional, Madrid, legajo 21,061.
[11] Azanza to Urquijo, Mexico, Nov. 30, 1799, A. G. I., Estado, Mexico, legajo 9.

that this small number of mere youths were incapable of any great undertaking. A recommendation for lenient punishment was finally approved. But the viceroy admitted that he was aware of the possibilities of danger due to the great distance from Spain, limited resources for defense, and "the influence of this unfortunate age which had declared for liberty."[12] It was the spirit of the age, then, that the Spanish and colonial officials had to struggle against.

A source of constant threat and danger at this time was England, who, the Mexicans knew full well, had lent an ear to the revolutionary proposals of Miranda. In 1797, to add to the fears of the anxious authorities, a report was started by one Benítez Gálvez that an agreement had been made between a republican organization in Mexico and the British government. A copy of a letter, supposedly sent by James Smith, secretary to the governor of Jamaica, to Barragán, a representative of the Mexican group, stated that the British government had agreed to give the aid requested by the *Caballeros Republicanos de México*.[13] Tampico had been selected as the place of rendezvous, and there the inhabitants had been prepared to meet their liberators and to give the necessary aid for an expedition inland.

That there was a close relationship between the English and the Mexicans, the viceroy said he knew, but Benítez Gálvez had aroused his suspicions so that he divided his efforts between the investigation of the plot and a careful check on the activities and reliability of the informer. After a long correspondence with the home government with frequent manifestations of willingness to protect the kingdom with his last breath, the viceroy discovered that his suspicions had been justified and that the reported plot was merely an opportune invention of Benítez Gálvez whose real name was Don Juan

[12] Berenguer de Marquina to Urquijo, Mexico, Oct. 27, 1800, *ibid*.
[13] Smith to Barragán, copied in Mexico, Aug. 27, 1800, *ibid*.

Vásquez Fernández, who merely sought revenge and remuneration. Previously condemned for bigamy and now discovered in an effort to deceive and defraud the government,[14] he was sentenced to eight years imprisonment and forbidden to return to the Indies.[15]

Another disturbance had been disposed of. But the English menace was no fiction of a disgruntled bigamist; it was a real and constant thing while the war lasted. British vessels hovered on the coast of Mexico, seemingly ready to put Miranda's project into action.[16] Even while belittling the reports of Benítez Gálvez, Berenguer de Marquina said he knew that the suspicious movements of the British agreed with the report, and were in keeping "with their former ideas concerning the Americas." It was also in accord with the sparks which he had observed, "indicating a hidden fire which desires the breath of independence." The prime movers of such ideas depend, he added, "on the uncultured and ignorant rustics, on the malcontents, on the delinquents, and on the naturally malevolent who are never lacking in a population, no matter how well organized."[17] This is only additional proof that revolutionary material existed, ready to be moulded according to the designs of the revolutionary leaders. And the viceroy was making all the military preparations he could with his limited means to prevent any outbreak.

Revolutionary propaganda had also been spread among the Tepic Indians where a project for independence was already under way. At the head of the conspiracy was Mariano, son of the governor of Pueblo de Tlaxcala in New Galicia. The English were suspected of having a hand in the affair because strangers were known to have mingled with the natives and the

---

[14] Berenguer de Marquina to Cevallos, Mexico, July 27, 1801, *ibid.*, legajo 10.
[15] Report by Domínguez, Ceuta, July 8, 1806, *ibid.*, legajo 20.
[16] Report from Orizava, April 14, 1798, *ibid.*, legajo 8; similar reports in legajos 9-11.
[17] Berenguer de Marquina to Urquijo, Mexico, June 25, 1800, *ibid.*, legajo 9.

English had frequently visited the Pacific coast.[18] Here again the authorities acted quickly and forcefully, and soon a large number of the conspirators were arrested. The affair ended with orders to the priests to be watchful and to inculcate the proper respect for the government.[19]

In the meantime a new danger had been added to the English menace, for the Russians were reported to have declared war on Spain; and this made the viceroy Azanza fear the loss of California where he had little means to defend the sparsely settled and distant province. Six frigates, he thought, would be enough to guard against the Russians and their allies, the English, who had formed establishments at Nootka, Galapagos, Sandwich, and other islands of the South Seas.[20] One might recall that Catherine of Russia was very much interested in Miranda's project when he was presented to her on his European visit.

Finally, there was the danger from the combined forces of England and the United States. The Spaniards, aware of the break between the United States and France, feared the consequences. The latter had given Spain sufficient warning of the Anglo-American danger in her effort to regain Louisiana. The French would have to "put up a dam which without them would submerge Mexico, Peru, and all their islands. . . . A double barrier must be established at once for in a few years it will be too late."[21] With this reminder one can again consider the efforts of Miranda to secure the coöperation of England and the United States in the liberation plan.

During the summer of 1799 the viceroy was informed from

---

[18] Berenguer de Marquina to Cevallos, Mexico, Feb. 26, 1801, *ibid.*, legajo 10; and cf. Alamán, *Historia de Méjico*, I, 135.

[19] Berenguer de Marquina to Cevallos, Mexico, Feb. 26, 1801, A. G. I., Estado, Mexico, legajo 10.

[20] Azanza to Urquijo, Mexico, Dec. 20, 1799, *ibid.*, legajo 9.

[21] Quoted from the correspondence of Létoube, June 18, 1797, by James, "Louisiana in American Diplomacy, 1795-1800," *The Mississippi Valley Historical Review*, I, 48.

two sources—the governors of Havana and Louisiana—that Major General Maitland and other English officers had arrived in Philadelphia. General Maitland had just completed some negotiations with Toussaint L'Ouverture in Santo Domingo, but the Spanish minister in the United States believed he had a more important mission in America, that of seeking an alliance between England and the United States against France, "and consequently against us."[22] He did not believe that the French island of Guadalupe would be "sufficient to tempt the two united nations," and he thought that the general had come to offer ships, money, and men.[23] The idea that there would be a combination against the Spanish colonies was not a novel one, then, for it was shared by France, England, the United States, Mexico, and the followers of Miranda. But in the viceroy's report to Urquijo in July there was a tone of hope, since President Adams had shown a desire for peace and a willingness to negotiate with France.[24] Still the military preparations were going on and Mexico was not safe. How far the American interest extended, varied with the individual —Hamilton, we remember, even suggesting that we ought to "squint at South America."[25] New Orleans appeared to be the objective for which the western army was being organized. "The differences with France offered a cover for the real design."[26]

The Spaniards became exceedingly disturbed when they observed the military preparations which were being made by their American neighbors. They sought information and an explanation from their former servant, General Wilkinson,

[22] Azanza to Urquijo, Mexico, July 27, 1799, A. G. I., Estado, Mexico, legajo 9. For Maitland in America see also King (ed.), *Rufus King*, II, 519 and 529.

[23] Yrujo to Conde de Santa Clara, Philadelphia, April 6, 1799, A. G. I., Papeles de Cuba, legajo 1708.

[24] Azanza to Urquijo, Mexico, July 27, 1799, A. G. I., Estado, Mexico, legajo 9.

[25] Hamilton to McHenry, New York, June 27, 1799, Lodge (ed.), *Works of Alexander Hamilton*, VII, 97.

[26] François-Xavier Martin, *The History of Louisiana* (2 vols., New Orleans, 1829), II, 174; see also Wandell and Minnegerode, *Aaron Burr*, II, 9.

whose reply could scarcely give them much confidence, no matter what its nature might be. He gave to the governor of Louisiana a report from the secretary of war, stating that the military preparations were not against Spanish America, but for the preservation of their own possessions.[27] This did not allay the Spanish suspicions, while the activities of Philip Nolan on the Spanish border certainly increased them.

In 1799 the governor of Louisiana sent orders to de Nava to arrest any American entering his territory, since he had heard rumors that they were coming to start an insurrection.[28] As for Nolan, the Spanish suspected him, resented his presence, and sought to capture him. De Nava was informed by the governor of Louisiana that Nolan was "a dangerous man and a sacriligious hypocrite" who was commissioned to make maps for Wilkinson. He ought to be captured because "the Knowledge he had acquired of the interior of parts of New Mexico, might one day be of injury to the Spanish Monarchy."[29]

Who knows how much of the information which Wilkinson gave to Hamilton came originally from Nolan? The Spaniards were probably correct in saying that Nolan was Wilkinson's agent. When Nolan entered the Spanish dominions, he might well be considered as a forerunner of the Miranda-Hamilton enterprise and as an entering wedge for the Americans. When he arrived with his band of followers the Spaniards naturally offered resistance, and Nolan was reported to have "been killed by a random shot."[30]

The most important factor in diverting the danger from the North was not the killing of Philip Nolan, but the *volte face* of Talleyrand and the willingness of Adams to trust the untrustworthy minister of foreign affairs of France. Happily for

[27] Azanza to Urquijo, Mexico, July 27, 1799, A. G. I., Estado, Mexico, legajo 9.
[28] Garrison, *Texas*, p. 113.
[29] *Ibid.*; and Daniel Clark to Jefferson, New Orleans, Nov. 12, 1799; "Concerning Philip Nolan," *The Texas Historical Association Quarterly*, VII, 315 (1903-1904).
[30] William Dunbar, Natchez, Aug. 22, 1801, *ibid.*

Mexico, Napoleon was as willing as Adams to avert war. There remained the greater projects of Miranda and the British, against which the Spanish authorities were equally vigilant and equally successful.

The plans of Miranda seemed to be maturing and promising success at the time when Caro left for America, April, 1798. Then there came a change. Secrecy seemed seldom to keep the Spanish authorities ignorant of the revolutionary activities. News of Caro's departure spread from France to Spain, to Santa Fé, to Havana, to Mexico—radio could hardly have served better. There was to be no surprise, and Caro had need for his disguise as a negro.[31] The home government, as well as Mexico, was warned by the viceroy of Peru,[32] and a description of Caro was sent in order that he might be arrested in case he came to Mexico.[33]

Besides the regular methods of securing information there were occasionally non-official informers who sought funds or favor by warning the government against any known plot. Such was Villery, an escaped French prisoner from Guiana, whose real name, he said, was D'Ossuanville. He had become aware of British preparations to make an attack on the Spanish authority in America, and on passing through London, his suspicions had been confirmed by the activities of Miranda in connection with the British cabinet. Then he had purchased copies of Miranda's papers from the latter's secretary, it seems, and was now offering them to the Spanish government through its minister in Austria. Campo Alange, the minister, examined them one by one and discovered that "they were copies of the correspondence between Miranda and Pitt, and other persons," containing "instructions, plans, and proclamations for a general insurrection in America," under the protection of the British forces and in agreement with a secret revolutionary

[31] Robertson, *Miranda*, p. 326, n. *a*.
[32] Azanza to Saavedra, Mexico, July 27, 1798, A. G. I., Estado, Mexico, legajo 8.
[33] Mendinueta to viceroy of Mexico, Santa Fé, March 19, 1798, *ibid*.

junta of Americans formed several years earlier in Madrid.³⁴ It was believed that they planned to make their first attack on the Isthmus of Panama, where all was in readiness, and two ships had already been sent as a preliminary step.

Although the whole disclosure was in keeping with the facts, with which the government was already somewhat familiar, the Spanish minister decided to be economical and not to reward the voluntary informer. Villery had come from London on the minister's request, but was now given slightly less than his expenses for the journey.³⁵ But then he had only copies of the papers and not the originals—such evidence could not be worth much in money.

In case the Spanish government did not have sufficient evidence, there was generally the accomplice who lost heart or found it more profitable to turn back. José Caro missed his boat for Philadelphia, but he did get to Trinidad, where British plans were centered. There, however, he came under the suspicion of Governor Picton, who believed that "he was an Emissary from the Court of Madrid, who had insinuated himself into the confidence of Miranda, the better to discover his Projects and the intentions of his Majesty's Government with respect to the South American colonies."³⁶ The governor therefore ordered him to leave the island. Caro returned to London; but a short time later, September 24, 1800, he wrote from Hamburg what seemed to be a confession or exposé of the whole Miranda scheme.³⁷ Ocariz, who received

---

³⁴ This was probably the one whose agents, Don Manuel de Salas, Don Pedro Caro, and Don José Pozo, together with Miranda, drew up the revolutionary plans in Paris, December, 1797.

³⁵ Campo Alange to Urquijo, Vienna, June 10, 1799, A. G. I., Estado, Caracas, legajo 4.

³⁶ Quoted by Robertson, *Miranda*, p. 345; see also n. *b* for the letter from Picton to Dundas, Sept. 28, 1800, *ibid*.

³⁷ On being asked the object of his visit he said he was an American and came from London, *"para remitir al Secretario del Despacho de Estado por su mano el adjunto pliego, importante por la revelacion de las tramas que conocido Dⁿ Francº Miranda, Dⁿ Pedro Fermin de Vargas, y el mismo interesada habian formado*

the confession, spoke also of Olavide, Quintana, Pozo, and Salas, and "several other Americans" who ought to suffer the death penalty as traitors. He began to describe the revolutionary plans but left them to be told more fully by the report of Caro and the documents which accompanied it. Caro asked for permission to confess and to be pardoned. In his own letter from Hamburg he referred to a conversation he had with a representative of the house of Turnbull in London, which had supported Miranda.[38] The agent's statements were guarded, but intimated that Miranda and his scheme had been discredited, and everything had been changed. Perhaps the English firm hoped to free itself from any serious charges, now that the whole scheme was being disclosed.

The reaction had set in, and the chance for a successful revolution had diminished. Diplomacy turned in favor of Spain; the officials had been warned and had prepared to defend their dominions; D'Ossuanville, alias Villery, had revealed the whole Miranda project; and now the rumors and suspicions had been substantiated by the confessions of Caro, one of the leading conspirators. Caro seems to have acted in good faith until he was suspected, but after that his usefulness might easily diminish to the point where it would be to his advantage to turn against his fellow-conspirators. His confessions, once begun, continued throughout the following year, and from Paris he informed the Spanish government that King and Hamilton had participated in the revolutionary project. And in support of Villery's opinion he said that a foothold was to be obtained in Panama from whence they could spread the germs of revolution.[39]

Caro had grown tired of the whole affair, and, pleading illness, asked for permission to retire to Spain. The authorities

---
y segundo cerca del Ministerio Britanico para obtener independencia de la America Española. . . ." A. G. I., Estado, Caracas, legajo 4.

[38] Pedro José Caro, Hamburg, Sept. 24, 1800, *ibid*.

[39] Caro, Paris, March 30, 1801, *ibid*.

were naturally anxious to know more, to know all, and poor Caro was now requested to return to London in order to keep the Spanish government informed about the revolutionary plans. Before leaving Paris he had time to write another report, saying that Miranda had returned to France to renew the plans of Brissot and Petion. He also had a consultation with Pickering, American secretary of legation in London and son of the former secretary of state. Finally, Caro had seen the papers of certain ex-Jesuits, Clavijero and Guzmán, in which revolutionary hope was again centered in the United States because of the transfer of the Mississippi to the French,[40] referring to the retrocession of Louisiana.

The Spanish dominions had been threatened by invasion and revolution, but the crisis had passed without the culmination of either. The bonds which held the colonies to the mother country were probably growing weaker, but they might last for a long time unless they were strained by foreign intervention. The ability of the government to keep fully informed on plans of insurrection and on plans of intervention was truly remarkable, and the colonial administrators were constantly put on their guard against the revolutionary activities of their own countrymen and foreigners.

[40] Caro, Paris, April 20, 1801, *ibid*.

CHAPTER XII

COMPETITION FOR THE KEY TO MEXICO

> "The day that France takes possession of New Orleans fixes the sentence which is to restrain her forever within her low water mark. . . . From that moment we must marry ourselves to the British fleet and nation . . . and . . . make the first cannon, which shall be fired in Europe, the signal for tearing up any settlement she may have made, and for holding the two continents of America in sequestration for the common purpose of the United British and American nations."—THOMAS JEFFERSON.
>
> "On the Continent . . . the supremacy of French influence in the determinations of the Spanish Court was of paramount importance. It made possible the peaceful acquisition of Louisiana. . . . But for this, Mexico and other Spanish colonies would have been earlier revolutionized."—WALTER F. MCCALEB.

THE peace with France, which had increased the ego of the egotistical John Adams, temporarily postponed consideration of participation by the United States with England in the Spanish American emancipation project. Had Miranda been permitted to go to the United States, he might have proved himself a "conjurer" with bewitching powers in spite of John Adams,[1] but the opportunity seemed now to have passed. When Hamilton lost his influence in the cabinet, Miranda lost his best supporter in the United States,[2] and England, too, seemed to be losing interest, leaving him helpless but not hopeless.

Towards the end of 1800 Miranda left England for France again, although his motives were not as well known this time as previously. One can hardly believe that he had suddenly given up his life work and his greatest ambition; it would be more reasonable for him to seek new supporters for his old scheme. His reception in France was most discouraging, for

---

[1] Adams had characterized him thus because of his influence over Pitt, Adams (ed.), *Works of John Adams*, I, 679-684.

[2] He had written to Hamilton on Oct. 4, 1799, asking to be notified if there was any chance for aid, Robertson, *Miranda*, p. 341.

he was suspected of being a British agent and was put into prison. Whatever the object of his visit to France might have been, he was given no opportunity to see it fulfilled. He was soon liberated through the influence of a friend, but was ordered to leave the country.[3]

England became again his asylum and the center of his activities. Her interest fluctuated, but it never ceased as long as the colonies were subject to Spain. In the beginning of 1801, under Lord Sidmouth's administration, the government resumed its consideration of the Spanish American project; "even the military operations were sketched and arranged; and the preparations far advanced for the expedition."[4] While Miranda was preparing to go to France, Lord Pelham was giving some attention to revolutionary plans, including those of Sir Ralph Abercromby. He said he was already familiar with the subject, as most of the officials must have been at that time, but he would not proceed without further consideration. If England were shut out from Europe, he said, it would be well if she had looked into this new field.[5] There was still some hope, then, for Miranda's dampened spirits.

Miranda's admirable courage had been severely tested. The United States had destroyed his best opportunity; England had given him hopes, only to shatter them; the king of Spain had issued an order for his punishment by death; and on returning to France he was thrown into prison as an emigré.[6] Then the tide turned. After he regained his freedom he returned to England, and "two of the latest arrived South American commissioners" returned with him. Others were sent back to keep their countrymen quiet until some favorable event took place from which he could profit by the aid of Great Britain or the

---

[3] Robertson, *Miranda*, pp. 347-349; and *Life of Miranda*, I, 212-220.

[4] *The American Register,* V (Part I, 1809), p. 385.

[5] Sept. 1801, Londonderry (ed.), *Correspondence of Castlereagh*, VII, 286.

[6] Robertson, *Miranda*, p. 346. He seems to have been promised protection (*ibid.,* p. 348; Villanueva, *Napoleón y la Independencia*, p. 105).

United States, "the only two countries on which he placed any reliance." He was again given hopes of British aid by the government under Addington. The preliminaries to the Treaty of Amiens, however, prevented any further action at that time.[7]

How Miranda must have hated the word "peace"! It seemed always to interrupt his play. He was in need of a war setting, for then only could the characters play their parts. But with Napoleon at large, he would not have to give up hopes, and the characters were not likely to forget their parts during the brief periods when peace interrupted their rehearsals. It was the peace between the United States and France that had really interrupted the project of 1798. But on October 1, 1800, the day after the treaty was signed with the United States, Napoleon gave rise to a new issue by the Treaty of Ildefonso, which finally brought success to the French efforts to regain Louisiana.[8] This was now to be "a bulwark for Mexico and a security for the tranquility of the Gulf."[9]

When the news of the retrocession leaked out, England expressed the opinion that the "two Americas ought to be alarmed at a change, which above all threatened the Spanish kingdoms of that great continent."[10] France now held New Orleans, which was "the key to Mexico." Here again were causes for apprehension and action and an opportunity for Miranda and his associates. Caro, who was informing Spain of revolutionary activities, spoke of the transfer of the Mississippi to the French as the opportunity about which the former Jesuit, Clavijero, wrote to his colleague, Vizcardo.[11] Their hopes lay now in Philadelphia, he said, where their friends, Mr.

---

[7] "Memorandum of Sir Home Popham," Oct. 14, 1804, *The American Historical Review*, VI, 511 (April, 1901); *The American Register*, V, 387.
[8] Since this treaty was kept secret there was no immediate threat of a rupture.
[9] Quoted by Barbé-Marbois, *History of Louisiana*, p. 170.
[10] *Ibid.*, p. 183.
[11] Probably Vizcardo y Guzmán, who wrote *"Lettre aux Espagnols."* Cf. *The Edinburgh Review*, XIII, 277 ff.

Hamilton, Mr. King, Mr. Smith, and others, assured them that there was no better time to arouse the United States than at a time when they could be stirred by the transfer of Louisiana to the French.[12] A note sent into circulation in September, 1801, declared that the cession of Louisiana and Napoleon's efforts to get territory bordering on the Amazon, "sufficiently disclose the intentions of the French Government with respect to the intermediate provinces . . . to excite the most serious apprehensions on the part of this country."[13] The note also referred to Miranda as saying that France had agents employed in Spanish America "to encourage the people to look to the Republic of France for liberation."[14] It was then advocated that England take a hand to prevent the revolution from being perverted by France. Fear was expressed that, through "the supremacy of France in the councils of the Peninsular courts," she would gain control of "the vast and rich colonies of Spain," lying between Louisiana and Brazil.[15]

The preliminaries to the Peace of Amiens, which restricted England's freedom in dealing with Spanish America, gave Napoleon a greater opportunity to consider prospects for an American empire. Spanish America was continually threatened by the one or the other. Napoleon planned first to secure a convenient base by subduing the Negro revolt in Santo Domingo. The slaves of this colony had been stimulated to revolt by the principles of the French Revolution,[16] and Toussaint L'Ouverture was setting a dangerous example for other European possessions. When asked about the influence of this revolt on the colonies, Lord Grenville admitted that "the

[12] Paris, April 20, 1801, A. G. I., Estado, Caracas, legajo 4.
[13] Londonderry (ed.), *Correspondence of Castlereagh*, VII, 287-288.
[14] Miranda's statement is substantiated by a report on Mexico by such an agent to Napoleon, "*Rapport du ministre de la marine,*" Archive Nationale, AF IV, 1211.
[15] A. T. Mahan, *Influence of Sea Power Upon the French Revolution* (10th ed., 2 vols., Boston, 1898), II, 78; see also Sloane, "Napoleon's Plans for a Colonial System," *The American Historical Review*, IV, 445 (April, 1899).
[16] T. G. Steward, *The Haitian Revolution* (2nd ed., New York, 1914), *passim*.

Colonial System must fall to the ground, we have seen it and nothing remains but to postpone it as long as possible."[17] Toussaint believed in action; and when he drew up a constitution, he made himself ruler for life; hence only in name was he still dependent on France. Bonaparte sent his brother-in-law, Le Clerc, with a large army to convince General L'Ouverture that France and Bonaparte were still supreme, even in Santo Domingo. L'Ouverture had conquered nearly the whole island and had shown remarkable ability as a general, but the "Buonaparte of St. Domingo" was unable to cope with the Buonaparte of Corsica. The French resorted to treachery to capture him, after which he was sent to France where he died in prison.

Bonaparte, like Caesar, was ambitious; and, having partially occupied Santo Domingo, he hoped next to restore or to create a French colonial empire by securing a foothold on the mainland. The retrocession of Louisiana afforded him a preliminary base. His actions were watched with suspicion by the United States and England, as we have seen; likewise, the Spanish authorities, his allies, feared that he would revive the pretentions of La Salle and Crozat in order to conquer Mexico.[18] His American activities might also threaten the Caribbean possessions of the British, and the vastness of the expedition he sent to Santo Domingo alarmed England.[19]

The presence in Mexico of a French observer, who was evidently serving as an agent for Bonaparte, tended to justify the suspicion of the rivals of France and Spain. A long report on the conditions of the country was sent to the French government, and the information given was such as a conqueror would desire. The writer stressed the lack of development,

[17] King to secretary of state, Jan. 10, 1799, King (ed.), *Life and Correspondence of Rufus King*, II, 499-500.
[18] I. J. Cox, "The Louisiana Texas Frontier," *The Quarterly of the Texas State Historical Society*, X, 10 (July, 1906).
[19] Mahan, *Sea Power and the French Revolution*, II, 79.

which he attributed to the policy of isolation and exclusion. There were discontent and a pronounced hatred for the Spanish government, and its authority had been greatly weakened during the recent wars. The result was that England carried on an extensive trade with Mexico—amounting to more than thirty-five million Spanish dollars. This flourishing trade, as one might expect, was carried on via Jamaica and Campeche, and little or no attention was paid to Spanish prohibitions. Efforts at restrictions gave only the outward appearance of efficiency. "The administration in this good country," the agent said, "is vicious in every phase," and in place of improving, it was retrograding. The garrison was weak and the "Spaniards would not be able to give a resistance to a conquest of the country as great as the resistance made when they conquered it."[20]

It was in 1801 that P. F. Page published a book in which he defended the colonizing ability of the French, making it appear greater than the English. He proposed the building of a world empire, "including such diverse regions as Egypt, Madagascar, the Island of Morphil in the Senegal River, Mexico, Peru and St. Domingue. His imagination rivaled that of Bonaparte himself."[21] The Peace of Amiens prevented the open adoption of such grandiose, colonial projects, but a beginning could be made.

Bonaparte's great scheme for a French empire in America met with reverses from the beginning. The long and persistent efforts of the United States to get an outlet on the Gulf were greatly stimulated by the rumors of the retrocession. When Morales, the intendant, withdrew the right of deposit at New Orleans, which the western Americans had had since 1795, there were many Americans who advocated war, to get by conquest what they could not get by negotiation. Yrujo,

[20] *Rapport du ministre de la Marine,* Archive Nationale, AF IV, 1211.
[21] C. L. Lokke, *France and the Colonial Question* (New York, 1932), pp. 231-232.

the Spanish minister at Washington, reported that the newspapers from north to south had spread the war cry and used every imaginable means to arouse the public. The West, in particular, wanted the United States to attack Louisiana.[22] Even Livingston agreed with the plan of Senator Ross that they ought to "acquire the country and negotiate afterwards."[23] It was believed that France was responsible for the order and that this would again bring the United States into the ranks of her enemies. This was important because it tended to renew the critical situation of 1798 with the possibility of a new project of Spanish American liberation. Spain, fearing this and trying to protect her colonies, sought the friendship of the United States by offering to pay the claims of American citizens against Spanish subjects.[24]

In case of war England could again seek the coöperation of the United States in the revolutionary projects; and the Peace of Amiens, which was signed in March, 1802, was known to be nothing more than a truce. Lord Hawkesbury, explaining the actions of the government, said, "We only wished to make an experimental peace."[25] Public discontent in England coupled with Napoleon's hostile attitude made war seem inevitable, and each country accused the other of not living up to the terms of the treaty.

Even Jefferson, who had generally looked upon France as an ally and a friend, recognized the possibility of war when he heard of the retrocession of Louisiana. It was then that he made the well-known statement: "From that moment we must marry ourselves to the British fleet and nation." And it is

---

[22] Yrujo to Captain General of Cuba, Jan. 25, 1803, A. G. I., *Papeles de Cuba*, legajo 1708.

[23] James K. Hosmer, *The History of the Louisiana Purchase* (New York, 1902), p. 138.

[24] Adams, *History of the United States*, II, 21-22.

[25] Barbé-Marbois, *The History of Louisiana*, p. 183. Details of the negotiations are told in Ward and Gooch (eds.), *Cambridge History of British Foreign Policy*, I, 309-327.

quite possible that he thought this marriage would be blessed by the birth of one or more new nations. His plans certainly were not limited to the Mississippi, for he said that the first cannon fired in Europe would be "the signal for tearing up any settlement she may have made, and for holding the two continents of America in sequestration for the common purposes of the British and American nations."[26] It would seem, therefore, that all the Spanish American possessions were dependent on the apparently small detail of a right of deposit at the mouth of the Mississippi, or, as Livingston said, on "a wilderness and an insignificant city."

Livingston informed the minister of foreign affairs that by seizing this territory France forced the United States to take the side of England, making the latter power the mistress of the New World.[27] He probably exaggerated for effect, but it is known that England had long sought to win advantages by liberating Spanish America. King wrote to Pickering that it was his "firm belief that if the war break out, that Great Britain will immediately attempt the emancipation and independence of South America,"[28] again meaning Spanish America, for Addington informed King that one of the first steps would perhaps be the occupation of New Orleans. Then King immediately warned the minister that the United States anticipated annexation of this territory.[29] And England would surely be willing to settle her differences with the United States in the face of her greater rivalry with France. Further assurance of American support was given when Livingston and Monroe were instructed by a letter of April 18, 1803, that if France failed to comply with the demands of the United States, they were to start negotiations for coöperation with

---

[26] Barbé-Marbois, *The History of Louisiana*, note by translator, p. 229.
[27] *Ibid.*, pp. 414-417.
[28] April 2, 1803, Robertson, *Miranda*, p. 352, n. *e*.
[29] *Ibid.*

England.³⁰ It was not, however, Jefferson's unusual threat of war which decided the fate of Louisiana.

It is more likely that the moderating influence of Jefferson's French friend, Du Pont de Nemours, contributed the most towards a peaceful settlement of the Louisiana question. Du Pont was especially interested in the success of American democracy, and he thought that a war for the conquest of Louisiana would give the military factions and the adventurers the upper hand; and these, he said, were anxious for the conquest of Mexico. He believed that the desire was quite general in America. There was also the prospect of Mexico's becoming independent as a result of a war over Louisiana. Then if she set up a monarchy she would not be a desirable ally of the United States, whose chief mission was to preserve liberty. And even if Mexico became a democracy there would be no real advantage to the United States, he believed, for it might fall into the hands of selfish military and political adventurers. Therefore, he added that it were best for the United States if Mexico remained in the hands of Spain, which she probably would not if a war were fought over the possession of Louisiana. He then suggested to Jefferson that, to deal successfully with Napoleon, he should offer to negotiate on a business basis, and not threaten war.³¹ It is reasonable to believe that Du Pont de Nemours deserves considerable credit for the remarkable success of the negotiations. On the other side, however, was the situation in which Napoleon found himself.

That Bonaparte's ambitions had made him look beyond Louisiana in planning his colonial empire was not only believed by his enemies but also substantiated by his agent's report from Mexico. Several factors contributed to the failure of his colonial plans. The desperate resistance of the natives

---

[30] Barbé-Marbois, *History of Louisiana*, Appendix No. 18, pp. 445-449.
[31] Gilbert Chinard (ed.), *The Correspondence of Jefferson and Du Pont de Nemours* (Oxford, 1931), p. xxxiii; see especially the letter of Du Pont to Jefferson, New York, April 30, 1802, *ibid.*, pp. 48-54.

under Toussaint L'Ouverture and Dessalines, coupled with the devastating influence of yellow fever, soon forced Le Clerc's army to give up in despair. The failure of the Santo Domingo expedition, the danger of war with England, the difficulty of defending distant possessions against a great naval power, and the immediate need for money made Napoleon decide to sell Louisiana. This he considered a blow at the English, and he said he would "prevent their ruling America as they rule in Asia."[32] Monroe and Livingston were exceedingly fortunate in their negotiations, and came to an agreement with Napoleon's representative, Barbé-Marbois, on April 30,[33] by which the "key to Mexico" was sold to the United States. This was a tremendous step for the United States, but the title was not entirely clear, and the conflicting boundary claims served as potential material for a future conflict with Spain.

The Louisiana Purchase again prevented the joint action of Americans and Englishmen in a liberation project, but the renewal of the war between England and France in May, 1803, created a greater incentive for English participation in such a project. Miranda felt encouraged and continued his efforts to arouse the British to action. He consulted Fullarton, who had been interested in Spanish America since 1781. Other material was available, for General Dumouriez was in England at this time and might have been amenable to revolutionary plans, but Miranda refused to see his former colleague of the French Revolution.[34] There were, however, a number of Englishmen who could be relied on for support and aid.

In November Sir Home Popham, who had been destined to lead one of the proposed expeditions of 1790, drew up plans for an expedition to the Plata. It is a long jump from La Plata to Mexico, but Popham considered the La Plata expedi-

---

[32] Barbé-Marbois, *History of Louisiana*, p. 260.
[33] Hosmer, *History of Louisiana*, p. 141, and Appendix, pp. 221-223.
[34] Christopher Gore to Rufus King, Aug. 30, 1803, King (ed.), *Life and Correspondence of Rufus King*, IV, 298-300 and 313-315.

tion secondary to the occupation of Caracas, and later they could continue on to Santa Fé and to Quito, "and ultimately establish a powerful and permanent post on the Isthmus of Panama." Among the points most suitable for military establishments on the Pacific, he had named Acapulco. It is quite evident, then, that the La Plata expedition was not limited to that region, but was to be one point of attack for the liberation of all Spanish America.[35] Mr. Davidson, a merchant, offered the government three or four Indiamen and two smaller vessels for the expedition. They would need only fifteen hundred men at first, "for the moment the expedition sails and that it can be made public, issue letters of service for a Mexican legion, and you will have 2000 recruits in a few weeks."[36]

During the Addington ministry plans were carried out for a revolutionary expedition according to promises made to Miranda after his last return from France. But on April 7 the government gave orders to suspend the preparations, very likely due to the change which was about to take place in the British cabinet.[37] For a short time England gave little heed to Miranda and he was becoming discouraged; but she had not given up his project, and waited only for the renewal of hostilities with Spain to resume the revolutionary plans.

In fact, similar ideas were being advocated by others during the summer. A document bearing the name of Donald Campbell and dated August 14, 1804, made a detailed description of England's relations with Europe and America. "I must premise," he wrote:

that Spain has long considered her Colonies in America as held by a very slender tenure; which must necessarily weaken with the increasing Naval Power of Great Britain; which power she is obliged to oppose from the more immediate influence in France; but she

---

[35] Sir Home Popham to Secretary Yorke, Nov. 26, 1803, Londonderry (ed.), *Correspondence of Castlereagh*, VII, 288-293.
[36] *Ibid.*, VII, 293.
[37] Villanueva, *Napoleon y la Independencia*, pp. 119-120.

consoles herself with the prospect of possessing Portugal by means of that very alliance, which may be the cause of depriving her of her Colonies.[38]

England, who was about to deprive Spain of her colonies because of her alliance with France, would also have to support Portugal to prevent France from taking Brazil, "an acquisition of such eminent importance, that we must consider it as impossible to have escaped the enterprising views of Bonaparte's overgrown ambition." Both the Portuguese and the Spanish colonies had now become the object of the old rivals, England and France. Spain, who for a time was frightened by the "revolutionary mania," considered moving her government to America until France was again a monarchy; but she had been caught in the Napoleonic scheme, not daring to oppose France because of ambition on one side and of fear on the other.[39]

Bonaparte's greatest objective and obstacle was, of course, England. She had prevented the funds of Mexico from reaching Spain and ultimately France. For a time, at least, Bonaparte thought he would gain all by an invasion of England. "Eight hours of night favourable to us would decide the fate of the world," he said.[40] The Anglo-French contest was indeed a world contest and the wealth of Spanish America was of utmost importance.

William Pitt was the man who saw the scope of the contest and he recognized the significance of the Spanish colonies and their wealth. When he replaced Addington he renewed the study of the revolutionary plans together with Lord Melville (Henry Dundas) and Sir Home Popham.[41] Just before Spain declared war on England in 1804, Miranda had a conference with Pitt and Lord Melville at Wimbledon. Sir Home Pop-

[38] London, Aug. 14, 1804, P. R. O., Chatham Papers, Vol. CCCXLV.
[39] *Ibid.*
[40] J. Holland Rose, *Pitt and Napoleon, Essays and Letters* (London, 1912), p. 120.
[41] *The American Register*, V, 387; Robertson, *Miranda*, p. 355.

ham was present, and gave a detailed memorandum[42] to show how England could harm France through Spain, "and at the same time improve British commerce by aiding Miranda's projects for the independence of the colonies."[43] He continued to emphasize the French danger and said that Napoleon was merely waiting for an opportunity "to offer some political plea for sending an army to Vera Cruz for the purpose of gaining possession of the rich province of Mexico, and putting an effectual stop to any expedition from the United States."[44]

A questionnaire, with complete answers, dated October 19, 1804, surveyed the political conditions of the time and stressed Spanish America. It was quite in keeping with the revolutionary plans, and spoke of a man who knew the language, the country, and the conditions, and who could be relied on for any information on revolutionary possibilities. If the English intended to make use of this man they would have to act at once, for he might not remain long in that part of the globe.[45] The writer of the questionnaire believed that the inhabitants of the Pacific coast were less devoted to Spain than those of the Atlantic coast, and therefore considered the former territory as the logical place for the introduction of revolutionary ideas. He suggested that the objective to hold out to the natives was independence and this should be done by means of pamphlets in Spanish to be distributed as soon as the expedition landed. At this time Pitt was making preparations to capture the Spanish treasure fleet because of Spain's help to Napoleon

[42] "Miranda and the British Admiralty, 1804-1806," *The American Historical Review*, VI, 509-517.

[43] Josceline Bagot (ed.), *George Canning and his Friends* (2 vols., London, 1909), I, 264-265.

[44] Popham referred to Napoleon's plans of conquest in South America, but, like many others, he meant all of Spanish America. See his explanation in "Miranda and the British Admiralty, 1804-1806," *The American Historical Review*, VI, 512.

[45] Murdoch to Eliot, Downing Street, Oct. 19, 1804, P. R. O., Chatham Papers, Vol. CCCXLV. Perhaps the man referred to was Miranda, who had recently considered leaving England; cf. Robertson, *Miranda*, p. 353.

and the French navy.[46] It would not be unreasonable to believe that Pitt hoped for more than a treasure fleet and sought the source of this wealth. He had sufficient reason for proceeding against Spanish America since Spain had been paying subsidies to his enemy, Napoleon, and had also helped to equip his fleet.[47] England was preparing for the time when hostilities would give her "a fair opportunity" to deprive Spain "of all her Continental Colonies."[48]

In the meantime William Jacob, "traveller and miscellaneous writer," suggested a threefold attack on Spanish America.[49] In October, 1804, when Spain declared war on England, Sir Home Popham drew up his memorandum on the revolutionary project. The details of the requirements had already been submitted to Lord Melville by Miranda. Popham raised a number of questions to which he gave his own answers to show that Spain and her American resources were under the control of France. After submitting his plan, he was willing to agree to any better one if its advantages were greater than those described of "ultimately annihilating one fleet, of cutting off fifteen millions from the Revenue of France, and probably adding to our own, and raising in that proportion our consequence in Europe."[50] In spite of her great interest England remained inactive, but Spain's possessions in North America were now threatened by revolutionists from the United States.

The Louisiana Purchase marked a decline in the interest of the United States in immediate revolutionary projects. It prevented her from going to war with Spain and France. "But for this," writes McCaleb, "Mexico and other Spanish-American colonies would have been earlier revolutionized."[51] Diffi-

---

[46] J. Holland Rose, *Wm. Pitt and the Great War* (London, 1911), pp. 513-514.
[47] Mahan, *Influence of Sea Power upon the French Revolution*, II, 138; Ward and Gooch (eds.), *The Cambridge History of British Foreign Policy*, I, 333-334.
[48] Quoted by Robertson, *Miranda*, p. 355.   [49] *Ibid.*
[50] For Popham's memorandum, see "Miranda and the British Admiralty, 1804-1806," *The American Historical Review*, VI, 509-517.
[51] W. F. McCaleb, *The Aaron Burr Conspiracy* (New York, 1903), p. 14.

culties with Spain were by no means at an end; in fact, the advance of the Anglo-Americans was to be an ever-present cause of friction and an excuse for hostile actions along an undetermined boundary.

Those who had once set their hearts on getting the American republic to spread her revolutionary influence to the neighboring country continued to foster the idea. There were still men in the United States who were interested, and Miranda continued to write to King about his needs, including "a hundred or two hundred brave Americans."[52] Rufus King, after returning to the United States, in touch with events in London through Christopher Gore, wrote to the latter in January, 1804, that Miranda "may yet see his wishes accomplished." He added that "Should he make a beginning, the news would electrify this country, which contains an immense number of individuals, who would be ready to take up their bed and walk."[53]

Such was the situation after this "bulwark," this "wall of brass," this "dam," and "key," which was to protect the Spanish colonies by being returned to France, had been handed over to the dreaded enemy—contrary to expectations, beliefs, and promises. Louisiana was no longer a barrier; it was a gateway. Further proof of the American menace to the Spanish Empire was soon to be seen in the Burr project.

[52] Aug. 23, 1803, King (ed.), *Life and Correspondence of Rufus King*, IV, 517-518.
[53] *Ibid.*, IV, 429.

CHAPTER XIII

BOUNDARIES AND BURR

"The Mexican project of 1806 was perhaps the most magnificent enterprise ever conceived upon the American continent—with the exception, possibly, of Citizen Genêt's, which had also included Canada within its scope."—SAMUEL H. WANDELL and MEADE MINNIGERODE.

"James Wilkinson . . . was an unstable foundation for the cornerstone of empire."—FREDERICK L. PAXSON.

THE American frontier was ever noted for its love of liberty, its irritation at restraint, and its scant respect for boundaries. The westerners were the personification of freedom, but they were not necessarily tolerant; in fact, they were quite intolerant of Spanish institutions and Spanish barriers, and they were filled with "painful solicitude for the unfortunate millions she held in bondage."[1] These independent Americans could be depended upon to sympathize with any opposition to privilege and the divine right of kings. Nor did they lack leaders to stir that sympathy to action: one is immediately reminded of Genêt, Clark, Adet, Blount, Kemper, Wilkinson, and Burr as some of the more conspicuous promoters of border hostilities. The Spanish government knew full well what class of neighbors it had to deal with, and it is not surprising that it should prohibit any inhabitant of Louisiana from entering Mexico, "for he had but one object in view—to strike a blow at Spain."[2]

While the boundaries of Louisiana remained undetermined there was a continual threat of conflict. Whenever Spain attempted to interfere with the freedom of the advancing frontiersman, she was considered a tyrant which ought to be removed. West Florida was one of the debatable lands which

[1] McCaleb, *The Burr Conspiracy*, p. 13.
[2] Salcedo to Cordero, Jan. 9, 1804, *ibid.*, p. 12.

was rapidly overrun by the irresistible stream of Anglo-Americans. In places like Baton Rouge they were more numerous than the Spaniards, and were "inclined to insubordination and prone to insurgency."[3] The Kemper insurrection during the summer of 1804 was largely one of border ruffians, "white Indians and river pirates." But when they were opposed by the Spanish authorities and driven into American territory, they returned at the head of thirty followers to march on Baton Rouge. They took themselves so seriously that they actually brought along a proclamation of independence and even carried a flag.[4]

The proclamation shows clearly the views of the dissatisfied Americans in the Spanish borderlands, and justified the Spanish policy of exclusion. Part of the declaration reads as follows:

> For a people to be free it is sufficient that they will it. Whereas, the despotism under which we have long groaned, has grown into an unsupportable burthen, and as it is long since admitted men are born with equal rights, we the undersigned, inhabitants of that part of the dominions called West Florida, have resolved to throw off the galling yoke of tyranny and become freemen, by declaring ourselves a free and independent people, and by supporting with our lives and property that declaration.[5]

Their "fellow sufferers" were then invited to aid in the "common emancipation." When they had accomplished their independence they would offer themselves "to some government accustomed to freedom." The Spanish authorities suspected the United States of encouraging the affair. It is quite possible that Jefferson merely anticipated it and regarded it with noncommital interest.[6] The rebels failed to arouse a general re-

---

[3] I. J. Cox, *The West Florida Controversy, 1798-1813* (Baltimore, 1918), p. 153.
[4] *Ibid.*, pp. 155-156.
[5] Professor Cox says the proclamation was "supposedly the work of Edmund Randolph of Pinckneyville, a partner of Daniel Clark." It was printed in the *Charleston (S. C.) Courier*, Sept. 2, 1804; cf. Cox, *The West Florida Controversy*, p. 155, n. 26.
[6] *Ibid.*, p. 151.

volt, and Grand Pré, captain of the Spanish army at Baton Rouge, successfully defended his country against the outlaws.[7]

A greater stir was created by the "Burr Conspiracy" which has generally been clothed in mystery, not on account of a lack of information, but owing to several contradictory views, depending on the group that was informed, and because the project was stopped before being realized. The apparent contradictions can be partly explained by the fact that Burr could not go through with his project without considerable aid, and especially the encouragement of a foreign power; and since he could not hope to keep it secret, he had to have a scheme ready for nearly every occasion and person—for the English he had one project, for the Spanish he had another, and for the westerners, who were to be his chief supporters, he had a third, probably the real one.

The disastrous duel with Hamilton had definitely ended Burr's career in national politics. But Aaron Burr, brilliant and ambitious, proceeded at once to occupy himself with a new project, that of Mexican independence. He is reported to have been interested in the liberation of Spanish America ever since 1796, when he had considered the subject together with Jay.[8] Hamilton's interest in the project was now assumed by his rival and slayer.

Now that the French "wall of brass" had been removed by the sale of Louisiana there was an opportunity to see if the French predictions had been correct. De Onís wrote that Louisiana had become a gateway for adventurers into Mexico.[9] Burr determined to make use of the gateway. He was bold enough to ask Casa Yrujo, the Spanish minister at Washington, for a passport to Mexico, pretending that he could no longer stay in the United States after his duel with Hamilton.[10]

During the summer of 1805 Burr traveled through the West

[7] For a more detailed account, see *ibid.*, pp. 153-163.
[8] M. L. Davis (ed.), *Memoirs of Aaron Burr* (2 vols., New York, 1837), II, 376.
[9] McCaleb, *Burr Conspiracy*, p. 14.   [10] *Ibid.*, p. 24.

to win support for his enterprise. He met Henry Clay in Kentucky, and by the end of May he had reached Nashville, where he spent several days with Andrew Jackson. Speaking of Jackson's sympathy for Burr, Henry Adams wrote: ". . . if his support was enlisted for the duellist who had killed Hamilton, his passions were excited in favor of the man who should drive the Spaniards from America."[11] Burr announced that this was the mission of his life, and, "as major-general of the Tennessee militia, Jackson looked forward to sharing his exploit."[12] The news spread rapidly, and to the frontiersmen in general, "it was a battle-cry they were only too eager to answer." They considered themselves as *adelantados* and *conquistadores* rather than adventurers and filibusters.

Next to Burr, General Wilkinson was, no doubt, the most important man for the success of the expedition. On May 28 he wrote to Adair about Burr. "Prepare to visit me," he said, "and I will tell you all. We must have a peep at the unknown world beyond me."[13] Wilkinson later met Burr at Fort Massac, where they spent four days, very likely talking over the plans.[14] When Burr left for New Orleans he had a letter from the General to Daniel Clark which was to serve as an introduction. Burr would enlighten him on "many things, improper to letter, and which he will not say to any other."[15] On June 24, the day before Burr reached New Orleans, Wilkinson signed the instructions for Pike, which, according to Timothy Kibby and John Adair, provided for his exploration of the way to Santa Fé and the mines of Mexico.[16] Others were consulted to get their views on the possibility of conquering Mexico and of establishing a military empire in Louisiana.

[11] Adams, *History of the United States*, III, 221.
[12] *Ibid.*   [13] *Ibid.*
[14] McCaleb, *Burr Conspiracy*, p. 27.
[15] In his defense Wilkinson asserted that the secret referred to elections. Letter of June 9, 1805, James Wilkinson, *Memoirs of my own Times* (3 vols., Philadelphia, 1816), II, Appendix lxxi.
[16] McCaleb, *Burr Conspiracy*, p. 28.

Burr was well pleased with his reception in New Orleans. It is quite likely that he came into contact with the Mexican Association. This was an organization of about three hundred Americans who were collecting information on Mexico which might be useful to the United States in case of war with Spain.[17] Lieutenant Spence admitted that there had been such an organization for several years and that its object was to discuss means of emancipating Mexico.[18] *The American Register* stated that the Association

> had assumed a character eminently elevated above all schemes of petty warfare and pillage. The object was ... to raise the standard of natural rights, political liberty, and free trade, in the face of opposing armies; and deliver one of the fairest portions of the globe from a most odious system of colonial bondage, conceived in tyranny, and nursed in fear, ignorance, and weakness.

The project required, "like the American Revolution, the sanction of success, to reflect immortal honour on all engaged in it."[19] Burr was believed to be a member of this organization, although he denied it. Daniel Clark disclaimed being a member, "but if his safety as a merchant required him to keep aloof, his sympathies were wholly with the Association," says Henry Adams.[20] Even the higher government officials, such as John Watkins, mayor of New Orleans, and James Workman, judge of the county court, were members. The existence of such an organization is a fairly good indication that Burr had come to a suitable place to get support for his project.

Burr selected an opportune time for his expedition. The king of Spain, hard pressed because of the European war and ignoring the economic and social conditions of New Spain, ordered the clergy to collect over forty-four million dollars owed to the church by landholders and others. T. Esquival

---

[17] *Ibid.*, p. 29. Dr. Watkins, mayor of New Orleans, said that an invasion of Mexico had always been considered in case of a war with "the dons," *ibid.*, p. 113.
[18] Wilkinson, *Memoirs*, II, 283 n.   [19] *The American Register*, II, 103 n.
[20] *History of the United States*, III, 223.

Obregon said of this that, "not only was he not obeyed, but fears lest agriculture be ruined aroused the ideas of independence among the aristocracy." He added this significant statement: "That unwise order was the death sentence of the power of Spain in Mexico."[21]

Burr's objective was to make use of all favorable circumstances and link them into one for a general movement which he wished to direct. Daniel Clark made several commercial voyages to Mexico and collected all the data he could. It is said that he had several conferences with military officials at Vera Cruz who were in favor of revolution.[22] And the viceroy of Mexico informed Casa Yrujo that Burr had been collecting information on Vera Cruz from Daniel Clark.[23] A Catholic bishop of New Orleans gave his support to Burr and, like Miranda, suggested the use of former Jesuits for agents.[24] The support which Burr was getting from all sides probably made him careless, and he must have trusted too many; for on September 7, 1805, shortly before he arrived in St. Louis on his return journey, Clark wrote to Wilkinson about some wild rumors. These rumors, which had already reached Spanish ears, intimated that the West was to separate from the Union and that it was "to be bribed with the plunder of the Spanish countries west of us." The following quotation from his letter will indicate what the rest of the rumors were:

But let not these great and important objects, these almost imperial doings, prevent you from attending to my land business. Recollect that you great men, if you intend to become kings and emperors, must have us little men for vassals.

He would need land and produce if he were to "buy a decent court dress" for the levée, he said. The imperial schemes were

[21] Obregon, "Factors in the Historical Evolution of Mexico," *The Hispanic American Historical Review*, II, 151.

[22] Davis (ed.), *Memoirs of Burr*, II, 382.

[23] Casa Yrujo to Someruelos, Philadelphia, Dec. 10, 1806, A. G. I., Papeles de Cuba, legajo 1708.

[24] Davis (ed.), *Memoirs of Burr*, II, 382.

probably interfering with Clark's trade, and his ironic treatment of the affair tended to make the cold facts seem incongruous. Such was undoubtedly his purpose when he added: "I hope you will have Kentucky men for your masters of ceremony."[25]

Burr's enterprise was getting a great deal of publicity.[26] Reports of his military preparations reached Texas in July. Merry wrote to England that the enterprise was under way. Casa Yrujo read the same reports as the others, and probably added some of his own to prevent Burr from doing anything contrary to the interest of Spain.[27] "The supposed expedition against Mexico," he wrote, "is ridiculous and chimerical in the present state of things; but I am not unaware that Burr, in order to get moneys from the English Minister or from England, has made to him some such proposition, in which he is to play the leading rôle."[28] McCaleb considers that both the British and the Spanish ministers were duped.[29]

Burr had sought financial aid from England, at first supposedly for an enterprise which involved the separation of the West from the Union. Cevallos, having received Casa Yrujo's report on Burr's attempt to get British aid, expressed the opinion that the British would not grant aid for this purpose.[30] Charles Williamson, Burr's representative in London, made a more reasonable appeal when he requested the British to support an American enterprise in Mexico, giving as his argument the same one which was used by Miranda for the rest of Spanish America, that such an undertaking would prevent the

---

[25] Wilkinson, *Memoirs*, II, Appendix xxxiii. Clark denied having any connection with the project. See his *Proofs of the Corruption of General Wilkinson* (Philadelphia, 1809), pp. 94 ff.

[26] Newspapers of the West took up the story, but Burr's enterprise lost little of its uncertainty or romance through publicity.

[27] Professor Cox has expressed the opinion that Yrujo was building a backfire to Burr's project. Letter to the author, Evanston, Ill., March 31, 1933.

[28] Yrujo to Cevallos, Aug. 5, 1805, quoted by McCaleb, *Burr Conspiracy*, p. 39.

[29] *Ibid.*, p. viii.

[30] Feb., 1806, Archivo del Ministro de Estado, legajo 213, L. of C. transcript.

French from getting control of the commerce of the Spanish colonies.[31] This plan could be equally advantageous to Americans and British, and particularly agreeable to the westerners.

By the middle of November Burr returned to Washington, apparently satisfied with the favor his project had received in the West. McCaleb writes:

> Everywhere through the Western country he had been applauded as the leader who was to march an army to the heart of the Kingdom of Mexico, giving freedom to her enslaved millions, and, incidentally, fortunes to his followers.[32]

While Burr was negotiating with Merry, the peer of plotters appeared in America.

Miranda left England to make use of the strained relations in which Spain and the United States found themselves, and appeared in New York in November, 1805. He was encouraged by some of his old acquaintances, such as Rufus King, Colonel Smith, and Christopher Gore.[33] Before he reached Washington, Jefferson was warned that Miranda's actions formed a link in "Burr's Maneuver's."[34] Burr met Miranda in Philadelphia and later admitted that he was "greatly pleased with his talents and colloquial eloquence,"[35] but was careful to avoid the subject of their common interest. Several of Burr's friends were attracted to the South American, but Burr did not want to play a secondary rôle to Miranda. Eaton reported in Burr's trial that when he had suggested Miranda as an impediment to the Mexican project, Burr's response was, "We must hang Miranda."[36] Yrujo said in January, 1806, that Miranda had returned to New York, "much piqued at finding that Col-

---

[31] I. J. Cox, "Hispanic-American Phases of the 'Burr Conspiracy'," *The Hispanic American Historical Review*, XII, 148-152 (May, 1932).
[32] McCaleb, *Burr Conspiracy*, p. 41.
[33] Robertson, *Miranda*, p. 362.
[34] *Ibid.*, p. 363.
[35] Henry Adams says he spoke of him with contempt, *History of the United States*, III, 189; cf. Robertson, *Life of Miranda*, I, 294.
[36] *Annals of Congress, 1807-1808* (10th Congress, 1st Session), I, 404.

onel Burr was very determined to have nothing to do with him."[37]

During the early part of the year 1806 Burr continued to negotiate with Yrujo and others for help, but with doubtful progress. He wrote to Blennerhasset and Wilkinson in April, saying that the project would not begin until December, "owing to want of water in Ohio," although the real reason was the lack of support from Merry and Yrujo.[38] The Spanish authorities were already suspicious. While there was probably no direct connection between Monroe's departure from Madrid and the arrival of Burr in the West, the reports of these facts caused no little uneasiness among the Spanish authorities. Officials on the border and Gulf Coast feared that Monroe's departure might be the first step towards hostilities, and the dissatisfaction of the American frontiersmen, because of Monroe's failure to secure a favorable settlement of the Louisiana boundary, added to this fear.[39] The frontier officials were urged to strengthen their defenses against ten thousand men from Kentucky who were preparing to invade the country. Morales wrote from Pensacola to the viceroy of Mexico that "there exists in New Orleans a strong party whose object it is to revolutionize the kingdom of Mexico, and the conditions on the frontier are entirely favorable to such a design."[40] The inspector-general of troops in Texas, Francisco Viana, supported the last statement and said: "I have neither munitions, arms, provisions, nor soldiers wherewith to uphold our authority."[41] Such were the opinions of Spanish officials who really knew the conditions on the frontier. The sanguine hopes of the conspirators were, therefore, not without foundation.

[37] Adams, *History of the United States*, III, 189. See also Cox, "Hispanic American phases of the 'Burr Conspiracy'," *The Hispanic American Historical Review*, XII, 161-164.

[38] McCaleb, *Burr Conspiracy*, p. 63.

[39] Isaac J. Cox, "The Louisiana-Texas Frontier during the Burr Conspiracy," *The Mississippi Valley Historical Review*, X, 274-276 (Dec., 1923).

[40] McCaleb, *Burr Conspiracy*, p. 64.

[41] Letter to Cordero, June 3, 1806, *ibid.*, p. 65.

Burr met with difficulties in the East. Cevallos had informed Yrujo that the king would not encourage Burr's designs;[42] and as for Merry, the answer he received from the British government was that of being recalled.[43] The death of Pitt and the impeachment of Melville were significant factors in the change of British policy. Burr, undaunted, now turned again to the West. He wrote to Wilkinson on July 29 that all was in readiness, even the naval protection of England. He would move down from the Falls with five hundred or a thousand men and would meet Wilkinson at Natchez in December, where they would determine whether to "seize on or pass by Baton Rouge." The people of the country to which they were going were ready to receive them, providing, as their agents had told Burr, that they could retain their religion and not be subject to a foreign power, then, "in three weeks all will be settled."[44]

The country referred to must have been Mexico. Herman Blennerhasset, too, who had hoped to recoup his dwindling fortune by participating in the enterprise, said that the design was "unequivocally against Mexico."[45] Many others were supporting the movement, and, as *The National Intelligencer* stated, they were men who would not be likely "to engage in a treasonable plot against their country."[46] While considering the real destination of Burr's expedition it might be well to speak here of the fact that he had three carefully made maps: one of Mexico from California to the Isthmus, one of the Gulf coast, and the third was a detailed topographical map of the territory from Vera Cruz to Mexico City.[47]

The separation of the western states from the Union was

---

[42] July 18, 1806, Adams, *History of the United States*, III, 249.
[43] *Ibid.*, III, 250.
[44] McCaleb, *Burr Conspiracy*, pp. 74-75; cf. *The American Register*, II, 90.
[45] McCaleb, *Burr Conspiracy*, p. 79.
[46] This article called it Burr's "expedition against Mexico," *ibid.*, p. 80.
[47] *Ibid.*, p. 85. The third is reproduced by McCaleb, *Burr Conspiracy*, frontispiece. See also *The American Register*, II, 90.

a reasonable project until 1795. The treaty of San Lorenzo had partially satisfied the settlers of the Mississippi Valley, but not sufficiently to insure their undivided allegiance. The purchase of Louisiana had, however, definitely established the national government as a friend of the West. There was henceforth very little chance of winning material support for an independent state in the Mississippi Valley. There was, nevertheless, on the part of the French in Louisiana, a feeling of hostility toward their newly acquired masters which could probably have been stirred to acts of resistance. The Anglo-Americans were by this time sufficiently loyal to the government not to have supported Burr in any project which threatened the Union, and without their support he could scarcely have hoped to succeed. Burr had purchased a large tract of land on the Washita, known as the Bastrop lands, which furnished him an excellent excuse for his interest in the West, and was to be a haven of refuge in case his project did not materialize. But the situation was still favorable.

Burr's hopes rested on the possibility of a war between the United States and Spain, and such an event was not at all unlikely. The United States had claims against the Spanish government for the seizure of American vessels. There were other claims for losses due to the suppression of the right of deposit at New Orleans in 1802. But what was more likely to give Burr his opportunity was the controversy over the boundary question in Louisiana.[48] Monroe had been unable to get any satisfaction at the Spanish Court; therefore, on May 18, he demanded his passports and received them with unusual promptness.[49] When he left for England Spain continued to plunder American commerce. Pinckney left in October and Spain continued her depredations. George W. Erving was sent

---

[48] These same difficulties were summed up by Robertson to show why Miranda might expect aid from the United States, *Miranda*, p. 361; and *Life of Miranda*, I, 293.

[49] Adams, *History of the United States*, III, 36.

from London as charge d'affaires, and still Spain continued to attack American commerce. Then Godoy calmly inquired how affairs were getting along, and said to Erving: "You may choose either peace or war. 'Tis the same thing to me. I will tell you candidly, that if you will go to war this certainly is the moment, and you may take our possessions from us."[50] This was the condition at the end of 1805, and the difficulties remained unsettled during the greater part of the next year so that Burr might well expect war.

Jefferson's message to Congress was most encouraging.[51] The president criticized Spain for her failure to settle their difficulties, for destruction of property, for obstruction of commerce, and for hindering the boundary settlement. Some of these injuries, he said, "are of a nature to be met by force only, and all of them may lead to it." And the thought of war, said the editor of *The American Register:*

... naturally fills the bold and adventurous mind with images of golden candlesticks and silver platters. Mexico is the native country of dollars, the treasures of which are only defended by unarmed monks or disaffected slaves. Its wealthy provinces are easily overrun by hardy soldiers, and the enemy is easily concealed under the mask of a deliverer. A rebellious temper will greedily listen to the promise of foreign succor, and blind them to the folly of confiding in the generosity of strangers and tyrants. Such were the images that naturally thronged the minds of many of the western people.[52]

What the people believed, and not the actual conditions, would determine their actions. Finally we have Colonel Burr's opinion in a letter to Senator Smith. "If there shall be a war between the United States and Spain," he wrote, "I shall head a corps of volunteers and be the first to march into the Mexican provinces. If peace should be proffered, which I do not expect,

[50] *Ibid.*, III, 38.
[51] Dec. 3, 1805, Daniel James Richardson, *A Compilation of the Messages and Papers of the Presidents, 1789-1897* (10 vols., Washington, 1899), I, 384-385.
[52] *The American Register*, II, 87.

I shall settle my Washita lands, and make society as pleasant as possible."[53] This sounds quite reasonable.

The Spaniards had forces across the Sabine on territory claimed by the United States, and "Every militiaman in the West was furbishing his accoutrements and awaiting the summons to the field."[54] Jackson, whom Burr was again visiting, thought war was inevitable.[55] The whole affair was to be started by Wilkinson's attacking the Spaniards at Arroyo Hondo. He had received orders to be on the defensive, but little was needed to make two hostile armies come to blows. On September 25 Wilkinson wrote that he would soon have a meeting with the Spaniards. The people of the United States expected war; many of them wanted war, some to vindicate the rights of the United States and others to free the Mexicans.[56]

Spain was not blind to her danger, and Godoy's frank statements were not as startling as they appeared, because the views expressed were common knowledge. Casa Yrujo, too, had heard that Burr had abandoned the plan of separating the western states and of taking Florida, and that he was planning an expedition against Mexico. The rumor still seemed ridiculous to him; but since it applied to a character like Burr, who was governed only by "impulse and his ambitions," it should be reported to the viceroy of Mexico in order that he might guard the Texas border and watch the conduct and movements of the suspect.[57] Yrujo sent an agent of his own, José Vidal, to the Ohio to watch the actions of Burr.[58]

The viceroy of New Spain was either better informed or more frank about the activities and plans of Burr than the

[53] Quoted by Wandell and Minnigerode, *Burr*, II, 96.
[54] Quoted by McCaleb, *Burr Conspiracy*, p. 81.
[55] It has also been suggested that Burr expected the government to sanction his project in case of war, *ibid.*, p. 84. Adair said of Burr's expedition to Mexico that "without a war he could do nothing," Davis (ed.), *Memoirs of Burr*, II, 380.
[56] McCaleb, *Burr Conspiracy*, p. 110.
[57] Yrujo to Someruelos, Philadelphia, Nov. 16, 1806, A. G. I., Papeles de Cuba, legajo 1708.
[58] Wandell and Minnigerode, *Burr*, II, 101.

Spanish minister in Philadelphia, and, being suspicious, sent additional warnings to the minister. Burr had been collecting information on Mexico for about a year, he wrote, and had shown special interest in Vera Cruz and its surroundings and in the port of Tampico or Pánuco. Daniel Clark or one of his companions, he believed, had furnished much of the data on Vera Cruz. The viceroy did not believe that Burr had any armed vessels for an attack, nor did Vera Cruz have an adequate number of vessels to defend itself, he added. That Burr could take four or five thousand adventurers from New Orleans to the coast of Mexico in merchant vessels did not seem at all unreasonable to him. Furthermore, he had good reason to believe, he said, that Burr had considered or had already secured the support of the American troops on the Texas frontier.[59] So he, too, linked Wilkinson's army with the Burr expedition. The marvelous network of correspondence kept the Spanish officials exceedingly well informed.

The departure of Monroe, who refused to listen to reason, as the Spaniards said, was followed by warnings sent to the colonial authorities to take the greatest precautions against American hostilities.[60] Iturrigaray, the viceroy, had been warned to look to the defenses of the Spanish provinces with the utmost care.[61] On October 1 Governor Folch informed him that the project to revolutionize Mexico "has not been lost sight of, and seems to be stronger than ever." The plan was that

> ... if the weather permits, in February or March ten thousand Kentuckians, three thousand regular troops, eight or ten thousand militia from Louisiana, who will be forced to go, will march for Mexico. They will raise a corps of five thousand blacks, who will be taken from the plantations and declared free.

---

[59] Casa Yrujo reporting the viceroy's letter to Someruelos, Philadelphia, Dec. 10, 1806, A. G. I., Papeles de Cuba, legajo 1708.
[60] Archives of California, Provincial State Papers (MS., Bancroft Library), XIX, 73.
[61] McCaleb, *Burr Conspiracy*, pp. 105-106.

The pretext for the invasion was to be the presence of Spanish troops at Los Adaes.[62] Congress probably intended to act only in the defensive, but it was believed that "once these troops are united they will march toward Mexico with great proclamations."[63]

By this time the United States government began to take notice of the project. Jefferson had been warned as early as January, 1806,[64] but warnings were not generally heeded. Judge Easton, who had conferred with Burr at St. Louis, wrote to a senator charging Wilkinson with being concerned in Miranda's project. He "was told in reply that the letter was burned and that the writer should mind his own business and take care how he meddled with men high in power and office."[65] Another person who attempted to warn Jefferson was told to "hold his tongue."[66]

Nevertheless, the affair was far from being a secret. One newspaper published the following statement:

A revolution in the Spanish provinces of North America will speedily when aided by Miranda, lead to one in South America, and the whole, along with the Western States in the Union organize into one empire, headed by a man of the enterprise and talents of Colonel Burr, will present a phenomenon in the political history of the globe perhaps only equaled by the modern Empire of France.[67]

All seemed in readiness for the rupture with Spain in September. The westerners were expecting war and were making preparations, Wilkinson was collecting an army at New Orleans, and the Spanish persisted in keeping their army on soil claimed by the United States. After General Herrera had crossed the Sabine River in July, 1806, Governor Claiborne came near bringing on the open break by recommending that

[62] *Ibid.*, p. 98.
[63] Wandell and Minnigerode, *Burr*, II, 101.
[64] McCaleb, *Burr Conspiracy*, pp. 99-101.
[65] Adams, *History of the United States*, III, 241.
[66] *Ibid.*, III, 242.
[67] Quoted by McCaleb, *Burr Conspiracy*, p. 180.

Lieutenant Cushing drive the Spaniards back, but the latter would do nothing without orders from General Wilkinson.[68] Nevertheless, action was expected and anticipated. The New Orleans *Gazette* for September 26 said that the president would seize the occasion to confer on the Mexicans "those inestimable blessings of freedom which we ourselves enjoy. Should the generous efforts of our government to establish a free, independent, republican empire in Mexico be successful, how fortunate, how enviable would be the situation in New Orleans."[69]

Wilkinson had it in his power to determine whether or not hostilities would be begun. And on September 28 he wrote to Adair: "The time long looked for by many and wished for by more, has now arrived for subverting the Spanish government in Mexico. . . . We cannot fail of success."[70] More details were given to Senator Smith, and after describing the military needs for the preliminary steps, he added that "from 20 to 30,000 will be necessary to carry our conquests to California and the Isthmus of Darien."[71]

Contrary to expectations, on the day before Wilkinson wrote to Adair, Herrera, the Spanish commander, gave orders for his troops to withdraw beyond the Sabine.[72] This was the turning point. Burr was not to become king of Mexico, nor his daughter the queen, as Blennerhasset had informed his gardener.[73] When Herrera's actions became known, Burr's opportunity was gone, for without war he could scarcely hope to succeed.

Wilkinson was enough of a schemer to profit by disaster. He turned informer and then he posed as the savior of the Union. He made an agreement with the Spanish officials

[68] Cox, "Louisiana-Texas Frontier and the Burr Conspiracy," *The Mississippi Valley Historical Review*, X, 283-284.
[69] McCaleb, *Burr Conspiracy*, pp. 125-126.
[70] *Ibid.*, p. 128.
[71] Wandell and Minnigerode, *Burr*, II, 102.
[72] McCaleb, *Burr Conspiracy*, p. 134.   [73] *Ibid.*, pp. 89-90.

which became known as the "Neutral Ground Treaty," signed on November 5, 1806.[74] A just reimbursement would be $111,000.00[75]—surely not an unreasonable sum for such a noble service! Then he sent a report on Mexico, supposedly from his messenger, Burling, to the president, inclosing a bill for fifteen hundred dollars—and he got it!

Jefferson received Wilkinson's revelations on November 25 and proceeded at once to check Burr's activities. His proclamation two days later was enough to turn many of Burr's supporters against him, and Wilkinson became zealous in his efforts to arrest and dispose of Burr's followers.[76] New Orleans was practically under martial law. Vincent Nolte, who in 1806 was in New Orleans to direct the transfer of Mexican silver, was suspected by Wilkinson of being a representative of the English house of Baring to supply Burr with the funds requested of England. In an interview with the general, Nolte cleared himself, but said that he came to the conclusion that Wilkinson was "an imposter."[77] Burr, however, continued with his project for some time before he heard of Wilkinson's duplicity and the president's proclamation. In December Jackson, hearing reports that Burr's plan had been against the Union, is reported to have said that "if this were true, he would hold no communication on the subject; but, if untrue, and his intentions were to proceed to Mexico, he would join and accompany him with his whole division."[78]

Burr reached the Mississippi in January and found the commandant of Chickasaw Bluffs still ignorant of the ban against him. He was even ready to join Burr, thinking the

---

[74] On this day the *Gazeta de México*, Nov. 5, XIII, 740, said that Salcedo was prepared to meet the invaders and that had they come they would have had their skulls crushed.

[75] Iturrigaray to Cevallos, March 12, 1807, McCaleb, *Burr Conspiracy*, p. 168.

[76] Among these were Ogden, Swarthwout, Bollman, Adair, Workman, and Kerr.

[77] Vincent Nolte, *The Memoirs of Vincent Nolte* (translated from the German, New York, 1934), p. 93.

[78] Davis (ed.), *Memoirs of Burr*, II, 382.

expedition was destined for Mexico.[79] By the time Burr reached the Mississippi Territory he found the country stirred by the proclamations of Wilkinson and Meade. He had already heard that Wilkinson had made peace with the Spaniards. Finding himself stopped by the militia from Natchez, he gave himself up to Meade, acting governor of the Mississippi Territory.[80]

Thus came the dream of empire to an inglorious end. Many believed that the project was not unreasonable, and even Jefferson considered it possible of execution. In a letter to Bowdoin, minister to Spain, he said that Burr had given up the idea of separating the West and "turned himself wholly towards Mexico and so popular is an enterprise on that country in this, that we had only to be still, and he could have had followers enough to have been in the city of Mexico in six weeks."[81]

Before Burr had been apprehended, Zebulon Montgomery Pike had been sent on his somewhat mysterious expedition to the Southwest which brought him into Mexico. It has been suggested that this expedition was another ramification of the Burr conspiracy.[82] General Wilkinson, as a participant in the project for revolutionizing Mexico, was naturally anxious to get as much information on the country as he could. In case of war New Mexico could be taken, he wrote to the secretary of war on September 8, 1805.[83] And some time before sending Pike he had written to Adair: "We must have a peep at the unknown world beyond me."[84] And Pike was evidently the

[79] McCaleb, *Burr Conspiracy*, p. 262.
[80] *Annals of Congress, 1807-1808*, I, 637.
[81] April 2, 1807, Ford (ed.), *Works of Jefferson*, X, 381-382.
[82] There were reports that Pike's enterprise "was a premeditated co-operation with Burr," Elliott Coues (ed.), *The Expedition of Zebulon Pike* (3 vols., New York, 1895), II, 826.
[83] I. J. Cox, "Opening the Santa Fe Trail," *The Missouri Historical Review*, XXV, 42 (Oct., 1930).
[84] May 28, 1805, Adams, *History of the United States*, III, 221.

one to "have a peep" for Wilkinson, as Nolan had done before him. Elliot Coues declares that it is well known that Pike had secret instructions from the general, "over and beyond those which were ostensible."[85] Pike's position on the right bank of the Rio Grande was at least suspicious.

Dr. Robinson was the first to reach Santa Fé, and while he and Pike were held there they took advantage of the hospitality of their guards to spread ideas which the officials considered dangerous and which brought on a warning to avoid political and religious topics. Pike also heard criticisms of the Spanish government and even discovered ideas of revolt, valuable information for the Americans.[86] When he was being escorted into Mexico he learned at Carrizal of Burr's conspiracy and realized why the Spaniards had treated him with such suspicion.[87] Whatever his motives were, Pike took pride in the information he had acquired in New Spain, "which," he said, "in case of a rupture between the United States and that Government will be of the highest importance." In case of peace it would "afford pleasing subjects of contemplation, for the statesman, the philosopher, and the Soldier."[88] Wilkinson warned Pike "that of the information you have acquired, and the observations you have made, you must be cautious, extremely cautious, how you breath a word."[89]

It is difficult to say what part Pike's expedition had in the Burr episode, but it is quite likely that Pike was innocent of any knowledge of participation with Burr. On the other hand, that Wilkinson was using Pike to supplement Burr's enterprise is also likely. When he was questioned by Timothy Kibbey about the object of Pike's expedition, "he smiled and said it

---

[85] Coues (ed.), *The Expedition of Pike*, II, 563, n. 2.
[86] Cox, "Opening the Santa Fe Trail," *The Missouri Historical Review*, XXV, 59-60 and 64.
[87] H. Whiting, *Life of Zebulon Pike* (Boston, 1848), p. 277.
[88] Coues (ed.), *The Expedition of Pike*, I, li.
[89] *Ibid.*, II, 826.

was of a secret nature."[90] Only one other person in the Territory knew, and Wilkinson added that even Pike was ignorant of the nature of his journey. He then declared that Pike was not sent by the government, but that it was his own plan. If Pike succeeded, Wilkinson said, he[91] "would be placed out of reach of his enemies and in the course of eighteen months he would be in a situation (if the plan succeeded) to call his Damned foes to an a/c [account] for their Deeds."[92] It is difficult to imagine what plan Wilkinson referred to here, except the one he was then planning in conjunction with Burr. The whole project, in spite of its failure, made a great impression, and it gave the oppressed inhabitants of Mexico the idea that they could rely on help from Americans in any struggle for independence.

[90] This is based on Timothy Kibbey's deposition, July 6, 1807, Herbert E. Bolton (ed.), "Papers of Zebulon M. Pike," *The American Historical Review*, XIII, 802 (July, 1908).

[91] Wilkinson.

[92] Bolton (ed.), "Papers of Zebulon M. Pike," *The American Historical Review*, XIII, 802.

CHAPTER XIV
PITT AND THE FAILURES OF 1806

> "Much of the affair was concerned with mistaken ideas as to bunting! The British proposed to offer the South Americans the Union Jack in place of the yellow and red of Spain. But the South Americans, although anxious enough to fight by the side of the Union Jack, had other ideas. They had it in mind to toss up the old Spanish flag and to let it explode in midair like a rocket, when it should send out quite new stars and brand new patterns of colors, which should be the property of the South Americans alone."—W. H. KOEBEL.
>
> "The war with Spain had opened vast colonial perspectives; and delirious enterprises swam constantly before their eyes. . . . Two forces starting in two separate hemispheres were to converge on Mexico."—PHILIP GUEDALLA.

THE revolutionary projects, in some form or another, were ever present, but the interest and the activity fluctuated with the international situation. No sooner had the United States been temporarily pacified than European rivalry prepared the way for the renewal of Miranda's plans in England. Numerous British officials, sympathetic with the revolutionary policy, waited only for a suitable opportunity to convert the plans into action. This opportunity appeared to have come with the termination of the Peace of Amiens, as we have seen, but was hindered and limited by occasional anticipations of peace or other diplomatic negotiations.

While Burr was making preparations for his invasion and emancipation of New Spain, England was occupied with her enemy across the Channel, and for a time the interest in Spanish America wavered. Napoleon was unquestionably the center of interest, and all other considerations were subordinated to the main object of defeating France and of saving England. During 1805 the Third Coalition under the supervision of Pitt was being prepared for the purpose of isolating Napoleon.

But England did not consider Spain as a permanent enemy,

rather as a country which might be induced to betray a treacherous ally. The very possibility of British action in Spanish America might serve as an inducement for Spain to seek peace with England in order to save her colonies. The British were willing to give up the revolutionary program if they could weaken Napoleon by depriving him of one of his allies and by adding one to their own coalition. Negotiations were actually begun with Baron Stroganoff acting as intermediary. It was understood that "His Majesty on His part will under those circumstances engage not to possess Himself during that period of any of the American colonies of Spain."[1] These negotiations put a temporary lull into the revolutionary plans, but they did not end them.

In January, 1805, a plan for the independence of America, proposed by a French émigré, Antoine Francois de Bertrand-Moleville, was presented to Lord Melville. It was argued that Napoleon's control of Spain made it necessary for England to take the Spanish colonies. The campaign should be begun by sending an English army to Mexico.[2] In order that the British government might keep informed on the Mexican situation it detained one Joseph Pavia, who knew Miranda and who had connections in Mexico where he had once lived.[3]

Miranda, however, was finally permitted to leave, not without some hope of receiving aid, but with the opinion that England would not immediately initiate a revolution in Spanish America.[4] The increasing prospects of war between Spain and the United States in 1805 aroused Miranda, as it had Burr, to the opportunity of securing aid from the latter country, and England could still give her support if she so desired.

While Pitt was at the helm, the British government was ever

---

[1] Downing Street, Oct. 4, 1805, P. R. O., F. O. 72 (Spain), Vol. LV. Preliminaries had been arranged earlier between England and Russia; cf. Ward and Gooch (eds.), *Cambridge History of British Foreign Policy*, I, 341.

[2] Robertson, *Life of Miranda*, I, 282.

[3] Robertson, *Miranda*, p. 359, and n. c.

[4] *Ibid.*, p. 361.

ready to consider the emancipation of Spanish America as a part of its foreign policy. The economic advantages, which would be tremendous during times of peace, were vital during the war. To be sure, England already had a great share of the prohibited trade, but not without considerable risk, since the Spaniards were at least justified in attacking the British traders, and the Caribbean swarmed with petty but annoying French privateers.[5] Shortly before the Battle of Trafalgar a royal order was sent to the viceroy of New Spain, "prohibiting, without any exception," the introduction of any foreign goods.[6] This was to countermand a previous order granting limited trade privileges. The opportunity to enforce such measures had been limited and soon became less.

The conflict between England and France culminated in two great battles, the Battle of Trafalgar, October 21, 1805, in which England upheld her naval supremacy, and the Battle of Austerlitz, December 2, 1805, which advanced Napoleon's domination over the continent. "Roll up that map; it will not be wanted these ten years" is a quotation attributed to Pitt upon seeing a map of Europe after Napoleon's victories.[7] Although Pitt had suffered from overwork, bad wine, and the gout, the news of Napoleon's success contributed to his decline and death. Canning had tried to create a ray of hope by intimating that Prussia might not submit to utter disgrace, and "if Russia does not give way," he added, "there may yet be an effort made to prevent Bonaparte from returning Emperor of the West."[8] The struggle now became more than ever an economic one. Pitt had recognized the significance of the

[5] Mahan, *The Influence of Sea Power upon the French Revolution and Empire, 1793-1812*, II, 109, 110.

[6] Royal order of Sept. 10, 1805, A. G. I., Estado, Mexico, legajo 11.

[7] This quotation appears in several forms and may be one of those popular phrases made to fit the ideas of a prominent man. Philip H. Stanhope (5th Earl Stanhope), *Life of William Pitt* (3rd ed., 4 vols., London, 1867), IV, 369. Cf. H. E. Bourne, *The Revolutionary Period in Europe* (New York, 1915), p. 377; and Mathews, *The French Revolution*, p. 365.

[8] Canning to Pitt, December 31, 1805, Stanhope, *Life of William Pitt*, IV, 365.

economic phase earlier, when he had said that France "must be separated from the commercial world . . . be blocked by land and sea."⁹ One of the immediate results was that much of the trade of the world was put on a smuggling basis.

England's supremacy on the sea gave her considerable freedom, and the losses in the Old World might be, at least partially, indemnified in the New. There was good reason for supporting Pitt's policy of sending expeditions against the enemies' colonies.¹⁰ In the summer of 1806, at the time when Burr, Popham, and Miranda were each directing their efforts against the Spanish colonies, William Jacob gave the British government a detailed report on Mexico. Two years earlier he had drawn up "Plans for Occupying Spanish America, with Observations on the Character and Views of its Inhabitants."¹¹ His second report recommended an attack on the eastern coast of Mexico. Winds and rain were taken into consideration, descriptions of fortifications and statistical tables were given, and other information which might be useful for anyone considering an attack was added. Jamaica was to be used as the base, and the force necessary for the undertaking was estimated at not less than eight thousand men. Finally there was a description of inland towns, supplemented with a table of distances from Vera Cruz to Mexico.¹² Such, then, was the information given to the British government during this memorable year of premature attacks on the Spanish Empire.

The French were completely aware of British activities in premeditating and promoting revolutionary projects. Inspired by the success of Napoleon, they, too, were preparing to participate in any possible change in the Spanish Empire. Once again they revived the arguments used to regain Louisiana, and

⁹ Quoted by W. E. Lingelbach, "Commercial History in the Napoleonic Era," *The American Historical Review*, XIX, 257 (Jan., 1914).
¹⁰ Mahan, *Influence of Sea Power upon the French Revolution*, II, 117.
¹¹ Robertson, *Miranda*, p. 355.
¹² July 11, 1806, Londonderry (ed.), *Correspondence of Castlereagh*, VII, 293-302. For evidence of preparations for a Mexican expedition, see *ibid.*, VII, 316.

proposed that Spain give a part of her colonies to Napoleon for his aid in saving the rest from the British.

M. DePons, a well-informed man who had spent four years in Spanish America, and the author of two works on Venezuela, gave several reports and recommendations to his government. His *Memoire sur las cession de la capitainerie generale de Caracas à la France*[13] is especially enlightening. England, he said, was trying to monopolize a quarter of the world. She was at that time (1806) attempting to free Spanish America from the motherland to gain control of its commerce. If the Miranda expedition were successful, he said, "all the Spanish colonies would detach themselves from the mother country successively," and "England would become a commercial power, equally threatening to France, Spain, and all commercial peoples." It was recognized that Spain possessed colonies too numerous and too distant to defend them "against exterior enemies, or interior factions." She had retained them up to the present because there had been no serious attempt to conquer them and because "religion and apathy of the inhabitants have prevented any ideas of independence." Now Spain was in a crisis and at the point of ruin, and France alone, he said, was interested in saving her from England. As a reward for this aid she might be given a colony—Venezuela was suggested. An army would have to be sent to make this exchange —only a small army, however, due to the great respect for French arms. Furthermore, the name of Napoleon, the symbol of valor, well-being, loyalty, and power, would win the respect of the people. Napoleon would restore order and preserve for Spain "all her overseas possessions," which were now being threatened by the British.[14]

French officials took the memoir under consideration. It was to be sent to the emperor together with a summary of its

---

[13] *Rapport du Ministre de la Marine,* Archives Nationale, AF IV, 1211.
[14] *Ibid.*

contents and a description of the author, who was to be recommended as a reliable person. Additional information was given, including an estimate of the population and the income of the country, and finally the project was described as one which could be accomplished with ease.[15] Here were new prospects for the satisfaction of Napoleon's ambition.

DePons must have been quite familiar with the British interest in Miranda's activities, and he believed that they were still giving encouragement and aid for the expedition of 1806. British support could generally be expected, but it had declined during the uncertain period of 1805, when England and Russia were assembling the third coalition. Miranda then departed for America. Pitt had discouraged his departure and urged him to be patient, "for the political affairs of Europe were not yet in the state of maturity to commence our enterprise."[16] Nevertheless, Miranda had become impatient and was anxious to see his project under way.

Upon reaching the United States in November, 1805, he renewed his old acquaintances, especially those who had encouraged him during his previous efforts to secure aid for his liberation project. Among his new acquaintances were President Jefferson and Secretary of State Madison.[17] Both Jefferson and Madison must have received information, either directly or indirectly, about the preparations being made by Miranda in New York for his revolutionary expedition. Jefferson, as president, would be expected to stop these activities or be obliged to deny any knowledge of them. Miranda, like Burr, was living in anticipation of an open break between the United States and Spain, a situation to which his own actions contributed. As we have already seen in connection with the Burr episode, there were numerous causes for ill-feeling between the two countries which might at any time precipitate

[15] *Ibid.*
[16] Miranda quoting Pitt's spokesman, Robertson, *Life of Miranda*, I, 290.
[17] Robertson, *Miranda*, p. 363.

a break. If the United States went to war with Spain, Jefferson could then support Miranda and Burr openly. The prospects seemed good, for as McHenry, the secretary of war, said: "The President is enraged with Spain, even to bloodshed," but war was averted.[18]

Without war Miranda was unable to get the government support which he desired, but he did get the secret aid of interested Americans. Colonel Smith, his former traveling companion on the continent, was active in securing recruits for the enterprise.[19] With men and supplies from both the United States and England, Miranda set out, early in 1806, on his unfortunate expedition to liberate Spanish America. He directed his first efforts to his home country, Venezuela, where the seeds of revolution were to be sown for the final emancipation of all the Spanish colonies in America. Such, at least, were his views when he was in England, and such were the views of contemporaries who expressed their ideas on the subject. Dionisio Franco of Caracas believed that, with a little aid from England, Miranda would be successful, "and it may happen," he added, "that this spark of fire, that appears nothing, may finish by devouring the whole continent."[20] The Richmond (Va.) *Enquirer* suggested that, if he were successful, Spain might "tremble for all her possessions in South America."[21] Other American newspapers frankly wished him success. DePons believed that the point of departure was to be the Island of Trinidad, where they would also have a meeting of delegates from Caracas, Santa Fé, and Mexico. It was believed, he said, that they were trying to establish the independence of all of Spanish America under the influence of England.[22]

[18] McHenry to Pickering, Feb. 19, 1806, Steiner, *The Life and Correspondence of James McHenry,* p. 533.

[19] Robertson, *Life of Miranda,* I, 299.

[20] *The American Register,* V, 388 n.   [21] Robertson, *Miranda,* p. 375.

[22] Paris, June 4, 1806, *Rapport du ministre de la marine,* Archive Nationale, AF IV, 1211. Stephen Sayre also declared, in a letter to the Richmond (Va.) *Enquirer,* that delegates were expected from Mexico, New Granada, and Venezuela (Robertson, *Life of Miranda,* I, 301).

The success of the project was nearly always spoken of as being dependent on British support, which would lead one to believe that without this aid it would surely end in failure. At the close of 1805 Miranda might have felt assured of British coöperation again, judging from the European situation; and when he consulted British officers in the West Indies he tried to create the impression that he was confident of receiving government approval for their aid. He met with varying success, a few giving him no encouragement, while others like Admiral Cochrane, who was later to become one of the most influential men in the wars for independence, considered the advantages to England too great to be allowed to pass without some share in the enterprise. Cochrane justified his action by pointing out, as others had before him, the great commercial advantages for England at a time when she was sorely in need of them, because European commerce was being closed to her. Most of the British officials refused to assist without orders from the home government, and the government left them in ignorance. Miranda must have felt confident that the orders would be favorable since he did not await them, but proceeded with only a few ships sent to his aid by Cochrane.[23]

Two attempts were made to conquer the country; both ended in dismal failure. Several good reasons may be found to explain the disasters. The authorities of Caracas were kept informed by their home government and by the indefatigable minister to the United States, Casa Yrujo, who may have been deceived about the activities of Burr, but who was certainly not deceived about the movements of Miranda.[24] He was aware that the expedition was directed against Venezuela, but took precautions to warn other colonies, including New Spain.[25]

[23] Londonderry (ed.), *Correspondence of Castlereagh*, VII, 315; for a general account of these events, see Robertson, *Miranda*, pp. 382-392, and also his *Life of Miranda*, I, chap. xiv.

[24] Philadelphia, Feb. 4, 1806, A. G. I., Papeles de Cuba, legajo 1708. Other references are given by Robertson, *Miranda*, p. 370.

[25] Robertson, *Miranda*, p. 370.

Being forewarned, the officials were prepared to resist. Another reason for failure was the lack of interest and support on the part of the colonists who were to be liberated. They did not flock to the standards of liberty as Miranda had anticipated. In the first place they were too ignorant of political changes in the world to understand and appreciate the full significance of the revolutionary movement, and in the second place they were so thoroughly imbued with respect for authority and fear of the government that they dared not take advantage of the opportunity to resist.[26] The lack of support from the United States and England has also been considered a determining factor. The British government had frequently approved the plans of Miranda, but because of its vacillating policy it failed at the crucial moment to give the coöperation and the aid necessary for the success of the enterprise.[27]

Before considering the changes in the British government which were partly responsible for this uncertain policy, another venture against Spain's colonies deserves attention. In discussing the proposed expedition of Popham and Baird to the Cape of Good Hope the authorities made repeated references to the naval needs in the Caribbean. Various points of attack were being considered in July, 1805, which might divert part of the expedition, but the tonnage would be immediately replaced, "in case we determine to detach to the West Indies," wrote Castlereagh to the governor of Jamaica.[28] Two days later he sent Pitt some information from Baird and Dundas, stating that a larger force would be necessary for the South

---

[26] Speaking of general plans to emancipate Spanish America, William Walton said that "its natives were neither predisposed, or even acquainted with what was premeditated so far off for the amelioration of their lot," *An Exposé on the Dissensions in Spanish America*, p. 69.

[27] For the attitude of the British government, see Londonderry (ed.), *Correspondence of Castlereagh*, VII, 314-315; and Duke of Wellington (ed.), *Supplementary Despatches and Memoranda of Field Marshal Arthur, Duke of Wellington* (15 vols., London, 1858-1872), VI, 63.

[28] Castlereagh to Sir Eyre Coote, July 20, 1805, Londonderry (ed.), *Correspondence of Castlereagh*, VI, 128-129.

African expedition. "These troops might first go to the Cape," he added, "assist in its reduction, and reach Barbadoes about Christmas."[29] The British may have had several good reasons for wanting reënforcement in the islands, but the concentration of British forces in the Caribbean could easily lead to the execution of any of the numerous revolutionary plans for Spanish America.

Indicative of his astonishing ability to secure information and his unusual insight into international affairs, Casa Yrujo notified Someruelos, the captain-general of Cuba and governor of Florida, of the British plans. When he heard of a large British expedition being prepared, ostensibly to attack France, he said he was inclined to believe that this report was spread to cover its real object, which was to send the whole or part of the expedition to attack the Spanish colonies in America. Someruelos was urged to send this information to the viceroy of New Spain in order that he might be ready to defend his country.[30] In his December report he suggested that the Popham expedition was intended for the Cape of Good Hope or for some point in Spanish America.[31] Had he said that it was destined for both, he would have been correct.

Sir Home Popham had for years been familiar with his government's interest in revolutionary plans for Spanish America, and had long been ready to head the proposed expeditions. He had reason to feel assured of the support of Pitt in any undertaking which would divert the commercial wealth of the colonies from the enemy to his own country, and he informed Miranda that Lord Melville took up the subject "very warmly."[32] Therefore, having occupied the Cape, Popham and Beresford proceeded to La Plata, where they captured Buenos Aires. This, as we have seen,[33] was to be only an

[29] Castlereagh to Pitt, July 22, 1805, *ibid.*, VI, 129-130.
[30] Philadelphia, Nov. 20, 1805, A. G. I., Papeles de Cuba, legajo 1708.
[31] Dec. 10, 1805, *ibid.*
[32] Quoted by Robertson, *Life of Miranda*, I, 268.
[33] *Supra*, pp. 200-201.

entering wedge for the emancipation of all of Spanish America. The ease with which the city was taken deceived the British, and they therefore did what diplomats and statesmen had warned against ever since the War of Jenkins' Ear—they came as liberators but remained as conquerors. In place of starting a colonial revolution which would spread over the whole of Spanish America and end in independence, the British found themselves confronted by a patriotic army which drove them out of the city.[34] The government had been extremely slow in deciding on a policy, and when it did decide, it made the same mistake as the leaders of the expedition by planning to send reënforcements to conquer and hold the country without any promise of freedom or protection.[35] Popham's venture, which had started so auspiciously, ended in failure, and the leader was called back to England to explain his actions before a court martial. The affair was not dropped immediately, however, since the troops which had been collected in La Plata were, according to Wellesley's more efficient plan, to serve in the revolutionary expedition which he was preparing for New Spain.

The events of 1806 gave rise to a long article in *The American Register,* indicating the opinions of the time.[37] The writer expressed some surprise that the dominions of Spain had not been formally attacked earlier, since they were known to contain the "richest mines . . . in the world," had numerous other advantages, and were supposed to be poorly defended. "The people are thought to be discontented with their government and ripe for any revolution," he said, and during a war, "would naturally present themselves as an easy prey. . . ." The explanation of their security was, he thought, the changed

---

[34] For a general account of this expedition, see W. H. Koebel, *British Exploits in South America* (New York, 1917), pp. 141-155.
[35] Londonderry (ed.), *Correspondence of Castlereagh,* VII, 315.
[36] Wellingon (ed.), *Supplementary Despatches,* VI, 37, 54.
[37] I, 24-25.

attitude about colonies after the American Revolution. The British had come to the conclusion that colonies were injurious and that there were no real advantages to the mother state equivalent to the hardships of war and the "enormous public expenses which they necessarily occasion." Two good examples were given as proof of the soundness of this theory. Twenty years after England defended her colonies from the French at great expense, she lost them.[38] It was then shown that Spain had become feeble since the establishment of her empire in the New World. He offered the following explanation:

> The imagination naturally supposes the colonies of Spain to be the cause of her decay.... As vast quantities of silver are manufactured and exported in the Spanish colonies, and none in those of other countries, we immediately fancy that the true cause of the decay of Spain is discovered, and that an extensive manufacture, or rather importation of the precious metals is the bane of industry, liberty, and science, and military virtue. These opinions have had a powerful influence on the conduct of states, and made the Spanish dominions rich, fertile, and extensive as they are, objects of abhorrence, rather than envy to their neighbors. These opinions contributed to their security from all external attacks.

The writer did, however, recognize certain advantages in alienating the Spanish colonies, one being the potential market for England's goods, especially at that time when European trade was closed to her; and a second advantage was that the conquest could also serve as pledges for an equitable peace.[39] The views of this writer were quite likely in harmony with those of British authorities.

The failures of Miranda and Popham, he believed, gave evidence of a mistaken notion held in America about the desire for independence in the Spanish colonies. "We have even harboured the great illusion," he said,

---

[38] The French loss of her American colonies might have been added as a third example.

[39] *The American Register*, I, 24-25.

that a wretched adventurer [Miranda?], at the head of two or three hundred men, picked up in our cities, could work a revolution in South America, and that the initial spark only was wanting to kindle a rebellion in Peru and in Mexico. The grossness of these delusions is now made evident by the failure of so many formidable expeditions to la Plata.

These experiences ought to inculcate a "proper caution and distrust with respect to similar projects," he added as a final warning.[40] For a real understanding of the failures of 1806 one has to consider British politics again.

The death of Pitt in January, 1806, marked the reaction from the liberation policy which had formed his "unceasing and favorite study."[41] Henry Dundas, later Lord Melville, had been an interested participant in the plans of Miranda,[42] he had been a promoter of Popham's expedition,[43] and he had also been approached by Colonel Williamson, Burr's agent in London.[44] Therefore his impeachment in 1806 was an additional blow to the revolutionary plans of the government. This incident, together with Pitt's death, may be considered as the principal cause for the failures of that eventful year.[45] The lack of support for Miranda in the Venezuela episode has also been attributed to the death of his most powerful British supporter.[46] And since Pitt and Popham had often considered together the prospects of separating the Spanish colonies from the motherland, it is possible that, had Pitt lived, he might have directed Popham so as to convert failure into success. Instead, an unsympathetic ministry changed encouragement to censure.

[40] *Ibid.*, II (Part II), 29-30.
[41] Walton, *An Exposé of the Dissentions of Spanish America*, p. 10.
[42] Robertson, *Life of Miranda*, I, 266-267.
[43] *Ibid.*, I, 268.
[44] Adams, *History of the United States*, III, 219, 234-235.
[45] Wandell and Minnigerode, *Burr*, II, 77, have also linked the death of Pitt with Wilkinson's playing the part of Judas in the affairs of Burr; see also Davis (ed.), *Memoirs of Burr*, II, 381.
[46] Wandell and Minnigerode, *Burr*, II, 65.

The significance of the passing of the great statesman becomes more evident when one considers the uncertain policy of his immediate successors. The ministry of "All the Talents" recognized the complicity of the previous administration, but hesitated to give its support. It waited over three months before sending any reënforcements, nor did it send any instructions.[47] Lord Grenville, the prime minister, raised the question, "How far shall we now countenance it, or engage in it?"[48] Charles James Fox, as the new minister of foreign affairs, was opposed to the war policy of the previous administration, and inspired a fleeting hope of peace. Little was to be gained, it seemed, on either side except the cessation of war; nevertheless, the way to peace was opened by a letter to Talleyrand.[49] Nothing came of this, however, and yet it had its influence in preventing the British support for the Spanish American expeditions, and therefore contributed to their failures.[50]

There was still a chance of coming to an agreement with Spain. Having been cut off from her colonies, Spain realized that it was useless to prohibit British trade, and tried to placate the enemy by offering commercial advantages which would be mutually beneficial. This proposal must have been a feeler in preparation for the later actions of Spain in her attempt to break from Napoleon and to join England in order to regain the much-needed wealth of her colonies. It was proposed that the British be allowed to carry a certain amount of goods between Spain and Mexico, half the cargo to be British and the other half, Spanish. The acceptance of this proposal of 1806 was postponed by the British until such time as they should have greater assurance that the Spanish government would

[47] Londonderry (ed.), *Correspondence of Castlereagh*, VIII, 315.
[48] Quoted by Robertson, *Life of Miranda*, I, 308.
[49] R. B. Mowat, *The Diplomacy of Napoleon* (New York, 1924), pp. 163-164; *The American Register*, I, 15-18.
[50] Wandell and Minnigerode, *Burr*, II, 65.

support it.[51] Napoleon's overwhelming military success in Prussia was the deciding factor in preventing the Anglo-Spanish *rapprochement*.

The international situation became more critical and the rivalry more keen during the latter part of the short ministry of Fox. The British found it necessary to revert to the old policy of Pitt. The Orders in Council and the Continental System provided the drastic rules for the mortal struggle of the great rivals. This terrific disturbance created a tidal wave which finally broke down the Anglo-American wall of neutrality and swept the Spanish colonies from their moorings, leaving them stranded, wrecked, and free.

[51] John Hunter to Lord Mulgrave, Madrid, Feb. 6, 1806, P. R. O., F. O. 72 (Spain), LV.

CHAPTER XV

CASTLEREAGH AND WELLESLEY

"Upon the Elbe and the Oder we have gained Pondicherry, our enterprises in the Indies, the Cape of Good Hope, and the Spanish colonies."—Napoleon to his troops on the anniversary of Austerlitz, December 2, 1806.

"But, while the territory of Old Spain is, in fact, a French province, and whilst not only the fleets and armies of Spain, but of France, are put in motion against us by the resources of Spanish America, we are *driven to consider* whether those resources may not be made the means of creating and supporting an amicable and local government, with which those commercial relations may freely subsist which it is alone our interest to aim at, and which the people of South America must equally desire."—Viscount Castlereagh, May 1, 1807.

NAPOLEON, winning victory after victory, threatened to crush all opposition on the continent. His allies were cowed into unwilling support, his opponents were whipped into submission, and his rivals waited in despair for the turning-point when they might combine against him in an attempt to save the world from the domination of a usurper. The declaration of war by Prussia in September, 1806, had kindled a hope in the hearts of both enemies and allies that the French army might yet be checked. Godoy, the prime minister of Spain, who, ever since the battle of Trafalgar, had sought an opportunity to turn against his ally, now decided that the time had come to break the bond which tied Spain to the chariot of France. A stirring manifesto called the patriots of Spain to arms, and mobilization was begun immediately. Although no enemy was mentioned by name, it was believed that Spain was at last to turn against her ally and to fight Napoleon.[1]

The faint hope which flickered for a short time was completely stamped out by the decisive battle of Jena. Napoleon,

---

[1] Mowat, *Diplomacy of Napoleon*, p. 208; H. E. Bourne, *The Revolutionary Period in Europe*, pp. 349-350; S. D. F. De Pradt, *Memoires historique sur la Revolution d'Espagne*, pp. 12-14.

flushed with victory, is said to have turned white with rage when he read the Spanish manifesto which called the people to arms. Godoy, seeing that the opportunity was lost, tried to cover up his action by making it appear as a movement to aid France. The emperor pretended that the explanation was satisfactory, his purpose being to retain Spanish support until he could dispose of it as he saw fit. His real feeling and intention are seen in his own words when he said: "I swore then that they would pay me for it."[2] And it was while addressing his soldiers on the anniversary of Austerlitz that he made the following bombastic but significant statement: "Upon the Elbe and the Oder we have gained Pondicherry, our enterprises in the Indies, the Cape of Good Hope, and the Spanish colonies."[3] His boast to the soldiers was not idle talk—it was a summary of his ambitious designs. In the meantime he made use of a part of the Spanish army which had been mobilized, and proceeded with his plans for the removal of the ruling families of Spain and Portugal.

England was still his greatest rival and the greatest hindrance to the realization of his ambitions. As the prospects for stopping Napoleon's victorious march through Europe declined, England turned again to the New World. After Pitt, the most prominent man to show an interest in Spanish America was Lord Castlereagh. He, too, based his policy on the actions of Napoleon. Sixteen days after the battle of Jena and a month before the emperor's speech to his soldiers, referred to above, Castlereagh wrote to his friend, Arthur Wellesley, for his opinion on the prospects of attacking New Spain.[4] On the same day, November 2, Wellesley was considering a propo-

---

[2] Mowat, *The Diplomacy of Napoleon*, pp. 208-209; De Pradt, *The Colonies and the Present Revolutions*, p. 15; Chapman, *History of Spain*, p. 407.

[3] E. G. Bourne, *Napoleon the First, a Biography by August Fournier* (New York, 1903), p. 370.

[4] Archibald Alison, *Lives of Lord Castlereagh and Sir Archibald Stewart* (3 vols., Edinburgh, etc., 1861), I, 229.

sition of combining an attack on Manila with one on New Spain. He raised certain objections to the combination of the two, believing, however, that the capture of Manila would be "a necessary consequence of the possession of New Spain." He then gave some consideration to the methods of attacking the latter and the forces which would be necessary. He believed it unwise at first to divide his forces between the eastern and western coast, and dangerous to travel overland from Panama. The best plan would be to concentrate the troops at Jamaica for a united effort.[5]

Sir Arthur Wellesley made a careful study of the Spanish American project and examined a great deal of correspondence on the subject in preparation for a report to Lord Castlereagh. Mr. Frazer, a merchant who had been trading on the coast of Mexico, gave him considerable information about the climate, the ports, and the routes.[6] Wellesley later supplemented this information with reports from others and then he wrote a memorandum in which he corrected some of Mr. Frazer's statements and rejected some of his proposals.[7]

By the twentieth of November he had his plans fairly well formulated. He reviewed the seasons and stated that the most suitable time for an attack would be in December and January since the unhealthful rainy season was then passed. Seven places for attack were considered and by a process of elimination he came to the conclusion that the most desirable, from the point of view of its strategic position, supplies, and its route to Mexico City, would be Vera Cruz. As a second choice he selected a point farther south, the Alvarado River.[8] The military force could be provided by soldiers from Europe, supplemented with Negroes from the West Indies, native troops from India, and

[5] Wellington, *Supplementary Despatches*, VI, 35-38.
[6] *Ibid.*, VI, 38-39.
[7] "Observations upon the Conversations with Mr. Frazer," Nov., 1806, *ibid.*, VI, 40.
[8] "Memorandum," Nov. 20, 1806, *ibid.*, VI, 42-44.

by sending north the troops at Buenos Aires.⁹ The La Plata expedition was to be saved from complete failure by sending the British forces to take part in the revolutionary movement in Mexico where independence offered them a greater chance of success than the unfortunate attempt at conquest. The population of Honduras was larger than necessary, he thought; therefore, a number would be willing to volunteer for service in the expedition to New Spain. He would not use many slaves, but would call for volunteers of free Negroes.¹⁰ Jamaica was to serve as a base for the expedition, except for the troops from India, which were not necessarily to aid in the conquest but to serve as reënforcements later. Judging from what he had read, the forces necessary would be not less than eight thousand infantry and one thousand light cavalry. A number of detailed memoranda were added, enumerating the needs of the expedition: number and size of transports to be ready to sail from Falmouth, August 20; beef, pork, and spirits for eleven thousand men for two months; biscuits for the same number for three months; and so on, including provisions for men, horses, and mules.¹¹ They should be ready to leave Jamaica for the coast of Mexico in January.

He was still somewhat uncertain about the point of attack, and suggested that the expedition might land north of Vera Cruz at Puerto Delgado, going from there to the more salubrious climate at Jalapa, since the good health of the troops was of utmost importance. He did, however, keep Vera Cruz in mind as the most desirable place to be conquered and gave full descriptions of its defense and of San Juan de Ulloa, the island fortress. The route to Mexico was considered suitable for the movement of an army, and only the city of Perote could give any material resistance, not great enough, however, to stop their advance.

⁹ *Ibid.*, VI, 45-47.
¹⁰ *Ibid.*, VI, 48-49.   ¹¹ *Ibid.*, VI, 54.

The preliminary plans were completed, including instructions to the victualling board for provisions,[12] but the final policy of the government seemed still to be undecided. Wellesley recognized the possibility of difficulties and emphasized the hostile attitude of the priests, who were numerous, "their influence powerful, and they have long been in the habit of vilifying the British nation," he said. The difficulty might be partially solved by following the suggestions of those who had communicated their ideas to the government, recommending a revolution instead of a conquest. Both Wellesley and Castlereagh seemed to be convinced of the necessity of following this plan. The first task would still be to remove the Spanish authority and to replace it with the British which was to serve during the transition. Wellesley was ready to put the plans into action and expected to command the expedition himself. "His Majesty's government," he said, "will, of course, instruct me in what manner they intend that His Majesty's authority shall be established in Mexico; the advantages which I am to hold out to the different classes of inhabitants to conciliate their attachment to the government."[13]

Lord Castlereagh had already given serious thought to the revolutionary schemes when he became minister of war and the colonies in 1807. In May he made proposals for the consideration of the government based on what he knew of past plans and attempts. In referring to Sir Arthur Wellesley's activities he said that "some progress had been made in arranging, though not in executing, an operation against Mexico."[14] The lack of any definite policy on the part of his predecessors was criticized, as was also their lack of support and direction in connection with the expeditions of Popham and Miranda.[15]

[12] Nov. 20, 1806, *ibid.*, VI, 54.   [13] *Ibid.*, VI, 50-55.
[14] "Memorandum, for the Cabinet, relative to South America," May 1, 1807, Londonderry (ed.), *Correspondence of Castlereagh*, VII, 315-316.
[15] The anticipation of a break between Spain and Napoleon might have contributed to the lack of British support for Popham's enterprise.

Some effort had finally been made to give military support to the British in La Plata by diverting an expedition intended for Chile, but again, "without instructions to hold out any particular hopes to the inhabitants, or to aim at more than a commercial intercourse, under the protection of a military occupation."[16] Castlereagh realized that the conquest of these vast countries was hopeless unless the desires of the natives were taken into consideration, and that success could be attained only by offering them independence with the assurance of British protection.

When it should be to England's advantage to establish American independence she would have to follow a definite policy in order to insure stability. If England should be shut out from European commerce it might be well, he said, "to carve out a separate existence," and open new channels of commerce, "less exposed to French power." The British should act as "auxiliaries and protectors. In order to prove our sincerity in this respect, we should be prepared to pursue our object by native force, to be created under our countenance."

Since he feared the revolutionary influence of democracy, he preferred to see an independent monarchy established in the colonies. The choice should not be made from the British royal family because such a person would have little in common with the people of Spanish America; but England might be willing to support a member of the Bourbon family, such a candidate being closely connected with the Spanish monarchy and having the same religion as the colonials. He went on to say that, "were such an enterprising individual as the Duke of Orleans, with their concurrence, to undertake it, the object might perhaps be accomplished, and, in that case, *must* prove beneficial to us." The Duke ought to begin only as a military man to aid in the revolution and then let circumstances, to be influ-

[16] Castlereagh's "Memorandum," May 1, 1807, Londonderry (ed.), *Correspondence of Castlereagh*, VII, 315.

enced by England, no doubt, pave the royal way to kingship. Numerous French officers would be expected to join him, "Dumouriez certainly would," and "Miranda might be induced to follow his fortunes."[17]

It is interesting to note in this connection the views of the Duke of Orleans and of Dumouriez. The former wrote a memoir on Spanish America with special emphasis on Mexico. His object, he said, was threefold: first, to prove that revolution was inevitable, which would endanger the new world with Jacobin ideas; secondly, to show the advantages of interference by Great Britain; and, thirdly, to point out the means to carry out the revolution without endangering the country. Spain's power over America was decreasing daily; therefore, the real question was, who should guide the revolution and who should reap the benefit, England or France? Merely the introduction of Jacobinism would be enough to give France a special connection. If England did not establish a stable government in these countries she stood the risk of losing the rest of her own American colonies. In addition to depriving Britain's enemies of resources and a base of attack, it would help to preserve her possessions and possibly add some new ones in the form of West India islands. The commercial advantages would be great enough to counterbalance the closing of the European ports. In becoming modesty the Duke said: "It is not for me to suggest what prince Great Britain ought to present to the Mexicans." But to make the revolution successful he did suggest that it should be on the principles of monarchy. Mexico should be the starting point because it was the most vulnerable, the most populous, and the most easily directed. Furthermore, "Mexico is the key-stone of the arch: when that is removed, all the other parts ... must fall to pieces." Finally

---

[17] *Ibid.*, VII, 323. Arthur Wellesley, too, said that "The French gentlemen who had turned their thoughts to this subject have recommended that one of the French princes should be established as king of New Spain," Wellington (ed.), *Supplementary Despatches*, VI, 50.

the Duke of Orleans offered his services to the British government, or to the prince that might be chosen as ruler.[18] Castlereagh had selected a willing candidate, it would seem, to become the king of Mexico; and Dumouriez likewise gave proof of his own willingness to support the project and the prospective ruler.

General Dumouriez had first shown his interest in the liberation of Spanish America in 1792, while leading the revolutionary army of France. And now, as an exile and an enemy of Napoleon, he found occasion to revive that interest and to make a careful survey of the naval stations and the conditions of the colonies.[19] His purpose was to arouse England to the necessity of a revolutionary expedition to these colonies to prevent their falling into the hands of Napoleon. England had no allies on the continent and would have to seek them or create them in America. He proposed that they begin their operations in South America, but added that they would not have completed a *moitie* of their object as long as they had not liberated Mexico,[20] this part of Spanish America being much more susceptible to revolution than the rest. He advocated a monarchical form of government, since a republic would become the natural ally of France or the United States.[21] After suggesting that a Bourbon be made a ruler, he gave a long list of qualifications, all of which were admirably fulfilled by the Duke of Orleans.[22] Four frigates and three thousand soldiers would be sufficient to establish this prince in Mexico, because a universal and spontaneous uprising would make opposition by the viceroy and the Peninsulars impossible.

---

[18] "Memoir on Spanish America, and the Viceroyalty of Mexico in Particular" by the Duke of Orleans, Castlereagh, *Correspondence*, VII, 332-344.

[19] This document is printed in French, *ibid.*, VII, 345-371.

[20] The part dealing with Mexico is found in *ibid.*, VII, 364-371.

[21] The failure of Miranda in Venezuela was blamed partly on his republican system.

[22] An additional note dated June 4, 1807, gave several reasons for selecting the Duke of Orleans as ruler of Spanish America, Londonderry (ed.), *Correspondence of Castlereagh*, VII, 374-376.

Another comment of his which deserves consideration is the one suggesting that the hostile attitude of the United States was a new incentive for sending troops to America.

The death struggle of the two great European rivals threatened to destroy the economic development of the United States by strangling her foreign trade, and she was now about to turn in righteous wrath against one or the other of the contestants. There was some uncertainty as to which side to resist, both being equally unreasonable in their demands. Wilkinson, whose statements are not always to be accepted at face value, wrote to Jefferson on March 12, 1807, proposing that "the United States and Great Britain should combine to preserve the western world from Napoleon and his unwilling ally, the king of Spain. With the aid of the British fleet they could preserve their own territory, occupy Cuba, reduce the Floridas, and give independence to Mexico."[23] Before the end of the month he made another proposal which might have been more in keeping with Jefferson's policy of avoiding European entanglements, suggesting "that an alliance composed of the independent states of Mexico, Peru, and Cuba might, with the aid of the United States, bid defiance to the Old World."[24] In harmony with this view was Jefferson's action of sending Wilkinson to warn the Spanish Americans against any close political or commercial relations with Great Britain, and to offer the friendly aid of the United States.[25] Troubles with Spain were continually irritating the president, and only respect for France, he said, has "kept our hand off her till now." He expected that the emperor would compel Spain to do justice to the United States, "or abandon her to us." And if this took place, "We ask but one month to be in possession of the city of Mexico."[26]

[23] Professor Cox thinks this suggestion was made to conceal the real purpose of Burling's mission to Mexico; see "The Pan-American Policy of Jefferson and Wilkinson," *The Mississippi Valley Historical Review*, I, 212-239 (Sept., 1914).
[24] *Ibid.*, I, 215. [25] *Ibid.*, I, 216.
[26] Jefferson to Bowdoin, April 2, 1807, Ford (ed.), *Works of Jefferson*, X, 381.

Dumouriez used the threat of war with the United States as an additional argument for sending British forces to the West Indies, and added that these troops might also serve for an expedition to Mexico. He continued to urge the British to immediate action in order to secure the benefits that might otherwise go to the United States or Napoleon. Even if they could not make complete preparations at once, it would still be advisable to send an expedition to Jamaica to prepare for the attack on Vera Cruz. He believed that the squadron being prepared by Napoleon at Rochefort was intended for Vera Cruz, which would afford him a base for collecting large amounts of cash.[27] With these inducements to stir the British to action the plans for the new nation continued. The Kingdom of Mexico should extend from Rio del Norte in the north to Guiana and should include all the islands except Cuba and Puerto Rico, the former to go to England and the latter to Denmark.[28]

Lord Castlereagh was by this time quite convinced of the desirability of executing the project for the liberation of Mexico, and his plans seemed to have been based on those of Wellesley.[29] He was soon given additional encouragement when the greatest of all the conspirators, Miranda, returned to England. His failure in Venezuela had undoubtedly convinced Miranda of the necessity of securing foreign aid, and on January 10, 1808, he renewed his pleas to urge British participation.[30] The best argument had now become the actions of Napoleon, and he made a great deal of the rumor that Spain was already disposing of her colonies to France in exchange for Portugal. To prevent this additional blow to British commerce, an expedition ought to be prepared at once for Terra Firma, his favorite point of attack; and then, he said, "we may expect to see, in a

---

[27] Londonderry (ed.), *Correspondence of Castlereagh*, VII, 364-371.
[28] *Ibid.*, VII, 376-381. His views of June 12, 1807, were repeated in a letter to Windham, June 21, *ibid.*, VII, 384-385.
[29] *Ibid.*, VII, 385-387.   [30] *Ibid.*, VII, 405-408.

very short time, the imitation in Mexico." To support his arguments and to make an effective appeal to the government, Miranda gave Castlereagh several letters from British officials, recommending participation.

J. D. R. Gordon, who had lived in Mexico for six years, gave him an excellent description of Vera Cruz and its surroundings, with full details of its military strength. Gordon's description of the people and their position was the conventional one, but he brought out the fact that the people dared not think of independence because they were so fettered by their religion that the threat of excommunication kept them thoroughly subjugated. "This," he said, "added to a stupidity inherent in their nature, renders them the most subservient and time-serving people on the face of the globe."[31] It would evidently take a great deal of propaganda to convince the people of the advantages of independence and of the safety in relying on the aid and protection of a foreign power which had generally been considered an enemy. What the Mexican people would not do for themselves, foreigners were about to do for them—fight for their independence.

Before Miranda's return to England, Wellesley had given some attention to a proposal for combining his Mexican expedition with one to Terra Firma.[32] He came to the conclusion that this was not practicable, and since Miranda's failure, the enterprise would meet with greater difficulties in South America. The one great argument for an expedition to Terra Firma, however, was the fear that if England did not act at once, France would, very soon; and this would place her in a strategic position to control an important commercial route. We have seen evidence of this French interest in the proposals of DePons.[33]

A year later, in February, 1808, after having talked with

[31] Jan. 26, 1808, *ibid.*, VII, 428-441.
[32] Wellington (ed.), *Supplementary Despatches*, VI, 57-61.
[33] *Supra*, pp. 230-231.

Miranda, Wellesley reviewed the whole Spanish America field to reconsider the point of attack. He was still confident that the colonies wanted their independence, although he admitted that he had little direct evidence to that effect. Wherever the revolution were started, it was believed that it would soon spread to the other colonies. Buenos Aires was taken under consideration again, and would have been a good place to start, except for the bad precedent of Popham's failure. Peru and Chile were too far away to promise success. The choice would be between Mexico and Terra Firma. The advantage of the latter lay in having Miranda to serve as an intermediary, and the people of that section were believed to be predisposed to revolution. The difficulty with this project was that, having landed troops in Caracas, "the French or Americans," he said, "will endeavour to obtain possession of Mexico either by the same method or by conquest." On the other hand, if the British began in Mexico, they would have a firm foothold which would enable them to keep others out of Spanish America. This attack would require a larger force, for which there would be ample compensation by greater results. There were other difficulties, one of which was that of withdrawing from Mexico in case of failure, and in case of success, Great Britain might be forced to defend it against the United States.[34] In spite of the difficulties, Wellesley continued with his preparations for the Mexican enterprise, which he considered to be the one of greater importance.[35]

He next devoted some attention to the organization of the new state. The form of government should be a monarchy "with such a representative body as will not be difficult to manage." The cabildos would serve as a basis for election. The upper house was to be composed of the ancient nobility

---

[34] Wellington (ed.), *Supplementary Despatches*, VI, 61-66.

[35] Robertson, *Miranda*, pp. 410-411, however, came to the conclusion that Wellesley favored the Venezuela project because of the difficulties he pointed out in connection with Mexico.

who should be named by the king, but who the king should be, he did not know. So, at least, he said to Miranda. Wellesley added new provisions for the project from time to time, but the general plan remained the same. Two measures seemed to him essential for the success of the enterprise: to obtain possession of Vera Cruz and the castle of San Juan de Ulloa and to remove the unseasoned troops from the coast to the more healthful territory in the neighborhood of Jalapa. The idea of independence would encourage the people to raise an army so that there would be no need of supplementary troops from India. But he had increased the estimate of troops needed to seventeen thousand, one-fourth of them to be Germans.[36] Sir Arthur Wellesley was now well on the way to make the project a reality.

Wars had for a long time encouraged England to consider plans for liberating Spanish America. For a decade, 1798-1808, there was a growing interest in the project until both statesmen and military men were agreed on the advisability of undertaking it. The general opinion was that it would be to the advantage of England both as an offensive and defensive measure, as well as for commercial gain. The international situation certainly favored the enterprise.

[36] *Ibid.*, VI, 66-67.

CHAPTER XVI

BRAGANZAS, BOURBONS, AND BONAPARTES

> Buanaparte has got the continent of Europe in his hand, he squeezes it at pleasure: when its resources are thus dried, they may be again replenished from the foreign settlements of the vassal States.—The London *Times*, January 9, 1808, quoted by W. S. Robertson.
>
> "*Un Bourbon sur le trone d'Espagne, c'est un voisin trop dangereaux.*"—NAPOLEON.

NAPOLEON and France have been mentioned not only as being the incentive for British action but also as having designs on Mexico similar to those of England. We recall Napoleon's words to his soldiers, his threat after the manifesto of Godoy, the suggestions of DePons, and the warnings of Dumouricz, Castlereagh, and Wellesley. It remains to be seen what actions followed these threats and warnings.

Before Napoleon could turn to the conquest of the Iberian peninsula, he had to settle his affairs with Prussia and Russia. The Treaty of Tilsit, July 9, 1807, was in part a recognition of what Napoleon had accomplished thus far, and it prepared the way for his new undertaking in the Spanish peninsula. The continental system had a bad leak as long as Portugal continued to be an ally of England, and Napoleon was not the kind of man to neglect such a detail without trying to apply a remedy. Secret articles of the treaty signed at Tilsit assured Napoleon of a new combination against England, and he probably decided then on the removal of the Bourbon and Braganza families from their thrones in favor of the Bonapartes.[1] When he tried to unite all the continental navies into one great federation, Napoleon showed that England was wise in seeking allies in America; and when the Portuguese refusal to close her ports to England was followed by a report in the *Moniteur*

[1] Alison, *Lives of Castlereagh and Stewart*, I, 216-217.

that the House of Braganza had ceased to reign,[2] Napoleon's plans began to reveal themselves. First he came as a friend of the Spanish and appealed to them for aid and approval for the partition of Portugal. He found the Spaniards amenable since they had never been quite reconciled to an independent Portugal. The king was led to believe that he would get a generous share of the spoils at the end of the war, territory which might be used in exchange for Gibraltar; and Godoy selfishly supported the division of the neighboring state, since he was to be given two of the southern provinces and be made the king of Algarves. The colonies would be provided for by making the Spanish king the "Emperor of the Two Americas."[3] The Spanish king, however, was soon to be a Bonaparte.

So far there was no indication of the impending danger to Spain, except the example of what would happen to those who dared resist the emperor. The Spaniards had given some evidence of being unwilling allies, and Napoleon would certainly take measures to secure their allegiance so that they could no longer turn against him at a critical moment. Napoleon probably had made no definite plan with regard to Spain, but he could act quickly when the need arose and would therefore await developments. The undignified quarrels of the royal family could easily develop into a favorable situation. Both factions had made appeals to Napoleon and there was some talk of Ferdinand's seeking a marriage alliance with a member of Napoleon's family.[4] The emperor decided to settle the Portuguese situation first and then be prepared for any contingency.

The expedition sent to depose the Braganza family and to

[2] *Ibid.*, I, 223; Mowat, *Diplomacy of Napoleon*, p. 210.
[3] Mowat, *Diplomacy of Napoleon*, p. 209.
[4] Louis Antoine Fauvelet de Bourrienne, *Memoirs of Napoleon Bonaparte*, ed. R. W. Phipps (revised ed., 3 vols., New York, 1891), III, 129-130. Bourne, *Napoleon the First*, p. 427. Albert Savine, *L'Abdication de Bayonne* (Paris, 1908), p. 112, refers to a letter by the Prince of Austria dated Oct. 11, 1807.

conquer Portugal was under General Junot. But his troops were not the only ones to cross the Pyrenees. Napoleon used this opportunity to send large forces into Spain and he ordered DuPont to establish headquarters at Vittoria with a force of twenty-five thousand men.[5] These were ostensibly to act as auxiliaries to Junot, but they could serve equally well to keep Spain in line. Portugal was quickly overrun by the French troops, although they arrived in Lisbon too late to capture the royal family, which, with the aid of the British navy, had left with its court and its treasury for Brazil on the previous day, November 29.[6] Portugal was, nevertheless, in the hands of the French.

Spain was to be dealt with next, and it is quite possible that the Portuguese episode was merely the introduction or the setting for the greater enterprise. The Spaniards had good reason for feeling uneasy since French troops were pouring into Spain along its whole frontier, even into Catalonia. Portugal did not seem to be sufficient excuse for all this; therefore a new one was invented in that these troops were intended for an expedition against Gibraltar.[7] This would of course give Napoleon an opportunity to take possession of the whole peninsula. That the invasion was the introduction for the removal of the Bourbons from the throne may be seen in the purpose of Napoleon's visit to Italy at this time, undoubtedly to offer the Spanish throne to his elder brother Joseph,[8] then king of Naples, where he had replaced another Bourbon. Louis XIV had once placed a Bourbon on the throne of Spain; why should not Napoleon place a Bonaparte on the same throne?

By the beginning of 1808 the situation in Spain was becoming critical because of the arrival of additional troops. The

---

[5] Mowat, *Diplomacy of Napoleon*, p. 210.
[6] *Ibid.*
[7] Bourne, *The Revolutionary Period in Europe*, p. 351.
[8] Mowat, *Diplomacy of Napoleon*, pp. 210-211.

appointment of Murat in February as lieutenant of the emperor in Spain must have opened the heavy eyes of Charles IV. Resistance seemed useless, for it was too late; therefore Godoy and the king decided to escape from Madrid. Perhaps they intended to imitate the Portuguese by taking refuge in America, which they could set up a court in one of the colonies, probably Mexico.[9] They had gone only as far as Aranjuez when their plans were suspected and a mob prevented their advance. Charles IV was forced to dismiss his unpopular minister, and, seeing that he was unable to cope with the situation, abdicated on March 19 in favor of his son, who then became Ferdinand VII.

This turn of affairs did not please Napoleon, for he would have a hand in any changes to be made in order to secure advantages for himself. He therefore decided not to recognize Ferdinand, but indicated his willingness to have a conference with him, supposedly in Burgos or Vittoria. Napoleon remained at Bayonne, where he made his headquarters, and Ferdinand was induced to cross the border to see him, submitting to Napoleon's wishes in hopes that he might thereby gain his good will and recognition. Murat, who was already in Madrid, handled the situation quite well, and it is possible that he hoped to become the successor of Ferdinand VII, who was to be dethroned.[10] A few days later Charles IV with his wife and Godoy also appeared at Bayonne where the family quarrels were renewed, whereupon Napoleon took advantage of the Bourbons to deprive them of the throne. Charles IV retracted his abdication, which he said had been forced, and was secretly induced to give up his claims to Napoleon who was supposed to be the only one who could restore order in the country. Ferdinand resisted stubbornly all attempts to make him renounce his newly acquired royal position, until

[9] A. Schalk de la Faverie, *Napoléon et l'Amérique* (Paris, 1917), p. 205.
[10] Bourrienne, *Memoirs of Napoléon*, III, 132.

the revolt in Madrid on May 2 gave Napoleon the advantage, and he threatened to try him for treason as being responsible for the uprising. The Spanish ministers tried to convince Napoleon that the abdication of Ferdinand would be invalid without the consent of the nation, a condition which he seemed unable to understand and which later contributed to his own downfall. By the treaty of May 5 Napoleon was free to dispose of the Spanish nation and empire.

A semblance of legality was upheld in the reorganization of the government. Murat had successfully and ruthlessly put down the rebellion of *Dos de Mayo,* leaving an undercurrent of fear and hatred but an outward appearance of submission. A junta of regency was appointed, whose duty it was to request that Joseph Bonaparte be made their king. Another group of notables were called to Bayonne to make the same request, and most of them did as they were instructed.[11] These actions were ostensibly to satisfy the people of Spain, but the whole affair bore an air of superficiality. On May 11, 1808, Napoleon wrote to his elder brother Joseph, king of Naples: "The nation, through the Supreme Council of Castile, asks me for a king. I destine this crown for you."[12]

In this seemingly simple way he disposed of one of the world's largest empires, which, instead of being a solution to his difficulties, became one of his most vexing and critical problems. Napoleon's method was to be condemned, and his whole arrangement to be challenged. He had acted cleverly but not wisely, as he was finally to recognize. His temporary mastery of Spain and the Indies was soon to be challenged in both continents. A constitution was drawn up at Bayonne and accepted by the group of notables, who probably thought there was no choice in the matter.

The Spanish people, however, refused to accept this instru-

[11] Bourne, *Revolutionary Period in Europe,* pp. 351-352.
[12] *The Confidential Correspondence of Napoléon Bonaparte with his Brother Joseph, sometime King of Spain* (2 vols., New York, 1856), I, 320.

ment of government imposed upon them by the emperor. "Their indignation rumbled hoarsely for a time, like a volcano in labour, and then burst forth in an explosion of fury."[13] The leading citizens of the provinces met in congresses or juntas where they took over the reigns of government and ruled in the name of Ferdinand VII and in defiance of the Bonapartes. Joseph had finally yielded to his brother's requests and accepted the crown of Spain, and in July he set out to rule a country which was already up in arms against him. His position was entirely dependent upon the support of France, and since Spain would not submit willingly she would have to be conquered. Napoleon was determined to rule Spain and to acquire the wealth of the Indies.

When the emperor began to make plans for the overthrow of the Bourbons in Spain, he already had his eye on the resources of the Indies. Both England and France had found sustenance in Spanish America: England, because of her control of the sea and by means of her smuggling, and Napoleon, indirectly through his influence over Spain, who was expected to share her resources during this critical period. Each feared the predominance of the other and made plans accordingly. On April 15, 1808, Napoleon wrote to the minister of the interior to request him to establish and encourage colonial trade with Spanish America. He suggested that commercial companies be organized at the leading French ports and offered them government subsidies. Special boats were to be built for this trade.[14] He was aware that the French might not be received with favor, but hoped to counteract this by sending agents to America to prepare the inhabitants for the inevitable. The agents were to make themselves familiar with the changes taking place in Spain and then show the colonists that these were to their advantage. It is not certain when he first sent

[13] Rose, *The Life of Napoléon* I, p. 154.
[14] *Correspondance de Napoléon Ier* (32 vols., Paris, 1865), XVII, 1-2.

agents to America, but on April 25 he wrote to Vice-Admiral Decrés, saying that he supposed he had sent agents to Mexico and to Montevideo and urged him to send additional ones.[15]

One of these agents, Octaviano D'Alvimar, attracted considerable attention in Mexico. His passport was dated November 27, 1807, at Bordeaux,[16] which shows that he was sent before the invasion of Spain. D'Alvimar, also known as "General Alvina," was a relative of Le Clerc and a man of considerable experience both in Europe and Spanish America.[17] He had been with Le Clerc in his unsuccessful expedition to Santo Domingo. He had also been in Caracas and Havana as well as other Spanish American centers in an effort to get aid for Le Clerc's expedition.[18] In the spring of 1808 he came to Philadelphia, where he had a conference with General Moreau, before continuing his journey to Mexico. Vidal, the Spanish vice-consul, was informed by Wilkinson and Claiborne of his presence, and wrote to the viceroy of Mexico of his proposed visit. He described him as being "a man of talent, high enterprise, with no morality; cruel, and with his apparent and assumed affability, capable of insinuating himself into the hearts of the most imperturbable and of playing upon the ignorant at will."[19] He was evidently worthy of the confidence of Bonaparte and well fitted for his task. At Baton Rouge he was treated kindly by Grand Pré, who was soon to regret his hospitality. D'Alvimar was even given a boat to go up the Red River on his way to the Provincias Internas.[20]

On August 5, 1808, D'Alvimar was arrested at Nacogdoches and taken to Monclova, where he attempted to escape, but was recaptured. He was ordered to be taken to the castle of Perote unless his papers gave reason for some other provision. The

[15] *Ibid.*, XVII, 47.
[16] Alamán, *Historia de Méjico*, I, 296.
[17] Cox, *West Florida Controversy*, pp. 313-314.
[18] Alamán, *Historia de Méjico*, I, 297.
[19] Cox, *West Florida Controversy*, pp. 313-314.
[20] *Ibid.*, p. 314.

examination of these papers did not lead to any clue as to his real purpose. They seemed to indicate that he was merely an adventurer or soldier of fortune. But he was suspected of being one of Napoleon's agents. He wrote four letters while he was a prisoner, one was addressed to Napoleon to inform him of his whereabouts, and the rest referred to his baggage. On opening one of his trunks at Baton Rouge it was found to contain some French uniforms, a copy of Machiavelli, and a treatise on the art of war[21]—a splendid combination for an emissary of Napoleon.

When he passed through Dolores as a prisoner, he was said to have had some conversation with Hidalgo. The latter in his trial declared that their conversation had been only about casual things, and this in the presence of several persons.[22] D'Alvimar was taken to San Juan de Ulloa, where his money and jewelry were taken from him. After he had been sent to Spain on an English vessel the authorities in Mexico received orders from Spain to sentence him.[23]

Napoleon did not intend to leave his agents without support, and urged Decrès to send "briggs, galleons, and frigates" to Spanish America.[24] He feared that the colonists might take advantage of the disturbed conditions in the peninsula to "deprive Europe forever of the advantages attached to their possession."[25] He also intimated that there was need for a strong monarch. He wanted the Spanish Americans to be informed of all these events and continued to urge Decrès to send boats with arms and a large number of letters and documents of information. These were to be sent particularly to La Plata and Mexico.[26] Six light and fast vessels should be built espe-

---

[21] *Ibid.*, p. 317.
[22] Alamán, *Historia de Méjico*, I, 359-360.
[23] Bustamante, *Supplemento*, III, 261. In 1822 he returned to Mexico and claimed a large sum for his confiscated property. He also requested that Iturbide make him a lieutenant colonel in the army, but this request was ignored.
[24] Napoleon to Decrès, April 25, 1808, *Correspondance de Napoléon Ier*, XVII, 47.
[25] *Ibid.*, XVII, 74.   [26] *Ibid.*, XVII, 110-111.

cially for communication with the colonies.²⁷ Junot, too, was urged to arrange for sending six boats to Spanish America, three to go to Vera Cruz. The boats were to leave eight days apart, and each was to contain letters for the viceroy.²⁸ On May 22 the Duke of Berg was instructed to announce at Madrid that six ships had already left French ports with letters, proclamations, and instructions for the Spanish authorities in America. The colonists were to be informed that everything was to their advantage since they no longer had anything to fear from France.²⁹ Furthermore they would receive protection against England.

The Mexicans did not trust the French and much less Napoleon. Every boat that came from Spain was carefully watched to prevent any action of his agents. In August, 1808, the *Gazeta* stated that large loans had been made by the agents of Napoleon from the Bank of France to be used in winning over the civil and military authorities of Mexico.³⁰ A French vessel arrived on August 10, 1808, carrying dispatches for the government, and there was considerable suspicion aroused by the actions of the captain of the ship and the commandant at Vera Cruz. The public made some attempt to break into the post office to get the papers intended for the viceroy. They condemned the captain, Cevallos, and made proclamations for Ferdinand VII.³¹ There was probably a greater opposition in Mexico than Napoleon expected, and the agents would find their task extremely difficult.

Napoleon certainly did not intend to leave the colonial administration without changes. He wrote to Gregorio de la Cuesta on May 25,³² asking him to accept the office of viceroy

---

[27] *Ibid.,* XVII, 104.
[28] Napoleon to Junot, May 15, 1808, *ibid.,* XVII, 157.
[29] Napoleon to Berg, *Correspondence de Napoléon Ier,* XVII, 157.
[30] *Gazeta de México,* Aug., 1808, XV.
[31] Pedro Alonso to Iturrigaray, Vera Cruz, Aug. 11, 1808; Garibay to Pedro Cevallos, Mexico, Feb. 20, 1809, A. G. I., 9-1-19, legajo 8.
[32] *Correspondance de Napoléon Ier,* XVII, 237.

of Mexico in order to secure it for the motherland and avoid the bad effects which might result from discontent with the present government. In other words, he wanted a viceroy of his own appointment to prevent the independence of Mexico. With this in mind we can better appreciate the difficult position of Iturrigaray, the viceroy of Mexico.

On the day after writing to Cuesta, Napoleon addressed a long letter to the Duke of Berg, telling him of the appointment. The latter should prepare the patents and commissions both for the viceroy and three or four colonels, brigadiers, or field marshals. The Duke had appointed a field marshal for Vera Cruz before this time, but Napoleon told him that "he was an officer without any merit and had gained his rank with money." He was also ordered to prepare the frigate *Flora* at Cadiz to carry the viceroy to Mexico, and in addition to this he should prepare despatch boats in the small ports between Cadiz and Portugal from whence they could easily leave for America. The *Flora* was to be prepared with three thousand guns and other things necessary for Mexico.[33] Napoleon urged haste above everything else because "America needs aid." He wanted to send officials, guns, boats, and proclamations to get possession of Mexico before it was too late. But Cuesta did not accept, because of poor health, according to his answer to Napoleon.[34] The emperor then requested him to name some other person in the army, not over fifty years of age or about fifty, who would be strong enough to hold the position.[35]

That this position was then offered to General Castañas is indicated by a report he gave to the British. Towards the end of May, he said, General Murat's aide-de-camp, Constantin, and another man came to Algeciras. General Castañas thought they came to arrest him, and therefore planned to kill the

[33] *Correspondance de Napoléon Ier*, XVII, 246-248.
[34] May 29, 1808, *ibid.*, XVII, 297.   [35] *Ibid.*

Frenchman and to escape to Gibraltar. To his surprise, the conversation took a different turn, and he was offered the appointment of the viceroyalty of Mexico with the assurance that Napoleon would approve and confirm it. Constantin added the interesting statement "that the measure of removing the whole of the Family of Bourbons from Spain had for three years past been the object of all Bonaparte's measures." And the House of Austria was to fall next. Dalrymple, who sent the report, would not comment on this, but said that as soon as order was established in Spain, the appointment of General Castaños to Mexico would certainly take place.[36]

Napoleon's plans to become master of Mexico were evident, and justified the fears of the Americans. But Spain proved to be the most difficult obstacle which he had encountered in Europe. Even his orders were not carried out. The difficulties of building ships as rapidly as Napoleon ordered them had been too great for the minister of marine, and he failed to comply with the orders. But he must have been thoroughly impressed by the power of Napoleon, since he compared him to a God, for which Napoleon kindly excused him, as well as for his neglect to send any ships to America; but he added that if he had had a minister of marine with any sense he would have had forty ships ready. As it was, Napoleon sent the only three boats which had been dispatched.[37] He had also mentioned that the sending of rifles and pistols to America was the best way in which to prepare the colonists to resist England.[38] He might well make this statement since Wellesley had already assembled an army at Cork destined for Mexico.

While Napoleon was preparing to arm the colonists against the British, the latter were preparing to support their inde-

[36] Copy of a letter from H. Dalrymple to Lord Castlereagh, Gibraltar, June 10, 1808, P. R. O., F. O. 72 (Spain), LXVIII.
[37] Napoleon to Decrès, May 22, 1808, *Correspondance de Napoléon Ier*, XVII, 212.
[38] *Ibid.*, XVII, 86.

pendence to prevent them from falling into the hands of Napoleon as Spain had.[39] Mr. Pavia, whom the British had detained in 1805, on account of his knowledge of Mexico, was now to be employed, together with Mr. Williamson, in preparing the Spanish colonies to accept British protection against Napoleon.[40] Burr, too, was reported to have gone to England to revive his Mexican project.[41] The occasion for active British aid was at hand, and Miranda called it a "grand and providential opportunity."[42] But he realized that they would have to get there before the enemy won the colonies by "some plausible scheme," and Napoleon was urging the same haste to forestall the British.

By June 1, 1808, Wellesley was making arrangements for the departure of his troops from Cork. He had now been instructed to consider an attack on Spain and, if this failed, to send the combined forces to the West Indies where they would proceed to liberate the Spanish colonies in the Gulf of Mexico.[43] The eight thousand troops at Cork should unite with those of General Spencer near Cadiz and those of General Prevost at Halifax, making an expedition of nearly seventeen thousand men, the force necessary for the attack on New Spain.[44] When Lord Melville heard that the expedition at Cork was to make a preliminary move to Spain, he addressed a letter to Lord Castlereagh in which he expressed some doubt as to the advisability of the plan. He did not think the Spaniards could make an effective resistance and that the effort would only

[39] The first point to be considered now was Cuba, both for its wealth and its strategic position. Lord Castlereagh to the Duke of Manchester, June 4, 1808, Castlereagh, *Correspondence*, VI, 364-368.
[40] *Ibid.*, VI, 368.
[41] Cox, "Jefferson and Wilkinson," *The Mississippi Valley Historical Review*, I, 216; Wandell and Minnigerode, *Burr*, II, 230.
[42] Miranda to Lord Castlereagh, May 16, 1808, Castlereagh, *Correspondence*, VII, 441-442.
[43] There was also a suggestion to send detachments to La Plata and Caracas which would later unite with the main corps in the Gulf of Mexico, Wellington, *Supplementary Despatches*, VI, 68-70.
[44] *Ibid.*, VI, 73, 74.

endanger the British troops. But in reference to the other project he said: "I am very sanguine in my expectations of success in effecting a separation of Spanish America from the mother country." If he were to decide "where the most beneficial exertions could be made," he "should be obliged to decide in favour of an attack on the province of Mexico," he said, although the preparatory steps could be at Mobile, Pensacola, or New Orleans.[45]

On June 4 Lord Castlereagh wrote a series of letters and recommendations to instruct British officials in the rôle they were to play with regard to Spanish America. The great catastrophe in Spain was described, and "Under these circumstances," he said, "it becomes the duty of his Majesty's Ministers to make every exertion for preventing the American provinces of Spain from falling into the same treachery which is subjecting Spain itself." Cuba was emphasized, a colony of great value, against which the French were already known to have designs. Fortunately, for the English, the inhabitants had shown great hostility to these French schemes and this was to be encouraged by the governor of Jamaica, even to the point of creating an open break. An English report of the events in Spain was to be translated into Spanish and given to the colonial officials. Besides fanning the flame of animosity into open hostility, the governor was to assure the colonials that Great Britain was the only power which could restore the independence of Spain. If the restoration in Spain became hopeless there would be only two lines of conduct left:

One, that the Spanish provinces should declare themselves independent, and place themselves under the dominion of some Prince of the Royal Family not in the power of Buanaparte—this independence to be guaranteed by Great Britain. The other, that the Spanish provinces should declare themselves independent, and erect Governments according to their own free choice—the independence of such Governments to be guaranteed by Great Britain.

[45] Londonderry (ed.), *Correspondence of Castlereagh*, VII, 442-448.

The first step should be to secure a declaration of hostility against France, with the assurance of British coöperation and support. If the Spanish officials were disposed to negotiate on this basis, they were to be assured that Great Britain formally disclaimed and renounced every attempt of conquering any of the colonies. British forces were to be sent to help Cuba resist any move on the part of France, and, if the officials of Cuba or the Floridas were willing to coöperate, the governor might also make advances for the payment of their troops. Every effort should be made to show the hopelessness of any support from Spain and that independence with British protection was unquestionably better than subordination to the usurper of Spain.[46] Charles Williamson was instructed to be ready to be secretly employed by the governor in promoting the resistance to the French.[47] Then the commander of the forces in the Leeward Islands was requested to coöperate and to be ready to send one thousand troops to Jamaica.[48] Everything seemed to be in readiness and Wellesley was prepared to sail.

On June 8, the day that Lord Melville informed Castlereagh that he preferred Mexico as the objective for Wellesley's expedition, an event occurred which changed British policy and left Mexico to face the crisis alone without the aid which England was ready to send her. This event was the arrival in London of two commissioners from the junta of Asturias at Oviedo,[49] who informed the British government that they had taken up arms against the invader and who asked for support in their struggle against Napoleon.[50] Any opportunity to strike a blow at the arch-enemy was certain to win favor in England, and four days after their arrival in London the commissioners

[46] *Ibid.*, VI, 364-368. The letter was to be brought by Mr. Pavia, who had been an intendant in Havana and who had "many connexions in Mexico," *ibid.*, VI, 368-369.   [47] *Ibid.*, VI, 369.   [48] *Ibid.*, VI, 369-370.
[49] The declaration of the junta was made May 25, 1808, Londonberry (ed.), *Correspondence of Castlereagh*, VI, 363-364.
[50] For a detailed account see William Spence Robertson, "The Juntas of 1808 and the Spanish Colonies," *The English Historical Review*, XXXI, 576 (Oct., 1916).

were assured of British assistance. Mr. Sheridan gave an excellent plea for the Asturians in Parliament on June 15. He wanted the government to cease "filching sugar islands" and devote itself to one mighty project and rescue the world.[51] The province of Galicia, as well as the junta of Seville, sent representatives to England, and when Canning decided to support them the plan to liberate Mexico was necessarily postponed or given up. The first object of England was to defeat Napoleon, and the future of Mexico would depend on the outcome of the Peninsular War. In the meantime England, as an ally of Spain, expected to share in the resources of the colonies.

Arthur Wellesley, who was accustomed to face danger and crises without flinching, said that he "never had a more difficult business" than when the government bade him tell Miranda of the changed policy. "I thought it best to walk out in the streets with him and tell him there," said Wellesley, "to prevent his bursting out. But even there he was so loud and angry, that I told him I would walk on first a little that we might not attract the notice of everybody passing."[52]

Others had to be notified, as illustrated by the letters which Lord Castlereagh now sent to the officials in the West Indies to inform them of the change of policy. The paper which he had sent for circulation in the Spanish provinces was written when there was little hope for the return of the Spanish monarchs, and therefore presented a view which "calculated to detach the provinces from the mother country," he said. Since the insurrection in Asturias there was some chance of restoring the Spanish monarchy; therefore, this paper should be withheld, or they could, he said, "circulate only such parts as relate to the recent conduct of the French and do not reflect on the conduct of the Spanish Court."[53] The colonies were to be urged to

---

[51] *Hansard's Parliamentary Debates* (London, 1812), XI, 887-888.
[52] Quoted by Robertson, *Life of Miranda*, II, 23.
[53] Castlereagh to the Duke of Manchester, June 20, 1808, Londonderry (ed.), *Correspondence of Castlereagh*, VI, 375.

support the cause of Asturias and the British in preventing the French from extending their detestable "system of perfidy and oppression to the American provinces."[54] Castlereagh next sent a message from the deputies of Asturias to Mexico.[55] In less than a month England had changed from an enemy of Spain to an ally, the formal treaty of alliance being approved on July 4. The Spanish uprising had given England an opportunity to fight Napoleon on land, and therefore Wellesley's expedition was diverted from the Mexican enterprise to that of the Spanish peninsula.

The spontaneous and scattered revolts of the Spanish provinces, coupled with the menace of a British army, created a most delicate situation for the French in Spain. The great armies of Austria, Prussia, and Russia had been no match for the superior military machine of Napoleon, and yet these rebellious Spaniards were to prove an insurmountable obstacle to the greatest military leader of modern times. Their lack of organization and of a national army contributed to Napoleon's failure, because at no one place could he strike a decisive blow that would destroy Spanish resistance. One must keep in mind, however, that after the first patriotic resistance the great burden of the war fell upon the British. On the Spanish side two battles deserve particular mention, the heroic resistance of the Aragonese at Saragossa and the defeat and capture of DuPont's army at Baylen. In the next month, August, the British forces under Wellesley reached Portugal, and from that time they endangered Napoleon's position in Spain.

Joseph Bonaparte, king of Spain and the Indies, found his throne exceedingly unstable. He had been in Madrid only three days when the French were defeated at Baylen, July 23, and only ten days when he decided to withdraw to safer territory in the north.[56] Napoleon did not approve of the retreat

[54] Castlereagh to commander of the forces of the Leeward Islands, June 20, 1808, ibid., VI, 374-375.   [55] Ibid., VI, 375.
[56] Bourne, *Revolutionary Period in Europe*, p. 354.

of his brother; but he could do nothing about it at that time because the French army had been driven out of nearly all except northern Spain, and he had other more pressing affairs to settle in Europe. This gave Spain three months in which to prepare her defense against Napoleon's new campaign, but she had great difficulty in getting unified action. The local juntas, which had sprung up like mushrooms, clung to their assumed sovereignty with a selfish tenacity which left the country in political chaos. "It was unfortunate," wrote Oman, "but inevitable, that the Juntas were largely composed of furious but incapable zealots, ambitious demagogues, and self-seeking intriguers."[57]

Having convinced the world of his greatness by a dazzling display at Erfurt and having made new agreements with the Czar and others for his own safety, Napoleon was free to turn again to the Spanish project. This time he led in person a veteran army which by December conquered Madrid. There he made a series of sweeping reforms, which failed entirely to win the expected support since they attacked tradition. He also helped himself to any wealth to be found, creating a deficit which was to be a great burden on both Spain and the colonies. His conquest of the rest of the peninsula was postponed by the necessity of concentrating his forces against the British, who were not only in possession of Portugal but who threatened also to reconquer Madrid. Furthermore, with too many irons in the fire, Napoleon was compelled to leave the conquest of the rest of Spain to his generals because the Austrians demanded his attention.

Spain had upset all his plans: she incited others to rebellion, she encouraged his enemies and gave them a place to fight from, and she made him change his policy with respect to the Spanish colonies. Napoleon's invasion had been accompanied by an attempt to win the colonies. The Spanish upris-

[57] Charles Oman, "The Peninsular War," *Cambridge Modern History*, IX, 435.

ing had made his colonial scheme untenable; therefore he, too, decided to work for the independence of the American colonies. The British had been prevented from executing the liberation project just what it was about to begin and when it might have had a fair chance of success. The change of revolutionary promoters from British to French also changed the method from armies to propaganda. Hence the events in Europe were of tremendous consequence in New Spain.

CHAPTER XVII

THE MEXICAN REACTION TO NAPOLEON

> "All the world is astir, and Mexico must be moving. . . . The leaven of liberty is working. . . . And where shall be found a leader? Here is opportunity; where is the man? . . . There is manifest every phase of feeling from loyalty, wholly or partially, to independence, wholly or partially."—HUBERT H. BANCROFT.
>
> "*Tanto el virey como los licenciados Azcárate y Verdad que dirijían al ayuntamiento, estaban en la persuasión de que España no podría resistir a los franceses. . . . Era pues, el plan de los individuos influyentes en la municipalidad, aprovecher las circunstancias en que España se hallaba para hacer la independencia. . . .*"—LUCAS ALAMÁN.

HAVING followed the foreign intrigues for some time, we may now consider the situation in Mexico and note the reaction to the European events. Both revolutionists and Spanish officials have failed to give a true picture of conditions in New Spain. The people were not as anxious for independence as the revolutionists would have the world believe, nor were they so universally devoted to the Spanish monarchs and as tranquil and peaceful as many of the official reports seem to indicate. Disturbances occurred, plots were discovered, and plans were obstructed by the watchful eye of the government. Officials had to exercise care in subduing or smothering the tendencies to disaffection in order to prevent the spread of hostile feeling. In many cases the people must have been ignorant of the international schemes for their liberation, but the events of 1808 were too significant to pass without a distinct reaction and a threat of revolution.

While the emperor of France and the authorities of England were plotting against one another with Spanish America as a pawn, the people of Mexico were left in the most unusual position of not knowing whether they were independent or still subject. And if they were subject, to whom did they owe allegiance? The viceroy of Mexico during these stirring times was José de Iturrigaray, a creature of Godoy, and "the last viceroy of the ancient régime." William Jacob, in discussing the possibilities of liberating Mexico, said that Iturrigaray had obtained his office through favoritism and that he was generally considered to be a weak man.[1] He was certainly not the man to cope with the problems which grew out of Napoleon's invasion of Spain. Had he been a forceful individual he might have separated Mexico from Spain for his own advantage.

The report on June 8 of Ferdinand VII's replacing Charles IV on the throne was received with a great demonstration of joy by most of the Mexican people.[2] Iturrigaray, on the other hand, manifested his disgust because his friend and protector, Godoy, had been removed with the king; and his position was, indeed, precarious. The viceroy was at San Agustín de la Cuevas when the news arrived from Spain, and for two days he made no public announcement of it in Mexico; but, seeing that the people were growing impatient, he found it necessary to make a formal manifestation of his allegiance to the new monarch. That the viceroy was an opportunist is clearly seen when he received the proclamation of Murat, Napoleon's representative at Madrid, announcing the removal of both the Bourbons.[3] He is said to have given this report in an exaggerated fashion to create a sensation, and he indicated that there was little hope now for Ferdinand VII or any other member of the royal family to return to the throne of Spain. The *real acuerdo,* the audiencia in executive capacity, considered this date as the beginning of the ideas of independence in Mexico.[4] The report of the abdication of the Spanish monarchs was veri-

[1] Londonderry (ed.), *Correspondence of Castlereagh,* VII, 300.
[2] Alamán, *Historia de Méjico,* I, 163.
[3] This report reached Mexico June 23, 1808, Genaro García (ed.), *Documentos Históricos Mexicanos, Obra Commemorativa del Primer Centenario de la Independencia de México* (6 vols., Mexico, 1910), II, 346-347.
[4] Report of the *real acuerdo,* Nov. 9, 1808, *ibid.*

fied by the arrival of the *Ventura* in Mexico, July 14, 1808.[5] Had the people been as ready for rebellion as some of the revolutionists would have us believe, they might have made Bastile Day doubly famous. Lethargy and the habit of submission prevented any action. On the following day the *real acuerdo* agreed that they ought not to recognize Murat nor any government except that of their own legitimate sovereign. The members must have anticipated trouble, for they recommended that the country be put into a state of defense.[6]

The Spanish colonies found themselves in a most extraordinary situation. Spain was left without a king and the crown was to be disposed of as Napoleon saw fit. Were the colonies free or were they not? This became the vital political question for the next two years. The allegiance of the Americans to Spain was not for love of country nor for love of the Spanish people, but due to their devotion to their king. In fact, Mexico was a kingdom, subject to the Spanish king, and the union with Spain was merely a personal one.[7] The king had been exalted to the position of a fetish, and was the only strong tie between the colonies and the mother country. The removal of the king, then, was equivalent to breaking the strongest bond for union. It was indeed an opportunity for those who desired freedom from the oppressive government in Spain as well as in America.

The ayuntamiento or municipal government, which was closest to the people, made immediate preparations for taking an active part in the coming events. Another question was, in which man or body of men did authority rest? The viceroy was the representative of the king, but without a king there could be no representative. Ideas of popular authority grew, and the ayuntamiento of Mexico City desired to represent all

[5] *Ibid.*
[6] *Ibid.*, II, 346.
[7] This was recognized by writers of the time such as Alexander von Homboldt and William Walton. Cf. Walton, *Exposé on the Dissensions of Spanish America*, p. 25.

of New Spain.[8] In the Spanish peninsula sovereign power had been taken over by the juntas whose members ruled in the name of the king, but who also considered themselves as representatives of the people. Sovereign power was a coveted prize in New Spain; the Spaniards wanted it as a symbol of the right to dominate, and the party desiring independence wanted it as a pretext to hide their true tendencies.[9]

A group of prominent men saw the opportunity for independence, but instead of proclaiming a revolution openly, they paved the way for a gradual change to self-government. Such were the desires and aims of Verdad y Ramos, Azcárate y Lezama, Fray Melchor de Talamantes, and Jacobo de Villa Urrutia. Their first objective was to set up a provisional government. The viceroy was flattered and cajoled into believing that only by calling a provisional congress could he be certain of holding his office. The ayuntamiento supported this view and went so far as to tell the viceroy that in the absence of the legitimate heir to the throne, sovereignty rested in the people and the officials, especially in the higher tribunals and in the ayuntamiento.[10]

This was, of course, political heresy in a Spanish country, and the members of the *real acuerdo* notified the viceroy and the ayuntamiento that no changes needed to be made in Mexico. A provisional body, they said, would weaken rather than strengthen the government and expose it to changes which were dangerous; and furthermore it would be not only impolitic but illegal.[11] This was the beginning of that long struggle between the privileged Spaniards and the creoles or Americans. The permanent *regidores* of the town council

---

[8] Vicente Riva Palacio (ed.), *México á través de los Siglos* (5 vols., Barcelona, 1888-1889; vol. III, by Julio Zárate), III, 40.
[9] *Ibid.*
[10] Report of the ayuntamiento, July 19, García (ed.), *Documentos Históricos*, II, 15-34.
[11] Report of the *real acuerdo*, July 21, *ibid.*, II, 37-38.

were nearly all Americans who had inherited their offices and who now became the champions of the creole element.[12]

While the French were in control of Spain, the colonists had an opportunity to discuss their affairs and prospects quite freely, and there were many who promoted the idea of independence in imitation of the United States.[13] Among the suggestions for a new government was the one made on July 15 by the *fiscal,* Robledo, to Villa Urrutia, that the Infante Dom Pedro of Portugal, then in Brazil, should be called to Mexico to rule as regent.[14] He had some right or claim, since he was related to the imprisoned kings of Spain. This proposal was rejected by the audiencia, but was later to be renewed by the Braganza family itself.[15] There was also an Indian, claiming direct descent from Montezuma, who considered himself a suitable candidate for the Mexican crown, now that Spain had no king.[16]

The numerous candidates for the royal office both in Spain and in Mexico added to the confusion. The outlying provinces of Mexico were also disturbed, and fantastic rumors spread without restraint and without foundation. Some spoke of independence, some of Iturrigaray becoming king, some proclaimed Ferdinand VII king, others predicted the ruin of the viceroyalty, and still others of religion. The people went so far as to hold popular meetings for discussions, but no decisions or plans for action were made. The importance of their meetings was in the acts themselves, for they were new and aroused popular interest in politics.[17] When some of the provinces,

[12] Riva Palacio (ed.), *México á través de los Siglos,* III, 41; Bernard Moses, "Government in Spanish America," *The American Political Science Review,* VIII, 206 (May, 1914).

[13] García (ed.), *Documentos Históricos,* II, 302.

[14] Riva Palacio (ed.), *México á través de los Siglos,* III, 42; Alamán, *Historia de Méjico,* I, 166.

[15] A. F. Zimmerman, "Spain and its Colonies, 1808-1820," *The Hispanic American Historical Review,* XI, 440-441 (Nov., 1931).

[16] Juan López Cancelada, *La Verdad Sabida* (Cadiz, 1811), p. 22.

[17] Riva Palacio (ed.), *México á través de los Siglos,* III, 42.

notably Jalapa, sent commissions to Iturrigaray, saying they were ready to defend their country and their religion and willing to obey orders, the peninsulars thought the ambition of the viceroy might lead him to use this support to make himself king of New Spain.[18] The vacillating viceroy, however, did not know which way to turn; he was tossed between the two factions, unable to direct his course. He allowed circumstances to determine his policy, and the news from Europe served as a barometer of action.

On July 29 the *Gazeta de México* published a special edition to inform the Mexicans of the heroic revolt of the Spanish people against the deceitful emperor of the French.[19] This reversed the whole situation and checked the growing ideas of independence. The government of Spain had been taken over by provincial congresses and juntas. In the name of Ferdinand VII these juntas called on all Spaniards to the defense of their country.[20]

The work for independence continued, although it was done with greater secrecy and care because the people were too much attached to their king to be put to the trial. The independence party, for so it might be called, continued to urge the viceroy to call a national junta which, by making use of circumstances, could easily drift towards independence.[21] The question of the necessity or justification for calling a general congress became the subject for bitter debate between the Spanish and American factions. Four local juntas were held as preliminary meetings to get some basis for action.

The first of these was held on August 9, and accomplished little except to emphasize the conflict between the two increasingly hostile parties. They agreed, however, to reject all claims

---

[18] Genaro García, *El Plan de Independencia de la Nueva España en 1808* (Mexico, 1903), pp. 17-18.
[19] *Gazeta Extraordinario de México*, XV, 501.
[20] García, *El Plan de Independencia*, p. 18.
[21] Alamán, *Historia de Méjico*, I, 181-183.

by the Bonapartes, to act in the name of Ferdinand VII, and to accept none but a Bourbon as sovereign. The peninsulars wanted to recognize the government of the Junta of Seville, but neither the viceroy nor the American faction would do this.[22] Iturrigaray published a report of the first junta in the *Gazeta* on August 12 and requested a formal celebration for the next day in order to make an official proclamation to the public.[23]

The reading of the proclamation was followed by three days of ceremony and celebration. Coins and medals were struck with a new effigy of Ferdinand VII. On the last day of the celebration a heated quarrel between some Spanish members of a commercial house and some peasants was followed by the firing of a few shots resulting in the death of two men. This has been considered as the first blood to be shed in the long struggle for independence.[24] It was not the first, nor was it necessarily for independence, but it was indicative of the ill-feeling which was to be fanned for another two years before breaking out into open revolt.

There was a great difference of opinion both in Mexico and in the provinces as to the accomplishment of the first junta. Talamantes, one of the most independent thinkers, would go much farther. He wanted a general congress as a basis for setting up a new government, partly to check the viceroy, who could no longer represent their king since they had none.[25] The Inquisition, on the other hand, would have neither a junta nor a congress, and wanted Talamantes brought before their court for his views.[26]

---

[22] Report of the junta published in the *Gazeta Extraordinaria de México*, XV, 559; and report of viceroy, Aug. 20, 1808, García (ed.), *Documentos Históricos*, II, 65; see also J. L. Cancelada, *Conducta del excelentísimo Señor Don José Iturrigaray . . . en Nueva España* (Cadiz, 1811), pp. 43-49.

[23] Proclamation, with notes attributed to Talamantes, and facsimile, in García (ed.), *Documentos Historicos*, II, 60-63.

[24] Riva Palacio (ed.), *México á través de los Siglos* III, 50.

[25] Alamán, *Historia de Méjico*, I, Appendix No. 9, pp. 34-35.

[26] *Ibid.*, I, 214.

When commissioners came from the Central Junta at Seville to get the oath of allegiance from New Spain, they were informed of the action at the meeting of August 9. The viceroy, however, agreed to call another junta for August 31 to give them a hearing. The members were still equally divided, and spent considerable time in a futile effort to define that elusive and intangible thing known as sovereignty. There had been a leaning towards a partial recognition of the Seville Junta,[27] thus dividing indivisible sovereignty, when, on the night of the Mexican meeting, Iturrigaray received a letter from the commissioners of Oviedo who had gone to England to get aid against France. Here was further evidence that sovereignty had been dismembered in Spain and that the provincial juntas were rivals for its favor, as were also the Mexicans. The viceroy called a third junta for September 1 to consider this news. He had found a loophole by which he could escape giving his allegiance to any junta, since no one could claim absolute supremacy in Spain. This was a blow to the European faction which had almost won its point on the previous day.[28]

On the same day the peninsulars were convinced that Iturrigaray was trying to create a government which in no way depended on Spain, for he sent out a call to the ayuntamientos of the provinces to name delegates to represent them in Mexico.[29] Talamantes, who wrote on the subject, intimated that the congress which was to be formed should bring with it the seeds of independence, but it should, however, avoid any system resembling the French Revolution.[30] In another pamphlet he drew up twelve cases in which the colonies could legitimately separate from the metropolis, all of which were based on ex-

[27] *Gazeta Extraordinario de México*, XV, 611; García (ed.), *Documentos Históricos*, II, 71.
[28] García (ed.), *Documentos Históricos*, II, 71-74; Riva Palacio (ed.), *México á través de los Siglos*, III, 51-52.
[29] García (ed.), *Documentos Históricos*, II, 74.
[30] *Ibid.*, II, 74-75.

isting conditions in Mexico.³¹ This was the situation into which Iturrigaray was being led by the American element. The peninsulars made great efforts to oppose the trend towards independence, and called attention to the fact that the French Revolution was caused by the calling of an assembly in 1789. It had destroyed monarchy and brought Louis XVI to the scaffold, the "wicked Napoleon" to the throne, and had caused the present misfortunes of Spain.³² This should have been sufficient evidence to show that the calling of a national congress was unwise.

A fourth and last junta met on September 9 to get the opinions on the previous ones. The heated debates and stormy discussions left all in confusion, and the contestants were no nearer to an agreement than they had been in the first meeting. Villa Urrutia became the chief spokesman for the American group desiring a congress. He was so mercilessly questioned, attacked, and abused that he finally asked for three days in which to prepare an answer to his opponents. The archbishop, seemingly a practical churchman, said that this meeting was undoubtedly an example of what would take place if a congress were called, and decided to oppose it. The junta ended with all the questions aroused but none settled, except that the viceroy agreed not to give up his position during this critical period,³³ as he had previously threatened to do.³⁴ On September 12 Verdad gave a long written argument on popular sovereignty to show that the municipality was its agent and could therefore act in calling a congress. Furthermore, he said that the Junta of Seville had also based its authority on the people.³⁵

---

[31] Alamán, *Historia de Méjico*, I, Appendix No. 9, p. 35.

[32] García (ed.), *Documentos Históricos*, II, 82.

[33] *Ibid.*, II, 135, 142-145; Riva Palacio (ed.), *México á través de los Siglos*, III, 54-55; Alamán, *Historia de Méjico*, I, 229-230.

[34] García, *El Plan de Independencia*, pp. 40-41; Alamán, *Historia de Méjico*, I, 226.

[35] García (ed.), *Documentos Históricos*, II, 147-168.

Thus the two parties were moulding public opinion and creating that restlessness and dissatisfaction which was soon to end in a long and bloody struggle for independence. While the king remained in captivity, it was easy for the members of the American party to develop their plans with apparent loyalty. In the meantime they were arousing a national spirit and self-consciousness of the group which had heretofore been relegated to an undesirable background. The people were getting political education as the controversy continued. When the juntas had been opened to the public, the proceedings and political views became knowledge of the common people. The power of the Americans continued to grow and their audacity increased accordingly.

Suspicions were aroused, and rumors spread about the viceroy's actions, which were interpreted by his opponents as being in preparation for his promotion to kingship. He gave the Spaniards further reason for suspicion when he proceeded to make appointments to high offices which had formerly been reserved to the king alone.[36] Then came the report that Iturrigaray had sent to the neighboring cantonments for troops which were probably to be used for his support in setting up the new government. It has been said that the Europeans retired every night with the fear of awakening to the cry of *"Viva José!"*[37]

The Spaniards realized that they would have to act quickly if they were to save the country for themselves. They finally decided on the drastic measure of removing the viceroy, and this would have to be done before the arrival of the troops and the meeting of the general congress. Without the viceroy as a protector and a cover, the revolution would not materialize, they believed. The task was now to find the man who was fit to take the leadership of such a dangerous enterprise. The rich merchants and gowned judges might

---

[36] Alamán, *Historia de Méjico*, I, 233.   [37] *Ibid.*, I, 235.

well tremble at the idea of paying with their heads for any unsuccessful attempt. Their search for a leader with the necessary energy and valor to insure success was rewarded in the person of Gabriel de Yermo, an elderly and wealthy Biscayan, who had a large estate near the city.[38]

The day set for the coup d'état was September 14, three days before the troops from Celaya were expected to arrive. The event was necessarily postponed one day because the captain of the guard for that night refused to coöperate, although he agreed not to interfere. The members of the guard were nearly all in the pay of the Spanish merchants and were therefore to be trusted.[39] The plot was carried out with clock-like precision, except for the killing of one guard who had not been properly directed. Iturrigaray was aroused from his sleep by his captors who handed him his clothes in a performance which was not unlike the *levée* of Louis XIV, except for the circumstances. This marked the end of his royal aspirations, if such they had been. The viceroy and has family were held as prisoners until they could be sent to Spain for trial.[40]

A small group of men had removed the highest official of the country in an unlawful manner to prevent that official from committing what seemed to them an unlawful act of much greater importance. It was a matter of using fire to fight fire. But their method of procedure was to have more far-reaching results than they had ever anticipated. Their work was only partly begun with the removal of Iturrigaray, for he was only the means by which more radical individuals hoped to carry out their designs. Several other important arrests followed, notably those of Verdad, Azcárate, and

[38] Riva Palacio (ed.), *México á través de los Siglos,* III, 56-57.
[39] *Ibid.,* III, 57-58; Bancroft, *History of Mexico,* IV, 53.
[40] A detailed account of the viceroy's capture is given in García (ed.), *Documentos Históricos,* II, 414 ff. A defense of Iturrigaray against the criticism of Cancelada was written by Servando Mier Noriega y Guerra, *Historia de la Revolución de Nueva España.* . . . (2 vols., London, 1813).

Talamantes. These men were not treated with the same consideration as the viceroy; and Verdad died shortly after his imprisonment, arousing some suspicion as to the acts of the peninsulars. Priests and soldiers were not exempt from accusations and arrests. The oidores of the audiencia, however, tried to avoid extreme measures so as to calm the creoles and to prevent an immediate counter-revolution.[41] Another group of the Europeans favored drastic measures.

The public had become interested in politics during the recent meetings of the juntas, and their attitude would have to be taken into consideration. It must have been with considerable surprise, however, that they read the proclamation of September 16 which stated that "The people" had requested the removal of Iturrigaray from office, and had convoked the *real acuerdo* and other authorities which had, in accordance with the royal order of October 30, 1806, given the command to the field-marshal, Pedro Garibay.[42] The oidores probably did not realize what a dangerous precedent they were setting up when they included "the people" in such unheard of activities.

The new government was soon recognized by the authorities of the city, by several army officers, and most of the provinces. Zárate says that the readers of the *Gazeta* were bored for several days by these manifestations.[43] There were, to be sure, numerous opponents of the new administration, but if they dared to criticize openly they were apprehended. Approval from Spain was being courted by sending nine million pesos to the Junta of Seville on the same ship which carried the

---

[41] *Ibid.*, II, 266; Riva Palacio (ed.), *México á través de los Siglos*, III, 61-62; Alamán, *Historia de Méjico*, I, 255-256.

[42] García (ed.), *Documentos Históricos*, II, facsimile opposite p. 204.

[43] Riva Palacio (ed.), *México á través de los Siglos*, III, 63. For the manifestations, see Hernández y Dávalos, *Colección de Documentos para la Historia de la Guerra de la Independencia de México* (6 vols., Mexico, 1877-1882), I, 594, 597, 599, and 600.

deposed viceroy to his trial.[44] Iturrigaray was later freed from the charge of treason and given his liberty under the general amnesty act of October 15, 1810, much to the disgust of the Spanish element in Mexico. This did not exempt him from paying a fine for certain irregularities during his term of office.[45]

It was almost impossible to prove that Iturrigaray had meditated treason. The most serious charge was his intention to convoke a national congress, and this might have been excused because of the example set by the provinces of Spain under similar circumstances. He, like others, was resisting Napoleon, probably to cover his designs while Mexico was drifting towards independence. It is difficult to determine what might have taken place had the congress been called; yet, as Alamán points out, one can get an idea by considering the results of similar bodies in other colonial centers.[46] Many believed with Iturrigaray that Spain could never resist the arms of Napoleon and that therefore there would be no disloyalty to the Bourbons in making Mexico independent. Yet the deposition of the viceroy must have helped Spain, for she probably would not have received funds as freely from the national congress as from the new administration under Garibay and his successor. One man wrote that had the Europeans hesitated six days more in removing the viceroy Mexico would have been lost to Spain.[47]

The removal of Iturrigaray had not put an end to the opposition to the Spaniards nor the work for liberation. Anger and bitterness were undermining the vestiges of habitual veneration which the people were accustomed to give to those who had dominated and oppressed them. Lampoons written and placed

---

[44] García (ed.), *Documentos Históricos,* II, 217, 252.
[45] Alamán, *Historia de Méjico,* I, 264-265, and Appendix, pp. 45-49; for Bancroft's criticism, see his *History of Mexico,* IV, 61.
[46] Alamán, *Historia de Méjico,* I, 270-274.
[47] García (ed.), *Documentos Históricos,* II, 298.

on prominent street corners continually brought before the public eye the bitterness against the Spaniards and won converts for the cause of America for the Americans. Strenuous efforts were made by the government and rewards offered in an attempt to root out the rebellious spirits, but with little success.[48] The idea of independence had become too firmly rooted to be easily eradicated. The dismissal of Iturrigaray checked the open action, but it added bitterness and determination to the second phase of the struggle; and the method of removing the viceroy became the most dangerous precedent which the Spaniards could have given.

Garibay had been chosen viceroy because he was expected to give full support to the European party. He was old, feeble, and poverty-stricken; and Bustamante says that he was stupid enough to be a good tool of the oidores.[49] Good-hearted and weak-willed, he became the mouthpiece of those who had put him into office, and the servant of Aguirre, the most dominating figure in the audiencia.[50] In one of his duties, at least, Garibay showed himself a master, that of collecting vast sums to be sent to Spain. By October Mexico had heard of the great victories won by the Spanish over Napoleon's army, and the viceroy made use of the enthusiasm engendered by this joyful news to raise more money for the struggling motherland. He published a proclamation in which he described the pitiful condition of the imprisoned king, and then he condemned the nefarious plans of Napoleon, hoping to arouse the people to such a state of anger that they would long to attack the perfidious tyrant and usurper. He must have known the art of war propaganda. He lamented the fact that the ocean, which separated them from the scene of action, prevented them from

[48] Hernández y Dávalos, *Colección de Documentos*, I, 608; Riva Palacio (ed.), *México á través de los Siglos*, I, 608; *Diario de México*, X, 508.
[49] Carlos María Bustamante, *Cuadro Histórico de la Revolución Mexicana* (2nd ed., 2 vols., Mexico, 1843), I, 8.
[50] Alamán, *Historia de Méjico*, I, 281.

being able to sacrifice their lives in the struggle and urged the people to aid Spain by giving generously and freely of their treasures.[51] England came in for her share of Mexico's wealth.[52]

This did not help the situation in Mexico. Whatever poor old Garibay tried to do for his country was certain to arouse opposition. The brief period of victories in Spain had been followed by defeats, and the American party sought to minimize Spain's ability to resist Napoleon, for then it might have an opportunity and a just cause for making New Spain independent. The viceroy asked the people to forget the odious titles of "creoles and gachupines" and to use the term "Spaniards" for all,[53] but the breach grew wider as time went on. The central junta in Spain made a last effort to win support and to secure the allegiance of the colonials by declaring that henceforth they were to be put on a basis of equality with the inhabitants of Spain and to become an integral part of the nation instead of a subject colony. Plans were also made for the calling of a cortes which should include representatives from the colonies.[54]

Criticisms of the opponents of Iturrigaray and of Garibay's administration continued until the government decided on drastic measures to destroy this growing menace. A special court, the *Junta consultiva,* was established for the purpose of trying all cases of disaffection or treason. It was composed of three judges and a number of spies, who began in June, 1809, their work of hunting down and of trying persons suspected of disloyalty. A few were apprehended, but it became in itself a new grievance which alienated many others.[55]

Garibay was a failure; even his supporters admitted it. There were rumors of deposing him in the manner of his

---

[51] *Gazeta de México,* XVIII, 739-740.
[52] Bustamante, *Supplemento,* III, 251.   [53] *Gazeta de México,* XVI, 365-367.
[54] *Ibid.,* XV, 326; Alamán, *Historia de Méjico,* I, 291-292.
[55] Alamán, *Historia de Méjico,* I, 294-295; Bustamante, *Supplemento,* III, 252.

predecessor. His appointment had never been formally approved in Spain; therefore it was comparatively easy to have him replaced. On July 19, 1809, he gave up his office to his successor, Lizana y Beaumont, the archbishop of Mexico.[56] This was seemingly a good choice since the ecclesiastics were generally held in veneration by the people and could be trusted by Spain. Nevertheless, Lizana was not fit for the office: he lacked the force of will power to deal with insurrection, he was timid and vacillating at a time when there was need for firmness, and he lacked an understanding of human character. One may read in Bancroft that "Had Spain specially desired to throw away Mexico, the appointment of Archbishop Lizana was the very thing to do. Old, sickly, as feeble in mind as in body, he was fitter for a hospital than for the viceregal palace."[57] This is probably an extreme view.

The new viceroy began with a conciliatory policy to allay the spirit of revolt. He soon came under the influence of the American faction, the *caballeros racionales,* who aroused his suspicion against the audiencia and Yermo's faction. He himself was loyal to Spain, although he played into the hands of her enemies. Like his predecessor he sent large amounts of money to Spain, part of which was carried by Lord Cochrane. He also tried to eradicate the disloyal element in the country by continuing the court started by Garibay, the *junta consultiva,* which he now renamed the *junta de suguridad,* a committee of safety with judicial powers. It was to be particularly alert in discovering and in stamping out French tendencies.[58]

In the meantime the subject of revolution continued to be a topic for conversation, and its chance of success became a subject for discussion or debate. As a result, revolutionary attempts could be expected at any time. In September, 1809, Valladolid, the capital of Michoacan, became the center of a

[56] Alamán, *Historia de Méjico,* I, 301.
[57] Bancroft, *History of Mexico,* IV, 77.
[58] *Ibid.,* IV, 80.

conspiracy to overthrow the government. The leaders, Vicento de Santa María, a Franciscan friar, and José María Obeso, captain of the militia, belonged to the organizations from which the government should have expected the greatest fidelity, the church and the army. Trusted agents were sent to neighboring towns, including Querétaro, to win support for the revolution. The response was good and gave promise of success. Up to twenty thousand Indians were expected to join, and the soldiers of Valladolid could be relied upon. The date of the uprising was set for December 21. On December 14 a priest warned the officials, and on the day set for the uprising the arrests began which nipped in the bud another revolution.[59] Again the participants were treated with leniency to prevent the spread of hostility. Nevertheless, the views and plans of the leaders were widely known and might at any time be resumed by others, as actually happened within nine months.

The disastrous events in Spain towards the end of 1809 contributed to the growing dissatisfaction in Mexico. The unpopular junta of Seville had been forced to take refuge on the island of Leon and resigned its authority to a regency of five members. This body had agreed to call the cortes, but it failed to win the support of the colonials because they were not given equal representation with the provinces of Spain. The later efforts to raise money in Mexico met with decreasing success, since the people were getting disgusted with the endless demands of the Spaniards and they were reaching the point where they were unable to spare any more.

Conditions did not improve in Mexico after the regency had acted on complaints and sent an order for the removal of Lizana.[60] The audiencia was in charge until the new viceroy, Venegas, should arrive. Suspicion, hostility, and division con-

[59] *Ibid.*, IV, 81-82. For an account by one of the participants, Michelena, see Hernández y Dávalos, *Colección de Documentos*, II, 5-7.

[60] Hernández y Dávalos, *Colección de Documentos*, II, 21.

tinued to weaken the government. Both Garibay and Lizana had tried to counteract the influence of Napoleon but with only moderate success. His agents worked secretly and effectively, in spite of the proclamations of Lizana against the "rapacious eagle of Corsica."[61]

[31] *Ibid.*, II, 11.

CHAPTER XVIII

JOSEPH BONAPARTE, KING OF SPAIN AND THE INDIES

"I embarked very badly on the Spanish affair, I confess: the immorality of it was too patent, the injustice too cynical."—NAPOLEON BONAPARTE.

"The object, which these agents are to aim at, for the present, is no other, than that of manifesting to, and persuading the Creoles of Spanish America, that H. I. and R. M. has solely in view, the giving of liberty to a people, enslaved for so many years, without expecting any return for so great a boon, other than the friendship of the natives, and the commerce with the harbours of both Americas. . . ."—JOSEPH BONAPARTE.

NAPOLEON'S military successes failed to give him possession of Spain, and with Spain, the Indies. His world conquest had been checked and his prestige given a blow from which it never recovered. Two governments continued to rule in Spain, one supported by French troops and the other by British troops. The colonies, instead of complying with Napoleon's desire for empire, gave their last and diminishing support to the provisional government of Spain and to England. America was out of Napoleon's reach as long as England controlled the sea, and only by propaganda could he hope to exert any influence on the colonies. The wealth of the Indies became a vital factor in the European struggle, which Napoleon sought by various means to divert from his enemies to France and himself.

One of the first plans of Napoleon to be reported was that of sending Charles IV to America to become the king of Mexico. The departure of a French fleet from Brest was followed by a warning in March, 1809, to the colonial authorities to be prepared against any hostile attempt on the part of that squadron or against any intrigue of the French.[1] By May 20 the

[1] Garay to Foronda, March 6, 1809, Archivo del Ministerio de Estado, legajo 216, Library of Congress Transcript (listed hereinafter as L. C. T.).

viceroy had been given more definite information, telling of the departure of a French squadron of eleven ships whose mission it was to convey Charles and María Luisa to Mexico. It had been pursued by the British and had taken refuge in Rochefort; nevertheless, the squadron might fulfill its mission at any time, and Garibay gave full instructions to his officials in case their former king should arrive. The presence of this undesirable royal personage would only complicate matters, and he would undoubtedly be serving the "infamous and astute Corsican." Charles and María Luisa had once been respected, he said, but having abdicated, they had lost all rights over their former vassals. Furthermore, having taken an oath to support his son, Ferdinand VII, the people would have to repel all actions by Charles as being against the fidelity and loyalty to their sovereign. The coast officials of Vera Cruz, Yucatan, and Campeche were ordered to prevent the French from landing, and they were allowed to use any means to oppose the French, even to the point of sinking the vessels if necessary.[2]

The *real acuerdo* took the matter under consideration and gave additional instructions on June 10, 1809.[3] If the royal family and followers did land, they were to be taken prisoners and sent to the castle of San Juan de Ulloa, with "the courtesy and decorum" befitting their persons. They should be carefully guarded to prevent escape and should be detained only long enough to secure a vessel and a responsible person to take them to Cadiz, where they could be left in charge of the supreme junta. If they came supported by warships and land forces, which might be expected of Napoleon, it would be necessary to concentrate the army at the points where disembarkation would be most probable. A military junta might also be called to consider the defense.[4] It would not have been unrea-

[2] Garibay's instructions, May 20, 1809, A. G. I., Estado, Mexico, legajo 11.
[3] A copy, Mexico, June 30, 1809, *ibid*. [4] *Ibid*.

sonable for Napoleon to have made such an attempt, and Charles IV might have been expected to support his captor.[5] The project evidently did not go beyond frightening the Spaniards and Mexicans, and Napoleon soon resorted to other means to gain influence in the colonies.

When the *real acuerdo* spoke of the military defense to prevent the coming of Charles IV, it also had in mind "to prevent any other aggression, which the Anglo-Americans might plan, especially if they join in the ambitious views of Napoleon."[6] The United States was, indeed, very much interested in the schemes of Napoleon, and there were those who expressed a hope that there might be a division of spoils. At first, however, the sentiment in the United States favored independence for Mexico. During the summer of 1808 Wilkinson wrote to Jefferson, expressing hopes that South America and Mexico would speedily gain their independence.[7] Referring to the Spanish Americans, Jefferson wrote to Claiborne in October, 1808: "We consider their interests and ours as the same, and that the object of both must be to exclude all European influence from this hemisphere."[8] This not only foreshadowed independence but also the Monroe Doctrine. Jefferson was undoubtedly worried about the great influence England might exert as an ally of Spain. General Wilkinson, on his way to Cuba to carry out some intrigues, stopping at Norfolk at a public dinner which was given in his honor, gave the toast: "The New World, governed by itself and independent of the Old."[9]

Such views were idealistic hopes, and in any actual disposition of territory, whether in the New World or in the Old, one should always consider the wishes of Napoleon. What

[5] Riva Palacio (ed.), *México á través de los Siglos*, III, 6.
[6] Report of *real acuerdo* for June 10, A. G. I., Estado, Mexico, legajo 11.
[7] Cox, *West Florida*, p. 286.
[8] L. A. Lipscomb (ed.), *Writings of Jefferson* (20 vols., Washington, 1903), XII, 186.
[9] Cox, *West Florida*, p. 291.

Jefferson thought of the situation in January, 1809, may be seen from his letter to Monroe. "And Bonaparte, having Spain at his feet," he wrote, "will look immediately to the Spanish colonies, and think our neutrality cheaply purchased by a repeal of the illegal parts of his decrees, with perhaps the Floridas thrown into the bargain."[10] And in April he wrote to Madison the following about Napoleon: "He ought the more to conciliate our good will, as we can be such an obstacle to the new career opening on him in the Spanish colonies. . . . But, although with difficulty, he will consent to our receiving Cuba into our Union, to prevent our aid to Mexico and the other provinces."[11]

There was cause for Spanish fear then. They had been suspicious of the American troops on the border ever since the government had refused to ratify the "Neutral Ground Treaty," which was only a temporary agreement between Wilkinson and Herrera.[12] With the concentration of additional troops at New Orleans, the governor of Florida, the commandant of the Provincias Internas, and the viceroy of Mexico were requested to maintain their frontiers in a state of defense. The Spanish government also requested an explanation from the United States for her military preparations.[13] Several reasons were given, such as the embargo, the possible revival of the Burr episode, and that a British squadron was said to be leaving Halifax for the West Indies.[14] Congress had determined to oppose any attempt of England to control the Spanish colonies.

The Spaniards, however, saw in the action of the United States either a hostile move on her part or a possible coöperation with Napoleon to get West Florida. The Spanish min-

[10] Lipscomb (ed.), *Writings of Jefferson*, XII, 241.
[11] *Ibid.*, XII, 276.
[12] Archivo del Ministerio de Estado, legajo 215, L. C. T.
[13] Garay to Foronda, April 12, 1809, *ibid.*, legajo 216, L. C. T.
[14] Cox, *West Florida*, pp. 287-288.

ister, Cevallos, condemned as hostile to the Spanish king, Ferdinand VII, any negotiation with France or the usurper relative to Spanish colonies.[15] Spain knew she could not trust Napoleon, who had once before acted as a realtor in disposing of Louisiana; nor could she trust the notorious Wilkinson with a large army at New Orleans. The colonial authorities were warned to take the greatest precautions against the intrigues in Louisiana, where there were a number of French agents, American adventurers, and a few malcontent Spaniards who were all taking advantage of Spain to create trouble in her possessions.[16]

The activities of the French under Napoleon caused considerable disturbance, and the colonial authorities exerted great vigilance in an effort to counteract their influence. Garibay said that one of his chief cares was to carry out the laws against foreigners; and he issued a proclamation on April 18, 1809, forbidding the landing of Frenchmen or other foreigners, whether they had passports or not. His efforts were directed especially against the French, whom he accused of being atheists, Jacobins, enemies of the church and crown, and members of the "contemptible order of freemasons."[17]

Louisiana had become a gateway for these intruders since Spain had allowed her citizens to migrate to Spanish territory after the retrocession. Unusual vigilance was required on the border and particularly in New Orleans to close the door to undesirables. Luis de Onís was pleased with the appointment of Don Diego Morphy as consul at New Orleans, "the most interesting point of the day," but he believed it was in need of two or three more to watch the activities of the French. The viceroy of Mexico and the captain general of Florida were warned to be on the lookout and to prevent any dangerous action because of this emigration.[18]

[15] *Archivo del Ministerio de Estado*, legajo 215, L. C. T.
[16] *Ibid.*, legajo 216, L. C. T.   [17] Alamán, *Historia de Mej.*, ., 298.
[18] Onís to Garay, Washington, Oct. 21, 1809, A. H. N., Estado, legajo 5635.

Napoleon in his methodical manner established a large organization of spies and emissaries which threw a network of propagandists over all of Spanish America. Before the end of 1809 his chief representative and the director of this organization, Captain Desmolard,[19] arrived in Baltimore with a staff of subordinates.[20] They came from Bayonne on the schooner *Tilsit* and some of the members landed at Norfolk, where they prepared for their enterprise, which was, according to de Onís, "nothing less than to revolutionize our Americas." Numerous proclamations and papers were brought for the purpose of converting the colonies to the support of Napoleon or opposition to Spain. They were expected to begin at Havana, where they had many partisans, and from there they would go to Vera Cruz, Caracas, and other colonial centers. The commander of the schooner went to Philadelphia, where he drew a considerable sum of money by letter or bills of exchange. He made his headquarters in Baltimore, where he and his officials, reported Onís, lived with great ostentation, wearing decorated livery and the tricolor cockade. The captain was called the ambassador of Joseph, but his cockade showed that this was not his official position. Nevertheless, he was an enemy of Spain as were all his followers, and de Onís took it upon himself to nullify their efforts to revolutionize the colonies.

The event was of such great importance that he chartered a special vessel, in spite of limited funds, to carry the news to Havana and to Vera Cruz. The authorities were warned in time to take proper precautions to frustrate the intrigues of the Bonapartes. He mustered his forces in the persons of the various Spanish consuls, who were instructed to watch the movements of the conspirators, to secure copies of the procla-

---

[19] Called Desmolans by Onís to Garay, Dec. 29, 1809, *ibid*.

[20] For a translation of Onís's report on the arrival of Napoleon's agents, see John Rydjord, "Napoleon and New Spain," *New Spain and the West*, ed. G. P. Hammond and others (2 vols., Los Angeles, 1932), I, 306-308.

mations, and to prevent, if possible, the execution of their plans. Bernabeu in Baltimore was commended for his success in collecting the first information on the French scheme.

Besides the French emissaries there were also disloyal Spaniards: two had been detected in January, 1810. Their descriptions were sent to the colonial governments, and the ports were to be watched with the greatest care to prevent their landing. Onis believed that three of the French agents had already set out on their iniquitous mission.[21] This vigilance was certain to bring results, and it was not long before he was in possession of a copy of a proclamation by Joseph Bonaparte, "King of Spain and the Indies."[22]

The content of the instructions of King Joseph to his agents shows an excellent understanding of the conditions of the colonies, but certainly not of their attitude towards the Bonapartes. The creoles were to be told that Joseph desired only to give them liberty after their long years of enslavement, and in return he expected only their friendship and their commerce. These were, to be sure, highly important during the Napoleonic wars. Joseph generously offered troops and war materials to aid in gaining their independence from Europe. Numerous advantages were to be pointed out to the colonists. They could increase their own funds by not sending any to Spain, and their commerce would develop by opening their ports. The freedom of agriculture from stifling restrictions, the establishment of manufactures, and the abolition of monopolies were all suggested as great economic advantages.

The agents could get the best results by making themselves acceptable to the officials of the church and state. Special emphasis was made on the point of winning the ecclesiastics.

[21] Onís to Garay, Dec. 29, 1809, A. H. N. Estado, legajo 5635.

[22] The proclamation is printed in Walton, *Exposé on the Dissentions of Spanish America*, Appendix, pp. ii-vii. A copy of these instructions was also sent by Luis de Onís to the Capt. General of Cuba, Philadelphia, Feb. 12, 1810, A. G. I., Papeles de Cuba, legajo 1708.

Here Joseph showed good judgment, since the clergy was the most powerful factor in deciding the allegiance of the people. The public should be made to believe that the Emperor Napoleon was sent by God "to chastise the pride and tyranny of monarchs," and that it was "a mortal sin, admitting of no pardon, to resist God's will." There was a special warning against criticising the Inquisition or the church, and the revolutionary banners were to be inscribed by the motto: "Long live the Catholic, Apostolic, and Roman religion, and destruction to bad government."

The harshness of the home government should be emphasized, and, to the Indians, the cruelty of the Spaniards. Freedom would give them happiness and exemption from the tyrannical tribute. The creoles should be reminded of the injustice shown them in the appointment to office, and their attention should be called to the progress and the comfort in the United States in comparison to Spanish America. Lastly, the people were to be reminded that their monarch was no longer in control of the government, but "in the power of the restorer of liberty and the universal legislator, Napoleon."

The agents throughout the colonies should keep records of those who accepted their proposals and transmit the lists to the principal agents who were in turn to send them to Desmolard for the information of Joseph. He would see that they were duly rewarded. The chief duties of the agents were to stimulate the feelings of dissatisfaction, to organize the people, and to get the revolution under way. They should keep one another informed so as to make the uprisings at different points take place on the same day. Where the officials were found to be hostile, their servants were to be won over, and their irreconcilable masters could be disposed of by poisoning.

Means and methods of communication had already been established with certain points on the coast as connecting links for vessels which kept in touch with Desmolard at Baltimore.

By October, 1809, the time of this proclamation, Desmolard had already reported great progress in Mexico. His report, as given by Joseph, stated that

the number of partisans already engaged, is immense, and those all of the first rank; he makes no doubt, that the insurrection will take place in the realm, that the success of the scheme at Vera Cruz, is quite certain; which will be the principal point of the whole expedition; that he, therefore, keeps ready a safe conveyance to advise those in New Orleans, where all necessary succours are ready, but that he thinks even these useless, from the promises of success held out by the party in his interest, as well as from the supineness of that government, which will not take any vigorous steps when the moment is arrived.

The Indian tribes which controlled the road from Vera Cruz, where they could cut off both treasure and correspondence from Mexico, had been secured as valuable allies. News from other sections of Spanish America, including California, was encouraging. Desmolard also believed that he could win the support of the army officers and thereby practically insure the success of the enterprise.

The optimistic note in this report from Desmolard does not seem justified. His agents won converts, no doubt, and they were scattered throughout Spanish America in spite of the vigilance of frontier officials; but they represented a ruler whose name was anathema, and could therefore expect little general support. Yet these agents advocating independence must have had some influence on the dissatisfied element of New Spain and other colonies. Independence, liberty, freedom, these were ideals to be accepted no matter who might offer them. The results promised to be the same whether they came from Castlereagh or Napoleon. Of course, Napoleon was merely urging the colonies to do what they were eventually to do at any rate. A revolution in 1809 or in 1810 would have been of considerable benefit to him, since he had encountered much unexpected resistance in the peninsula.

The Spanish authorities worked assiduously, and for a time successfully, to counteract the influence of Napoleon. A "royal" order from Spain to the colonial officials, dated April 25, 1810, renewed the warnings against his agents.[23] This was scarcely necessary, however, since the Spanish-American authorities had already taken practically every precaution within their means. On April 21, 1810, the viceroy, Lizana y Beaumont, gave an order that on the twenty-fifth there should be a public and formal burning of Joseph's proclamation[24] as an official act of justice. It was a great event. The royal army band led the procession of civil and military officials to the public square before the palace. An effigy of Ferdinand VII, *"el amado y deseado,"* was placed on the official stand. A large brasero was brought from the prison and placed on a special platform. An appropriate address was given to the large crowd which had assembled; and then, in the proper atmosphere, the hangman burned the dangerous proclamation of the usurper.[25]

On the previous day he had answered the appeal of Joseph by a counter-proclamation. His method was ridicule, a weapon he used most effectively. He picked the proclamation to pieces and made it appear as an insult to the Mexican people, and he became eloquent in his denunciation of Joseph's recommendation that servants poison their masters. He sent a challenge to Joseph and his "revolting brother" in which he placed the Mexican people on a much higher plane than had been done by the Bonapartes.[26] The Inquisition came to the aid of the viceroy and issued an edict which condemned the proclamation of Joseph.[27]

---

[23] Report of Oct. 24, 1810, *Guatemala*, 100-6-3, A. G. I.

[24] This was the general proclamation: *"Españoles de mis Posesiones de América— Vuestro legítimo Soberano os exorta a la sumisión,"* dated Oct. 2, 1809. For the viceroy's order, cf. Hernández y Dávalos, *Colección de Documentos*, II, 32-33.

[25] Report signed by Manl. de la Baldera (rubric), Mexico, April 25, 1810, *Historia*, CLXI, No. 421, Archivo General, Mexico.

[26] Hernández y Dávalos, *Colección de Documentos*, II, 28-32.

[27] *Diario de México*, XII, 463-464, 465-468.

This might put an end to one proclamation, but where there had been one before there were soon to be several. Joseph addressed the next one to the upper clergy who were to inform their parishioners that it was a mortal sin to oppose the will of God who had sent Napoleon and his brother to regenerate the Spanish nation. One paragraph was devoted to a condemnation of the English and a warning not to be deceived by the "insidious insinuations" of their agents whose Machiavellian instructions cause the wars of Europe.[28] There was another, supposedly by a creole, calling his countrymen to action. Luis de Onís had heard of these, but said that he had been unable to procure any copies.[29] He thought that the first was sufficient to show the "Machiavellian or infernal spirit with which our enemies try to revolutionize the loyal and precious colonies of H. M. in this part of the world."

One of the agents, Josef Muentes, a Spaniard by birth, had recently come from Mexico by way of Havana with a package of letters, and Desmolard, the supposed ambassador "del Rey Pepe," had immediately sent him to San Sebastián in an American vessel to report to Joseph's government. Of the hundred and fifty officials expected by Desmolard, twenty-four had already arrived by the middle of March, and among these, one general and two colonels had set out immediately for their respective destinations. Four of the arrivals were Spaniards, acquaintances or associates of Joseph's official supporters. Most of them were to go to New Orleans, in keeping with the former instructions of their king. Onís gave further evidence that Desmolard was getting results and reported that the chief envoy had received packages and letters which appeared to

[28] Onís to Captain General of Cuba, Philadelphia, March 9, 1810, Papeles de Cuba, 1708, A. G. I. And Onís to Saavedra, March 14, 1810, E 5636, No. 83, A. H. N. See also Facsimile, opposite p. 300.

[29] Onís to Saavedra, Philadelphia, March 14, 1810, A. H. N., Estado, legajo 5636. Extracts from *"Avisos y Exhortaciones de un Criollo Español a sus Conciudadanos de América"* was discovered by the Spanish consul at New Orleans. Copy by Deigo Morphy, *Historia*, CLXI, Archivo General, Mexico.

PROCLAMA

De Don JOSEF NAPOLEON, *Primer Rey de España y del Continente de America, dirigida al Clero en general de todas sus posesiones en America.*

O Vos ARZOBISPOS, OBISPOS y PRELADOS de todas las denominaciones de mis posesiones de América, los que soys destinados por estado en predicar la palabra de Dios, oid la voz de la razon! Vuestro Rey legítimo quien solo anhela la felicidad de sus súbditos, qualquiera que sea la distancia que los tiene separados de él; como padre benéfico y tierno, os exhorta á atraer vuestras ovejas respectivas á la sumision. Hacedles saber por medio de vuestros consejos espirituales que es ofender á Dios gravemente, el no someterse voluntariamente á la obediencia de un soberano, el que ese mismo Dios que están adorando, les tiene destinado.

Y en efecto respetables eclesiásticos, qué fruto recogerian así ellos como vosotros, si los unos y los otros persistierais en una tan rea rebelion? Otro no seria sino una punicion exemplar en este mundo, y unos castigos harto merecidos en aquel endonde nosotros todos havemos de ir y parar. Bastantemente esclarecidos soys para conocer y preveer las funestas consequencias que resultarian de una criminal obstinacion: en vos es, ministros de paz, que pongo mi confianza para restablecer mis súbditos á la sumision; y si contra mi expectacion descuydareis ese deber sagrado, temblad! pues mi venganza seria terrible para con los infractores.

Y qué objeccion valedera podiertis hacer contra mis pretensiones legítimas: seria la del juramento de sumision y obediencia que haveis tomado para con Fernando? Os desempeñó de él en cediendo libremente todos sus derechos á favor de mi augusto hermano Napoleon *Emperador de los Franceses* quien lealmente me los confirió. Seria la esperanza que al fin la metrópoli conseguirá el privarme de ellos, para entregarlos á un simulacro de rey, el que ni capacidad ni deseo de mandaros tiene? Mas aquella esperanza seria tanto menos sensata quanto frívola pues vuestros hermanos de Europa se han todos rendido á la voz de la justicia y de la razon deplorando el error que les ha tenido los ojos fascinados. Ademas del gozar de la dicha inapreciable del haver sido colocados en la clase de los pueblos regenerados, se están ahora congratulando de haver tenido harto sano juicio para rehacerse al rededor de un tierno padre que los ama, y los hace gozar de las dulzuras inseparables de los Estados bien governados. He! porque no induciriais mis súbditos de las posesiones que estais habitando en seguir un exemplo tan christiano? Solo los eclesiasticos de mis colonias serian los que no quisiesen ceder á la voz de la razon y de la humanidad? Ellos solos tendrian el corazon tan endurecidos contra la verdad, que en vez de predicar la moral y la sumision, no predicarian sino la rebelion y el levantamiento? No, respetables prelados: mejor opinion tengo de vuestros sentimientos generosos. Estoy perfectamente persuadido que retraereis al corral las descarriadas ovejas, si tales se hallaren, quando conocereis nos sentimientos paternales hácia todos mis hijos. Imitad esos dignos pastores de la metrópoli, los que han sacrificado su reposo y las recreaciones inherentes á la vida humana para retraer á la obediencia por medios persuasivos hijos desagradecidos que havian tenido la osadia de rebelarse contra su padre comun. A los que se han entregado á vuestro govierno, persuadid así mismo que su felicidad y la vuestra, penden de una pronta sumision. Decidles que vuestros hermanos de Europa han todos logrado su perdon, y que no dexamos caer nuestro brazo vengador que sobre los refractores á las leyes y los perversos reos. Nuestra real clemencia se extenderá en todas nuestras posesiones, y nunca castigaremos mas que los que se opusieren á la execucion de nuestros secretos.

Un pueblo que persiste en su rebelion contra su legítimo soberano, ha de atraer tras sí la venganza celestial y la rigurosidad de las leyes. Qué ha de ganar en tener una conducta reprovada de las leyes divinas y humanas? Nada mas que acarrear miseria y desolacion en su infeliz patria. Mil exemplos memorables nos demuestra la historia cuyas resultas no sirvieron sino en engratificar los intereses de algunos ambiciosos quienes havian sido engañados y descarriados. Desconfiad de aquella dañosa y peligrosa casta de que se acostumbra hacer melosos y enredados discursos al pueblo solo para engañarlo; sed los primeros en denunciarlos á los magistrados, si tal vez alguno se tuviese encubierto entre vos, paraque se le castigue segun que lo requiriere el caso.

Dignos Prelados: vuestro rey os exhorta á desconfiaros de las insinuaciones insidiosas de los emisarios ingleses. En todas partes esta hormigueando esa peste de los humanos, uniendo instrucciones de su govierno las mas machiavélicas que han jamas existido, y son el fomentar discordias civiles con la mira de retardar su tan merecida caida la que se está acercando. Son ellos los que fomentan las guerras en Europa, provocandolas en todas partes. Ellos son los que retardan el cumplimiento de la regeneracion universal de los pueblos la que nuestro augusto hermano con sabiduria concibió, ayudado é inspirado de la divinidad que yo y vosotros adoramos. Ellos mismos enfin son la causa de que las quatro partes del mundo estén anegadas con torrentes de sangre, para disminuir el numero de los hombres, y tener mas facilidad en governarlos. Y no merece tal govierno el que á mas de menospreciar nuestra santa religion es el enemigo declarado de quantos la profesan, no merece de ser aniquilado? Sin duda lo merece; y estoy perfectamente enterado de que no tardará en castigar de sus crímenes la venganza de Dios, combinada y coadyuvada de la de los hombres.

De vuestros esfuerzos confio resultará el mas completo suceso; y así me reposo con confianza que las primeras noticias que llegarán de todas mis posesiones lejanas, tendre la dulce satisfaccion de aprender que haveis restablecido mis fieles y muy amados subditos á una obediencia implícita. Lleno de una alegria sin igual será entonces mi corazon, porque se me dispensará de obrar con una severidad que repugna tanto mas á mis principios, quanto que es funesta á la humanidad; y sobre todo á demas de que haveis hecho una accion meritoria delante de ese Dios de paz quien recompensa las buenas obras, haveis adquirido igualmente la estimacion y benevolencia de un rey que sabrá recompensar generosamente á todos los que se hayan mostrado mas zelados; haviendo impedido por medio de sus exhortaciones evangélicas la efusion de la sangre de mis súbditos.

Dado en nuestro Palacio Real de Madrid, el dia 3 de Oct. de 1809.

JOSEF.

contain "great reports from his emissaries in all of our Americas."[30] The Spanish minister spent freely of time and money to frustrate the plans of the French,[31] with only moderate success.

De Onís was greatly disturbed over the arrival of General Demotier as minister plenipotentiary of Napoleon. The object of his mission was uncertain, but Onís thought of a number of possible activities, nearly all against the interests of Spain. It first occurred to him that he was to aid in directing the revolution which was already, according to reports, beginning to materialize under the influence of the French agents. A second possibility was that Napoleon, having almost drawn the United States into the war by the confiscation of American property, was willing to return both prisoners and property providing that the United States would recognize Joseph as king of Spain, accept one of his ministers, and send Onis away.[32] The United States had tried to remain neutral in the Spanish conflict and had therefore refused to recognize de Onis, allowing him, however, to remain in the country.[33] If Napoleon could have gotten Onís out of the way, he would have had a great deal more freedom in his revolutionary activities in the colonies. The United States hesitated to accept his offer, perhaps in fear of further trouble with England; and even the viceroy of Mexico threatened to declare war if Joseph were recognized as king.[34]

Neither faction was recognized, and both remained in the country to work against one another. Desmolard had spent some time in New York, where, according to Onís, he had some difficulty in securing lodgings since the acceptance of such a "rascal" would drive out all the others. He finally found a

[30] To Saavedra, Philadelphia, March 14, 1810, A. H. N., Estado, legajo 5636.
[31] Onís to Saavedra, Philadelphia, April 30, 1810, *ibid*.
[32] Onís to Marques de las Hormazar, Philadelphia, May 31, 1810, *ibid*.
[33] F. E. Chadwick, *The Relations of the United States and Spain* (New York, 1911), p. 112.
[34] Onís to Hormazar, Philadelphia, May 31, 1810, A. H. N., Estado, legajo 5636.

place in a French inn, where he reviled Onís for undermining his position and interfering with his plans. Onís evidently wanted his government to feel that he was extremely influential in America. He frankly takes the credit for having been the means of preventing the success of Napoleon's schemes. Desmolard was supposed to have left for France before the end of May, and Turreau, another Frenchman, had gone to Boston, where he too was expected to leave for France. This was considered by Onís as further evidence that the plot had failed.[35] The Spanish minister was, however, too optimistic.[36]

While the Napoleonic agents were spreading their influence, a revolution was actually under way in Venezuela. Onís criticized the captain general of that province for allowing suspicious characters to remain free. If Orea, one of the deputies from Venezuela, should ask for a passport to Mexico it would surely be refused, and Havana and Vera Cruz were to be put on their guard against him or any of his compatriots.[37] Here then was a new danger since the rebellious colonists would be working for the same cause as Napoleon's agents.

The papers in the United States were enthusiastic about the revolution in Caracas, much to the disgust of Onís. He had other news, however, which might cause the Americans some worry. A French vessel had arrived in June with eighty French and Spanish passengers. They were believed to be spies of Napoleon, who were to make their headquarters at New Orleans. Onís said that their object was to attack Louisiana and the Floridas. The French would have one believe that Charles IV had made a cession or sale of the territory before his abdication and that he had recognized this after his surrender to Napoleon. The growing alarm in America was

[35] *Ibid.*
[36] When Desmolard arrived in Spain, he helped to improve and strengthen Napoleon's revolutionary organization in America. Rydjord, "Napoleon and New Spain," *New Spain and the West,* I, 300. See also translation of instructions to the new leader, D'Amblimont, *ibid.,* I, 309-312.
[37] Onís to Hormazar, Philadelphia, June 18, 1810, A. H. N., Estado, legajo 5636.

encouraged by Onís in hopes of turning the United States against France. In this way the colonies might be saved, "for it is certain," he added, "that without the approval of this government, the French can do nothing, neither against the Floridas, nor against Mexico from Louisiana." He found that the lethargy of the United States was such that large numbers of Frenchmen were entering Louisiana under the pretext of fleeing from the tyranny of Europe. It was his belief that they were sent expressly for the purpose of starting a revolution. The border provinces of the Spanish were in constant danger, and they were again warned.[38]

From New Orleans came an account of the efforts of one of the agents, Monsieur Lestique, who had arrived in Philadelphia in March on the American schooner *Lovely Matilda*. This man pretended to have a secret commission from the central junta to the authorities in Mexico and that he was awaiting a passport in order to travel with greater security. He also pretended to know many Spanish officials intimately, including de Onís. He had the reputation of being a man with considerable ability, but he spoke so freely that he aroused the suspicion of Don Diego Morphy, consul at New Orleans. Onis denied that he knew him, thereby confirming the consul's suspicion that he was a spy of the French government, seeking an opportunity to enter Mexico.[39]

The home government was vitally interested in these revolutionary schemes, and praised Onís for his achievement in keeping the authorities informed and hoped he would thwart the schemes of these "disturbers of mankind."[40] The Spanish authorities did their share in warning the colonial officials against Napoleon's agents. In April Saavedra, the Spanish minister of state, informed the colonials of the departure of

[38] *Ibid.*
[39] Onís to Bardoxi, Philadelphia, July 12, 1810, *ibid.*
[40] Bardoxi to Onís, Sept. 5, 1810, Archivo del Ministerio de Estado, legajo 217, L. C. T.

Don Francisco Belmont for the United States, where he was going with instructions from the "pretender" to the people of New Spain, and perhaps to Havana, Florida, or Terra Firma.[41] Later the colonies were warned against Don Josef María Navarro, a retired surgeon on his way to the Provincia Internas or to Mexico.[42] The reports from Onís generally contained additional names.[43]

The information about the emissaries which was sent to the leading colonies bore fruit. The names and the descriptions of the men who had come on the *Tilsit* were sent to the frontier officials who were put on their guard. On the first of May the viceroy of Mexico and the captain general of Cuba informed Onis of their success. The report dealt chiefly with a person called Don Manuel Rodríguez de Peña, who had gone to the consul at Norfolk for a passport to Mexico. He was thoroughly familiar with the military movements of the French in Spain and was believed to have been an assistant of General Moncey. He spoke Castilian without any accent, but passed as a Frenchman among the French. He was a vigorous partisan of Napoleon, and spoke highly of the philosophy of the usurper, Joseph. Perhaps he was actually a Spaniard, but, if he were, he must have been one of those unworthy ones who had embraced the cause of Napoleon—so thought the officials. Onís was confident that he was one of the secret agents, but ordered the consul to give him a passport to Vera Cruz. This was merely a trap, for he sent full instructions to the colonial officials in order that they might apprehend him. The results were most gratifying to the Spaniards. The agent was arrested at Havana and a large number of revolutionary papers were found in his possession. In a postscript to this report Onís was

---

[41] Saavedra to Onís, April 20, 1810, *ibid*.
[42] Aug. 8, 1810, *ibid*.
[43] His report of July included LeRoy, Larue, Lanno, Pere Charle, Luis Dupar, Lafonta, and Geofrey, A. H. N., Estado, legajo 5636.

able to add that he had just learned that Alemán de la Peña had "expiated his crime on the gallows."[44]

Don Nemicio de Salcedo reported from Chihuahua the arrest of four other spies from the list sent by Onís, now more proud than ever of his achievement. Onis admitted that the peace and tranquility in America, as well as the increasing patriotism were largely, if not entirely, due to his efforts. But he had not finished the task. In order that the arrests would have the proper effect on other agents of Napoleon, he had the newspapers of the United States publish accounts of what had taken place.[45] His actions and his success met with the most hearty approval of Spanish authorities. The hanging of Alemán de la Peña was also approved, and the minister of state urged the officials to repeat the performance whenever they caught similar spies, since it would make people hesitate to undertake such projects and warn those who were easily misled.[46]

Nevertheless, the number which had been apprehended was very small in comparison to the number continually arriving in American ports. On the very day that he wrote home to the government, praising his own success, de Onís reported the presence of another French vessel which had just arrived from Bordeaux with fifty-four passengers of which forty-nine were French, four Americans, and one, a young Spaniard who was reported to be of very bad character—perhaps because of his company. A few of the passengers were priests, but the rest were "suspicious characters," some having announced that they were on their way to Kentucky, and others to Spanish America.[47] Here was more work for the vigilant Spanish authorities.

[44] Onís to Bardoxi, Philadelphia, Aug. 14, 1810, *ibid*.
[45] *Ibid*.
[46] Bardoxi to Onís, Nov. 15, 1810, Archivo del Ministerio de Estado, legajo 217, L. C. T.
[47] Onís to Bardoxi, Philadelphia, Aug. 14, 1810, A. H. N., Estado, legajo 5636.

Several persons were employed by Onís to watch these new arrivals and to keep him and the colonial officials informed. The consuls were ordered to give no passports to any except responsible persons, and they were to examine the passenger lists with the greatest care so that the "Apostles of Bonaparte" could not enter the Spanish colonies under assumed names, as was their custom.[48] By September the revolutionary agents had scattered to the West Indies and to the western part of the United States on their way to their fields of action in Spanish America. In the meantime new arrivals were constantly increasing the ranks of Napoleon's supporters.[49]

It is possible that the revolutionary agents of Joseph, these "Disciples of Bonaparte," contributed to the desire for independence, but their influence was merely one of a large number of contributing causes and their work was in a field which was already being prepared. While these agents were encouraging independence as a friendly act to Napoleon, most of the revolutionists sought their independence as an act of hostility to the Bonapartes. The results would be the same. Their attitude towards Joseph and Napoleon was the same, and these names were continually used interchangeably; and well they might, for the work of Joseph, even as the king of Spain, was largely directed by his younger and more energetic brother, Napoleon. The revolutionary agents worked in the name of Joseph, but by the will of Napoleon.

In Mexico the conditions were growing critical, and, contrary to the declarations and hopes of Onís, the country was on the verge of revolution. Causes for dissatisfaction and rebellion were prevalent, as we have seen, and the people needed only to be shown that independence were possible, to throw off the Spanish yoke. The long-suffering inhabitants were gradually emerging from their lethargic attitude of blind submis-

[48] *Ibid.*
[49] Onís to Bardoxi, Philadelphia, Sept. 9, 1810, *ibid.* Onís to viceroy of Mexico, Sept. 5, 1810, *Historia,* CLXI, No. 64, Archivo General, Mexico.

sion to a control they obeyed from fear. The all-powerful and Divine Right monarchs of Spain had been deposed by an unscrupulous army officer who was a self-made emperor. And when Spain had been overrun by a foreign invasion, "the people," and not the king, had risen to defend their country and their honor. If the people of Spain could set up a government and fight the enemy without a king, what might not the Mexican people do if they chose to act?

Ever since its conquest Mexico had fostered a subconscious hope of independence, a hope which was occasionally to flare up into conscious but feeble attempts to secure the coveted liberty. But the power of the government and the church had been too well established to be thrown off easily. The masses had been too deeply submerged in ignorance and slavery to appreciate the significance of liberty and independence or to dare think of its realization. With the gradual penetration of modern ideas there was an awakening of the desire for freedom which was eventually to break the last feeble bond holding New Spain to the Old.

An artificial stimulus was given to the movement by the extraordinary actions of Napoleon in Spain, but the foreign influence had long been active in urging and inciting the colonies to independence. The commercial influence of England, the example of the United States, the ideas of the French Revolution had all contributed to the same movement. Finally the Napoleonic war cut Mexico off from Europe, making her almost independent in fact, if not in theory, an act which reached its climax in the removal of the last bond of unity, the king.

The revolutionists who met at Querétaro covered their designs by assuming the name of a literary society. It was believed by contemporaries that the revolutionary plan at Querétaro was one and the same with Napoleon's and by the same head or source. And since Captain Allende was involved, the authorities recalled the communications he had had with Napoleon's agent, D'Alvimar.[50] Among the occasional visitors was the priest from Dolores, Miguel Hidalgo y Costilla, a philosopher, a dramatist, and a practical economist. He was quite familiar with French literature, thus arousing the suspicion of the Inquisition, in spite of which he had retained his freedom. He became the leading spirit among those who sought to make use of the chaotic situation in Europe to win freedom for Mexico. When the plot was discovered, as plots generally are discovered, Hidalgo decided to risk all and bring the issue before the public. On the morning of September 16, 1810, exactly two years after the deposition of Iturrigaray, Hidalgo issued his battle cry, *El Grito de Dolores,* and started that terrific struggle for freedom which was to last for a decade before being crowned with success.

The preliminaries have been told, the revolution was under way, and for the third time since 1775 the world witnessed a tremendous struggle of mankind in an effort to gain that oft misconceived and ever elusive ideal of liberty.

[50] José Luyando and Juan Antº. Yandiola to Venegas, Mexico, Oct. 5, 1810 (copy by Velázquez de León, Mexico, Nov. 10, 1810), Mexico, 90-7-21, A. G. I.

BIBLIOGRAPHY

Bibliographical Note

The guides to materials in European archives published by the Carnegie Institution of Washington have been used, as well as the guide to source material in the Archives of the Indies, *La Independencia de América* (1924), edited by P. Torres Lanzas.

In the bibliography the manuscript material has been listed in collections and divisional classifications as far as possible, and the specific references have been left to the footnotes.

A. Primary Sources

1. Manuscripts

Archivo del Ministero de Estado, legajos 215-217, Library of Congress transcripts.

Beliardi Papers, Fr. 10769, Bibliotheque Nationale, Paris; Bancroft Collection transcripts, Berkeley.

Chatham Papers, Vol. CCCXLV, Public Record Office, London.

Colonial Office, 137, Vol. LXXVII, Public Record Office, London.

De Pons, M., "Memoire sur le Cession de la Capitainerie Generale de Caracas a la France." In *Rapport du Ministre de la Marine*, Archives Nationale, Paris, AF IV, 1211.

Estado, legajos 5635-5636, Archivo Histórico Nacional, Madrid.

Estado Caracas, legajo 4, Archivo General de las Indias, Seville.

Estado Mexico, legajos 1-23, Archivo General de las Indias, Seville.

Foreign Office, 72 (Spain), Vols. I, LV, LXVIII, Public Record Office, London.

Guatemala, 100-6-3, Archivo General de las Indias, Seville.

Historia, Tomo 161, Archivo General, Mexico.

King, Rufus, Correspondence, Huntington Library, San Marino.

Mexico, 90-7-21, Archivo General de las Indias, Seville.

Miscellaneous, legajos 9-1-19, 90-2-20; Archivo General de las Indias, Seville.

Papeles de Cuba, lejajo 1708, Archivo General de las Indias, Seville.

Provincial State Papers, Vol. XIX, Archives of California, Bancroft Library, Berkeley.

Representacion umilde que hace la Ymperial Novilisima y muy Leal Ciudad de México en favor de sus Naturales a su Amado

Soberano el Señor Don Carlos 3. en 2 de Mayo de 1771, Mexico, 1771, Bancroft Collection, Berkeley.

2. PRINTED MATERIAL

Adams, John. *The Works of John Adams, Second President of the United States: With a Life of the Author, Notes and Illustrations, by his Grandson, Charles Francis Adams,* ed. Charles Francis Adams. 10 vols. Boston, 1852-1865.

American Historical Review. "Documents on the Blount Conspiracy, 1795-97," X, 574-606 (April, 1905).

—— "Documents on the Relations of France to Louisiana, 1792-95," III, 490-516 (April, 1898).

—— "Miranda and the British Admiralty, 1804-1806," VI, 508-530 (April, 1901).

—— "Observations of London Merchants on American Trade, 1783," XVIII, 769-787 (July, 1913).

—— "Santiago, and the Freeing of Spanish America, 1741," IV, 323-328 (Jan., 1899).

American Register or General Repository of History, Politics, and Science. Vols. I-VII. Philadelphia, 1807-1811.

American State Papers, Foreign Relations. Vols. I and II. Washington, 1833.

Annals of Congress, Fifth Congress, 1797-1799. 3 vols. Washington, 1851; and *Tenth Congress.* 3 vols. Washington, 1852-1853.

Aulard, François V. Alphonse, ed. *Recueil des actes du Comité de Salut Public avec la Correspondence Officielle des Representants en Mission et le Registre du Conseil Executif Provisoire,* in *Collection de Documents Inédits sur l'Histoire de France.* 26 vols. Paris, 1889-1923.

Bagot, Josceline, ed. *George Canning and his Friends, Containing Hitherto Unpublished Letters, Jeux d'Esprit,* etc. 2 vols. London, 1909.

Barbé-Marbois, Francois. *The History of Louisiana, particularly of the Cession of that Colony to the United States of America...* (translated by an American citizen, W. B. Lawrence). Philadelphia, 1830.

Beveridge, Albert J. *The Life of John Marshall.* 5 vols. New York, 1925.

Bolton, Herbert E., ed. "Papers of Zebulon M. Pike, 1806-1807," *The American Historical Review,* XIII, 798-827 (July, 1908).

Bourrienne, Louis Antoine F. *Memoirs of Napoleon Bonaparte I.* Revised Edition. 3 vols. New York, 1891.
Brissot de Warville, J. P. *New Travels in the United States of America in 1788.* Dublin, 1792.
Cancelada, Juan López. *Conducta del Excelentísimo Señor Don José Iturrigaray.* Cadiz, 1812.
—— *La Verdad Sabida y Buena Fé Guardada. Origen de la Espantosa Revolución de Nueva España comenzada en 15 de Septiembre de 1810.* Cadiz, 1811.
Chinard, Gilbert, ed. *The Correspondence of Jefferson and DuPont de Nemours.* Oxford, 1931.
Clark, Daniel. *Proofs of the Corruption of Gen. James Wilkinson, and of his Connexion with Aaron Burr.* Philadelphia, 1809.
Coues, Elliot, ed. *The Expeditions of Zebulon Montgomery Pike to headwaters of the Mississippi River, through Louisiana Territory, and in New Spain during the Years 1805-6-7.* 3 vols. New York, 1895.
Davis, Mathew L., ed. *Memoirs of Aaron Burr with Miscellaneous Selections from his Correspondence.* 2 vols. New York, 1837.
Dexter, Franklin Bowditch, ed. *The Literary Diary of Ezra Stiles.* 3 vols. New York, 1901.
Diario de México, Vols. X-XII. Mexico, 1808—.
Diplomatic Correspondence of the United States of America, from the signing of the Definitive Treaty of Peace . . . to the adoption of the Constitution, March 4, 1789. 7 vols. Washington, 1833-34.
Edinburgh Review. "Letters Illustrative of the Reign of William III from 1696 to 1708," LXXIV, 128-159 (Oct., 1841).
—— "Emancipation of Spanish America, a review of *'Lettre aux Espagnols Américains, par un de leurs Compatriots,'*" XIII, 277-312 (Jan., 1809).
Gage, Thomas. *A New Survey of the West Indies or, the English American, his Travel by Sea and Land. . . .* Third Edition. London, 1677.
García, Genaro, ed. *Documentos Históricos Mexicanos, Obra Commemorativa del Primer Centenario de la Independencia de México.* 6 vols. Mexico, 1910.
—— *Tumultos y Rebeliones acaecidos en México,* Vol. X in *Documentos Inéditos o muy raros para la Historia de México.* 35 vols. Mexico, 1905-1911.

García Icazbalceta, Joaquín, ed. *Colección de Documentos para la Historia de México.* 2 vols. Mexico, 1858-1866.

Gazeta de México, Compendio de Noticias de Nueva España y Europa. Vols. XV-XVIII. Mexico, 1806—.

Hamilton, Alexander. *Works of Alexander Hamilton, Comprising his Correspondence and his Political and Official Writings,* ed. John Church Hamilton. 7 vols. New York, 1850-1851.

—— *The Works of Alexander Hamilton,* ed. H. C. Lodge. 9 vols. New York, 1885-1886.

Hansard, T. C. *Parliamentary Debates,* XI (1808). London, 1812.

Hernández y Dávalos, Juan E. *Colección de Documentos para la Historia de la Guerra de Independencia de México de 1808 a 1821.* 6 vols. Mexico, 1877-1882.

Humboldt, Alexander de. *Political Essay on the Kingdom of New Spain* (translated from the original French by J. Black). Second Edition. 4 vols. London, 1814.

Jefferson, Thomas. *The Works of Thomas Jefferson,* ed. Paul Leicester Ford. 12 vols. New York, 1904-1905.

—— *The Writings of Thomas Jefferson,* ed. Andrew A. Lipscomb. Library Edition. 20 vols. Washington, 1903.

Kellog, Louise Phelps, ed. "Letter of Thomas Paine, 1793," *The American Historical Review,* XXIX, 501-505 (April, 1924).

King, Rufus. *The Life and Correspondence of Rufus King, Comprising his Letters, Private and Official, his Public Documents and his Speeches,* ed. Charles R. King. 6 vols. New York, 1894-1900.

Leonard, Irving A., ed. *Alboroto y Motín de México del 8 de Junio de 1692. Relación de Don Carlos de Sigüenza y Gongora.* ... Mexico, 1932.

Londonderry, Second Marquess of. *Memoirs and Correspondence of Viscount Castlereagh, Second Marquess of Londonderry,* ed. Charles William Vane, Third Marquis of Londonderry. 12 vols. London, 1848-1853.

Mier Noriega y Guerra, José Servando Teresa de. *Historia de la Revolución de Nueva España, Antiguamente Anáhuac, ó Verdadero Origen y Causas de ella con la Relación de sus Progresos hasta el presente Año de 1813.* 2 vols. London, 1813.

Napoleon I. *The Confidential Correspondence of Napoleon Bon-*

aparte with his Brother Joseph, Sometime King of Spain. 2 vols. New York, 1856.
—— *Correspondance de Napoléon Ier, Publiée par ordre de l'empereur Napoléon III.* 32 vols. Paris, 1865.
Nolte, Vincent. *The Memoirs of Vincent Nolte . . . or Fifty Years in Both Hemispheres, translated from the German.* New York, 1934.
Paine, Thomas. *The Writings of Thomas Paine,* ed. M. D. Conway. 4 vols. New York, 1894-1896.
Pradt, Dominique G. F. de. *Memoires Historique sur la Revolution d'Espagne.* Paris, 1816.
—— *The Colonies and the Present American Revolution* (translated from the French). London, 1817.
Present State of Revenues and Forces by Sea and Land of France and Spain, Compar'd with those of Great Britain. London, 1740.
Raynal, Guillaume Thomas François. *A Philosophical and Political History of the Settlements and Trade of the Europeans in the East and West Indies* (translated by J. O. Justamond). 8 vols. London, 1788.
Recopilación de Leyes de los Reynos de las Indias. 3 vols. Madrid, 1791.
Richardson, James Daniel. *A Compilation of the Messages and Papers of the Presidents, 1789-1897.* 10 vols. Washington, 1899.
Rojas, Aristides, ed. *Miranda dans la Revolution Française.* Caracas, 1889.
Rolt, Richard. *A New and Accurate History of South America and Mexico.* London, 1756.
Rydjord, John. "Napoleon and New Spain" (I, 289-312), *New Spain and the West,* ed. George P. Hammond. 2 vols. Los Angeles, 1932.
Sinclair, John. *The History of the Public Revenue of the British Empire.* London, 1785.
Steiner, Bernard C. *The Life and Correspondence of James McHenry.* Cleveland, 1907.
Stevens, B. F. *Stevens's Facsimiles of Manuscripts in European Archives relating to America, 1773-1783.* 25 vols. London, 1889-1895.
The Texas Historical Association Quarterly (Austin), "Concerning Philip Nolan." VII, 308-317 (1903-1904).
Turner, Frederick J., ed. "Correspondence of Clark and Genet,"

Annual Report of the American Historical Association, 1896. (2 vols., Washington, 1897), I, 930-1107.

——— "Correspondence of the French Ministers to the United States, 1791-1797," *Annual Report of the American Historical Association, 1903.* (2 vols., Washington, 1904), II.

——— "English Policy toward America 1790-1791," *The American Historical Review,* VII, 706-735 (July, 1902).

——— "The Mongourit Correspondence in Respect to Genet's Projected Attack upon the Floridas," *Annual Report of the American Historical Association, 1897.* Washington, 1898.

Walton, William. *An Exposé on the Dissentions of Spanish America.* ... London, 1814.

Wellington, Duke of. *Supplementary Despatches and Memoranda of Field Marshall Arthur, Duke of Wellington,* ed. Duke of Wellington. 15 vols. London, 1858-1872.

Wilkinson, James. *Memoirs of My Own Times.* 3 vols. Philadelphia, 1816.

B. Secondary Sources

1. Articles in Periodicals and Publications of Learned Societies

Brown, Vera L. "Anglo-Spanish Relations in America," *The Hispanic American Historical Review,* V, 325-348 (Aug., 1922).

——— "Contraband Trade: a Factor in the Decline of Spain's Empire in America," *The Hispanic American Historical Review,* VIII, 178-190 (May, 1928).

Bustamante, Carlos María. "El Venerable Señor Don Juan de Palafox y Mendoza," *Voz de la Patria* (Suplemento Num. 5), Mexico, 1831.

Cox, Isaac Joslin. "The American Intervention in West Florida," *The American Historical Review,* XVII, 290-311 (Jan., 1912).

——— "Hispanic-American Phases of the 'Burr Conspiracy'," *The Hispanic American Historical Review,* XII, 145-175 (May, 1932).

——— "The Louisiana-Texas Frontier," *The Quarterly of the Texas State Historical Association,* X, 1-75 (July, 1906).

——— "The Louisiana-Texas Frontier during the Burr Conspiracy," *The Mississippi Valley Historical Review,* X, 274-284 (Dec., 1923).

——— "Opening the Santa Fe Trail," *The Missouri Historical Review,* XXV, 30-66 (Oct., 1930).

―― "The Pan American Policy of Jefferson and Wilkinson," *The Mississippi Valley Historical Review*, I, 212-239 (Sept., 1914).

Desdevises du Dezert, Gaston. "L'Eglise Espagnole des Indes a la fin du XVIIIᵉ Siècle," *Revue Hispanique*, XXXIX, 111-293 (Feb., 1917).

―― "Vice-Rois et Capitaine Généraux des Indes Espagnole a la fin du XVIIIᵉ Siècle," *Revue Historique*, CXXV, 225-264 (July-Aug., 1917).

Fortescue, J. W. "The Expedition to the West Indies," *Macmillan's Magazine*, LXIX, 184-197 (Jan., 1894).

Hale, Edward Everett. "The Real Philip Nolan," *Publications of the Mississippi Historical Society*, IV, 281-329 (1901).

James, James Alton. "French Opinion as a Factor in preventing War between France and the United States, 1795-1800," *The American Historical Review*, XXX, 44-55 (Oct., 1924).

―― "Louisiana in American Diplomacy, 1795-1800," *The Mississippi Valley Historical Review*, I, 44-56 (June, 1914).

Lingelbach, W. E. "Commercial History in the Napoleonic Era," *The American Historical Review*, XIX, 257-281 (Jan., 1914).

Manning, William Ray. "The Nootka Sound Controversy," *Annual Report of the American Historical Association, 1904* (Washington, 1905).

Masson, Marjorie, and Jameson, James F. "The Odyssey of Thomas Muir," *The American Historical Review*, XXIX, 49-72 (Oct., 1923).

Moses, Bernard. "Government in Spanish America," *The American Political Science Review*, VIII, 204-215 (May, 1914).

―― "Social Revolution in South America," *Annual Report of the American Historical Association, 1915.* Washington, 1917.

Nettels, Curtis. "England and the Spanish-American Trade, 1680-1715," *The Journal of Modern History*, III, 1-32 (March, 1931).

Obregón, T. Esquivel. "Factors in the Historical Evolution of Mexico," *The Hispanic American Historical Review*, II, 135-172 (May, 1919).

Posey, Walter Brownlow. "The Blount Conspiracy," *Birmingham-Southern College Bulletin*, XXI, 11-21 (1928).

Riley, Franklin L. "Spanish Policy in Mississippi after the Treaty of San Lorenzo," *Annual Report of the American Historical Association, 1897* (Washington, 1898).

Rives, George L. "Spain and the United States in 1795," *The*

American Historical Review, IV, 62-79 (Oct., 1898).

Robertson, William Spence. "The Juntas of 1808 and the Spanish Colonies," *The English Historical Review,* XXXI, 573-585 (Oct., 1916).

Rusk, Ralph Leslie. "The Adventures of Gilbert Imlay," *The Indiana University Studies,* X, 3-26 (March, 1923).

Shepherd, W. R. "The Cession of Louisiana to Spain," *The Political Science Quarterly,* XIX, 438-458 (Sept., 1904).

Sloan, William M. "Napoleon's Plan for a Colonial System," *The American Historical Review,* IV, 439-455 (April, 1899).

Strong, Frank. "The Cause of Cromwell's West Indian Expedition," *The American Historical Review,* IV, 228-245 (Jan., 1899).

Temperley, H. W. V. "The Relations of England with Spanish America, 1720-1744," Vol. I, pp. 231-237, *Annual Report of American Historical Association.* 2 vols. Washington, 1913.

Thomas, Alfred B. "Spanish Exploration of Oklahoma, 1599-1792," *The Quarterly of the Oklahoma Historical Society* (reprint, June, 1928).

Turner, Frederick Jackson. "The Diplomatic Contest for the Mississippi Valley," *The Atlantic Monthly,* XCIII, 676-691; 807-817 (May and June, 1904).

——— "The Origin of Genet's Projected Attack on Louisiana and the Floridas," *The American Historical Review,* III, 650-671 (July, 1898).

——— "The Policy of France Toward the Mississippi Valley in the Period of Washington and Adams," *The American Historical Review,* X, 249-279 (Jan., 1905).

Zimmerman, A. F. "Spain and its Colonies 1808-1820," *The Hispanic American Historical Review,* XI, 439-463 (Nov., 1931).

2. GENERAL WORKS

Adams, Henry. *History of the United States of America.* 9 vols. New York, 1909-1911.

Addison, Joseph. *Charles the Third of Spain.* Oxford, 1900.

Alamán, Lúcas. *Historia de Méjico desde los primeros movimientos que prepararon su Independencia en el año de 1808 hasta la época presente.* 5 vols. Méjico, 1849-1852.

Alison, Sir Archibald. *Lives of Lord Castlereagh and Sir Charles Stewart, the Second and Third Marquesses of Londonderry....* 3 vols. Edinburgh, 1861.

Bancroft, Hubert Howe. *Essays and Miscellany*, Vol. XXXVIII, *Works*. San Francisco, 1890.
——— *History of Central America*. 3 vols. San Francisco, 1882-1887.
——— *History of Mexico*. 6 vols. San Francisco, 1883-1887.
Becker, Jerónimo. *España é Inglaterra, sus Relaciones desde las Paces de Utrecht*. Madrid, 1906.
——— *Historia de las Relaciones Exteriores de España durante el Siglo XIX, Apuntes para una Historia Diplomática*. Madrid, 1924.
Bemis, Samuel Flagg. *Pinckney's Treaty, a Study of America's advantage from Europe's Distress, 1783-1800*. Baltimore, 1926.
Bolton, Herbert E., ed. *Athanase de Méxières and the Louisiana-Texas Frontier, 1768-1780*. 2 vols. Cleveland, 1914.
Bolton, Herbert E., and Marshall, Thomas M. *Colonization of North America, 1492-1783*. New York, 1921.
Bolton, Herbert E., and Ross, Mary. *The Debatable Land*. Berkeley, 1925.
Bolton, Herbert E. *History of the Americas, A Syllabus with Maps*. Boston, 1928.
——— *The Spanish Borderlands, a Chronicle of Old Florida and the Southwest* (Vol. III in *Chronicles of America*). New Haven, 1921.
——— *Texas in the Middle Eighteenth Century*. Berkeley, 1915.
Bourne, Edward Gaylord. *Napoleon the First, a Biography by August Fournier*. New York, 1903.
——— *Spain in America, 1450-1580* (Vol. III in *The American Nation*, ed. A. B. Hart). New York, 1904.
Bourne, Henry E. *The Revolutionary Period in Europe*. New York, 1915.
Bustamante, Carlos María de. *Cuadro Histórico de la Revolución Mexicana comenzada en 15 de Septiembre de 1810 por el Ciudadano Miguel Hidalgo y Costilla.* . . . 2 vols. Mexico, 1843.
Carman, Harry J., and McKee, Samuel, Jr. *A History of the United States, 1492-1865*. Vol. I. Boston, 1931.
Caughey, John W., *Bernardo de Gálvez in Louisiana, 1776-1783* in *Publications of the University of California at Los Angeles in Social Sciences*, Vol. IV. Berkeley, 1934.
Cavo, Andrés. *Los tres siglos de México durante el Gobierno Español, hasta la entrada del Ejército Trigarante . . . , con Notas*

y Suplemento, el lic. Carlos María Bustamante. 4 vols. in 2. Mexico, 1836-1838.

Chadwick, F. E. *The Relations of the United States with Spain.* New York, 1911.

Chandler, Charles Lyon. *Inter-American Acquaintances.* Sewanee, 1917.

Channing, Edward. *A History of the United States.* 6 vols. New York, 1905-1930.

Chapman, Charles E. *The Founding of Spanish California.* New York, 1916.

—— *A History of Spain.* New York, 1918.

Collins, Sister Mary Austin. *The Reforms of Charles the Third in New Spain in the Light of the Pacte Famille.* (MS. thesis), University of California, 1927.

Conway, Moncure D. *The Life of Thomas Paine, with a History of his Literary, Political and Religious Career in America, France and England.* Third Edition. 2 vols. New York, 1893.

Corwin, Edward S. *French Policy and the American Alliance of 1778.* Princeton, 1916.

Cox, Isaac J. *The West Florida Controversy, 1798-1813.* Baltimore, 1918.

Coxe, William. *Memoirs of the Kings of Spain of the House of Bourbon, from the Accession of Philip V to the death of Charles III, 1700-1788.* Second Edition. 5 vols. London, 1815.

Doniol, Henri. *Histoire de la Participation de la France à L'établissement des États-Unis d'Amérique.* 5 vols. Paris, 1885-1892.

Dunn, William E. *Spanish and French Rivalry in the Gulf Region of the United States, 1678-1702; the beginning of Texas and Pensacola.* Austin, 1917.

Fish, Carl Russel. *American Diplomacy.* Fourth Edition. New York, 1923.

Fisher, Lillian Estelle. *The Background of the Revolution for Mexican Independence.* Boston, 1934.

—— *Viceregal Administration in the Spanish-American Colonies.* Berkeley, 1926.

Ford, Worthington C. *The United States and Spain in 1790.* Brooklyn, 1890.

García, Genaro. *El Plan de Independencia de la Nueva España en 1808.* Mexico, 1903.

Garrison, George P. *Texas, a Contest of Civilizations*. Boston, 1903.
Gayarré, Charles. *History of Louisiana*. Fourth Edition. 4 vols. New Orleans, 1903.
Gerard, James W. *The Peace of Utrecht: A Historical Review of the Great Treaty of 1713-14, and of the Principal Events of the War of the Spanish Succession*. New York, 1885.
González Obregón, Luis. *D. Guillén de Lampart, La Inquisición y la Independencia en el Siglo XVIIe*. Paris, 1908.
——— *Los Precursores de la Independencia Mexicana en el siglo XVI*. Paris, 1906.
Hart, F. R. *The Disaster of Darien*. Boston, 1929.
Hosmer, James K. *The History of the Louisiana Purchase*. New York, 1902.
Hume, Martin A. S. *Modern Spain, 1788-1858*. New York, 1900.
James, James Alton. *The Life of George Rogers Clark*. Chicago, 1928.
Keller, Albert G. *Colonization, a Study of the Founding of New Societies*. Boston, 1908.
Koebel, W. H. *British Exploits in South America*. New York, 1917.
Kroeber, A. L., and Waterman, T. T. *Source Book in Anthropology*. Berkeley, 1920.
Latané, John Holladay. *A History of American Foreign Policy*. Garden City, 1928.
Lea, Henry Charles. *The Inquisition in the Spanish Dependencies*. New York, 1922.
Leonard, Irving A. *Don Carlos de Sigüenza y Góngora*. Berkeley, 1929.
Leroy-Beaulieu, Paul. *De La Colonisation chez les Peuples Modernes*. Fifth Edition. 2 vols. Paris, 1902.
Lokke, Carl Ludwig. *France and the Colonial Question: A Study of Contemporary French Opinion, 1783-1801*. New York, 1932.
Lyon, E. Wilson. *Louisiana in French Diplomacy, 1759-1804*. Norman, 1934.
McCaleb, Walter F. *The Aaron Burr Conspiracy*. New York, 1903.
Mahan, A. T. *Influence of Sea Power on History*. Boston, 1902.
——— *Influence of Sea Power upon the French Revolution and Empire, 1793-1812*. 2 vols. Boston, 1898.

Mancini, Jules. *Bolívar y la Emancipación de las Colonias Españolas desde los Orígenes hasta 1815.* Paris, 1914.
Martin, François-Xavier. *The History of Louisiana.* 2 vols. New Orleans, 1829.
Mathews, Shailer. *The French Revolution, 1789-1815.* New York, 1924.
Medina, José Toribio. *Historia del Tribunal del Santo Oficio de la Inquisición en México.* Santiago de Chile, 1905.
Merriman, Roger B. *The Rise of the Spanish Empire in the Old World and New.* 3 vols. New York, 1918-1925.
Mora, José María Luis. *Méjico y sus Revoluciones.* 3 vols. (I, III, IV). Paris, 1836.
Moses, Bernard. *The Establishment of Spanish Rule in America.* New York, 1898.
——— *Spain's Declining Power in South America, 1730-1806.* Berkeley, 1919.
Mowat, R. B. *The Diplomacy of Napoleon.* New York, 1924.
Navarro y Lamarca, Carlos. *Compendio de la Historia general de América.* 2 vols. Buenos Aires, 1910-1913.
Newton, Arthur Percival. *The European Nations in the West Indies, 1493-16.* London, 1933.
Noll, Arthur H., and McMahon, A. P. *The Life and Times of Miguel Hidalgo y Costilla.* Chicago, 1910.
Oman, Charles. *A History of the Peninsular War.* 7 vols. Oxford, 1902-1930.
——— "The Peninsular War," *Cambridge Modern History* (IX, 428-482), ed. A. W. Ward. 14 vols. London, 1902-1912.
Orozco y Berra, D. Manuel. *Noticia Histórica de la Conjuración del Marqués del Valle, Años de 1565-1568.* . . . Mexico, 1853.
[Palacio, Manuel.] *Outline of the Revolution in Spanish America, or an Account of the Origin, Progress, and actual State of the War carried on between Spain and Spanish America . . . by a South American.* London, 1817.
Parra-Pérez, C. *Miranda et la Revolution Française.* Paris, 1925.
Phillips, Paul C. *The West in the Diplomacy of the American Revolution.* Urbana, 1914.
Priestley, Herbert I. *José de Gálvez.* Berkeley, 1916.
——— *The Mexican Nation: A History.* New York, 1923.
Renaut, F. P. *Le Pacte de Famille et L'Amérique; la Politique Coloniale Franco-Espagnole de 1760-1792.* Paris, 1922.

BIBLIOGRAPHY 321

Rivera y Cambos, Manuel. *Historia Antigua y Moderna de Jalapa y de las Revoluciónes del Estado de Vera Cruz.* 5 vols. Mexico, 1869-1871.
—— *Los Gobernantes de México.* . . . 2 vols. Mexico, 1872-1873
Robertson, James A., ed. *Louisiana under the Rule of Spain, France, and the United States, 1785-1807.* 2 vols. Cleveland, 1911.
Robertson, William. *The History of America.* 2 vols. London, 1777.
Robertson, William Spence. "Francisco de Miranda and the Revolutionizing of Spanish America," *Annual Report of the American Historical Association for the Year 1907* (I, 189-539). 2 vols. Washington, 1908.
—— *The Life of Miranda.* 2 vols. Chapel Hill, 1929.
—— *Rise of the Spanish American Republics, as told in the Lives of their Contemporaries.* New York, 1918.
Roscher, Wilhelm. *The Spanish Colonial System* (translated and edited by E. G. Bourne). New York, 1904.
Rose, J. Holland. *Pitt and Napoleon, Essays and Letters.* London, 1912.
—— *William Pitt and the Great War.* London, 1911.
Rousseau, François. *Règne de Charles III d'Espagne.* Paris, 1907.
Salcedo y Ruiz, Angel, and Angel y Alvarez, Manuel. *Historia de España é Historia de la Civilización Española.* Madrid, 1914.
Savine, Albert. *L'Abdication de Bayonne.* Paris, 1908.
Schalk de la Faverie, Alfred. *Napoléon et L'Amérique.* Paris, 1917.
Sierra, Justo, ed. *Mexico, Its Social Evolution.* 3 vols. Mexico, 1900-1904.
Sinclair, Marguerite C. *French Commercial Relations with the Spanish American Colonies.* (MS. thesis.) Berkeley, 1922.
Sorel, Albert. *L'Europe et la Revolucion Française.* 7 vols. Paris, 1887-1904.
Soulange-Bodin, André. *La Diplomatie de Louis XVe et le Pacte de Famille.* Paris, 1894.
Spears, John R., and Clark, A. H. *A History of the Mississippi Valley from its Discovery to the End of Foreign Domination.* New York, 1903.
Stanhope, Philip Henry (5th Earl). *Life of the Right Honourable William Pitt.* Third Edition. 4 vols. London, 1867.

Steward, Theophilus G. *The Haitian Revolution.* Second edition. New York, 1914.
Temperley, H. W. V. "The Age of Walpole and the Pelhams" (VI, 140-189), *Cambridge Modern History,* ed. A. W. Ward. New York, 1925.
Trescott, William Henry. *The Diplomacy of the Revolution.* New York, 1852.
Villanueva, Carlos A. *Historia y Diplomacia: Napoléon y la Independencia de América.* Paris, 1911.
—— *Fernando VII y los Nuevos Estados.* Paris, n.d.
Wandell, Samuel H., and Minnigerode, Meade. *Aaron Burr, a Biography compiled from Rare, and in many cases, Unpublished Sources.* 2 vols. New York, 1925.
Ward, A. W., and Gooch, G. P. *The Cambridge History of British Foreign Policy, 1783-1919.* 3 vols. New York, 1922.
Weiss, Charles. *L'Espagne depuis le Règne de Philippe II jusqu'a l'avénement des Bourbons.* 2 vols. Paris, 1844.
Whitaker, Arthur Preston. *The Spanish-American Frontier, 1783-1795; the Westward Movement and the Spanish Retreat in the Mississippi Valley.* Boston, 1927.
Whiting, Henry. *Life of Zebulon Montgomery Pike.* Boston, 1848.
Winsor, Justin, ed. *Narrative and Critical History of America.* 8 vols. Boston, 1884-1889.
Zamacois, Niceto de. *Historia de Méjico desde sus tiempos más remotos hasta nuestros días.* 18 vols. Mexico, 1877-1882.
Zárate, Julio. *La Guerra de Independencia,* vol. III in *México á través de los Siglos,* ed. Vicente Riva Palacio. 5 vols. Barcelona, 1888-1889.

INDEX

Abadi, Juan, Frenchman in Mexico, 130.
Abdication, Charles IV, 257, 273, 291; cession of lands before, 302.
Abercromby, Sir Ralph, on liberation of South America, 175, 192.
Acapulco, in revolutionary plans, 90, 91, 153, 201; soldiers at, 73; trade with Orient, 45, 96.
Acayucan, Olaeta in, 135.
Adair, John, relations with Wilkinson, 209, 221, 223.
Adams, Henry, quoted, 209, 210.
Adams, John, minister to England, report to Jay, 97-98; president, on revolutionary plans, 156-157, 159, 161; X. Y. Z. affair, 163; and Miranda's plans, 165-169, 172, 175, 177; and peace with France, 169, 174, 177, 185-187, 191.
Addington, Henry, ministry of, and Miranda's plans, 193, 198, 201, 202.
Adet, French minister to Philadelphia, retrocession of Louisiana, 125; Genet's project, 126-127; Blount's conspiracy, 127; protest to Spanish, 147; warnings of, 150, 157; and the West, 206.
Agents, revolutionary, to New Spain, 21, 91, 134; Mendiola, 100; Mexico, 100-101, 104; of Genêt, 114, 121; of French Revolution, 132-134, 194, 301; Caro, 160, 188; in Europe, 154-155, 157, 192; of Burr, 212, 215; of Napoleon, 195, 259-260, 262, 289, 295-306; to Querétaro, 288; in Louisiana, 294.
Aguirre, Guillermo, 285.
Agriculture, Joseph, for freedom of, 296.
Alba, Duke of, opinion on Louisiana, 68.
Alburquerque, Duke of, viceroy, 47.
Alcudia, Duke of, Carondelet reports to, 122; information on the French, 145-146; *see also* Godoy.
Alemán de la Peña, execution of, 305.
Alexander, glory of, 50.
Algarves, Godoy, king of, 255.
Algeciras, agent of Murat to, 263.

"All the Talents," ministry of, and policy, 239.
Allaire, P., informs English, 107.
Allegiance, of New Spain, 279.
Allende, Captain, with D'Alvimar, 307-308.
Alliance, rearranged, 48-49; France with Spain, 53, 147, 148, 152, 170, 195, 202, 227, 241; Spain and United States, 86; France and United States, 93; France seeks English, 110; for liberation, 112; Anglo-American, 157, 164, 167, 248; England and Russia, 184; England and Spain, 227, 268-269; England with Portugal, 254.
Alvarado, illicit commerce near, 135.
Alvarado River, Wellesley's point for attack, 243.
Alvimar, Napoleon's agent in Mexico, 260-261, 308.
Alvina, *see* Alvimar.
Amazon, Napoleon's interest in, 194.
America, Spanish control of, 23, 47, 202, 237, 247, 302; French interest in, 43, 45, 47, 113, 119, 259; British interest in, 45, 48, 157, 185, 200, 216, 249, 254; independence of, 198, 227, 274; Napoleon and, 263, 270-271, 290, 295-306; *see also* Spanish America.
American Register, The, quoted, 210, 217, 236.
American Republic, to spread revolution, 205.
American Revolution, example of, 77; link with D'Aubarde, 92; loyalty of Mexico during, 100; and changed attitude on colonies, 236-237.
Americans, against Europeans, 8-9; education of, 12; westward movement of, 102; fear conquest by, 193; policy of, 108; and Louisiana, 115, 123, 186, 196, 200; Genêt recruiting, 136; violate exclusion act, 149; and Spanish posts, 164; Nolan, a wedge for, 186; Miranda and, 205, 232; against Spain, 206; in Mexican Association, 210; ad-

vantages of Burr's plan to, 213; warnings against, 219; and New Mexico, 224; and Mexico, 225, 252; arrive from Bordeaux, 305.
Americas, emperor of the Two, 255; agents to revolutionize, 295.
Amiens, Peace of, 193, 194, 196, 255; Treaty of, 193.
Ancien régime, in New Spain, 139.
Anglo-American, plan of coalition, 87; 185; French warning against, 184; neutrality of, 240.
Anglo-Americans, advance of, 205; into West Florida, 206-207; loyal to Union, 216; defend Mexico against, 292.
Anglo-Saxon, penetration, 42; example of, 105.
Anglo-Spanish, *rapprochement* prevented, 240.
Anson, Commodore, expedition of, 50, 75; independence plan of, 51.
Antigua, British, 45.
Antilles, British in, 41.
Apaches, Spain seeks aid of, 48.
"Apostles of Bonaparte," Spanish consuls to watch, 306.
Aragon, excluded, 17.
Aragonese, resist French at Saragossa, 269.
Aranda, Count, and Raynal, 13; on government, 17; on Louisiana, 68; Spanish minister to France; fears American Revolution, 80-81, 104; prophesy of, 94, 99; plans kingdoms in America, 95; approves frontier plan, 103.
Aranjuez, abdication of Charles IV, 257.
Archbishop, report on French, 142, 143; praises Inquisition, 143; opposed to a congress, 280.
Archduke, British support Austrian, 46.
Archives, to be destroyed, 25.
Aristocracy, for independence, 211.
Armada, defeat of, 40.
Armola, *see* Villaroel, 72.
Armies, agents equal to, 91.
Arms, purchased by Portuguese, 31-32; amount necessary, 100; for rebellion, 154; England to supply, 156.
Army, officer in, discovers plot, 34; lack of, in Indies, 57; reforms of, 73-74; agency for rebellion, 74; posts on frontier, 74; and taxes, 74; Hamilton to lead, 165, 170, 172; United States to supply, 168; in the West, 171; to New Orleans, 185; defeat of Le Clerc's, 200; Spanish, across Sabine, 218; of Wilkinson, 220; English to Mexico, 227; defeat of British, 236; for Mexican expedition, 244; for Mexico, 253; Wellesley's, 264; capture of Du Pont's, 269; British, in Spain, 269; defeat of Napoleon's, 285; in conspiracy, 288; at New Orleans, 294; Desmolard to win support of, 298.
Aroche, Juan, French in inn of, 130, 138.
Arroyo Hondo, Wilkinson to attack on, 218.
Asia, English rule in, 200.
Asiento Treaty, 16.
Assembly, French, influences of, 109, 138, 140, 143, 280.
Association, Mexican, 210.
Asturias, junta of, agents to London, 267; insurrection of, 268; colonies to support, 268-269.
Asturians, British support of, 268.
Atheists, French as, 294.
Atlantic Coast, loyalty to Spain of, 203; England on, 209.
Aubarde, Marquis de, conspiracy of, 62-64, 73, 92.
Aubrey, French governor of Louisiana, 65; aids Ulloa, 66, 70; opposition to a republic, 69.
Audiencia, and conspiracy, 25; criticized, 27; on abdications, 273; rejects Dom Pedro, 276; caution, of, 283; leader of, 285; control over Mexico by, 288.
Austerlitz, Battle of, 228; speech on, 242.
Australia, Muir escapes from, 129.
Austria, and Spanish succession, 45; English support of, 46, 47, 49; prince of, for Mexico, 49, 51, 61; for liberation, 97; Spanish minister in, 187; Napoleon and, 264, 269.
Austrian Succession, 51, 61.
Austrians, distract Napoleon, 270.
Auto-de-fé, 36.
Avila, Alonso de, leader of American faction, 23; plans rebellion, 24-26.
Avila, Gil González, arrested, 26.
Ayuntamiento, authority in Mexico, 274; and Mexican congress, 275, 279.

INDEX

Azanza, viceroy, fears loss of California, 184.
Azcarate y Lezama, for independence, 275, 282.
Aztec, crown, 25.

Baird, expedition of, 234.
Baltimore, provisions for British in, 151; headquarters for Napoleon's agents, 295, 297; Bernabeu in, 296.
Bancroft, H. H., quoted, 23, 287.
Bank of France, funds for Napoleon's agents, 262.
Barbados, Modyford of, 41; troops for Africa to, 235.
Barbé-Marbois, on sale of Louisiana, 200.
Barbuda, British, 45.
Baring, Nolte and house of, 222.
Barlow, Joel, revolutionary activities of, 115, 116, 123.
Barragán, agent of Mexican revolutionists, 182.
Bartholemy, French representative at Basle, 125.
Basle, Treaty of, 124-125.
Bastile Day, Mexico on, 274.
Bastrop lands, Burr's purchase of, 216.
Baton Rouge, Kemper insurrection in, 207-208; Burr and, 215; D'Alvimar at, 260, 261.
Battle of Austerlitz, 228, 242.
Battle of Trafalgar, naval supremacy of England, 228.
Baylen, Du Pont's defeat at, 269.
Bayonne, Napoleon's headquarters, royal family at, 257; constitution for Spain at, 258; Napoleon's agents from, 295.
Beaumarchais, example of, 98.
Beaupoils, revolutionary plans of, 116.
Béliardi, Abbé, French agent in Madrid, 59.
Belmont, Francisco, to United States, 303-304.
Benbow, Admiral, report on Indies, 46.
Berenguer de Marquina, viceroy, belittles conspiracy, 181; suspects British, 183.
Beresford, General, to La Plata, 235.
Berg, Duke of, 262; and Napoleon's appointments for Mexico, 263.
Bernabeu, information on French agents, 296.

Bertrand, Moleville, revolutionary plan of, 52, 227.
Bishops, favored, 4.
Blennerhasset, Herman, with Burr, 214, 215, 221.
"Bloody O'Reilly," 71; won apparent loyalty, 114.
Blount, conspiracy of, 127; and Genet with Burr, 150; and Chisholm, 151; impeachment of, 152; and the westerners, 206.
Bogotá, starting point for revolution, 155. *See also* Santa Fé de.
Boissi d'Anglas, Discurso por, read in Mexico, 139.
Bonaparte, Napoleon, agent of, in Mexico, 195; and Santo Domingo, 195; failures in America, 196; invasion of England, 202; views on Brazil, 202; Emperor of the West, 228; Castlereagh on, 266; removal of Bourbons and House of Austria, 264; for throne of Spain, 255, 256; D'Alvimar and, 260; watch "Apostles" of, 306; *see* Napoleon and Joseph.
Bonapartes, for peninsular throne, 254; juntas in defiance of, 259; Mexican junta rejects, 277-278; intrigues of, 295; answer to, 299.
Bolton, H. E., quoted, 49.
Bonet, Pedro, accusation of, 140.
Bonneville, Nicholas, with Paine in Paris, 115.
Books, prohibited, 120-123.
Booksellers, and Inquisition, 12.
Bordeaux, D'Alvimar from, 260; French agents from, 305.
Borderlands, 3; French extend, 48; Genet to spread French views in, 117; Genet and Florida, 120; plans fail on, 121; defense of, 74, 149, 214; intrigues on, 150; American troops to, 151, 205; independence of, 151; warned against British, 153; Nolan on, 172, 186; Russian threat on, 184; to arrest Americans in, 186; dissatisfied Americans in, 207; fear of Burr in, 214; danger to, 303.
Borica, Diego de, governor of California, entertains Muir, 179.
Boston, Miranda in, 111; Turreau leaving, 302.

Botany Bay, Thomas Muir to, 178.
Bott, Edmund, interested in plot, 96.
Boundary, Louisiana, 200, 205, 206, 214, 216, 217.
Bourbons, influence in Spain, 12, 16, 18-19, 47-48, 59, 136; influence in Mexico, 18-19, 49, 89, 142, 273, 277-278, 284; opposed by British, 46-47, 77, 95; Family Compact of, 53, 57-58, 75, 88, 109; and American Revolution, 78-83; for throne of Mexico, 246-248; removal from Spain, 246, 254, 256-257, 259.
Bowdoin, minister to Spain, Jefferson on Burr to, 223.
Bowles, William, on Florida border, 107.
Braganza, family, removal of, 254-255; offers Pedro to Mexico, 276; Duke of, related to viceroy, 31; letter to, 34.
Branciforte, viceroy, on education, 12; against French influence, 131, 137-139, 144, 146, 147; on British menace to Mexico, 149.
Brazil, revolutions in, 31; French interest from Louisiana to, 194, 202; Braganzas to, 257; Dom Pedro in, 276.
Brest, French fleet from, 290.
Brissot de Warville, interest in the West, 103; head of Girondists, 110; and Miranda, 111, 112, 190; guillotined, 121; Muir describes, 179.
British, relations with the United States, 15, 150-151, 197-198, 212-215, 249; commerce of, 16, 46, 50, 149, 203; relations with Spain, 16, 38-40, 239, 265, 267-269, 290-291; and independence of Spanish colonies, 46, 47, 49-51, 56-57, 60, 95-98, 100, 107, 149, 152, 180, 182, 227, 229, 235-237, 245-246, 250, 252, 265-267; policy of, 51-52, 201, 215, 227, 234, 236, 240, 266-267, 271; colonies of, 74, 87, 234; and Miranda's plans, 106, 168, 169, 187, 226, 233, 251; relations with Napoleon, 195, 230, 250, 254, 263, 265, 270; and Burr's project, 212-215.
Brown, Senator of Kentucky, favors Genêt, 120.
Bucareli, viceroy, French cook of, 137.
Buccaneers, French in Caribbean, 42.
Buenos Aires, British expedition to, 235, 244, 252.

Buonaparte, of Santo Domingo and Corsica, 195.
Burgos, Ferdinand VII to meet Napoleon at, 257.
Burgoyne, General, defeat of, 85.
Burke, Edmund, and Thomas Paine, 128.
Burling, Wilkinson's messenger, 222.
Burr, Aaron, comparison with conspiracy of, 150; seeks army command for Spanish American expedition, 165-166; conspiracy of, 205-227, 229; and Jefferson, 223, 232; and Williamson, 238; reported in England, 265; and army, 293.
Bustamante, Carlos, on Garibay, 285.

Caballeros racionales, American faction, 287.
Caballeros Republicanos de México, revolutionary organization, 182.
Cabildo, to govern New Orleans, 71.
Cabinet, John Adams and, 167; Hamilton to consult with, 171; Dundas gives plans to British, 176.
Cadiz, and French system, 140; deportation of French to, 146; Berg to send viceroy from, 263; British troops near, 265; take royal family to, 291.
Caesar, and Napoleon, 195.
California, defense against foreigners, 75, 149, 153, 179, 184; to Isthmus, map of, 215; Wilkinson on conquest of, 221.
Calvin, heresies of, 36.
Campbell, Donald, on England's foreign relations, 201.
Campbell, Sir Archibald, plan of, 107.
Campechano, brigantine, 135.
Campeche, and English trade with Mexico, 196; warnings against French, 291.
Campeche Coast, British logwood on, 56.
Campo Alange, Spanish minister to Austria, buys Miranda's papers, 187.
Canada, add to United States, 117; troops from, to Mexico, 151.
Canal, right of navigation of, 156.
Canning, George, on checking Napoleon, 228; to support Spanish juntas, 268.
Cap, George, Frenchman in Mexico, 137, 148.

Cape of Good Hope, British expedition to, 234-235; Napoleon and, 242.
Capet, Louis, executed, 119.
Captain-general, Marquis del Valle proposed for, 24; of Venezuela, criticized, 302; of Cuba, reports arrest, 304.
Caracas, and La Plata expedition, 200-201; captain-general, on cession of, to France, 230; delegates to Trinidad, 232; warned against Miranda, 233; difficulties in taking, 252; D'Alvimar in, 260; Napoleon's agents to, 295; American newspapers support, 302.
Cardinaux, Francisco Louis, report on D'Aubarde, 62; plan of, 92.
Caribbean, British in, 41, 45, 58; French in, 42; Admiral Vernon in, 50; Jamaica and smuggling in, 56; and Napoleon, 195; trade rivalry in, 228; British needs in, 234-235.
Carmichael, William, commissioner to Spain, Jefferson to, 120.
Caro, Pedro José, revolutionary agent in London, 155; serving Miranda, 155, 160, 161, 165, 168, 175; Spanish government and, 187; expelled from Trinidad, 188; confession of, 188-189; and ex-Jesuits, 190, 193.
Carolina, Bourbons oppose prosperity of, 59.
Carolinians, advance of, 49.
Carondelet, Baron, governor of Louisiana, on French influence, 122; defense of Louisiana, 123, 124.
Carrizal, Pike hears of Burr at, 224.
Carry, James, Blount's report to, 150.
Carthagena, revolution in, 31; galleons from, 45; Admiral Benbow to, 46.
Caciques, aid to revolt, 91.
Castañas, General, appointed viceroy by Napoleon, 263.
Castejón, Marquis de, on American Revolution, 82-83.
Castile, and immigration, 16-17; king of, 24; Supreme Council of, 258.
Castilians, oppose Portuguese, 31.
Castlereagh, Lord, and Pitt, 234; links West Indies with Popham's expedition, 234; and Wellesley's plan, 243, 245; and Duke of Orleans as king for Mexico, 248; minister of war and colonies, and revolution for Spanish America, 242, 245, 246, 250, 266-267; Miranda's appeal to, 250-251; warnings of, 254; Melville on plans to, 265; new policy of, 268-269; and Napoleon, 298.
Castro, Antonio de, and Inquisition, 13.
Catalonia, rebellion of, 30; French troops entering, 256.
Catherine of Russia, and Miranda's project, 184.
Catholic, church opposes Lampart, 35; ministers of, 133; country, 142; Juan Kendrick becomes, 180; bishop of New Orleans supports Burr, 211; Joseph Bonaparte's appeal to, 297.
Celaya, troops expected from, 282.
Central America, England's interest in, 106.
Central Junta of Seville, commissioners to Mexico, 279; on equality of colonials, 286.
Cevallos, Spanish minister, on British aid to Burr, 212; report to Yrujo on Burr, 215; opposes negotiations with France, 294.
Cevallos, Captain, at Vera Cruz, 262.
Chagres River, England's interest in, 106.
Channel, enemy across English, 226.
Chapetón, 4.
Chargé d'affaires, Erving to Spain as, 216-217.
Charles II, last of the Spanish Hapsburgs, 18, 43, 45.
Charles III, appeal to, 177; reforms of, 14, 15, 19, 59, 72; and independence, 19; and Anglo-French rivalry, 53; and France, 59, 75; sees danger in West, 75; wants Jamaica, 75; and defense of America, 78; treaty with Portugal, 85; D'Aranda's report to, 94.
Charles IV, character of, 19; escape and abdication, 257; report in Mexico on abdication of, 273; Napoleon plans Mexican kingdom for, 290-292; report of cession to French by, 302.
Charles V, 18, 21.
Charleston, Spanish boundary to, 109; Genet in, 120.
Châtelet, Count of, minister to England, suggests republic for Louisiana, 65, 68.

Chesterfield, Lord, *Letters of*, on index, 129.
Chickasaw Bluffs, commandant of, and Burr, 222.
Chihuahua, Napoleon's agents in, 305.
Chile, economic restrictions, 14; in revolutionary plots, 57, 63, 113, 246, 251.
Chisholm, Captain, inherits Genet's schemes, 150-151.
Choiseul, foreign minister of France, 53; and Spanish alliance, 53, 58, 59; and independent Louisiana, 65.
Church, agency of state, 9-10; against new ideas, 14; and the French, 142, 143, 294, 296; collections in New Spain, 210; and independence, 288, 307.
Citizens, Spanish, migrate from Louisiana, 295.
Claiborne, governor of Louisiana, recommends attack on Spaniards, 220-221; reports on D'Alvimar, 260; Jefferson to, 292.
Claims, United States against Spain, 197, 216.
Clark, Daniel, to aid revolution, 115; and Genet, 120-121; and Wilkinson, 209, 211; and Mexican Association, 210; viceroy's report to Yrujo on, 211; interest in Mexico, 211-212; information to Burr, 219.
Clark, Elijah, and Genêt's plan, 123.
Clark, George Rogers, leader of Genêt's project, 115, 117-118, 124; in Chisholm's project, 151; and Westerners, 206.
Class distinction, 4, 6, 8.
Clavier, friend of Brissot, quoted, 103.
Clavijero, Jesuit, on retrocession of Louisiana, 193.
Clay, Henry, meets Burr in Kentucky, 209.
Clergy, position of, 4, 10, 73, 184; and the French, 142, 147, 300.
Coahuila, list of French in, 145; English interest in, 153-154.
Coast Guard, against foreign intrusion, 134-135, 179.
Cochrane, Admiral, to aid Miranda, 233; carries funds to Spain, 287.

Colleges, 11.
Collot, General, Adet's agent on the Mississippi, 150.
Colonies, Spanish, rule of, 14, 32-34, 57, 60, 122, 144, 167, 169, 187, 194-195, 201, 236-237, 239, 255, 266, 268-269, 272, 274, 276-277, 284, 293; British interest in, 42, 44, 45, 46, 49, 52, 75, 153, 159, 167, 185, 194-195, 202, 204, 227, 229, 234, 235, 237, 250, 264-265, 267-269, 293, 296; French interest in, 48, 49, 53, 84, 122, 124-125, 157, 164, 195-196, 202, 227, 242, 250, 257, 259, 262, 264, 266, 270, 290, 293-295, 302; United States and, 77-78, 116, 163, 167, 169, 185, 190, 211, 214, 218, 219, 229, 232.
Colonies, French, 54, 65, 157.
Colonies, British, Bourbons against, 85-86.
Colonies, *see* Spanish America.
Colonists, and Indian vassals, 21-22; and Spain, 22, 25, 276, 286; ignorance of, 234.
Colony, Scotch, 44; value of Cuba as a, 266.
Commander-in-chief, George R. Clark for Genêt's expedition, 118; Washington, with Hamilton, 172.
Commerce, Spanish policy for, 39, 66, 216; Anglo-French rivalry for, 46, 95, 212-213; English and Spanish American, 52, 156, 175, 203, 230, 239, 246, 307; French seek advantages, 110, 259; equality of, in new Hispanic states, 154, 159, 166, 167; advantages to England and United States, 156; *see* trade.
Commissioners, replace viceroy, 27; United States, to Paris, 160; South American, with Miranda, 192; from Asturias to London, 267; from Central Junta to Mexico, 279.
Committee of Public Safety, plan proposed to, 112-113, 124; speech by member of, 139; organized in Mexico, 287.
Commons, House of, for Mexico and Peru, 158.
Communication, Napoleon with America, 263, 297.

INDEX

Condorcet, Marquis de, writings on index, 129; Muir describes, 179.
Confession, of Miranda's scheme by Caro, 188-189.
Congress, United States, and British policy, 104; Jefferson's message to, 217; on frontier defense, 220; Mexico to call a, 275, 277-281; examples of, in Spain, 284; opposed England in Spanish colonies, 293; *see* juntas.
Conquerors, sons of, and encomienda, 21-23.
Conquest, of Mexico, and independence, 20, 54; and trade, 50; American threat of, 196; failure of La Plata, 236; advantages of, 237.
Conspiracy, of Alonso de Avila, 25-26; Mexican, 60-62; failure of Louisiana, 70; Blount's, 126; Burr's, 150, 208 ff.; Spanish information about, 178; of the Knives, 181; among Tepic Indians, 183-184; in Valladolid, 287-288; of Querétaro, 308; *see* revolution.
Constantine, aide-de-camp to Murat, on Napoleon's plans, 263-264.
Constitution, of conspirators, like United States, 181; by L'Ouverture, 195.
Continent, Napoleon's victories on, 241.
Continental system, 240, 254.
Contraband, lucrative, 16; British rival French in, 46; trade, 52, 135.
"*Convención Nacional Americana,*" conspiracy of, 181.
Cork, Wellesley's army for Mexico at, 264-265.
Corn, shortage of, and riots, 37.
Corsairs, English, 153.
Corsica, Bonaparte of, 195; proclamations against eagle of, 289.
Cortes, called for Spain, 286; to be called by regency, 288.
Cortés, Hernando, independence of, 20; loyalty questioned, 21; impersonated, 25.
Cortés Martín, encomendero, 22; in conspiracy with Avila brothers, 23-29.
Coste, Mateo, revolutionary plot by, 133-134.
Costi, translated Locke's works, 130.
Coues, Elliot, quoted on Pike, 224.
Council of the Indies, and New Laws, 22, 26.

Courbiene, Andres, with de Mézières, 137.
Courrier de l'Europe, on American Revolution, 83.
Courts, corruption of, 18; for treason, 286.
Creoles, classification of, 4, 5, 286; revolutionary activities of, 23, 37, 73, 99, 181, 275, 283; Joseph's appeal to, 297.
Croix, viceroy of New Spain, warned, 61; French servant of, 137.
Cromwell, Oliver, and English commerce, 41; relations with Spain, 41-42.
Crown, Mexican, candidates for, 276.
Crozat, Napoleon revives interest of, 195.
Cruíllas, viceroy, and defense, 73.
Cuba, warning of plot from, 133; Yrujo warns governor of, 235; and New World against the Old, 249; United States to occupy, 249; excluded from Mexico, 250; Castlereagh's interest in, 266; British to aid against French, 267; Wilkinson to, 292; agent arrested in, 304.
Cuesta, Gregorio de la, Napoleon's choice for viceroy of Mexico, 262-263.
Cushing, lieutenant, to attack Spaniards, 220-222.
Czar, Napoleon's agreements with, 270.

Dalling, Governor of Jamaica, plans of, 91.
Dalrymple, Alexander, on Napoleon's viceroy for Mexico, 264.
D'Alvimar, *see* Alvimar.
Danton, G. J., Muir describes, 179.
D'Aranda, *see* Aranda.
D'Argis, Pierre, Frenchman in Kentucky, warns Spain, 102.
Darien, Isthmus of, Scotch colony on, 44; Wilkinson on conquest of, 221.
D'Aubarde, *see* Aubarde.
Davidson, English merchant, offers vessels to government, 201.
Decrés, vice-admiral, to send agents to Mexico and Montevideo, 260-261.
Defense, against Scotch in Panama, 44; weakened Spanish, 48; of border, 74, 219, 293; viceroy asks for, 132; of Mexico, 149, 274; of Spanish America, 178; of California, 184; limited

330 INDEX

resources for, 182; of Vera Cruz considered, 244.
D'Egalité, Muir describes, 179.
De Mézières, French with, 145-146.
Democracy, Du Pont on, 199; for Mexico, 199; Castlereagh's fear of, 246.
Demotier, General, minister of Napoleon, 301.
Denmark, to aid in liberation of Spanish colonies, 97-98, 112; to get Puerto Rico, 250.
De Onis, *see* Onis.
De Pons, author, recommendations to French, 230; information on British, 231; on Miranda's expedition, 232; on French interest in Venezuela, 251, 254.
Deportation, of French, 146.
De Pradt, M., on example of United States, 102.
Deputies, from Mexico, 60; revolutionary, in Madrid, 156; of Asturias, message of, to Mexico, 269.
Deputy, Orea from Venezuela, 302.
Desmolard, captain, leader of Napoleon's agents in America, 295; revolutionary activities of, 297-298, 300-302.
Dessalines, opposition to Le Clerc, 200.
D'Iberville, Pierre Le Moyne, 44.
Diego, Captain, war on Spain, 44.
Diplomacy, game of, 49; and Spanish possessions, 124; in favor of Spain, 189.
Diplomats, warn against conquest, 236.
Directors, French, seek Louisiana, 125.
Directory, replaced by Napoleon, 177.
"Disciples of Bonaparte," influence of, 306.
Divine right, of kings, opposed by Americans, 206; monarchs deposed, 307.
Dolores, curate of, 14; D'Alvimar with Hidalgo at, 261; link with Querétaro, 308.
Dominions, *see* colonies.
Don Juan, revolutionary agent to England, 93, 95-96.
Dorr, Captain, trader in Pacific, 179.
Dos de Mayo, 258.
D'Ossuanville, alias Villery, informer of Miranda's plans, 187, 189.
Drake, Francis, a warning to Spain, 40.
Duke of Alburquerque, loyal viceroy, 47.

Duke of Berg, instructions to Spanish America, 262; *see also* Murat.
Duke of Orleans, as monarch for Spanish America, 246, 248; memoir on Spanish America, 247.
Dumouriez, General, for English alliance, 110; with Miranda against Bourbons, 111; and Genet mission, 113; plan of, 116; and Muir, 179; in England, 200; wants Bourbon monarch for America, 247; as enemy of Napoleon, 248; Mexican plan by, 248, 250, 254.
Dundas, Henry, secretary of war, on revolutionary plans, 176, 202, 234, 238; *see* Melville.
Dunn, William E., quoted on France, 42.
Du Pont de Nemours, on Louisiana question, 199.
Du Pont, General, in Spain, 256; defeat at Baylen, 269.
Dupont, Victor, to stop Genet project, 126; consul-general to United States, 163; warning Talleyrand, 169.
Durand, French minister to England, 65.
Durrey, surgeon, Frenchman in Mexico, 140-142, 148.
Dutch, English alliance with, 46; in Pacific, 75.

East Indies, expedition from, 90.
Easton, Judge, report on Wilkinson, 220.
Eaton, William, report on Burr, 213.
Ecclesiastics, support for independence, 26, 61; warned against the French, 143; trust in, 287; Napoleon's agents and, 296.
Economic, restrictions, 14; advantages of encomienda, 22; improvement, 58; France seeks favors, 58; conditions of New Spain, 210; Pitt and advantages of Spanish America, 228; and British aid to Miranda, 233; United States, harmed by European rivals, 249.
Edinburgh, Muir from, 179.
Education, restrictions on, 11-12.
Egalité, 179.
Egypt, French Empire, 196.
El Desengaño del Hombre, prohibited, 128-129.
El Grito de Dolores, battle cry for independence, 308.

El Guarico, Santo Domingo, plot in, 133; linked with Genet, 136.
Elbe River, Napoleon on, 242.
Elizabeth, Queen, aid rebels of Flanders, 86.
Elliot, Hugh, British minister to Berlin, for independence of all colonies, 92.
Embargo, and military preparations, 293.
Emigré, Talleyrand as, 164; revolutionary plan by French, 227.
Emissaries, of Napoleon, warnings against, 304; *see* agents.
Emperador de los Mexicanos, 33.
Emperor, Napoleon as, of the West, 228; DePons memoir to, 230; Spanish policy of, 242; of the Two Americas, 255; and Portugal, 255; Murat as agent of, 257; opposed by Spanish people, 259, 277; plotting against England, 272; deposed kings, 307.
Empire, for Louisiana, 209; to be organized in the West, 220; of France, comparison with, 220; Burr's dream of, 223; cause of Spain's decline, 237; colonies oppose Napoleon's, 290; *see* Spanish Empire.
Encomienda system, 7, 21-24.
England, trade of, 15, 52, 56, 175, 196, 202, 230, 286, 307; rulers of, 31; aid from, 34; relations with Spain, 40, 45, 48, 58, 88, 116, 153, 202, 204, 226-227, 239, 269; foothold in America, 41; on Florida border, 44; and Darien colony, 44, 45; in Caribbean, 45; and opposition to Bourbons, 45, 47, 49, 53, 81, 88, 95, 110-111, 116, 176-177, 203; allied with Netherlands and Austria, 46; for independence of Spanish America, 50, 52, 63-64, 73, 75, 92, 100, 106, 125, 148-149, 154, 156-157, 182-184, 194, 203, 236, 253, 259; encroachments of, 52; and Cuba, 53, 250, 266; and Louisiana, 54, 55, 67, 69, 164, 193, 200; and plans of Guiller, 61, 63; and loss of colonies, 65, 237, 247; relations with France, 88, 119, 164, 194, 197, 202, 226, 272; relations with United States, 136, 157-159, 163, 165, 167, 184-185, 191, 197-199, 216, 292, 301; and Blount Conspiracy, 150; and Miranda, 152, 157, 167, 191-192, 226-228, 232, 234, 260;
interest in Texas, 153-154; and Philip Nolan, 173; and Muir, 179; and Napoleon, 195, 200, 202, 242, 248, 254, 262, 264, 268, 300; Dumouriez in, 200; and Brazil, 202; and Burr, 208, 212, 215; naval supremacy of, 228, 229, 290; and Portugal, 254; and junta of Asturias, 267, 279; *see also* Great Britain.
Englishmen, ability in revolution, 165; from Nootka, 181; to support Miranda, 200.
Enquirer, Richmond, on success of Miranda, 232.
Equality, principles of, 140, 142.
Erfurt, Napoleon's display at, 270.
Erving, George W., to Spain, 216-217.
Escalona, Duke of, viceroy, 30-31.
Española, French base, 43.
Espinosa, evils of work by, 130.
Esprit des Lois, 13.
Esquisse d'un tableau historique, by Condorcet, prohibited, 129.
Essai philosophique, by Locke, prohibited, 129.
Europe, Louis XIV in, 43; wars in, 97, 210, 290, 308; Miranda and events in, 165, 233; liberating possessions of, 194, 198, 211, 243, 261, 277, 290, 296, 308; England and, 204, 233, 247, 300; Napoleon in, 242, 247, 249, 264, 270; United States and, 249, 292, 303; D'Alvimar in, 260.
Europeans, envy Spanish trade, 39; conspiracy against, in Mexico, 181.

Faction, American, 23, 277-278, 280, 287.
Falkland Islands, and war threats, 75.
Falses, Marquis de, viceroy, 27.
Family Compact, 53, 57-58, 75; and American Revolution, 88; and Nootka Sound Controversy, 109.
Far East, trade route to, 44.
Fauchet, French minister, to replace Genêt, 123; proclamation of, 123; on Anglo-American alliance, 157; warning Talleyrand, 169.
Fayden, maps by, 173-174.
Federalist, John Adams a, 163.
Ferdinand and Isabella, unification of Spain, 18.

Ferdinand VII, plans a Bonaparte marriage, 255; and Spanish throne, 257-258; juntas rule in name of, 259, 277-278; proclamations for, 262; Mexican allegiance to, 273, 276, 291, 299; Cevallos on, 294.
Fish, C. R., quoted on Franco-American peace, 174.
Flanders, English aid to, 86.
Flassau, for French aid to Spanish colonies, 123-124.
Fleet, arrival of Spanish, 24; British attack on, 48-49; aid Napoleon, 204; British, to California, 149; treasure, 203-204; French, from Brest, 290.
Flora, frigate, to carry viceroy to Mexico, 263.
Florida, French interest in, 27, 42, 85, 120, 294, 303-304; Spanish in, 43-44, 89, 92, 235, 293-294; American interest in, 83, 94, 107, 108, 120-121, 123, 126, 156, 171, 218, 248, 293, 303; British to pay troops of, 267; Napoleon and, 293, 302; *see* West Florida.
Floridablanca, Count of, views on American Revolution, 82, 84, 87-88; and frontier defense, 102.
Folch, governor, on revolutionary project for Mexico, 219.
Folney, French revolutionary agent, 132.
Fonseca, minister of Indies, 21.
Foreigners, restrictions on, 16-17, 39, 59, 136, 138, 145, 147, 149, 153, 178-180, 294; intrigues of, 40, 44, 60, 251, 272.
Fort Massac, Burr and Wilkinson at, 209.
Fournier, Juan, Frenchman in Mexico, 140, 141, 146.
Fox, Charles James, minister of foreign affairs, policy of, 239-240.
France, literature of, 13, 128-129; trade of, 15, 16, 204, 212-213, 230, 296; privateers of, 20, 228; and Spanish colonies, 27, 38, 42, 43, 45-46, 48, 57-59, 110, 128, 136, 155-156, 176, 193, 194, 230, 246-248, 250-252, 254, 262, 266, 267, 290-291, 296, 305; rulers of, 27, 31, 45, 53; colonies of, 42, 54, 195, 196; Spanish relations with, 45, 46-48, 53, 57, 75, 77-89, 109, 125, 152, 158, 160, 164, 169, 174, 184, 194, 201, 202, 249, 254, 259, 269-270, 276, 277, 279, 290, 294; English relations with, 46, 49, 64, 65, 79, 85, 87, 109, 116, 119, 158, 185, 201, 203, 212-213, 226, 228-229, 230, 235, 237, 251, 267-269, 272; and Louisiana, 48, 65, 66, 122, 136, 190, 208; people from, 61, 119, 136, 139-140, 181, 216, 287, 303; United States relations with, 87, 93, 157, 160, 163, 164, 167, 169, 170, 174, 184-186, 191, 197-198, 249, 302, 303; and Miranda, 109, 112, 152, 175, 190-192, 200; theories from, 130-132, 140-143, 160-161, 266, 271, 287; and Muir, 179, 180; *see also* French Revolution.
Franciscan, Vicento de Santa Maria, leader of conspiracy, 288.
Franco, Dionisio, on success of Miranda, 232.
Franco-American, war, 163ff.
Franklin, Benjamin, appeal to British, 60, 65; with Sayre, 116.
Frazer, British merchant, information to Wellesley, 243.
Freebooters, 20, 52.
Freemasons, 13, 143, 294.
French Assembly, *see* Assembly.
Frenchmen, on borders, 43, 114, 137; in Mexico, 130, 135, 138, 140, 143-148, 294.
French Revolution, and the church, 10, 13, 128; influence of, 19, 110-112, 127, 128-129, 132, 133, 136, 158, 168, 178, 194, 279, 280, 307; Genet and, 117.
Frontier, dangers on, 43, 206, 214, 219, 256, 293, 298; American, Spain to absorb, 102; French plan separation of, 114; to aid New Orleans, 114.
Fullarton, Colonel, Spanish American interest of, 200.

Gachupín, 4, 286.
Gage, Thomas, report on Mexico, 5, 29, 41.
Galapagos, British in, 184.
Galicia, representatives to England from, 268.
Gálvez, Benítez, alias Vásquez Fernández, reports plot, 182-183.
Gálvez, Bernardo de, conquest of Florida, 92.

INDEX

Gálvez, José de, visitor-general, reforms of, 72, 74, 75, 100.
Garibay, Pedro, field-marshal, as viceroy, 283-287, 289, 291, 294.
Gazeta de México, cited, 129, 262, 277, 278, 283.
Gazette, New Orleans, quoted on Mexican independence, 221.
Genêt, French minister to United States, revolutionary project of, 113-114, 117-118, 120-121, 123-124, 126, 136, 150, 206.
Genoa, trade of, 15.
George III, United States opposition to, 117.
Georgia, Spanish claims to, 49.
Gérard, C. A., on United States expansion, 88.
Germain, Lord, and revolutionary plans, 89-90, 92.
German, troops for British expedition, 253.
Gerry, Elbridge, commissioner to Paris, Miranda's plan to, 160.
Gibraltar, Spanish interest in, 89, 255; and French, 256; Castañas to, 263.
Girondists, for Spanish liberty, 110; disavowed, 123.
God, intervention of, 142, 143; Napoleon and, 264, 300.
Godoy, Manuel, Spanish minister, 19; and the French, 125-126, 147, 164, 241-242, 255, 257; and United States, 217-218; and Iturrigaray, 273; *see also* Alcudia.
González Obregón, cited, 28.
Gordon, J. D. R., description of Mexico to Castlereagh, 251.
Gore, Christopher, and Miranda's project, 205, 213.
Government, Spanish, 14, 17, 18, 95, 202, 258; opposition to, 24, 29, 34, 283; theory of, 24, 142, 148, 199, 252, 275; Mexican defense of, 25, 26, 28, 37, 142, 178, 211, 214, 221, 224, 272, 274, 283, 285-286, 291, 296, 304; English, Scotch colony lacks support of, 45; and trade, 48; British, to aid revolutionists, 96, 173, 192, 193, 201, 252, 266, 267; Spanish, aid to Inquisition, 131; French, feared, 143; United States, loyalty of West to, 216.

Grand Pré, Captain, defends Baton Rouge, 208; treatment of D'Alvimar, 260.
Grantham, British diplomat in Madrid, 84.
Great Britain, haughtiness of, 91; and plans for liberation of Spanish America, 97, 151, 156, 160, 162, 192, 247, 252; naval power of, 201; to restore independence of Spain, 266; *see also* England.
Grenville, Lord, and revolutionary plans, 106, 158, 160, 165, 176; Bowles report to, 107; against French, 158; on colonial system, 194-195; prime minister, 239.
Grievances, of colonies, 38, 60, 74, 105.
Grimaldi, Spanish minister, on Bourbon aid to British colonies, 82-83.
Guadalupe, interest in, 185.
Gual, Manuel, appeal to England by, 176.
Guanajuato, and expulsion of Jesuits, 72.
Guardiola, Marquis de, agent to England, 101.
Guarico, El, revolutionary plot in, 133.
Guatemala, under New Spain, 3; England's interest in, 106.
Guazacualcos, and illicit commerce, 135.
Guerrero, Juan, plot of, 140-141, 181.
Guiana, French, Villery from, 187; extent of Mexico, 250.
Guiller, conspiracy of, 61, 73.
Gulf Coast, fear hostilities on, 214; Burr's map of, 215.
Gulf of Mexico, British interest in, 50, 59, 265; fear United States in, 94, 102, 193, 196; French to protect, 193.
Gulf of Pánuco, expedition to, 117.
Guzmán, Lombardo, *see* Lampart.

Hague, William Van Murray at, 167.
Haiti, nest of revolution, 42-43.
Hakluyt, Richard the Younger, quoted, 39.
Hale, E. E., report on plan to invade Mexico, 167, 172.
Halifax, and British troops, 265, 293.
Hamburg, trade of, 15; Caro's confession from, 188.
Hamilton, Alexander, favor England, 108; and Miranda's project, 158, 161-

334   INDEX

162, 164-170, 172-174, 177, 185, 189; and Louisiana, 193-194; and Burr, 208-209.
Hammond, George, English minister to United States, 136.
Hammond, Samuel, and Genêt, 121, 123.
Hancock, John, smuggler, 40.
Hapsburgs, end of, in Spain, 18, 45; favored in Mexico, 49.
Havana, galleons from, 45; and British, 53, 79, 184-185; and revolutionary plots, 134, 187; and Napoleon's agents, 260, 295, 300, 303-304.
Hawkins, John, and Spanish monopoly, 39-40.
Hawksbury, Lord, on Peace of Amiens, 197.
Herrera, General, and Louisiana boundary, 220-221, 293.
Herron, Captain, and Genet's plan, 118.
Hidalgo y Costilla, Miguel, and colonial restrictions, 13, 14; and D'Alvimar, 261; starts revolt, 308.
Hippisley, Captain, on Jesuit plans, 90-91.
Hispanic America, see Spanish America.
Hobbes, Thomas, writings of, condemned, 130.
Holland, trade of, 15; and alliance for liberation, 97, 112; war with, 116; satellite of France, 159.
Honduras, British and, 56, 244.
Hos, Nicolas, serving de Croix, 137.
Hosier, Admiral, blockade Porto Bello, 49.
House of Lords, for Mexico and Peru, 158.
Humboldt, Alexander von, on Mexico, 4, 11.
Hume, David, quoted, 19.
Huss, John, heresies of, 36.
Hussey, chaplain, agent to England, 88.

Iberian peninsula, Napoleon and, 254.
Iberville, Pierre Le Moyne, after La Salle, 44.
Imlay, Gilbert, on revolutionary plans, 115.
Independence, ideas of, 19, 32, 50, 56-58, 92, 133, 151, 175; victims of, 26, 36; Portuguese, influence on, 31-32; Pacheco and, 31; supported by Lampart, 33-34; of Mexico, 46, 49, 104, 112, 183, 221, 225, 251, 263, 273, 275, 277, 278, 280, 284, 292, 296, 306; British support of, 51, 198, 203, 246; Louisiana and, 68, 69, 114, 123, 200; revolt in Pátzcuaro, 72; of British colonies, 79, 85, 93; of Flanders, 86; of Santo Domingo, 167; in West Florida, 207.
Index, books on papal, 12, 129.
India, troops from, to Mexico, 153, 243, 244, 253.
Indians, classification of, 7-8; and encomienda, 21-22; and revolution, 33-34, 37, 44, 117, 183, 276, 288, 297, 298; and expulsion of Jesuits, 72; and frontier defense, 74, 75.
Indies, laws of, 17; and European rivalry, 39, 41, 46, 75, 290; Napoleon and, 242, 258-259, 269, 290, 296; see Spanish America.
Infante, Dom Pedro of Portugal, regent for Mexico, 276.
Inquisition, and literature, 12, 13, 102, 128-129, 142; persecutes Portuguese, 32; charges against Lampart, 35; government aid to, 131; Olavide suspected by, 156; opposed to Talamantes, 278; and Napoleon, 297, 299; suspects Hidalgo, 308.
Insurrection, see revolution.
Intendants, warned against foreigners, 138; Morales, 196.
Italy, Napoleon visits Joseph in, 256.
Iturrigaray, José, viceroy of Mexico, 219, 263, 273, 276, 278-279, 281-286.

Jackson, Andrew, and Burr, 209, 218, 222.
Jacob, William, report on Mexico by, 204, 229, 273.
Jacobins, French party, influence of, 121, 122, 142, 247, 294.
Jalapa, British plans for, 244, 253; supports Iturrigaray, 277.
Jamaica, British base against Spanish America, 42, 45, 64, 75, 100, 106, 182, 229, 243, 244, 250, 266-267; smuggling, 56, 196; competition with France, 59.
Jamestown, British against Spain at, 40-42.

INDEX   335

Jay, John, revolutionary plans, 97-98; and Burr, 208.
Jay's Treaty, 124-125.
Jefferson, Thomas, and revolutionary plans, 98-99, 104, 108, 119-121, 213, 231, 249, 292, 293; and Louisiana, 163, 197-199; interest in West Florida, 207; and Burr, 217, 222, 232; policy of, 249.
Jena, Battle of, 241-242.
Jenkin's Ear, War of, 49.
Jesuits, revolutionary influence of, 10, 62, 72, 90-91, 104, 106, 111, 159, 190, 193, 211.
Joseph Bonaparte, king of Spain, 256, 258-259, 269; appeal to colonies, 295-297, 300, 301, 306.
Joudenes, Spanish minister, protests to, 147.
Junot, General, conquers Peninsula, 255-256, 262.
Junta, called by Croix, 61-62; revolutionary, 155; of regency, for Joseph Bonaparte, 258; Spanish, 259, 270, 275, 278, 279, 283, 286, 288, 291; of Asturias, 267, 268; in Mexico, 277, 278, 279-281, 283, 291.
Junta Consultiva, special court, 286.
Junta de Seguridad, 287.

Kaye, Captain, revolutionary plan by, 89-90.
Keller, A. G., quoted on kings, 18.
Kemper, and westerners, 206; insurrection of, 207.
Kendrick, John, explorer of Columbia River, 180; in service at San Blas, 180; to Spain as interpreter, 181.
Kentucky, to march on Mexico, 219.
Kentuckians, Nolan's return to, 173; Burr project in, 209, 212, 214; Frenchmen to, 305.
Kersaint, Admiral, plan of independence, 112; head of agents to Mexico, 133.
Key, to Mexico, West Indies, 44; Havana, 54; Louisiana, 115, 124, 193, 200.
Kibby, Timothy, report on Pike, 209, 224.
King, of Spain and Mexico, 23, 27-28, 31-32, 34, 60, 135, 144, 210, 274, 275, 278, 281, 307; and Portugal, 31, 255, 276; and the British, 40, 42, 76, 153; death of, 46; Philip V, 47; views on Louisiana, 69; suspects Jesuits, 72; and Miranda, 192; and Burr, 215; ally of Napoleon, 249; Joseph, 255, 258, 269, 296, 301; Charles IV, 257, 273, 290; Ferdinand VII, 281; people rule in absence of, 307; for Mexico, 24, 29, 31, 95, 211, 221, 276, 290; of France, and M. Cortés, 27; laws and Louisiana, 66; execution of, 131, 139; of England, to support independence, 101, 154; Bourbon, 136; of Algarves, Godoy to become, 255.
King, Rufus, United States minister to England, and Miranda's plans, 158-160, 164-165, 168-169, 172-174, 189, 193-194, 198, 205, 213; report on Portugal and Spain to, 158-159.
Kingdom of Mexico, independence for, 213, 214, 250.
Kingdoms, D'Aranda plans, 95.
Kings, divine right of, 206.
Knox, General, and revolutionary plans, 108, 111, 161-162, 166.

La Crise de l'Europe, pamphlet on liberation, 97.
"La Marseillaise," in Mexico, 138.
La Plata, Popham's expedition to, 200, 235-236, 238; and Mexico, 236, 244; and Chilean expedition, 246; Napoleon's orders to, 261.
La Salle, a threat to Mexico, 43; and Napoleon, 195.
Laborra, Pedro, Frenchman in Mexico, 137.
Lafayette, General, ideas of, 94, 130, 138; and Muir, 179.
Lafrénière, revolutionary leader in Louisiana, 66, 69.
Lampart, Don Guillén de, alias Lombardo Guzmán, revolutionary plan of, 33-37.
Lampoons, propaganda for Americans, 284-285.
Las Casas, Bartolomé de, and New Laws, 21.
Latin America, *see* Spanish America.
Lausel, Juan, Frenchman in Mexico, 137, 142.

Laws, 11; enforcement of, 22; new code for Louisiana, 71; of the Indies, and the French, 146.
Lawyers, 11.
Le Clerc, General, Santo Domingo, 195, 200, 260.
Lea, Henry C., on protection of Indians, 8.
Leavenworth, on liberation plan, 23.
Lebrun, C. F., and liberation plans, 111-113, 119-120.
Lee, Arthur, seeks Spanish aid, 85; with Sayre, 116.
Lee, General Charles, appeals to Spain, 80; and Miranda, 161.
Leeward Islands, aid of, 267.
Legion, "Independent and Revolutionary, of Mississippi," 119; British, for Mexico, 201.
Lemée, Nicholas, with de Mézières, 137.
Lemos, Gayoso de, governor of Natchez, 113.
Lemos, Gil de, viceroy of Peru, on education, 12.
Leon, island of, Spanish regency in, 288.
Les Ruines, ou Meditations, prohibited, 130.
Lestique, M., French agent to Mexico, 303.
Letters of Lord Chesterfield, prohibited, 129.
Lettre aux Espagnols, by Viscardo y Guzman, 159.
Liberation, *see* independence.
Liberty, glory of, 50; in America, 103; United States and, 114, 206; French and, 110, 119, 161; Thomas Paine and, 115; theory of, 122, 141-142, 156, 182; not popular in Venezuela, 234; Mexican struggle for, 307-308.
"Liberty and Equality," pamphlet in Louisiana, 122.
Lisbon, report on French from, 158-159; Braganzas escape from, 256.
Liston, Robert, reports revolt in Mexico, 100; British minister to United States, 151, 160-161.
Livingston, R., and Louisiana purchase, 197-198, 200.
Lizana y Beaumont, archbishop of Mexico, as viceroy, 287-289; and Napoleon, 289, 299.

Locke, John, writings of, 13, 129.
Logan, Benjamin, to aid revolution, 115.
London, and revolutionary plans, 61, 64, 102; colonial deputies to, 85; Pinckney to, 125; Spanish Americans in, 155; Chisholm to, 151; house of Turnbull in, 189; Caro returns to, 190; King to Gore in, 205; Williamson seeks aid in, 212, 238; commissioners from Oviedo to, 267.
Los Adaes, Spanish troops at, 220.
Louis XIV, interest in Spanish America, 43; grandson of, king of Spain, 47, 256; *levée* of, 282.
Louis XV, Spanish appeal to, 75.
Louis XVI, opposition to, 109; life of, pictured, 131.
Louisiana, French policy for, 48, 113-115, 118, 122, 123, 164, 184, 195, 229-230, 294; Spanish policy for, 54-55, 65, 67, 68, 70-71, 122-123, 185, 186, 206; British interest in, 56, 150, 154, 185; government of, 62, 65, 66; and plans for independence, 65, 67, 68, 70, 115, 122, 123; a gateway, 80-81, 205, 208, 294; American interest in, 83, 103, 108, 156, 171, 186, 197, 208-209; and Treaty of San Lorenzo, 125; retrocession of, 125-127, 190, 193-194; French influence from, 136-137, 145, 194, 216; purchase of, 199-200, 204, 216; boundary of, 206, 214, 216; and Burr, 208-209, 214, 216, 219; Napoleon and, 294, 302-303.
Louisville, Wilkinson papers in, 172.
L'Ouverture, Toussaint, in Haiti, 195, 200.
Lower California, plan attack on, 90.
Luther, heresy of, 36.
Lyonnet, and revolutionary plans, 116, 121.

McCaleb, W. F., quoted on Louisiana and Burr, 212, 213.
McHenry, James, secretary of war, on United States support of Miranda, 166, 167, 170-171, 232.
Machiavelli, D'Alvimar has copy of, 261; principles of, 300.
Madagascar, for French empire, 196.

INDEX

Madison, James, secretary of state, and Miranda expedition, 231; Jefferson to, 293.
Madrid, Mexican appeal to, 60; and British colonies, 80; Pinckney leaves, 125; revolutionary agents in, 155-156, 187-188; Charles IV, escape from, 257; revolt of May 2, 258; and Napoleon, 262, 269, 270, 273.
Mahan, A. T., cited, 57.
Maitland, General, to Philadelphia, 185.
Malvert, Juan, on equality, 139.
"Manifest Destiny," seeds of, 104.
Manifestoes, British, to Mexicans, 91; Godoy to Spaniards, 241.
Manila, Wellesley plans attack on, 242-243.
Map, of Spanish America, 173-174; for Wilkinson by Nolan, 186; Burr's, of Mexico, 215.
María Luisa, to Mexico, 291.
Mariano, head of Tepic conspiracy, 183.
Marquis, Captain, for republic in Louisiana, 69-70.
Marshall, John, commissioner to Paris, 160.
Martial law, in New Orleans, 222.
Masserano, Prince of, Spanish ambassador to England, 64.
Mayorga, Martin de, viceroy, loyal to Spain, 100.
Meade, Cowles, acting governor of Mississippi Territory, arrest of Burr, 223.
Melville, Lord Henry Dundas, revolutionary plans for Spanish America, 154, 202, 204, 227, 235, 238, 265-267; impeachment of, 215, 238.
Memoire, of De Pons, on Caracas, 230.
Méndez, Captain Felipe, reports on Lampart, 34-35.
Méndez, Juan, captain of *Campechano,* 135.
Mendiola, Francisco, agent to England, 100.
Mereghal, Servain, *History* by, prohibited, 120.
Merry, Anthony, English minister, and Burr's project, 212-215.
Mestizos, classification of, 6-7.
Mexanes, theories, 141.
Mexican Association, purpose of, 210.

Mexico, revolutionary influence in, 5, 29, 30, 34, 44, 46, 47, 49, 51, 54, 59, 60, 61, 64, 90, 96-97, 100, 104, 108, 132, 155, 158, 181, 182, 204, 208, 210, 219, 221, 238, 247-249, 250, 273, 279-280, 284, 306-307; and economic conditions, 8, 14, 15, 52, 100, 211, 286; University of, 11; French interest in, 13, 43, 49, 83, 112, 113, 130-132, 138, 140, 145, 148, 170, 184, 193, 195, 202, 252, 291, 294, 303; English interest in, 17, 54, 56, 58, 61, 79, 86, 96-97, 101, 106, 107, 112, 149, 152-153, 158, 163, 182, 185, 200-201, 212, 227, 229, 232, 239, 244-245, 248, 249, 250-252, 264, 266-269, 286; government of, 20, 23, 211, 247, 257, 276, 284, 287, 290-291; conditions in, 20-22, 27-28, 33, 128, 130, 288, 308; conquest of, and defense of, 25, 54, 68, 116, 123, 127, 184, 193, 200, 206, 214, 219; and Jesuits, 72, 90; United States relation with, 103, 104, 161, 163, 172, 176, 185, 200, 217-218, 221, 223, 249, 292, 301, 303; maps of, 174, 215; Napoleon's interest in, 195-196, 199, 203, 260-264, 290, 292-293, 300, 303-304; Burr and independence of, 208-225, 265; and French invasion of Spain, 272-279, 284-288, 290-291; *see also* New Spain.
Mexico City, riots in, 37, route to, 215, 243, 244, ayuntamiento of, 274-275.
Michaux, André, with Clark, 119.
Michoacán, Bishop of, complaint by, 6; conspiracy in, 287-288.
Milhet, Jean, agent from Louisiana, 66.
Military, against negroes, 29; and Portuguese, 31; and rebellion, 61, 73, 183, 251; American, preparations of, 185; dangerous to democracy, 199; British expedition planned, 192; preparation of Burr, 212; of Napoleon, 269.
Militia, in Mexico, 73; Jackson, and Tennessee, 209; stops Burr, 223; in conspiracy, 288.
Mines, needs of, 29-30; Pike to Mexican, 209; wealth of Spanish, 236.
Mirabeau, Muir describes, 179.
Miranda, Francisco de, on conditions in Mexico, 12, 13; and United States support for revolution, 94, 105, 108, 116,

160-162, 166, 168-169, 173, 193, 205, 213, 220, 227, 231-232; and British revolutionary projects, 106, 154-158, 162, 165, 167, 175, 176, 182, 192, 200-204, 211, 226-227, 231, 233, 235, 238, 245, 250-253, 265, 268; and France, 109-112, 115, 119, 152, 156, 190-194, 230, 247, 250; other revolutionary activities of, 105, 153, 177, 178, 181, 184, 187-188, 211, 227, 229, 232, 234, 237, 250-251.

Mississippi River, French interest in, 43, 117, 119-120, 150, 190, 193; navigation of, 86, 102, 107, 119, 124, 126, 198, 216; as a boundary, 103, 106, 164, 198, 216; British troops via, 151; posts on, Spanish withdrawal from, 164; Burr to, 222-223.

Mississippi Valley, independence of, 216.
Mobile, attack on, 266.
Modena, rulers of, related to Pacheco, 31.
Modyford, Colonel, supports Cromwell, 41.
Monarch, see king.
Monarchy, danger to Spanish, 23; for Mexico, 61, 158, 199, 246-248, 252; and French Assembly, 143, 202, 280.
Moncey, General, 304.
Monclova, D'Alvimar to, 260.
Mongourit, French consul, and Genet, 120.
Moniteur, report on Braganzas, 254-255.
Monopolies, Spanish, burdensome, 14; challenged, 38; and British, 40, 51, 97, 165, 230.
Monroe, James, instructions to, 198; purchase of Louisiana, 200; departure from Spain, 214, 216, 219; Jefferson to, 293.
Monroe Doctrine, Jefferson and, 292.
Montecino, Manuel, taken for Miranda, 153.
Monterey, California, British visit, 149, 179.
Montesquieu, writings of, 13.
Montevideo, Napoleon's agents to, 260.
Montezuma, impersonated, 25; Conde de, and independence, 46, 47; descendant of, for Mexican crown, 276.
Montmorin, and American Revolution, 84, 88.

Montserrat, British and, 45.
Morales, intendant, closes Mississippi, 196; report on New Orleans, 214.
Moreau, General, D'Alvimar meets, 260.
Morel, Estevan, Frenchman in Mexico, 130, 139, 143.
Morgan, Colonel, settlement of, 103.
Morphil, Island of, for French, 196.
Morphy, Diego, consul at New Orleans, 294, 303.
Moses, Bernard, quoted, 50.
Mosquito Coast, British on, 56, 106-107.
Motolinia, Toribio de, on government, 17.
Moultrie, governor of South Carolina, and Genêt, 120.
Muentes, Josef, agent of Napoleon, 300.
Muir, Thomas, experiences of, 178-180.
Mulattoes, revolt of, 37.
Muniain, Juan Gregorio, on Louisiana, 68.
Municipality, of Mexico, 274, 280.
Muñoz, Alonso, replaces viceroy, 28.
Murat, Napoleon's lieutenant in Spain, 257, 273, 274.
Murray, William Van, on colonies, 167; to France, 174.
Muzquiz, Miguel de, favors return of Louisiana, 68.

Nacogdoches, report from, 151; D'Alvimar in, 260.
Naples, Joseph, king of, 256, 258.
Napoleon, and Mexico, 17, 203, 250, 254, 258, 261-265, 270-271, 273, 284-286, 289, 290-292, 294-295, 297, 300-302, 304-307; and Spain, 19, 193, 202-204, 227, 229, 239, 241-242, 250, 254-259, 267, 269-271, 284, 290, 297, 299, 301, 302; and United States, 120, 169, 177, 186-187, 199-200, 249, 292-293, 300-302; interest in Amazon, 194; and Peace of Amiens, 194, 197; and Santo Domingo, 194; and the British, 195, 226-228, 240-242, 248, 250, 264-265, 267-270, 298; and Louisiana, 195, 199-200; and Europe, 229, 241-242, 254, 270, 280; and Venezuela, 230-231; and World empire, 242; see also Bonaparte.
Nariño, Antonio, agent in London, 155.
Narváez, and Cortés, 20.

INDEX 339

Nashville, Burr in, 209.
Natchez, report from, 113-114; and Burr, 215, 223.
National Intelligencer, The, quoted on Burr, 215.
Natives, classification of, 6, 8; treatment of, 21; resistance of, in Santo Domingo, 200; offer to, 203.
Nava, Pedro de, governor, list of Frenchmen, 137, 145; to protect borderlands, 153, 186.
Navarro, Josef María, colonies warned against, 304.
Navy, offices held by Portuguese, 31; Bourbons build, 75; British, 168, 200, 201, 215, 228, 249, 256, 293; French, 203-204, 291.
Negroes, classification of, 6; and revolution, 29, 34, 37, 133-134, 194; sold by France, 46; as British soldiers, 243-244.
Nemours, Du Pont de, and Jefferson, 199.
"Neutral Ground Treaty," 222, 293.
Neutrality, of United States, 108, 120, 123, 151, 177, 240, 301; French plan British, 111.
Nevis, British island, 45.
Newcastle, Earl of, and Anson's plan, 51.
New Galicia, conspiracy in, 183.
New Granada, Spanish king for, 95; and revolt, 96.
New Laws, 21, 22.
New Mexico, defense against French, 43; and General Clark, 113, 118; list of French in, 145; Wilkinson on conquest of, 223.
New Orleans, revolutionary activities in, 67-68, 114, 122, 214; and Falkland Islands, 75; influence on Mexico, 101, 107, 129, 193, 219, 221; danger of attack on, 114, 118, 123, 171, 185, 266; United States and, 120, 123, 171, 185, 196, 209, 216, 220, 222, 293, 294; French and, 193; British interest in, 198, 266; and Napoleon's agents, 294, 298, 300, 302, 303.
New Spain, description of, 3; conditions in, 6, 11, 15, 22, 30, 72, 76, 123, 139, 180, 181, 210, 224, 271-279; and Spain, 21, 46; and Florida, 27; security of, 28, 32, 47, 233; and Portuguese, 30-32; revolutionary trends in, 31, 34, 37, 51, 62, 77, 118, 142, 272, 286, 307; French interest in, 43, 46, 48, 54, 128, 133, 140, 286, 298, 303-304; British interest in, 44, 56, 86, 112, 153, 235-236, 242, 244, 265; United States and, 77, 89, 123, 218-219, 224, 226, 228; *see also* Mexico.
New World, destiny of, 5, 125, 159, 160, 164, 198, 292; depredations in, 39, 229; Spain's empire in, 237; England turns to, 242; independence of, 292.
New York, possession of, 86; Miranda in, 213, 231; Desmolard in, 301.
Newspapers, American, against France, 197; on revolutionary plans, 220, 232, 302, 305; *Gazeta de México,* 262, 277, 278, 283; *Moniteur,* 254; *The National Intelligencer* on Burr, 215; New Orleans *Gazette,* 221; Richmond *Enquirer,* 232.
Nicaragua, British to occupy, 154; canal of, 156.
Nolan, Philip, expeditions of, into Spanish territory, 172-173, 186, 224; and Miranda's project, 172-173.
Nolte, Vincent, meets Wilkinson, 222.
Nootka Sound, Controversy of, 106-110; British in, 181, 184.
Norfolk, Wilkinson in, 292; Napoleon's agents in, 295, 304.
North America, example of independence in, 99; Spain's possessions in, threatened, 204.
North, Lord, and America, 87.
Nouveau voyage en Espagne, prohibited, 129.
Nueva Vizcaya, list of French in, 145.

Obeso, José María, captain, in conspiracy, 288.
Obregón, T. Esquivel, on Mexico, 210-211.
"Observations," by Imlay, 115.
"Occidental Circle," British interest in, 52.
Ocariz, receives Caro's confession, 188-189.
Oder, River, Napoleon on, 242.
O'Fallon, brother-in-law of Clark, grievances against Spain, 117.

340 INDEX

O'Fallon, Dr. James, to aid revolution, 118.
Oglethorpe, aid to free Mexico, 51.
Ohio River, troops stationed on, 171; Burr's project on, 214, 218.
Oidores, enemies of viceroy, 27; actions of, 283, 285.
Olaeta, Captain Ignacio, to guard against Coste, 134-136.
Olavide, Pablo de, with Miranda, 156; report on, 188-189.
Old World, relations with the New, 39, 229, 292.
Oman, C., quoted on juntas, 270.
Onís, Luis de, Spanish minister, on Louisiana, 208; opposes Napoleon's agents, 294-296, 300-303, 306.
Oracion in tempora Belli, against French, 142.
Orea, Telesforo de, deputy from Venezuela, 302.
Orders in Council, 240.
O'Reilly, Alexandro, to govern Louisiana, 70-71.
Orizaba, escaped Negroes in, 29.
Ossun, French minister to Spain, warned against British, 78.
Otter, escape of Muir in, 179.
Oviedo, commissioners from, 267, 279.

Pacheco, Duke of Escalona, viceroy, 30-32.
Pacific, foreign intruders in, 50, 75, 109, 149.
Pacific Coast, British interest in, 149, 153, 184, 201; Kendrick's knowledge of, 181; revolutionary center, 203.
Page, P. F., on French colonial empire, 196.
Paine, Thomas, and liberation plans, 115; writings of, prohibited, 129.
Palafox y Mendoza, viceroy, and plots, 30-33.
Pamphlets, on independence, 97, 203, 279.
Panama, Scotch colony in, 44; and revolutionary plans, 50, 91, 106, 188-189, 200-201, 243; canal for, 156.
Panes, governor of Vera Cruz, and English, 153.
Pánuco, 117; Burr's interest in, 219.

Paris, revolutionary influence in, 12, 115, 156-157, 160, 189-190; Treaty of, 94; Muir in, 179.
Parliament, British, aid to Asturians, 268.
Pasquinades, posted in Mexico, 140.
Patterson, William, colony at Darien, 44.
Pátzcuaro, movement for independence in, 72, 74.
Pavia, Joseph, in England, 227, 265.
Peace, between England and Spain, 49, 239; and Spanish reforms, 76; between France and Spain, 126; Franco-American, 169, 174, 176-177, 186-187; between United States and Spain, 217, 223.
Peace of Amiens, and Miranda, 193, 226; and Napoleon's colonial plans, 194, 196, 197.
Pedro of Portugal, for Mexico, 276.
Pelagius, heresies of, 36.
Pelham, Lord, and liberation plans, 192.
Peñalosa, renegade Spaniard, 43.
Peninsula, Spanish, and Napoleon, 254, 256, 261, 270, 298.
Peninsulars, favoritism of, 4, 99; opposition of, 248; and Seville junta, 278-279.
Peninsular War, 268-271.
Pensacola, expedition to Darien, 44; and Louisiana, 67; and plans of conquest and liberation, 91, 118, 214, 266.
People, political interest of, 23, 28, 272, 276, 280, 281, 283, 299, 307.
Peralta, Gastón de, viceroy, 27.
Pereyrat, revolutionary plans of, 116.
Perignon, General, and retrocession of Louisiana, 125.
Peroté, resistance of, 244; D'Alvimar to, 260.
Peru, restrictions on, 14; and Scotch colony, 44; and revolution, 57, 63, 154, 158, 187, 238, 249, 252; Spanish king for, 95; and United States, 103, 161; and France, 170, 184, 196.
Pétion, and Miranda's plans, 111, 190.
Petit, and Louisiana, 67, 70.
Peyron, and *Letters of Lord Chesterfield,* 129.
Philadelphia, revolutionary activities in, 113-115, 122, 136, 138, 162, 168, 213, 218-219, 260, 295, 303; British

INDEX

minister in, 150, 173; Wilkinson called to, 172.
Philip II, and colonies, 18, 28, 39.
Philip III, father of Lampart, 34-35.
Philip IV, related to Pacheco, 31; related to Lampart, 34-35.
Philip V, and Mexico, 47-48.
Philippines, viceroy to save, 149.
Philosophers, eighteenth century, 12.
Pickering, John, American secretary of legation, London, 190.
Pickering, Timothy, secretary of state, and Chisholm, 151; and Miranda's plan, 160-161, 165, 167, 168, 198.
Picton, Thomas, governor of Trinidad, and revolutionary plans, 154, 188.
Pike, Zebulon M., and Burr conspiracy, 223-224.
Pinckney, Charles, departure from Spain, 216; on peace with France, 174.
Pinckney, Thomas, instructions to, 120; leaves Madrid, 125; and the army, 166.
Piracy, 29, 42.
Pitt, William, Spanish American policy of, 106, 111, 157, 160, 175, 187, 202-204, 227-229, 234-235, 238, 240, 242; Brissot and plans to, 112; death of, 215, 228, 238; and Napoleon, 226, 228.
Platte River, Villasur massacre on, 48.
Political Herald and Review, reports spread of revolution, 99.
Pompadour, Madame, Americans in mansion of, 115.
Pondicherry, Napoleon and, 242.
Pope, bishop of Mexico to become, 31; seek aid from, 34; donation to Spain by, 42.
Popham, Sir Home, and La Plata expedition, 200-202, 204, 229, 234-238, 245, 252.
Portilla, Pedro, leader of conspiracy, 181.
Porto Bello, report from, 44-45, blockade of, 49.
Portugal, independence of, and Mexico, 30-32, 34; relations with Spain, 85, 250, 255; relations with England, 95, 98, 158, 201-202, 254, 269, 270; relations with France, 158-159, 174, 242, 254-256, 263; Dom Pedro of, for Mexico, 276.

Portuguese, in Mexico, 30-32, 36; Charles IV to imitate, 257.
Pownall, governor, and Spanish colonies, 92.
Pozo y Sucre, Joseph del, revolutionary agent, 155-156, 188-189.
Presbyterian Colonies, support independence of, 92.
President, John Adams, and Miranda's project, 159, 161-162, 166-168, 170; Jefferson, relations with Spain, 217, 232, 249; and Miranda, 231; and Burr, 221, 222; Washington, and Muir, 180.
"Pretender," instructions of, 304.
Prevost, general, at Halifax, 265.
Priests, defend Indians, 21; against foreigners, 143, 245; suspected, 283.
Priestley, Joseph, comparison with, 157.
Principality, for D'Aubarde, 63.
Prisoners, Martín Cortés, 27; Portuguese, 32; plan to liberate, 143, 181; deportation of French, 145-146.
Privateers, French, 20; in Caribbean, 228.
Privateering, and New Spain, 47.
Proclamation, of French convention, 119; by Fauchet, 123; against Burr, 222, 223; for Ferdinand VII, 262; of Murat in Mexico, 273; of Iturrigaray, 278; of European faction, 283; by Garibay, 285, 294; against Napoleon, 289; for Napoleon, 295, 296, 299, 300; of independence, in Baton Rouge, 207.
Propaganda, French, in Mexico, 131-132, 138, 271, 290, 295; by British, to Spanish America, 154, 183; for Mexico, 251; by viceroy, 285.
Property, of Frenchmen in Mexico, 144, 147-148; Napoleon's confiscation of American, 301.
Protector, to head Louisiana republic, 69.
Protestants, hostility to, 39.
Provinces, organize juntas, 259, 279, 288.
Provincias Internas, French in, 137, 145, 260; protection of, 153, 293, 304.
Provisional government, colonies support of, 290.
Prussia, to aid in liberation project, 97, 112; and Napoleon, 228, 240-241, 254, 269.

342 INDEX

Pueblo de Tlaxcala, conspiracy in, 183.
Puerto Delgado, Mexico, point of attack, 244.
Puerto Rico, for Gibraltar, 89; to Denmark, 250.
Puglio, James, book by, 128.
Pyrenees, French cross, 256.

Quebec, French in, 42.
Queen, Burr's daughter, 221; of France, reputation of, 139.
Querétaro, revolutionists in, 288, 307.
Quintana, reports on, 188-189.
Quito, and Popham's plans, 200-201.

Raleigh, Sir Walter, settlement of, 40.
Races, classification of, 3.
Raynal, Abbé, on Indies, 5, 9; *History* by, 13; on British plan for Mexico, 54.
Real Acuerdo, of Mexico, relations with Napoleon, 273-275, 291; and Anglo-Americans, 292.
Rebellion, spirit of, 15; threatened in Mexico, 22, 24-26, 28-30, 33, 37, 44, 72; Catalonian, 30; Portuguese, 30; in Louisiana, 69-71; in West Florida, 207; in Madrid, 258; *see* revolution.
Red River, D'Alvimar on, 260.
"Reflections on Louisiana," 55.
Reforms, of Charles III, 14, 15, 19, 59, 72; French ideas for, 59; and stability, 76.
Regency, in Spain, 258, 288.
Regent, Dom Pedro, for Mexico, 276.
Regidores, Americans, 275-276.
Reign of Terror, in Mexico, 28.
Religion, controversy over, 30; French views on, 139; in Burr Project, 215; Pike to avoid topic of, 224; to prevent independence, 230, 251; ruin of, 276; Joseph's appeal to, 297.
Representation, of colonies in Spain, 288.
Representatives, colonial, to Spain, 22, 286; from Spanish juntas, 268; of the people, 275.
Republic, for Mexico, 54, 61, 143, 182, 248; admired by Miranda, 105; for Louisiana, 65, 69, 122; French, maxims of, 156; United States war on, 167; for liberation of Spanish America, 194.
Residencia, of Cortés, 21.

Retrocession, of Louisiana, 125, 126, 190, 193, 197, 294.
Revilla Gigedo, viceroy, and French in Mexico, 114, 132, 137, 142.
Revolution, Mexicans plan, 27, 29, 60-63, 124, 127, 134, 139, 141, 181, 211, 272, 281, 287-288, 308; by Portuguese, 30; in Cartagena, 31; in Brazil, 31; British plan for Spanish American, 52, 57-58, 63, 89-90, 95-96, 104, 107, 116, 154-158, 165, 173, 176, 178, 182, 187, 192, 201-204, 226-229, 232, 245, 253; Peru and Chile to follow Mexico, 63; in Louisiana, 67, 70; for Spanish America, 92, 95-96, 159; United States and plans for, 150, 152, 159, 165-166, 186, 197, 219, 232; in Spain, 158, 187-188; French to start, 303; *see* American and French.
"Rey Pepe," Joseph, 300.
Right of Deposit, United States at New Orleans, 196, 198, 216.
Rights of Man, by Paine, 115, 128.
Rio del Norte, boundary of Mexico, 250.
Rio Grande, Pike on, 224.
Riots, in Mexico, 29, 37, 72, 74.
Rippis, Dr., revolutionary interest of, 96.
Robertson, W. S., quoted, 105, 157.
Robespierre, 121, 179.
Robinson, Dr., with Pike to Santa Fé, 224.
Robledo, fiscal, Dom Pedro for regent, 276.
Rochefort, Napoleon's squadron at, 250, 291.
Rochford, Lord, British ambassador to Madrid, 55, 64.
Rodríguez de Peña, Manuel, experiences of, 304.
Roelas, Pedro de las, arrival of, 24.
Rolands, with Paine in Paris, 115.
Rojas, José Antonio, in United States, 101.
Rome, messengers to, 25.
Ross, Mary, quoted, 49.
Ross, Senator, for conquest of Louisiana, 197.
Rouen, France, agent arrested in, 98.
Rousseau, works of, 13, 130.
Roxas y Rocha, Francisco, arrest of, 140-141.

Rubí, Marquis de, and frontier defense, 74.
Russia, on west coast, 75, 184; to aid liberation, 97; Miranda in, 184; Napoleon and, 228, 254, 269.

Saavedra, Spanish minister of state, 303-304.
Sabine River, Spanish forces across, 218-221.
St. Domingue, for French empire, 196.
Saint Germain, Comte de, and Vergennes, 79-80.
St. Kitts, part British, 45.
St. Louis, Clark to capture, 118; Burr to, 211, 220.
Salas, Manuel Joseph de, revolutionary agent, 156, 188-189.
Salcedo, Nemicio de, reports of, 305.
San Agustín de la Cuevas, viceroy at, 273.
San Blas, Juan Kendrick, pilot at, 180.
San Diego, British visit, 149.
San Francisco, British visit, 149.
San Juan de Ulloa, in British plans, 63, 244, 253; D'Alvimar to, 261; and royal family, 291.
San Lorenzo, Treaty of, 124, 216.
San Luis Potosí, insurrection planned, 72.
San Martín de Acayucan, mission to, 134.
San Miguel, Fray Antonio de, on Indians, 8.
San Sebastián, Napoleon's agent to, 300.
Sandoval, Manuel Antonio, on Indians, 8.
Sandoval, Tello de, and New Laws, 22.
Sandwich Islands, British in, 184.
Santa Fé de Bogotá, Caro to, 162, 187; and Popham's plans, 200-201; and Trinidad, 232; *see* Bogotá.
Santa Fé, New Mexico, Pike to, 209; and Robinson, 224.
Santa Helena, Florida, 27.
Santa María, Vicento de, leader of conspiracy, 288.
Santiago, Conde de, agent to England, 101.
Santo Domingo, feared conquest of, 80-81; French interest in, 111, 125, 133, 167, 194, 195, 200, 260; English negotiations with, 185.
Saragossa, resistance to French, 269.
Satan, emissaries of, 143.
Saugrain, M., on American frontier, 103.
Savoy, rulers of, and Pacheco, 31.
Sayre, Stephen, and revolutionary plans, 116.
Scotch, at Darien, 44.
Sea power, importance of, 57.
Self-government, in Mexico, 275.
Senegal River, island in, for French empire, 196.
Seven Years' War, influence of, 52, 56, 60, 73, 92.
Seville, junta of, 268, 278-280, 283, 288.
Shelburne, Earl of, secretary of state, and conspirators, 64.
Shelby, governor of Kentucky, Jefferson to, 121.
Sheridan, M. P., plea for Asturians, 268.
Ships, American, capture French, 163; Spanish seizure of, 216; to Spanish America, from Napoleon, 261.
Short, W., commissioner to Spain, 120.
Shrewsbury, Duke of, 46.
Sidmouth, Lord, and Spanish American project, 192.
Sigüenza y Góngora, cited on riots, 38.
Silver, harmful to Spain, 237.
Sinclair, John, liberation plan by, 98.
Slaves, natives as, 21; English trade in, 48.
Smith, Colonel William, and Miranda's project, 111, 119, 158-159, 165-166, 193-194, 213, 232.
Smith, James, secretary to governor of Jamaica, 182.
Smith, Senator, and Burr conspiracy, 217, 221.
Smuggling, and independence, 16; extent of, 52, 229; from Jamaica, 56; British control of, 259.
Society of the Friends of the People, principles of, 178-179.
Somueruelos, Captain-general of Cuba and governor of Florida, 235.
Sonora, list of French in, 145; British threat to, 149, 153.
South Africa, British and, 50, 161, 170, 175, 188, 220, 232, 248, 251; and France, 57-59; United States and in-

dependence of, 151, 161, 170-171, 173, 185, 232, 292.
South Sea, attack Mexico from, 97; British posts in, 184.
Southwest, Pike's expedition to, 223.
Sovereign, of Mexico, 23; allegiance to, 24; Mexico for a Bourbon, 277-278; Ferdinand VII as, 291.
Sovereignty, English promise of, 154; theory of, 275, 279, 280.
Spain, relation to colonies, 3, 18, 20, 22, 24, 25, 27-29, 32-33, 34, 43-44, 54, 57, 60, 65, 101, 113, 123, 155, 170, 187, 196, 199, 201, 202, 211, 221, 224, 236-237, 247, 259, 273, 274, 278, 283, 284, 286, 287, 288; policy of, 8, 10, 13, 15, 40, 46, 52, 62, 63, 68, 76, 97, 102, 103, 106, 119, 133, 180, 189, 202, 207, 226, 241, 279, 286, 288; relations with France, 13, 43, 48, 53, 54, 57, 59, 75, 119, 126, 140, 147, 148, 152, 158, 160, 164, 174, 194, 249, 280; rulers of, 18, 23, 45-47, 202, 242, 256-257, 259, 264, 268, 272, 273, 274, 276, 279, 290, 307; and Portugal, 31, 255; British relations with, 41, 44, 48, 49, 75, 88, 95, 106, 109, 116, 150, 160, 189, 192, 201, 202, 203, 204, 226, 234, 239, 240, 245, 249, 265, 266, 268, 269, 292; and Austria, 49; United States relations with, 77, 119, 125, 151, 167, 171, 185-186, 197, 200, 204, 206-209, 212-214, 216, 217, 218, 220, 223, 224, 231, 232, 293, 301; and Napoleon, 193, 195, 202, 229-230, 241-242, 254-261, 264-266, 269, 270, 273, 276, 284-286, 288, 290, 292, 301, 307.
Spaniard, in Mexico, 4-5, 22, 29, 37, 51, 144, 275, 281, 282, 284-285, 296, 300, 305.
Spanish America, economic conditions of, 20, 58, 202, 203, 259; threat of revolution in, 38, 102, 124, 155, 204, 220, 227, 236, 269; French interest in, 43, 176, 194, 272; British interest in, 50, 51, 53, 57, 154, 158, 161, 187, 192, 197-198, 200-204, 212, 226-228, 230, 232, 235, 239, 242, 246-249, 251-253, 259, 266, 272; and Spain, 106, 274-275, 277-278, 280-281, 287; United States and, 152, 158, 161, 165-166, 174, 177, 178, 186, 197, 198, 208, 249, 292, 297; and Napoleon, 259, 260-262, 295, 298, 305; *see also* colonies.
Spanish Armada, 40.
Spanish Empire, organization of, 18; threatened, 29-31, 105; to Bourbons, 45; Burr project and, 205; French interest in, 229; Napoleon and, 258.
Spence, Lieutenant, on Mexican Association, 210.
Spencer, General, troops to join, 265.
Stiles, Ezra, president of Yale, and Miranda, 12.
Stormount, British diplomat in Paris, 84.
Stroganoff, Baron, intermediary between Spain and England, 227.
Subsidies, to French companies, 259.
Superior Council, of Louisiana, 66.
Superior junta, for funds, 134.
Supreme Council, of Louisiana, 68; of Castile, supports Napoleon, 258.
Sutil, coast guard, San Blas, 179.
Sweden, to aid in liberation, 97, 112.

Tabaco, guardas de, 14.
Talamantes, Fray Melchor de, for independence, 275, 278-279, 282.
Talleyrand, foreign policy of, 163-164, 169, 186, 239.
Tallien, and Muir, 179.
Tampico, threatened by revolution, 153, 182, 219.
Tapia, Christobal de, 21.
Tate, William, and Genet, 121, 123.
Taxes, 15, 30, 33, 74, 100.
Teachers, lack of, 11.
Temperley, H. W. V., quoted, 45.
Tennessee, Jackson in, 209.
Tepic, Indians, rebellion of, 8, 183.
Terra Firma, British and Miranda's expedition to, 250-252; French instructions to, 303-304.
Terror, French, and Miranda, 152.
Texas, Spanish oppose French in, 43-44, 145; English interest in, 153-154; defense against Burr, 212, 214, 218-219.
Theology, in colleges, 11.
Third Coalition, against Napoleon, 226, 231.
Tilsit, carries Napoleon's agents, 295, 304; Treaty of, 254.

INDEX 345

Tobacco, monopoly of, 14.
Torre Cassio, Conde de la, agent to England, 101.
Tortuga, buccaneer base, 43.
Toussaint L'Ouverture, 185, 194-195.
Tovar, Captain José, and Muir, 179.
Town council, Americans in Mexican, 275-276.
Trade, Spanish American, regulation of, 15, 25, 34, 40, 92, 228; French interest in, 39, 46, 58, 59, 259; British interest in, 39, 48, 50-52, 59, 89, 91, 156, 196, 228, 237, 239; Clark, with Mexico, 211; see commerce.
Trafalgar, Battle of, 228.
Treason, examples of, 26, 188-189, 284, 286.
Treaty, Spain and France, 53, 258; France and United States, 87; Spain and England, 89, 269; agent seeks, from England, 101.
Treaty of Amiens, 193, 197.
Treaty of Basle, 124-125, 147, 148.
Treaty of Ildefonso, 193.
Treaty, Jay's, 124-125.
Treaty, Neutral Ground, 222, 293.
Treaty of Paris, 94.
Treaty of San Lorenzo, 124-125, 160, 216.
Treaty of Tilsit, 254.
Treaty of Utrecht, 48-49.
Trinidad, revolutionary influence from, 154, 162, 188, 232.
Troops, British, to Mexico, 151, 253, 265, 267; to Barbados, 235; to Jamaica, 243; American, on frontier, 219, 293; Spanish, on Sabine, 220-221; German, to aid British, 253; French, in Spain, 256, 290; Mexican, 281-282.
Turnbull, John, and Miranda, 161, 168.
Turnbull, house of, London, and Miranda, 189.
Turreau, to France, 302.

Ulloa, Antonio de, governor of Louisiana, 61, 65-67; see San Juan de.
Union, West to break from, 211-212, 215-216, 221-222.
United States, relations with France, 87, 116, 120-121, 125, 129, 156-158, 160-169, 190-194, 195, 203, 292, 303, 305-307; threat to Spanish colonies, 93, 94, 97-99, 101, 102, 104, 106-107, 125-126, 164, 172, 191, 197, 199, 203-205, 211, 248, 249, 276, 292, 297; relations with England, 97-98, 112, 151-152, 158, 160-169, 175-176, 184-185, 249-250, 252; and Miranda, 105, 161, 166, 176, 191-194, 231, 234; and Genet, 116, 121; relations with Spain, 119, 151, 185, 213, 216-218, 220, 226, 231-233, 293; and Floridas, 120, 156, 207; and Louisiana, 156, 164, 190, 193-194, 196; constitution of, 181; and Burr, 208, 216, 220, 224, 232.
University, of Mexico, 11, 13.
Urquijo, reports to, 185.
Uruapan, recruiting in, 74.
Utrecht, treaty of, 48.

Valderrama, visitador, 23.
Valenzuela, report on conspiracy, 141.
Valladolid, expulsion of Jesuits, 72; conspiracy in, 287-288.
Valle, Marquis del, son of Cortés, 22, 24, 26.
Vancouver, George, on Pacific coast, 149.
Vansittart, Nicolas, plans of, 150, 152-153.
Vara, Juan, in Guerrero's plot, 141.
Vásquez Fernández, Juan, alias Benítez Gálvez, 182-183.
Velasco, viceroy, 22; Luis, son of, 24.
Velásquez, governor of Cuba, 20.
Venegas, viceroy, 288.
Venezuela, French interest in, 230; revolt in, 302-303.
Ventura, dispatches from Spain, 273-274.
Vera Cruz, founded, 20; conquest and defense of, 25, 73, 90, 149, 203, 219, 242, 250, 291, 295; escaped Negroes in, 29; trade in, 45, 52; and revolt, 61, 133, 141, 211; England's interest in, 106, 153, 229, 243-244, 251, 253; and the French, 131, 141, 203, 250, 262-263, 291, 295, 298, 302, 304; map of, 215.
Verdad y Ramas, for independence, 275, 280, 282-283.
Vergennes, foreign minister of France, policy of, 78-79, 83-88.
Vernon, Admiral, and Indies, 46, 50, 51.

346 INDEX

Viana, Francisco, inspector general of troops, 214.
Viar, Ignacio de, Spanish representative in Philadelphia, 136, 147.
Vicente, Juan, on French ideas, 131.
Viceroy, office of, 4, 23.
Viceroy, Gastón de Peralta, 23, 27-28; Duke of Escalona, 30-32; Count of Galve, 37; Count of Montezuma, 46-47; Baltasar de Zúñiga, 48; Marquis of Croix, 61; Marquis of Cruíllas, 73, 74; Martín de Mayorga, 100; Revilla Gigedo, the second, 114, 132-135; Branciforte, 123, 131, 137; and French in Mexico, 144-148; and security, 151, 153, 179-180; Bucareli, 137; Berenguer de Marquina, and revolutionary plots, 181-183; Azanza, 184-185; of Peru, warns Mexico, 187; Iturrigaray, and Burr, 211, 214, 218-219; and relations with Spain, 228, 274-275, 277-283; warnings to, 235; and English plans, 248; and Napoleon, 260, 262, 263, 273; policy of, 277-283; Cuesta, Napoleon appoints, 262-263; Garibay, 283, 285-286, 291, 293; Lizana y Beaumont, policy of, 287, 294, 299, 301, 304; Venegas, 288.
Vidall, Luis, plan of, 96.
Vidal, José, 218, 260.
Villalba, Juan de, reform of army, 73-74.
Villanueva, Carlos, cited, 64.
Villa Rica de Vera Cruz, 20.
Villaroel, Pedro Soria, governor of Pátzcuaro, 72.
Villasur, expedition of, 48.
Villa Urrutia, Jacobo de, for independence, 275-276, 280.
Villena, Marquis de, 34, 36.
Villery, D'Ossuanville, on Miranda's plans, 187-189.
Visitador, Valderrama, 23, 26; Palafox, 30; José de Gálvez, 72, 74, 75, 100.
Vittoria, French in, 256, 257.
Vizcardo y Guzmán, Jesuit, 104, 159, 193.
Volney, French deputy, works prohibited, 130.
Voltaire, 13, 130, 157.

Walling, Thomas, Miranda and, 161.
Walpole, favors independence of Mexico, 51.

War, of Spanish Succession, 45-47; Spain against England, 48, 75, 88, 119, 150; of Jenkin's Ear, 49, 51, 236; and revolutionary plans, 50, 52, 106, 109, 163, 193, 198, 216, 221, 253, 307; of the Austrian Succession, 51; Seven Years', 52; France and Spain, 116, 119, 147, 268; chance of, United States with Spain, 151, 196-197, 210, 216-217, 220-223, 231; United States with France, 157, 160, 163, 167, 169, 196-197, 199; between England and France, 176, 202, 296, 307; Russia on Spain, 184.
Washington, Yrujo, Spanish minister in, 196, 208; Miranda to, 213; Burr's return to, 213.
Washington, George, neutrality policy of, 108-109; and Genet, 121; on Miranda's project, 166, 171; and Muir, 180.
Washita River, Burr's land on, 216-217.
Watkins, John, mayor of New Orleans, 210.
Wealth, sought by viceroy, 30; for war, 50; British interest in Spanish American, 97, 204; Spanish American, and world contest, 202; aids Spain against Napoleon, 285-286.
Weiss, Charles, on foreign trade, 15.
Wellesley, Sir Arthur, plans for liberation of Mexico, 17, 236, 242-245, 250-254, 264-268; in Peninsular war, 269.
West, conditions in the, 108, 171, 197, 206, 211, 220; and Burr, 208, 211-218, 223.
West Florida, French danger in, 122; revolt in, 206-207; and United States, 293.
West Indies, British interest in, 39, 44-45, 233-234, 243, 247, 250, 265, 268, 293; and the French, 131, 306; Miranda to, 175; French agents to, 306.
Westward movement, Spanish precaution against, 102.
Weymouth, Lord, 64, 81.
White, Robert, revolutionary plan of, 90.
Wilkinson, General, and Genet, 114; and Miranda's plans with Hamilton, 165-167, 170-172, 186; and Burr's conspiracy, 206, 209, 211, 214-215, 218-225, 293; on independence of Spanish

America, 249, 292; and D'Alvimar, 260; and Spaniards, 185-186, 293, 294.
Williamson, Colonel, Burr's agent in London, 212, 238, 265, 267.
Williams, Roger, and Cromwell, 41.
Wimbledon, Miranda and Pitt at, 202.
Windham, W., on revolution, 176.
Wollstonecraft, Mary, with Paine in Paris, 115.
Workman, James, and Mexican Association, 210.
World, rivalry for control of, 202, 268, 290.

X. Y. Z. Affair, 163.

Yale, visited by Miranda, 12.
Yellow fever, in Le Clerc's army, 200.
Yermo, Gabriel de, leader of conspiracy, 282, 287.
Yrujo, Casa, Spanish minister to United States, 151-152, 196-197; and Burr, 208, 211-215, 218; and Miranda, 233, 235.
Yucatan, conquer, for trade, 91; warned against French, 291.

Zapo, hacienda of Coste, 133.
Zarate, Julio, cited, 283.

F 1231.R93 1972

circ Foreign interest in the independence of
Bergen Community College Library

3 5936 000 627 244

**Library and Learning
Resources Center
Bergen Community College**
400 Paramus Road
Paramus, N.J. 07652-1595

Return Postage Guaranteed